START-TO-FI LANDSCAPE CONSTRUCTION

ORTHO®

Des Moines, Iowa

Ortho Start-to-Finish Landscape Construction
Writer: Martin Miller
Contributing Graphic Designer: Tim Abramowitz
Senior Associate Design Director: Tom Wegner
Assistant Editor: Harijs Priekulis
Copy Chief: Terri Fredrickson
Copy and Production Editor: Victoria Forlini
Editorial Operations Manager: Karen Schirm
Managers, Book Production: Pam Kvitne,
    Marjorie J. Schenkelberg, Rick von Holdt
Contributing Copy Editor: Ro Sila
Contributing Proofreaders: David Krause, Elise Marton,
    Anne Terpstra
Indexer: Donald Glassman
Editorial and Design Assistant: Renee E. McAtee,
    Karen McFadden

Additional Editorial Contributions from
Art Rep Services
Director: Chip Nadeau
Designer: lk Design
Illustrator: Dave Brandon

Meredith® Books
Editor in Chief: Linda Raglan Cunningham
Design Director: Matt Strelecki
Executive Editor, Gardening and Home Improvement:
    Benjamin W. Allen
Executive Editor, Home Improvement: Larry Erickson

Publisher: James D. Blume
Executive Director, Marketing: Jeffrey Myers
Executive Director, New Business Development:
    Todd M. Davis
Executive Director, Sales: Ken Zagor
Director, Operations: George A. Susral
Director, Production: Douglas M. Johnston
Business Director: Jim Leonard

Vice President and General Manager: Douglas J. Guendel

Meredith Publishing Group
President, Publishing Group: Stephen M. Lacy
Vice President-Publishing Director: Bob Mate

Meredith Corporation
Chairman and Chief Executive Officer: William T. Kerr

In Memoriam: E.T. Meredith III (1933-2003)

All of us at Ortho® Books are dedicated to providing you
with the information and ideas you need to enhance your
home and garden. We welcome your comments and
suggestions about this book. Write to us at:
    Meredith Corporation
    Ortho Books
    1716 Locust St.
    Des Moines, IA 50309–3023

If you would like to purchase any of our home improvement,
gardening, cooking, crafts, or home decorating and design
books, check wherever quality books are sold. Or visit us at:
meredithbooks.com

If you would like more information on other Ortho products,
call 800-225-2883 or visit us at: www.ortho.com

Photographers
    (Photographers credited may retain copyright ©
    to the listed photographs.)
L = Left, R = Right, C = Center, B = Bottom, T = Top
Pamela Barkentin-Blackburn: 30BL
Laurie Black: 6TR, 168TR
Bob Braun: 20B
Ernest Braun Photography: 51TL, 38BR, 41TR
R. Christman: 151TL
Josephine Coatsworth: 144BL
Crandall & Crandall: 19C, 40TR
Stephen Cridland: 7BR, 14BR, 30TR, 35BL, 35BR, 60T, 219BR
Grace Davies: 130BL
Todd Davis: 24BL
Catriona Tudor Erler: 22T
Richard Felber: 168BR
D. Randolph Foulds Photography: 6TC
John Fuller: 28BL
Susan Gilmore: 24BR, 45T
Edward Golich Photography: 23T, 37T, 145TL
Jay Graham: 16BL, 21T, 21B,
Bob Greenspan: 34BR
Hedrick-Blessing Studios: 7TL, 39TL
Bob Hawks Photography: 29BR
Jerry Harper: 33BR
Sue Hartley: 58TC
Shelly Hawes: 67T
Carol Highsmith: 66B
Saxon Holt: 25BL
William Hopkins Sr.: 201BL
Inside/Out Studio: 56BL
Jerry Howard/Positive Images: 12T, 53T, 54T, 200CL
Roy Inman: 15LC, 56TL, 152TL
Mike Jensen: 4T
Bill Johnson: 35T, 38TL, 154C
Jenifer Jordan: 27TL, 41TL
Jim Kaskoutas: 201TL, 201CL
Pete Krumhardt: 43BR
Susan M. Lammers: 27BL
Michael Landis: 26B
Lee Lockwood/Positive Images: 18CR
Mark Lohman: 32TR
Bryan McCay: 39TC, 45B, 83CR, 83BL
Charles Mann: 22B
Janet Mesic-Mackie: 14LC
Mike Moreland: 14BL, 29C
Clive Nichols: 168BL
Jerry Pavia: 29BL, 49BR
Robert Perron/Positive Images: 42BR
Mary Carolyn Pindar: 16BR, 184BL
Portland Cement Association: 153T
Ken Rice: 5CR, 40TL, 51BR
Eric Roth: 27BR, 31BR, 33TL, 146TL
Marvin Sloben: 50T
Pam Spalding/Positive Images: 42TL
William Stites Photography: 4B
Steve Struse: 7C, 25BR, 39TR, 232TR
Rick Taylor Photography: 4C, 35C, 220TL
Al Teufen: 37CR
Tom Tracy: 148TL
Joan Hix Vanderschuit: 64T
Jessie Walker: 23CR
Judy Watts: 62TR
Zane Williams: 28TR, 43TR, 43C
James Yochum: 18T, 23B, 31BL, 218BL

Whether you want to create a tranquil getaway for small gatherings or a large expanse for entertainment, you'll find the space more enjoyable if all the elements work together to enhance that purpose. Here, tall roses soften the hard fence surface, and an off-brown paint brings a muted complement to the red brick and the understated furnishings.

No matter the kind of outdoor structure you plan, blend it with its natural surroundings. Enhance its appearance with colorful furnishings, built-in planters, and other decorative accents.

LIFESTYLE AND MATERIALS

As you plan your landscape, remember that the shapes, colors, textures, and patterns of the materials you use will enhance both its style and comfort. Brick, concrete, flagstone, tile, wood, and gravel all express different styles, but some materials are better suited to certain purposes than others.

For example, you may like the rustic look of flagstone, but if you're planning a summer full of dance parties, its rough surface may not fit the bill. If you have to have both, extend your patio with a "danceable" platform deck. Consider safety too. Wood gets slippery when wet, so flagstone may prove safer for a hot tub or pool border.

There's no limit to what you can accomplish when you unify function and aesthetics. The size, materials, and location of this shed complement the maintenance requirements of the large woodland garden. Cedar shakes add rustic character and make the shed appear as if it has grown naturally out of its surroundings.

PLANNING TO SUIT YOUR STYLE

Building an outdoor structure is not a complicated process, but it does require careful planning. It's especially important that you build the structure to complement the rest of your landscape—that it not only act as a functional addition to your yard but also appear as an integral part of the outdoor design.

You should consider many questions. Where exactly should you locate it? How big should it be? What special features do you want to include? How will it tie in with the overall landscape? Will the area contain other structures? What materials should you use? And finally—how do you build it?

Finding answers to all of these questions will prove much easier if you make plans with your lifestyle in mind. All outdoor structures should start with the answer to one question: "How will you use your landscape?"

Whether you plan to use the outdoors for family dining, entertainment, recreation, quiet contemplation—or all of these activities— you'll enjoy it even more when you create it to meet specific needs. If you're not sure of those goals yet, don't start shopping for materials.

Consider how you want your landscape to function, how you want it to look and feel, how your project will complement your home and garden, and what kinds of weather and surface conditions will affect its comfort, appearance, accessibility, and durability.

Ask yourself: "What will make me want to spend time in it?" Build on that answer.

When you plan an outdoor structure, make sure style and practicality go hand in hand. The umbrella not only shades the spot but adds to its sense of enclosure.

ADD VALUE TO YOUR HOME

Well-designed outdoor structures—especially decks and patios—can increase the value of your home because they add living space. The more work you do yourself, the more of your investment you'll recoup. A $3,500 patio built by a professional can return about 40 percent of its cost. But if you do the work yourself, you can cut your costs to about $1,000 and add about $1,500 to the value of your home.

How much you get back can vary from as little as 40 percent to as much as 150 percent, depending on two factors:

■ The area of the country in which you live.
■ The average resale value of homes in your neighborhood.

One of the key considerations is how long you plan to stay in your home. If you're going to stay there forever, how much you get back on your investment may not be important. But if you plan to sell your home in the foreseeable future, do a little research before building your patio. Ask a local realtor if patios are an improvement potential buyers want and will pay for. Then add the cost of the patio to the average resale value of homes in your neighborhood.

As a general rule, the total patio costs plus the current market value of your house should not exceed the value of any home in your neighborhood by more than 20 percent. Selling a house priced well above neighboring houses will be difficult.

HOW WILL YOU USE YOUR LANDSCAPE?

Even an addition that's strictly functional can be dressed up at little cost. Here an understated coat of paint and colorful plantings do the trick.

Here's a novel way to enhance a small space for gatherings. The painted design on the decking calls attention to itself and creates an attractive area that is continually inviting.

A special place to relax with your morning coffee; a shaded retreat for catching up with your favorite book; a place for storing outdoor tools and equipment; an area for hosting festive parties, large and small—your landscape can serve any one or all of these purposes. How you design the elements of your landscape will depend largely on how you want to use it.

A GETAWAY

If your needs are simple—adding space for getting away from it all, or simply going outdoors to enjoy the weather—a small unused section of the lawn such as a narrow side yard might be the perfect spot for a deck or patio. Keep the area private with a minimum investment— a few screening plants will do the trick. Add paving that fits the style of the surroundings and some built-in or moveable seating, and you have transformed an area you used to mow into a low-maintenance private room.

Wherever you place your getaway, don't forget that even small areas

require comfortable seating. And if the space will double as a spot for family gatherings, you'll want enough seating and table space to accommodate everyone. If dining is on the agenda, you'll need room for a grill too.

ENTERTAINING

Ample space for parties is like guacamole dip—there never seems to be enough of it. So if you entertain, even infrequently,

Outdoor entertainment often means outdoor cooking. Brick, tile, casual, open furnishings and background plants bring warmth and comfort to this entertainment area.

SHAPING SPACES

Most decks and patios serve multiple purposes. They're called upon to function as private retreats, family gathering spots, and entertainment centers. Defining spaces will enhance your enjoyment of them. Use walls, fences, planters, even container plants arranged along the edges of specific areas to help them maintain their individual identities.

consider guests in your plans—both those who come for specific gatherings and those who simply drop by. Patios and decks—even gazebos—are a great way to relieve a cramped kitchen. They can quickly turn an overflow crowd into a festive gathering.

Small groups may not require much more space or furnishings than your family would need. But for large gatherings, increase the size of the seating, cooking, and dining areas. Remember teenagers too—a patio or deck can offer them privacy and at the same time reward you with some peace and solitude.

PLAY SPACE FOR CHILDREN

The outdoors is perfect for children's play, but your landscape plans need to account for both the ages of the kids and their number.

A single outdoor structure can serve several purposes. The back room of this 15-foot gazebo, for example, is a storage shed for toys and equipment used in a nearby pool.

designed deck, patio, or gazebo can include ample room for things that would otherwise clutter up the view. And with no more than a little imagination, you can build an attractive shed that contributes to the beauty of your backyard.

Divide your patio space into separate sections with implied "walls." Moving furnishings in and out of the squares on this patio offers endless possibilities for both large- and small-group get-togethers.

Sandboxes are great for toddlers, but when the kids grow up they'll need tree forts and things to climb. Plan your space so you can phase in these activities in the future.

STORAGE

No landscape is complete—or comfortable—without ample space for storing garden tools, equipment, and outdoor toys that won't fit into indoor closets or under the bed. Now's the time to design a space to keep those items out of sight when they're not in use. A well-

This quiet setting is flexible enough for many uses. Movable furniture and flower pots allow a fresh look for every season and every occasion.

SIZING UP A DECK OR PATIO

How much space will you need for your deck or patio? Some designers say an outdoor living space should be about the same size as the interior room it adjoins. Others suggest it should be roughly one-third the size of the main floor of the house. The primary guideline? Make your deck or patio large enough to accommodate all of the functions it will need to serve.

FUNCTION FIRST

How many functions will take place in your outdoor room? To get an answer, start with a list of the activities you enjoy. Assign different activities to different parts of the area, allowing ample space for
■ the activity itself,
■ traffic flow through and around the area, and
■ outdoor furniture (which tends to be a little larger than indoor furniture).

Perhaps you'd just like a place for family dining. In that case you might get by with an area as small as 6×10 feet. But soaking in a hot tub will call for a substantial addition.

Personal relaxation may not work well in the same space where children play, and a basketball hoop could be disastrous near a dining area.

Where different functions must take place close to each other, separate their spaces with planters, trellises, benches, or even a change

PLANNING TO SCALE

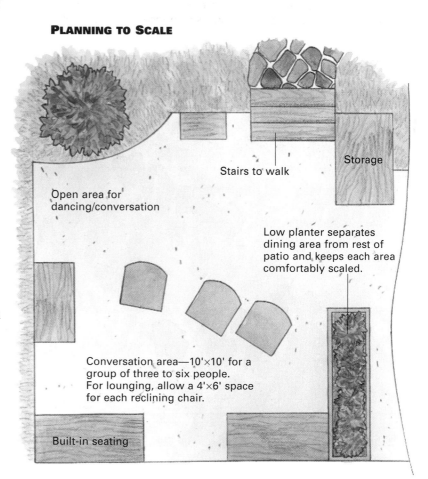

Stairs to walk

Storage

Open area for dancing/conversation

Low planter separates dining area from rest of patio and keeps each area comfortably scaled.

Conversation area—10'×10' for a group of three to six people. For lounging, allow a 4'×6' space for each reclining chair.

Built-in seating

LEGALITIES

The design of any outdoor structure will, of course, be affected by your lifestyle and budget—things over which you have control. But it may also be affected by factors outside your control—building codes, zoning ordinances, deed restrictions, and easements. These regulations can have a major effect on where you put any outdoor structure and how you build it. A little preliminary research will save you time, effort, and frustration later.
■ **Building Codes.** Almost all communities enact building codes to ensure the safety of their residents. You may find regulations that define footing depths, material choices, and fence heights. Check with your local building department before you start, and submit your plans for approval.
■ **Zoning Ordinances.** These provisions govern the use of property and the placement of structures. They can

establish minimum setbacks from property lines, easements, and the size of your structure. In recent years many communities have become strict about the size of hard scape surfaces because large areas of hard scape increase runoff into storm sewers.
■ **Deed Restrictions.** These regulations control local property values or architectural style. You may find restraints on the kind of structure you want to build, its style, and the materials you want to use.
■ **Easements and Right-of-Ways.** These rules guarantee access by local utilities to their service lines. If a utility company has a line running through your yard, you might not be able to build any part of a structure above it. It is possible, however, that sand-set installations, which allow quick access to utilities below, would be allowed in areas where concrete would be forbidden.

in paving patterns. Or employ structural solutions to separate one area from the others. Build a T-shaped patio or deck or set the surface on different levels and connect them with stairs or sloping pathways.

PLANNING TO SCALE

Once you've computed the approximate size of your outdoor room based on its intended uses, step back and consider its scale. The structure should be proportionate to the house and grounds. A small space can be overwhelmed by a huge house, and a lavish site will likely seem out of proportion to a modestly sized home. Your budget and lot size may provide the most help in solving this problem. Start with a design that fits the uses you envision and then scale back to fit the limits of your budget and terrain.

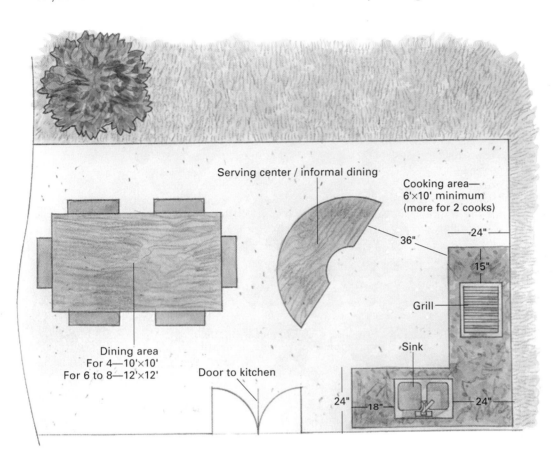

Serving center / informal dining

Cooking area—
6'×10' minimum
(more for 2 cooks)

36"

24"

15"

Grill

Sink

Dining area
For 4—10'×10'
For 6 to 8—12'×12'

Door to kitchen

24"

18"

24"

TESTING THE FIT

The best way to find out if the size of your proposed deck, patio, or gazebo is large enough is to rope off or spray-paint the space in its approximate location. No matter what kind of structure you plan to build, don't be concerned with marking the exact location yet—you still have some other decisions to make.

Once you've marked the area, tie helium balloons in places where new trees and shrubs will go and move in the furniture and equipment you will use—tables and chairs, barbecue grill, lounges, and recliners. If you haven't purchased the furniture yet, use interior furnishings and add about a foot more space for each item. You can generally figure about 2 feet square for each outdoor chair, plus about a foot or two to push it back from a table.

Imagine the floor space as it will be when finally furnished. Does everything seem to fit? Imagine it with family and guests. Can people move around or will they be reduced to elbowroom only?

If you're building a shed, mark its perimeter on the ground and evaluate its size. Bring out your tools, the lawn mower, and other equipment and put all of them between the painted lines to make sure everything fits. Will all your current or planned equipment fit comfortably, or should you enlarge the space so you don't have to crawl over things to get to the tool you want?

Adjust the size of the painted imprint until you get it right for your current and planned needs, then draw the plan on paper.

DESIGNING A DECK

Decks can assume a limitless number of shapes and forms. Your design will depend on the terrain and landscaping of your property, your proximity to neighbors, and how you plan to use your deck.

GROUND-LEVEL DECKS: Typically associated with flat yards and single-level homes, ground-level decks present fewer design and construction challenges than do raised or multilevel decks.

Ground-level decks make pleasant entryways, breakfast spots, and outdoor mudrooms. Construction is uncomplicated, and because they are low to the ground they may not require railings (but check your local codes to make sure). Bring together two or more independent ground-level decks and experiment with decking patterns to create a cascading effect down a gentle slope, or form a pattern to define a garden space.

When it comes to supporting a ground-level deck, you have several options—traditional post-and-pier foundations,

continuous footings, or existing concrete slabs. To make a structure that seems to float above the terrain, extend the edges beyond the posts or footings. Be sure to check with your building department to see what your local codes have to say about how far the cantilevered sections can extend.

RAISED DECKS: Raised decks provide access to upper-level rooms and can also solve landscape problems caused by steep terrain. Making tall supports look graceful can be an exciting challenge.

Slopes that fall away sharply from a house present special design and deck-building challenges. The easiest solution is to build a single-level deck attached to the house and supported by piers and posts. Perched on a sloped lot, even a simple deck offers great views and increases your living space.

Safety concerns increase with elevated decks. Be sure the height of the railing and the space between balusters comply with local building codes.

Although the design of this redwood deck is simplicity itself, it took careful planning. The forward platform spills easily into the surrounding yard, but the rear section, which vaults over a slope, required railings for safety. Note the comfortable cushions—an innovative approach to seating that can be permanent or temporary, depending on the family's needs and budget.

MULTILEVEL DECKS: Multilevel deck designs fix problems caused by rolling terrain or naturally terraced landscapes. Add interest to your design by building the sections in different sizes and shapes and connecting them with stairs or walkways.

Multilevel decks are ideal for sloping lots. Try out designs that cascade down the hill in stages—they can give you stunning views from different vantage points along the way. Multilevel decks are complex, however, and require precise planning. Stairs, railings, and structural components must come together correctly.

You don't need a sloped lot to build a multilevel deck, however. Such a design can create an easy, smooth transition from the ground to an upper level of your house. Instead of one long stairway, consider building a series of platforms leading up the elevation.

WRAPAROUND DECKS: These are built along more than one side of a house and often feature multiple entries to the home. Wraparound decks are the perfect solution for lots that receive varying amounts of strong sunlight at different parts of the day. They also provide an easy answer for families that need spots for both private gathering and parties on the same structure.

This multilevel deck contains several small areas. Each is designed to accommodate its own function, and all of the areas provide a unique view of the rest of the property.

A landing divides up this long stairway ascending to a raised second-story deck. Landings make the climb less tedious and the design more attractive, breaking up the large expanse of the siding.

Not all decks cling to houses. This freestanding redwood deck takes advantage of a setting with views into a wooded glade.

SINISTER SHADOWS

An upper-level deck can plunge the interior rooms beneath it into a darkened gloom. If you're designing a second-story deck— and your site and sun pattern allow it— try slimming down the width of your design. Narrow structures can offer plenty of room for seating and enjoying the view, and they cast a smaller amount of shade. A deck no wider than 8 feet can strike a good compromise, offering ample floor space without darkening any of the rooms below.

DESIGNING A PATIO

Once you have settled on an approximate size for your patio, it's time to address its shape. Start by revisiting the contours of your house and yard. There are things you may not have noticed the first time that may affect where you put the patio.

HOUSE AND GARDEN

First the shape of your house may suggest a configuration for your patio. Second, you may have overlooked areas of your yard that have had no purpose other than to get you to fire up the mower on weekends.

Front-yard patios can extend the driveway or open up the area around the entrance to your home. Patios on the side of the house can turn wasted space into more room for outdoor living. And, of course, in any area a patio makes an excellent location for flower beds and plantings.

ATTACHED PATIO: The typical attached patio is located next to the house with access to the interior—usually the kitchen or family room. U-shaped or L-shaped houses come with ready-made opportunities for maintaining privacy, but that doesn't mean that the contour of the patio has to be uniformly rectangular. Round off the corners, create flowing patterns with your paving, and add shrubs to soften hard edges.

Not all patios have to be designed with square corners. Here sweeping curves, low walls, and a small pool combine to suit this site to both formal and informal gatherings—large and small.

ATTACHED PATIO

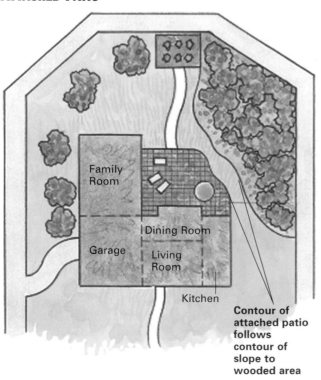

Family Room

Dining Room

Garage

Living Room

Kitchen

Contour of attached patio follows contour of slope to wooded area

DETACHED PATIO

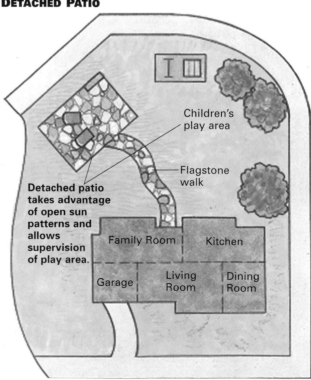

Children's play area

Flagstone walk

Detached patio takes advantage of open sun patterns and allows supervision of play area.

Family Room

Kitchen

Garage

Living Room

Dining Room

DETACHED PATIO: A detached patio offers a quick fix for sun and shade problems. Consider moving the patio away from the house and into the natural surroundings to take advantage of the changing shade patterns cast by existing trees. A detached patio also makes a good retreat, allowing you to separate yourself from the business of the household.

Even though it's situated away from the house, your detached patio should have the same general architectural tone as the house. Its very distance from your home lets you create stunning patterns on its surface that harmonize and contrast with the overall design of the property. But be sure to connect the patio to the house with a path or walkway that complements the look of your overall landscape—formal brick or rustic wood chips, for example.

COURTYARD PATIO: A courtyard is a great solution for townhouses, condos, apartments, or any home with a small lot. A courtyard needs walls, of course, but if you don't have them, you can make them with fencing or tall hedges. Garden beds or planter boxes will make this spot your private oasis, but if garden beds won't do, use potted plants or small trees to bring greenery and flowers into the space.

Install trellises and let vines climb the walls. Add the splash of falling water by installing a small recirculating fountain available in most garden centers. If running water lines and putting in a pump aren't feasible, consider an ornamental wall fountain. If the courtyard is small, keep the paving subdued and the furniture simple to avoid overwhelming the space.

WRAPAROUND PATIO: A wraparound patio is a made-to-order option for the family that wants patio access from several rooms or has plans for multiple uses—a quiet retreat outside the master bedroom, family dining off the kitchen, and parties that flow from the family room.

If the size of your patio won't quite fit the open areas of your yard, this style is for you. It allows you to keep space for smaller gatherings on the least-used side of the house

COURTYARD PATIO

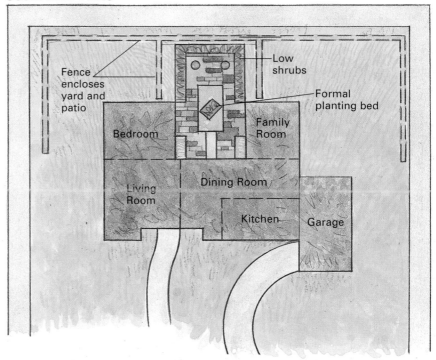

Fence encloses yard and patio

Low shrubs

Formal planting bed

Bedroom

Family Room

Living Room

Dining Room

Kitchen

Garage

WRAPAROUND PATIO

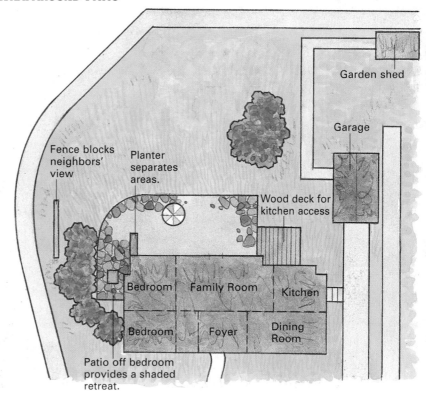

Garden shed

Garage

Fence blocks neighbors' view

Planter separates areas.

Wood deck for kitchen access

Bedroom

Family Room

Kitchen

Bedroom

Foyer

Dining Room

Patio off bedroom provides a shaded retreat.

and still have enough room for large parties. Curved corners, garden beds, planter boxes, and low walls—placed independently or in combination with each other—will separate each area and give each space its own character.

DESIGNING SHEDS AND GAZEBOS

When you choose a design for your shed or gazebo, the appearance of the structure takes second place on the list of things to consider. The most important determination is: What do you want the building to do? The answer to that question affects the appearance of the project.

FUNCTION AND FORM

If you want to build a structure for storage, make a list of what you want to store. A small 3×6-foot shed attached to the garage will be perfect for storing rakes, shovels, trowels, and bags of fertilizer. It might even be roomy enough for a medium-size push mower. But a riding mower, garden tractor, wheelbarrow, or other large equipment will increase your need for space dramatically. And if it's only a place for potting plants you plan, you should know that most potting sheds eventually become storage sheds too. Plan the shed with enough room for potting *and* storage. Similarly a gazebo with an 8- or 9-foot floor diameter will comfortably accommodate a family of four but quickly confines a group of party guests.

Design factors will affect the structure as well. For instance, a small shed with a single or double entry door probably won't have enough wall space for a window. A larger structure allows a window and larger doors, letting in light and improving access.

Then there's what goes inside a shed. Worktables, shelving, cabinets, and so forth affect not only the size of the structure but also its exterior appearance.

The materials used, too, can limit design. Physical limitations complicate window installation in openings larger than about 3½ feet, for example. If you're planning an enclosed 12-foot gazebo, its 60-inch openings will require windows with a center support (unless you're willing to spend a lot of money), and you may not like the way the support breaks the line of the opening. To avoid problems, plan the project in as much detail as possible before you start construction.

Screened openings make this gazebo a pleasant, bug-free place to view the garden. Steps lead down from an adjacent deck to the gazebo, which has been raised to overlook the garden.

This playhouse is simply an 8×8-foot shed built on an 8×12-foot platform to provide a porch. The porch roof, trim, and colorful paint scheme disguise its utilitarian structure. When the children outgrow the playhouse, it can serve as a storage shed and potting area.

Built with both new and salvaged materials, this shed fits the overall look of the garden and adds its own touch of charm.

CHOOSING A SITE

The placement of a shed or gazebo is a crucial consideration that affects the building's usefulness as well as the character of the surrounding area.

GETTING STARTED

Go outside and stand next to your house and casually survey your yard for what seems to be the best location for the shed or gazebo. This first step in site selection sounds almost too simple, but you'll refine the process later.

LOCATING A SHED: Look for a location that's convenient and, if you have garden beds, makes a logical connection to them. For example, centering the shed between two garden beds would unify the garden district in your landscape. For new-garden, new-shed additions, treat the space as one area and plan accordingly. If you don't have beds and don't plan to make any, a location at the rear or edge of the property usually makes sense. Remember—a freestanding shed is a design element in its own right. Its location should maintain its own identity without appearing to be an adjunct to the house or garage.

LOCATING A GAZEBO: Trust your instincts when considering the best place for your gazebo. From the moment you started thinking about building a gazebo, you probably had a notion—perhaps only dimly perceived—of where you would build it. Stand next to your house and find that spot. You may end up changing your mind, but that instinctive location is a good place to start.

LEVEL GROUND

In most cases it's best to build a shed or gazebo on level ground. Building on sloped ground increases the difficulty of construction, plus grading a slope is expensive. Avoid areas that require removal of large trees or rocks, preparations that often cost more than the project itself.

THE ROOM WITH A VIEW

How a shed or gazebo looks from the house and the yard undoubtedly is important, but the reverse is also true.

Stand at the planned site and observe the other elements in your yard. Even if you're building a basic shed, you probably don't want to see the utility boxes behind the garage every time you use it. And if you build a potting shed, you'll want to see an attractive view from the work space. That goes double for the views from a gazebo. Take your time and look out from every side. Changing a gazebo's location by a matter of feet often makes a significant difference in the view.

This freestanding pavilion, a cousin to a formal gazebo, is tied to the house with a boardwalk, proving that small elements can enhance an already pleasant location.

SIZE UP YOUR SHED

When you plan your shed, think big from the start. In just a few years, you'll probably outgrow a shed that seemed too large when you built it, so plan for the future.

The whimsical painting on this shed makes it an attention-getter in the garden. Here, the shed is an important accent in the garden design.

PRACTICAL PATHWAYS

Paths solve problems. They provide a way to travel from one place to another, unify design elements of the landscape, and reduce landscape maintenance. A path or network of paths is also a great way to add something new to an existing landscape without disrupting its character.

A path should have a purpose. To determine that purpose, start by asking yourself these questions:
- How will the path be used?
- Who will use it?

The answers will help you determine the path's route through the yard and what kind of surface it should have.

HOW WIDE?

Two people can easily pass each other on a 3-foot-wide path. They can walk together comfortably on a 4-foot surface. A person in a wheelchair needs a 40-inch walk, and one using a walker requires a path at least 27 inches wide.

FUNCTION FIRST

A footpath worn into the grass is a sure sign that you probably need to put in a path or sidewalk, even one that is strictly functional. Many landscapes will benefit from one or two utilitarian, single-purpose paths—those that simply get you from one place in the yard to another. Walks from the house to the garage or from the garage to the garden shed are typical examples. Such paths get frequent use. They should be wide, feel comfortable and secure underfoot, and allow you to proceed quickly from one point to another.

Unless you plan to include new elements in your design, working paths like these are best laid in straight lines. For example, if getting groceries from the garage to the house is the main purpose of the walk, having it meander through a cottage garden will almost ensure that people will step off the path and take shortcuts through the plantings. If you already have a sidewalk that connects such locations but it isn't attractive, consider ways to improve its appearance.

Nonutilitarian paths can take a more circuitous route. A path joining informal flower beds, for example, might call for a design more suited to a leisurely pace. Gentle curves will slow the pace of traffic yet make it easy to move materials and equipment along the path. And if you won't need to move materials and equipment along the path, you can make it narrow and winding.

Function also affects surface and construction choices. A path for children running barefoot between the pool and the house should not be surfaced with sharp crushed quartz, rough bark, or slick tile, for

Materials must suit the purpose of the path. If you're going to push wheelbarrows along a path, continuous hard paving will make the work easier. If the path is meant for strolling among the flowers, soft materials or stepping-stones like these are good choices.

Paths need both a place to start and a place to end. When these features don't exist naturally in the landscape, create them. This rustic arbor marks the start of a path to a most relaxing destination— a hammock in the trees.

instance. Stepping-stones spaced for child-size steps or brick laid in a sand bed would be a better choice. If you want a path so you can wander through the gardens, but you will also be moving wheeled equipment along it, closely spaced pavers or stepping-stones are a better choice than redwood bark.

A path with closely spaced stones lends itself to a leisurely stroll; placing the stones or pavers farther apart will speed up foot traffic.

WHAT'S ALONG THE WAY?

Think of your path as part of the floor in your landscape when you pick materials.

Then think of the path as a trail when you're planning its course. A trail invites you to take a journey—it hints of the unknown, the unexpected, the mysterious. When planning a new path for your landscape, include elements that increase the interest and provide surprises along the way.

Curves—gentle or abrupt—and tall plants can hide the view around the corner, creating a sense of anticipation. The surprise can be anything you choose—a shaft of sunlight piercing through the trees and falling on a gazing ball, a water feature, or some other accent. A spectacular view always provides sufficient reward at the end of a path. Simple elements—like randomly placed cut-stone stepping-stones—lead the eye along the path and entice you to follow it. Any kind of pattern will make you want to follow the path. And if you include places for resting along the way—a bench, a tree stump sawn at a height for sitting, or even a wide spot in the path—you will create a rhythm within the walk that will add to its charm.

Instead of leading to just a dead end at the fence, this path brings you to a pair of chairs— a nice place to sit in the garden.

destination should provide an experience— something to anticipate as you get closer to it.

Paths can lead to areas for family play in the yard, or they can take you through a wooded area to a secluded spot. They can lead to gazebos or other outdoor structures, or to entryways to public areas framed by pilasters or gates.

Some paths lead circuitously back to their starting point. Such paths are, in effect, ends in themselves. This is a good way to provide a destination when your landscape lacks features you consider dramatic or exciting. You may find that the lack of an astounding ocean view, for instance, doesn't matter as much when the paths in your urban backyard lead you around and through a colorful array of flower beds.

WHERE DOES IT END?

Imagine walking along a path that simply ends in an open expanse of lawn or comes up to a chain link fence with the neighbor's yard just beyond. You probably would be disappointed following a path that doesn't lead to anything of interest.

Once you've started down a path, you expect it to take you somewhere. That destination can be a dramatic overlook above a river or lake, a simple herb garden, or the entrance to a vine-covered garden shed. (Even a utility shed can be charming.)

No matter what the style of your path, it should have a definite end point. Ideally the

WORKING WITH THE TERRAIN

Most yards are not perfectly flat. Variations in terrain may look like obstacles to your path, but with careful planning you can turn most of them into opportunities.

Steps will make any path safer, easier to climb, and more architecturally interesting. Bending your path around sloped contours will save you time and effort in cutting into the soil and will make your path look as if Mother Nature herself put it there. Even a gentle slope can be made more appealing by running the path back and forth across it rather than straight up.

SOLUTIONS FOR SMALL SPACES

If your proposed structure seems like it will look cramped in your small yard, don't throw away your plans. There are numerous ways you can make small spaces seem larger and feel more secluded and comfortable. The key to small-space design is simplicity.

■ Create one large area from two smaller ones. If, for example, you can design your patio or deck so it spills out into your yard, the open yard space will make it seem larger.

■ Draw attention to the structure, not the property line. Instead of letting the lawn end undramatically at the property line, sculpt the perimeter of the lawn with planting beds. This will redirect attention to the patio or deck, where you want it.

■ Use plants with interesting textures to focus attention on the surrounding landscape rather than on the limits of your property.

■ Concentrate color in a patch instead of scattering flowers throughout the landscape. Groups of flowers create more impact than scattered blooms. If you use color in more than one location, repeat two or three colors to tie the areas together.

This rough-textured house provides an interesting backdrop for a small deck. Smaller, more intricate furnishings and container plantings complement the scene without cramping it.

Oversize pavers make the "floor" space of this patio seem larger than it is, and the statuary draws attention away from the narrow edges.

Leave room for greenery in small spaces. Here a patch of grass and a vine clinging to the wall keep a small patio looking fresh.

Create an illusion. This small patio looks deeper than it really is because the artful placement of the plants and containers not only conceals part of the view, but it hints at another destination.

■ Whenever possible, borrow nearby views. For example, if you live next to an attractive pond or rolling lawn, make the most of what that surrounding scenery has to offer by leaving the view open.

■ Instead of walling off a deck, gazebo, or patio entirely, place screening strategically to enhance privacy and block only those sights that are distracting.

■ Hang wind chimes or install a fountain. The soothing sounds will subdue any close-by neighbor or street noise.

■ Install built-in seating. It takes up less space than freestanding furniture. The same goes for round tables. They'll leave you more room than rectangular ones.

■ Keep paving patterns scaled to the size of your patio. A lot of small patterns and contrasting textures will leave you feeling dizzy and hemmed in.

DETAILS...DETAILS...

Details—those special decorative touches—must work extra hard in small spaces because there's no room for clutter. Finishing touches—artwork, found objects, or architectural salvage—give small spaces personality. And a small patio or deck might be perfect for an object that would get lost in a larger setting.

Overdoing the details, however, can ruin an otherwise artful patio. To avoid overwhelming the space, step back and view the surface in its entirety. Look for noticeable bare spots. Do they function better as empty areas that draw attention to your decorating scheme, or would a potted plant, artwork, or other accent improve the setting?

Leave room for each detail or collection to breathe. For example, if you line a wall shelf with shells, don't put a lot of small items on the table below it. And if you have more things to display than you have space, store the surplus for a while and rotate it with other elements of your decorative stock every two or three months.

Even small lots can meet a variety of needs. This side-yard deck makes good use of limited space, providing a play area and container-gardening opportunities. It allows parents to supervise younger children and provides a small herb garden within a few steps of the kitchen.

FORCING PERSPECTIVE

Forcing perspective is one way to make a small area seem larger. Narrowing the line of sight through a small space, *left*, is a technique that goes hand in hand with this optical space-saver.

The stepping-stones that curve around the house make this space seem larger by seeming to connect it to a hidden area. Small plants in the background and large ones in the foreground would enhance the effect, as would placement of coarse textures in front, fine textures to the rear.

In this way an empty side-yard space becomes a cozy garden getaway.

This little patio looks big. Tucking large items off to the sides keeps the center space open and avoids overcrowding.

ACCESS AND COMPATIBILITY

Bring the interior of your home into the outside world—and vice versa. Here the brick pattern flows smoothly from the family room into the adjoining patio, creating a natural extension of the indoor space. The large windows and open doorway act to bring the outdoors in.

Even the most basic landscape structure will provide ample enjoyment if you can see it from the inside, if you can easily access it, and if its uses complement the uses of the adjacent interior room. These factors—visual access, actual access, and compatibility—can spell the difference between a successful and unsuccessful design.

VISUAL ACCESS

At its most basic level, *visual access* means that you can see the structure—or a portion of it—from the inside. Ideally, however, visual access should also extend a palpable invitation into the space.

Windows and see-through doors provide visual access, but you don't need to see the entire deck or patio to want to get out and enjoy it. Just a glimpse of the space can draw you in more effectively than a complete view.

When planning your landscape, include ways to entice guests outdoors by providing visual hints of the destination. At least some of the area should be visible from more than one interior room. The most complete view should be from the room that adjoins it.

ACTUAL ACCESS

Actual access refers to the physical method by which you get from inside your home to the outdoor living space.

Actual access should be easy. Whenever possible, you should not have to step too far up or down to move from the interior to the exterior of your home. That means that the level of any adjoining surface should be as close as possible to the level of the interior floor. (From the doorway to the edges, however, the surface should slope slightly away from the house for proper drainage.)

If a deck or patio is significantly lower than the doorway on the house wall, add a landing or an entry deck to avoid having to step down immediately as you go outside. Such a threshold gives you the opportunity to get your bearings as you move from indoors to outdoors. If a landing is out of the question, build steps—and make them wider than the doorway to create an illusion of spaciousness. Each tread (the part you step on) should be no less than 12 inches deep so the stairs don't appear too steep.

COMPATIBILITY

The success of an outdoor space may depend on how you use the nearest indoor room. That's because you'll most likely use your deck or patio more often when the general purpose of both the indoor and outdoor spaces is similar. If the primary purpose of the outdoor area differs substantially from that of its connecting indoor room, you're less likely to make full use of the space.

A small deck for coffee and the morning paper, for example, will feel just right if it's adjacent to your bedroom. But the same site would not work for party space. For frequent dining put the deck close to the kitchen. Even if you plan a completely self-contained outdoor kitchen, place it close to the indoor kitchen. And don't forget to build in storage for the trash. That way you avoid carrying it inside, only to have to carry it outside on collection day. For entertaining plan a location that's close to the public rooms of the house. Make spaces that serve more than

Create safe access by building interior and exterior floors as close as possible to the same level.

Broad double doors offer visual and actual access to a private deck outside a bedroom. The deck gets lots of use because it's easy to see and to enter. In your situation, consider whether so much use is desirable.

one function large enough to be accessible from several rooms.

For private areas look for ways to limit access—shield your deck behind hedges or fencing. For entertaining look for ways to increase access, with doorways from rooms where you would entertain guests and with interior "walkways" that allow guests to move to and from your outdoor room without traipsing through the house.

EASY AND INVITING

Any outdoor living space that's difficult to get to probably won't be used. Start by making sure the main door to the structure is wide enough to permit an easy in-and-out traffic flow as well as to provide an inviting view from inside the house. French doors, atrium doors, and sliding doors work especially well because they give a sense of continuity between the indoors and outdoors. If your house does not already have such openings, consider including them in your plans and budget.

CREATING A STYLE

Who says parallel lines have to look uneventful? This 2× tread decking is a good example of how texture creates interest. The decking ties the tiers together and complements a dazzling array of plant colors.

Your outdoor living space needs to be practical, of course, but you'll enjoy it and use it more when it possesses a style that appeals to you and reflects your personality.

STYLE AT A GLANCE

Categories of style abound. Some take their origins from pure geometry. Others grow from geographic or historical factors. Here's a quick summary of some of the primary variations:

FORMAL: Formal design employs straight lines, right angles, regular geometric shapes, and decorative objects arranged in even numbers.

INFORMAL: Characterized by curved lines, irregular and free-flowing shapes, and odd-numbered groupings, informal styles emphasize balance instead of symmetry.

TRADITIONAL: Think Greek or Roman and you'll conjure up an approximate image of what traditional means. Imagine a formal courtyard accented with urns, fountains, columns, and lush foliage.

CONTEMPORARY: Cool, serene, and comfortable, a contemporary design might include bold shapes and colors, sleek lines, and abstract accents with an emphasis on color, texture, and light instead of representational forms.

■ Regional: Evolving from local climate and cultures, regional styles can offer a handsome solution to design problems because they fit their surroundings so well.

CREATING HARMONY

A successful landscape design will combine all its elements into a unified whole. Achieving that harmony requires an artful blending of the shape of the structure and its materials. Shape and materials impart form, mass, and texture and define the relationship of an outdoor space with the house and landscape.

■ To achieve a sense of unity, repeat or blend contours of the structure with dominant forms—the rectangles of the house; curves, angles, and shapes suggested by swimming pools; garden beds; or sloping lawns.

■ Select materials that complement the style of your home in the context of the yard. For example, a quarry-tile patio might look out of place with a Victorian house but would look perfect with a Southwestern adobe home.

■ Select accessories and furnishings that harmonize with the space and tie together the house and yard.

Here in the rustic desert, the house and pool offer the comforts of modern living. The design is formal but uses organic, regional shapes as accents. Like most successful patios, this one is built to fit its surroundings—not contradict them.

Paths create movement in the landscape. Straight paths give a formal look and lead to a destination quickly; curved paths are more casual and invite leisurely strolls through the garden.

■ Combine classic and modern styles to create space with old-style charm and modern convenience. Mix different regional accents to spice up the outdoor space with surprises.
■ Create a sense of continuity with materials, colors, shapes, and textures. Use small, carefully placed elements to contrast color, shape, or texture.
■ Arrange walls, plants, and walkways so that they lead to a focal point, a destination—any object or view you want to call attention to.

How will you know when the design you've created is harmonious? It will look soothing rather than jarring. It will present a cohesive blend more than a jumbled clutter of parts, and its general impression will be inviting and comfortable.

Color is an important design element and usually the first to be noticed. The right paint color or stain can dramatically improve the overall look of any outdoor structure.

Repeated patterns and finishes can help unify a design theme. Here the unstained but treated pine doors on the service island blend with the rear privacy fence and the furnishings.

FINDING YOUR STYLE

The best way to discover your personal style is to tour your neighborhood and mentally note things you like. Then jot down your impressions. Clip and file photos and diagrams from magazines. When you're ready to make your final design decisions, take the folder and spread its contents before you. Discard what doesn't appeal to you. You'll notice a general consistency in the images left over. Use the elements of that style in your paving patterns, fences, and overall landscape plan.

The plants surrounding a garden shed connect it to the landscape design. Enlist all the design elements—color, texture, line, and form—when developing a planting plan.

PLANTS IN ALL THE RIGHT PLACES

Without a connection to the other elements in your yard, even the most attractive outdoor structure ends up looking like an add-on in your landscape. With the addition of plants, however, you can easily integrate your new outdoor space into the landscape.

Plants solve design problems too. They can function as dividers, separating one area of the landscape or an outdoor structure from another. They can create privacy, add design interest, screen out unwanted views, and make small areas feel more intimate. Foliage offers a pleasing contrast in both color and texture to the materials used in the construction of any structure and provides a gentle visual transition to the rest of the yard.

SELECTING PLANTS

Plant selection depends on your personal preference. You might like contrast—a bed of white blooms in front of a dark-stained redwood—or complementary elements—a white flower bed around the base of a white Victorian gazebo. Red tulips or roses set off a white structure, making it a stronger visual accent, while shrubs along the side of a shed help to break up the lines of horizontal siding and add a textural contrast. Consider combining textural and color variations—for instance, using large yellow variegated foliage to smartly set off a coat of hunter-green paint.

Only inches high, variegated hosta surrounds a brick patio, forming an attractive divider.

Imagine this setting without the plantings and the resulting image is a stark, uninviting patio.

GET TO KNOW THE CULTURE

Culture—the conditions of soil, light, and water in which a plant thrives—is the most important consideration in selecting plants. Plants suited to the conditions in your landscape are more likely to grow successfully. And though plants native to your area have a greater chance of success than those from different regions, they are not the only good choices. The staff at your local garden center will help you choose plants that are compatible with the climate zone of your region and that will work in your setting.

Turn to the U.S. Department of Agriculture climatic zones map on page 237 to find the zone in which you live and compare it with the hardiness zone of any plant you are considering. There's a little leeway in the designations. If you live in Zone 4, for example, you may still be able to grow plants from warmer zones. Check with your garden center to be sure.

Plants and climbing roses naturally tie this gazebo to the landscape. Instead of standing out, it becomes an integral part of the garden.

ROOM FOR VINES

It takes only a small opening cut into paving to grow plants within a patio. Vines thrive in openings as small as 8 inches across.
A single vine can cover the face of a wall with a cloak of leaves.
Or plant one at the foot of an arbor to twine up a post and grow overhead.

For a tasteful, professionally designed appearance, aim for a unified color scheme in flowers and containers.

PRIVACY
CREATING A SENSE OF ENCLOSURE

Outdoor structures—decks and patios especially—need definition. Without definition both above and at the edges, you can feel exposed and uncomfortable. If your site lacks natural attributes that enhance privacy and a sense of enclosure, you can create them. Now is the time to build them into your plans.

Consider privacy first. Is your outdoor living space effectively screened from the street and from the neighbors' view? If your proposed site is on the least exposed side of the house or tucked behind a retaining wall or hedge, you may not have a privacy problem. And if your

site is located at a distance from the house or on a hillside above the surrounding views, you may not need to alter your design at all. But if you want to increase your privacy, add a fence, a wall, or trees and shrubs to your plans.

These elements will also produce a sense of enclosure, of course. But so will benches, garden beds, and other features. And remember to look up. Overhead space will have an impact on your comfort too. Open sky above your deck may cause you to feel unprotected. That's when you need an outdoor "ceiling" such as an arbor, a pergola, or tree limbs.

DON'T BUILD A FORTRESS

To avoid turning your yard into "Fort Redwood," avoid unnecessary barrier-style screens—solid walls, high fences, and dense, straight hedges. Use these only in areas that require the absolute maximum screening.

A deck shouldn't put you on display. Use a living barrier to screen you from the neighbors. Here a standard entrance to a deck mimics a hallway and creates an intimate sitting spot solely because of the surrounding vegetation.

Combine fences or walls with plantings for the best of both worlds. Walls offer instant privacy, and plants soften their hard surfaces. Use vines for a quick cover.

"UP" SCALE

Overhead space, both indoors and out, has a psychological impact. Indoors we feel most comfortable in rooms with 8- to 10-foot ceilings. Outdoors we're accustomed to higher ceilings, but we still feel more comfortable when the overhead space is somewhat closer to the indoor standard. In general make sure that space for intimate activities has some kind of cover over it, from 10 to 12 feet high. Areas for parties will feel more comfortable with ceilings up to 20 feet high. A rule of thumb for covering your patio from above: Shelter at least a third of the surface.

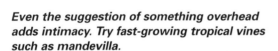

Even though the latticework on this gazebo provides some built-in privacy, this site needed the slat fence to shield it from the neighbors' view. The metal fence to the right provides visual definition without making the site feel closed in.

Even the suggestion of something overhead adds intimacy. Try fast-growing tropical vines such as mandevilla.

A privacy fence covered with dense foliage solves two problems at once. It creates privacy and also muffles unwanted noise.

WALLS AND FENCES

Walls and fences make beautiful additions to an outdoor design, connecting your living space to the larger landscape and adding a vertical contrast to the horizontal expanse of lawn.

Walls and fences can solve problems too:
■ They define space—giving it an identity that suits its purpose.
■ They can tame slopes, create privacy, reduce annoying winds, form backdrops for decorative accents, and hide utility areas.
■ They can make large areas seem less imposing by dividing them into smaller ones.

DEFINING SPACE

More than any other design element, walls and fences delineate space. For example, without a clearly defined perimeter, a ground-level deck may seem just an extension of the lawn. Without something to set your family dining space apart from entertainment areas, your weekend patio brunch can feel exposed. Both inside an outdoor structure and beyond it, you need something that visually separates one area from the others.

There are obvious walls, such as fences and the sides of the house. Then there are walls that are not so obvious, perceived walls:
■ ankle-high hedges
■ built-in seating
■ planters
■ posts that support an overhead
■ a change in decking pattern
■ even plants and small trees
Anything that separates your deck or patio

Subtle "walls" in this space define the seating area. The simple redwood planter, the terraced planting beds, and the open-topped fence all create a sense of intimate enclosure.

This fence is a design feature in itself. It hides a utility area and offers a garden seat plus a cozy nook with a table for two.

from the rest of the world—or separates one area from another—is behaving like a wall.

A low shrub hedge, for example, becomes a living wall that divides the deck from the rest of the lawn. A row of trees can do this too, filtering the views without blocking them.

Built-in benches and raised planters can keep your party space from encroaching on the private areas of your deck. Freestanding benches create the suggestion of a wall or fence and divide areas without completely enclosing them. They're especially useful when you need to separate two spaces that have closely related purposes.

Erecting solid walls, fences, or closely knit hedges to divide your property into bits of space can result in separate but isolated areas. Perceived walls imply the separation without isolating spaces from one another.

SCREENING FOR PRIVACY

The amount of privacy you'll need will depend on how you plan to use each of the areas on your deck.

HOW HIGH?

Let the purpose of a wall dictate its height. For security, a windbreak, or total screening, build a structure 6 to 8 feet tall. To separate spaces build walls as low as 6 inches or as high as 3 feet. In general any wall or fence should be either well above or well below eye level. There's nothing worse than having a wall or fence cut your view in half.

■ Cozy, intimate spots for reading, conversation, sunbathing, or meditation should provide plenty of privacy. Screen these areas with walls, high fences, or dense evergreen plantings.

■ Active areas, such as rooms for parties, family gatherings, or children's play, require less privacy. For these areas, partial screening should do the trick—latticework fences, airy trees, or seat walls.

Where you put privacy screens matters too. The closer to the deck area, the more privacy you'll get. The farther from the surface, the less privacy.

Very few patios will require screening around the entire perimeter. Before you plant a hedge all the way around your deck, figure out the angle from which other people can see you. Then plan the screening to block the most revealing views first. Remember your goal: Enhance privacy without barricading your outdoor space. Lattice, picket, and ornamental iron fencing form a friendly, see-through screen.

SCREENING OUT UNSIGHTLY VIEWS

When you're enjoying your outdoor room, you won't want to be looking at the garbage cans, the dog run, a heat pump, your neighbor's open garage, or parked cars. Consider the angles from which you see these sights, then strategically place screens to hide them from view.

A high, solid fence can turn your private retreat into a stockade. Here the owners have softened the potential isolation with painted lattice panels.

Simple built-in benches and lattice panels clearly separate this space from the lawn. Colorful flowers unify the elements in this design.

The panels on this deck offer privacy and safety. Those at the rear of the yard define the property without blocking the view.

A brick planter defines the shape of this planting bed and separates the small dining area from larger spaces on the patio.

OVERHEADS AND SHADE STRUCTURES

Whether you call it an arbor, pergola, lanai, or canopy, an overhead will enhance your deck with a minimum of materials and work.

FUNCTION FIRST

Let the use of your outdoor space determine whether it needs an overhead. The sky might be considered the ultimate ceiling for all of the outdoors, but many times it's too high for a deck or patio. Active areas, such as those designated for entertaining large numbers of guests or for children's play, can, of course, function well if left open. But more intimate areas, such as those planned for dining, talking, or relaxing, will feel more inviting and cozier with an overhead.

Protection from the elements is also a reason for an overhead.

If an open roof doesn't fit your landscape design but the cost of shingles isn't in your budget, let vines grow up the posts and cover the roof.

STYLE

No matter what your reason for building an overhead, make sure its design reflects and

Even a simple prefabricated arch makes a statement. A well-marked entrance, such as this arbor, lets everyone know they're entering a special place.

complements the overall architecture of your home. An overhead structure should appear to be an integral part of the design, not an add-on. By repeating some detail of your house—a molding or post style, pitch of the roof, accent color, or building material—you can link the overhead to your home.

Curved overheads lend a romantic cottage style to an outdoor space. Dressed and painted lumber suggest formality. Rough cedar or bentwood lends a rustic air to an archway. A modern metal framework or masonry arch adds a touch of old-world charm.

COMING TO TERMS WITH OVERHEADS

An arbor is a shelter of vines or latticework covered with climbing plants. A pergola is an overhead framework supported by columns. A lanai (a Hawaiian word) is a porch or veranda, uncovered or covered, and a canopy is either a solid roof or the roof of any of these structures.

RAFTER ANGLES

If you want an overhead to provide shade, take the time to experiment to find how to get the maximum amount of shade in the heat of a summer day and the minimum amount when it's cooler.

Monitor your proposed deck area to see when the sun makes the deck site too hot and bright to use. Note the season, the time of day, and the angle at which the sun shines on the area. Then position the overhead and design it to block the sun's rays from that angle by shading the areas where it's most needed.

Control the amount of sunlight reaching a sheltered area by varying the size, spacing, and orientation of framing members. Build the structure and then experiment with different slat configurations before attaching them to the roof.

Lattice slats oriented east to west will shade the area underneath for most of the day. Oriented north to south, they will provide the same amount of shade as east-to-west slats in the morning and evening but will allow some sun through to the area

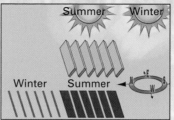
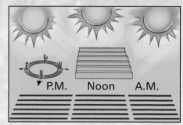
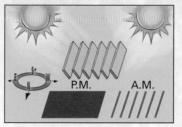
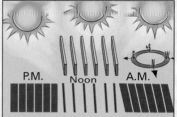

below at midday. Setting rafters at a 30-degree angle blocks more sun. Spacing slats close together will also provide more shade.

Attach louvers or lattices to the sides of the structure to filter low-angle rays on late summer afternoons, or plant vines to sprawl across the top and the sides.

Thanks to a careful analysis of sun and shade patterns, this design offers shady comfort with open, airy views.

ROOFED STRUCTURES

Structures with solid roofs—corrugated metal or plastic, cedar shakes, asphalt shingles, or slate tiles—offer more physical protection than open roofs. They keep you dry when it rains and totally block out the sunlight. They're especially helpful above outdoor cooking areas.

Solid-roofed structures create miniature environments underneath them. Shadows cast by the roof may cool nearby paving but may also darken the interior of your home. If possible, locate solid roofs away from the main portion of your deck so that the space is versatile for use in both fair and inclement weather.

GROWING PRIVACY AND ENCLOSURE

Should you build a wall or fence to increase your privacy or let plants do the job? The answer depends on your budget, your patience, and the look you are trying to achieve.

Plants grow. Fences and walls don't. For that reason privacy plantings make good economic sense. If you have the patience, you can start with small plants and wait for them to grow. Or you can invest in a few large plants to block critical areas and set out smaller plants to fill in where you don't mind waiting for a living screen to mature.

Then there are the neighbors. A substantial fence can create sore feelings next door. Trees, shrubs, and other plants create a softer look than fences or walls, so it might not be as evident to the neighbors that you're putting up a privacy screen. Plantings also remove the possibility that your neighbors (or you) won't like looking at the back side of a fence. If your yard already has a lot of paving or decking, using plants instead of fencing keeps the hard scape from overwhelming the space.

Privacy planting doesn't mean you have to enclose your deck completely. Tree trunks, branches, and foliage can filter views for natural privacy.

VINES FOR ARBORS AND PERGOLAS

Common Name	Botanical Name	Features	Zones
Armand clematis	Clematis armandii	Fragrant flowers, evergreen foliage	7–9
Bougainvillea	Bougainvillea glabra	Winter flowers	9–10
Carolina jessamine	Gelsemium sempervirens	Spring flowers	8–10
Clematis	Clematis hybrids	Spring flowers	4–8
Climbing roses	Rosa hybrids	Showy flowers	Varies
Confederate jasmine	Trachelospermum jasminoides	Fragrant flowers	8–10
Coral vine	Antigonon leptopus	Summer flowers	8–10
European hop	Humulus lupulus	Bright foliage	5–8
Hyacinth bean	Lablab purpureus	Purple fruit; rapid-growing annual	7–10
Moonflower vine	Ipomoea alba	Summer flowers; rapid-growing annual	8–10
Morning glory	Ipomoea tricolor	Summer flowers; rapid-growing annual	4–10
Silver lace vine	Polygonum aubertii	Summer flowers	4–8
Sweet autumn clematis	Clematis terniflora	Fall flowers	6–9
Trumpet honeysuckle	Lonicera sempervirens	Summer flowers	4–9

SELECTING PLANTS

If you've decided to plant a screen but aren't sure how to choose the plants, consider the amount of privacy you need.

■ If you need year-round and total privacy, evergreens will yield the best results. These species shed their foliage discreetly throughout the year instead of dropping the leaves all at once. You may have to put up with a small trade-off, however—many evergreens grow at a slower pace than deciduous plants.

■ If seasonal privacy will suffice, plant deciduous species. Their screening ability increases in spring and summer when they bear leaves and decreases in autumn and winter when foliage falls. Even without leaves, the structure of the plant forms a visible barrier that defines space.

Some tree species, such as serviceberry, feature multiple trunks that lend themselves beautifully to separating areas and creating a sense of enclosure. They offer a measure of privacy too. Deciduous trees permit winter rays to warm your deck and allow sunlight to reach inside your home. Mixing evergreen and deciduous trees and shrubs together gives you the best of both worlds.

The fronds of a potted palm serve as a perceived wall. This simple barrier focuses attention within the outdoor room.

EVERGREEN SCREENS

Common Name	Botanical Name	Zones
TREES		
Canadian hemlock	*Tsuga canadensis*	3–7
Colorado blue spruce	*Picea pungens glauca*	3–7
Douglas fir	*Pseudotsuga menziesii*	4–6
Eastern red cedar	*Juniperus virginiana*	3–9
Leyland cypress	× *Cupressocyparis leylandii*	6–10
Loquat	*Eriobotrya japonica*	8–10
Norway spruce	*Picea abies*	3–8
White pine	*Pinus strobus*	3–8
SHRUBS		
American arborvitae	*Thuja occidentalis*	3–7
Hick's yew	*Taxus × media* 'Hicksii'	5–7
Inkberry	*Ilex glabra*	3–10
Leatherleaf viburnum	*Viburnum rhytidophyllum*	6–8
Lusterleaf holly	*Ilex latifolia*	7–9
Nelly R. Stevens holly	*Ilex* 'Nellie R. Stevens'	6–9
Oleander	*Nerium oleander*	8–10
Yew pine	*Podocarpus macrophyllus*	8–10

GOOD DECK AND PATIO TREES

No tree is completely mess-free, but these trees come pretty close. They mature at 30 to 35 feet tall or less and adapt to confined conditions.

Common Name	Botanical Name	Features	Zones
American yellowwood	*Cladrastis lutea*	Fragrant flowers	5–8
Amur maple	*Acer tataricum ginnala*	Shade, fall color	3–8
Apple serviceberry	*Amelanchier × grandiflora*	Spring flowers, fall color	3–8
Chinese elm	*Ulmus parvifolia*	Interesting bark	4–9
Crape myrtle	*Lagerstroemia indica*	Summer flowers, sculptural form	7–9
Eastern redbud	*Cercis canadensis*	Spring flowers	4–9
European mountain ash	*Sorbus aucuparia*	Fall color	3–6
Japanese maple	*Acer palmatum*	Fall color, sculptural form	5–8
Sargent cherry	*Prunus sargentii*	Spring flowers	5–8
Sweet bay magnolia	*Magnolia virginiana*	Fragrant summer flowers	5–9
Yaupon holly	*Ilex vomitoria*	Winter berries; prune into tree form	7–9
Washington hawthorn	*Crataegus phaenopyrum*	Winter berries	4–9
Wax myrtle	*Myrica cerifera*	Fine-textured, evergreen foliage; prune into tree form	8–10
Wax-leaf privet	*Ligustrum lucidum*	Glossy evergreen foliage; prune into tree form	7–9
Yoshino cherry	*Prunus × yedoensis*	Spring flowers	5–9

Flowering trees and shrubs can add intimacy to a seating area without the formal feel of clipped hedges. Combine deciduous plants with fences or with evergreens. You'll have both seasonal interest and year-round structure.

ADDING AMENITIES

Amenities bring many of the comforts of the indoors into the beauty and spaciousness of the outdoors. Which amenities you choose will depend on how you want to use the space.

Outdoor kitchens allow the cook to escape the heat and isolation of the indoor kitchen and enjoy more time with guests. An outdoor cooking area with a propane grill and cabinetry can be as easy to use as an indoor kitchen. With a working sink outdoors, you can cook entire meals without dashing in and out of the house.

Outdoor lighting adds decorative beauty as well as extra hours to the enjoyment of a patio or deck. Easily installed low-voltage systems can set just the right mood.

Consider including a fireplace, chiminea, or fire pit in your patio plans. Just as a fireplace inside provides a cozy gathering point, firelight outside draws guests and family to its dancing flames and crackling embers.

Just off the patio or deck—or anywhere in your landscape for that matter—a small pool with a fountain adds charm. So does a container or tabletop fountain, which are available at home centers. Research a water feature first to find suitable plants and fish—species that require minimal maintenance.

If your design includes any of these amenities but your budget doesn't, plan for them now and add them later. At a minimum, you'll probably want outdoor electrical receptacles and running water.

An outdoor kitchen lets the cook prepare food and mingle with guests instead of being consigned to the indoors.

PLANNING FOR AMENITIES

Many patio amenities require plumbing, electrical, or natural-gas installations, and all of these requirements should be included in your plans before you start building your outdoor living space.

For example, a spa requires running water and a drainpipe. Spas, ponds, fountains, and waterfall pumps require electrical outlets with ground fault circuit interrupters (GFCIs). Lighting systems require electric lines. A permanent natural-gas line for a gas grill might be preferable to propane tanks. An exterior phone jack is useful for households that haven't yet gone wireless. If outdoor activities include watching TV, you'll need an electric outlet and perhaps an exterior cable connection.

Utilities are best run underground to the site—both for safety and to avoid clutter. Plot the utility run so that it does not interfere with anything else in the area. Rough-in the systems after excavation and finish them before laying any foundation.

Outdoor lighting not only extends the use of your deck into the evening hours but it also creates its own special ambience, giving your deck an entirely different character at night than during the day.

This pool and waterfall may look complex, but their installation requires only a few basic skills. Start with a pool liner as shown on page 233 and surround it with mortared flagstone. Set the flagstone steps at a slight angle toward the pool to direct the water downward.

This outdoor storage closet has a split personality. The doors closest to the yard (right) provide access to lawn equipment. The back side holds deck furniture (left). The closet separates the private sitting area on the deck from the entry area.

OUTDOOR KITCHENS

Cooking and serving food outdoors provide an easygoing alternative to indoor food preparation. Incorporating an outdoor kitchen in your landscape plans requires only a little creativity and perhaps some minor modifications to make the space easy to use, efficient, and pleasurable. You can equip the kitchen with facilities ranging from a plain charcoal grill to a fancy gas range and complete the kitchen with an outdoor sink.

Your deck becomes a favorite dining room if it's conveniently close to the kitchen and offers cooking facilities.

LOCATION, LOCATION

Because a moveable grill—gas or charcoal—will fit just about anywhere, you might think it doesn't make much difference where you put it. But portable or permanent, using a grill can have disastrous consequences if its location is poorly planned.

First find the safest spot. Convenience is important, but safety is more important. Locate a portable grill so it's far enough away from flammable surfaces and little ones' hands. Construct a built-in with fire-prevention methods that conform to your local building codes.

Whether portable or permanent, put grills out of traffic paths and views. Take care that they don't pose other hazards—you don't want anyone to get smoked out. Install an overhead shelter with a vent or locate the grill under overhanging eaves. This way you can continue grilling if it starts to rain. And if your unit is portable and you don't have room to store it somewhere, you'll need a waterproof cover when it's not in use.

Your outdoor kitchen should include enough room for preparing and serving food as well as storage space for utensils. If you're adding a portable grill to your plans but lack space for full-blown serving areas, keep cooking items handy but out of sight by tucking them inside a potting bench or other cabinetry or behind a screen. Large potted plants will do a good job of hiding the grill too. Set them on platforms with casters for easier maneuverability.

BUILT-INS

Permanent fixtures, such as outdoor cooktops, ovens, and refrigerators, offer a host of options that will turn your patio into a summer kitchen. You'll find compact cooktop-only units as well as combination units with a built-in rotisserie, grill, or griddle that fit into a relatively small space.

Look for outdoor-grade equipment that meets building codes and withstands all weather conditions. Choose from cooktops fueled by wood, charcoal, electricity, or natural gas. Have electric or gas lines installed before setting up the unit.

Even weather-resistant appliances need shelter—waterproof countertops made of marble, metal, or tile will prove to be an investment that gives you plenty of elbowroom for preparing meals. Have your contractor help you calculate the expense of building the countertop large enough to form a 15- to 18-inch overhang opposite the cooking area for a bar or buffet. Waterproof cabinets prove useful too. So will storage made for a kitchen-size garbage can. Close cabinets with screen door hooks or a sliding bolt to keep critters out.

Cooking out is easier when your outdoor room contains built-in cooking space. Whether it's a spot for charcoal grilling or a gas stove top, there are many choices of equipment available for fresh-air use.

ADDING AN OUTDOOR KITCHEN

When retrofitting your landscape for outdoor kitchen space, think small. You may need only a modest extension to an existing deck or patio surface. Build a grill-size spot from the same materials as your deck. Or add a kitchen patio. Use concrete stepping-stones or precast pavers on a sand base—they will go with almost any design scheme.

The best outdoor cooking areas offer plenty of weather-proof storage as well as room to prepare and serve meals. After all, you don't want to tote supplies every time you cook out.

Arranging an outdoor kitchen is a lot like arranging one indoors. But you may need extra countertop room for shared work space if family members enjoy cooking together out-of-doors.

LIGHTING

Low-voltage lights can transform your landscape. They enhance views from within your house and give outdoor spots an after-hours glow.

Lighting extends the use of your landscape into the evening hours and makes it safer and more secure at night, even when you're not using it.

Adding lights to an outdoor structure takes planning and care, but it's not difficult. Choose the lighting system you prefer, review the installation guidelines, and prepare to enjoy your outdoor living space any time of day or night.

LIGHTING SOURCES

Decorative and concealed light fixtures lend style and atmosphere to outdoor space as well as bolster home security.

CONCEALED: Concealed light sources focus attention on an object or area, not the fixture itself. Tucked among plants, in a tree, or at ground level, strong lightbulbs typically cast their beams a long distance. Place the fixtures carefully so the bulbs aren't visible from any angle.

DECORATIVE: Decorative fixtures throw a more diffused and weaker light than concealed fixtures. You should be able to look at them without squinting. They come in two forms—either as freestanding units mounted on short pillars or made for mounting on posts or walls. Decorative fixtures should fit their setting. For example, small lanterns perched atop chunky pilasters or hanging on a large empty wall will look out of proportion.

LIGHTING STRATEGIES

Getting the right light in the right places on your patio or deck means combining light from various sources in different strategies.

UPLIGHTING: This technique, in which a concealed fixture casts light up into an object from its base, adds drama to your patio. Use uplighting to draw attention to an area or decorative object. Position the fixture so its beams graze trees or artwork to highlight their shapes. Or aim the light toward a wall or

NEW LIGHT FOR AN OLD DECK

When building a new deck, you can lay PVC pipes through the area before installing the paving so you can run wires easily for lighting. But if it's too late for that, you can hide wiring by attaching it to the underside of structures.

You can install perimeter low-voltage lighting at any time. And where the space gets at least six hours of sun, consider installing solar fixtures. They don't require any wires at all.

LIGHTING WITH STYLE

Low-voltage lights are available in styles that range from Victorian revival to high-tech. Most are designed for in-the-ground installation, but many can be mounted on deck railings, under stairs, or along fences. Halogen bulbs cost more initially but are less expensive to operate.

Lighting steps, stairs, or decking to prevent stumbling requires bright lights wherever there's a change in level.

Concealed fixtures and path lighting (left) combine to illuminate the outdoor room and turn the upper-story deck into a sculptural element.

Conventional path lighting (above left) runs off an electrical system. Solar path lighting (above right) operates on special batteries that store the sun's energy during the day.

fence silhouetting the shapes of plants, trees, sculptures, or fountains.

Position the fixture in front of the object so that the beam shines away from viewing areas. Or use can lights, which are recessed into the ground and shine upward at an angle while shielding the bulb from view.

DOWNLIGHTING: Downlighting casts a soft, indirect glow on horizontal surfaces such as steps, paths, floors, balconies, and tabletops. Mount the fixtures on tree trunks, branches, or overhead rafters.

A special type of conduit is available for running wiring up trees without harming them. On arbor rafters, thread wires through the center of hollow columns or cut a rabbet along the length of a solid post to create a channel for the wiring.

Keep downlighting fixtures out of sight so that they don't draw attention from the illuminated object. As with other lights, aim

them to illuminate your yard and outdoor rooms, not those of your neighbors.

PATH LIGHTING: These low-level decorative fixtures cast light directly along a walkway, linking your outdoor room and other parts of your yard such as the driveway, parking area, or pool. Use a single or matched pair of path lights to illuminate short flights of exterior steps or to mark points of entry.

BEWARE THE GLARE

Artfully placed fixtures cast gentle pools of light that transform your deck into evening-friendly space. Choose lighting that improves the setting and helps guests feel comfortable. Mounting bright spotlights to shine on the deck will provide plenty of light, but that's all. Your guests will feel uncomfortable under the glare.

LINE VOLTAGE AND LOW VOLTAGE?

Lighting systems come in two forms: line voltage, which uses the 120-volt AC power in your house, or low voltage, which uses power reduced by a transformer to 12 volts of direct current. Working with line voltage is easy enough for homeowners with experience doing their own electrical work. But it can be dangerous to use outdoors; you may want to hire professional electricians.

■ Most outdoor line-voltage installations require approval from a building inspector. Because low-voltage systems are safer for outdoor use, they seldom require inspection unless you add a new 120-volt circuit to feed the low-voltage system. Even with low-voltage circuits, you need to use care and follow all manufacturer's instructions carefully.

■ Low voltage is safe, easy to install, and inexpensive to operate. Line voltage is compatible with the wiring you already have, and it's useful for outdoor appliances and power tools as well as lighting. If you can't decide which

system to use, think about which one matches your needs best.

■ A line-voltage system requires conduit, fittings, junction boxes, receptacles, fixtures, bulbs, wire, and connectors. Your supplier can tell you what other materials, tools, and hardware you'll need. Low-voltage systems are designed for use outdoors and require fewer accessories.

■ Several kinds of fixtures are available for both systems, but low-voltage systems generally offer more options. You can find lights to illuminate patio surfaces, walkways, and stairways. Others are made to show off plantings, walls, fountains, and other special features. Fixtures are available in many different materials, from molded plastic to hand-finished teak to cast bronze.

■ A retailer who handles outdoor lighting may offer free design advice to customers. Take your plan along in case you need to ask for help.

FIRELIGHT

Outdoor fireplaces bring warmth and intimacy to fresh-air rooms. The style of an outdoor fireplace, especially if it's near the house, should match the style of the home. Its design shouldn't look like you're trying to use up leftover brick.

No artificial light source can match the comforting glow of a controlled fire. Firelight brings instant coziness and extends your landscape's potential for use.

Firelight is most appealing at night, encouraging after-hours use of the outdoor room. Fires also take the chill out of spring and fall evenings.

Most homeowners don't think about including a fireplace or fire pit when planning their landscape. But it's easy enough to do, in either new or existing installations.

FIREPLACES

Unlike interior fireplaces, which are built into a wall, most outdoor fireplaces are freestanding, although you can build a fireplace into a wall or use it to accent a retaining wall against a hillside. Made of mortared brick or stone, outdoor fireplaces resemble conventional fireplaces. A hearth provides a fireproof safeguard against burning embers that tumble out. Andirons hold logs in place. A fire screen contains exploding embers and sparks that fly from burning logs. A damper controls drafts. If you like, include a rotisserie and a brick-lined warming oven in the plan, and use your fireplace for cooking and keeping food hot.

Build the outdoor fireplace so it will suit the way you use your outdoor living area, as a warming place near the pool or the backdrop for an outdoor room. Whether you construct your fireplace of masonry, firebrick, or other material, it should match the style of your home. Choose a rustic look with a wide stone-ledge mantel for a log home. Or design a neat brick structure if your home is more traditional. Cover masonry with a stucco finish, if you prefer, but consult a contractor about fire retardation before applying finishes. Cap the chimney as you would a house

FIRES AND CODES

Before building a fireplace or fire pit into your plans, check local regulations.

Many communities have setback and construction requirements as well as seasonal burning rules. Arid, fire-prone areas may restrict outdoor fires altogether.

AN OVERWHELMING ACCENT?

Outdoor fireplaces are imposing features that draw attention year-round. Remember to treat your fireplace as a focal point so its presence doesn't overwhelm the rest of the space. Position it where it won't compete with other accents.

Follow this rule: Step into your proposed or existing deck or patio location. Glance around. What do you see? An outdoor fireplace and chimney will probably dominate the scene. If that's the case, plan to put other items of interest, such as a sculpture, a fountain, or outstanding specimen plants where people won't see them within the same initial glance.

Once limited to the Southwest, chimineas are available just about anywhere. These wood-burners cost less than a fireplace and are convenient for open or roofed areas. Use a vent pipe in closed or roofed areas.

Build a raised pit for safety. Raised pits prevent guests from accidentally stepping into the fire, and they contain sparks as well.

chimney and screen it to keep out birds and other animals. Dress up the mantel with potted greenery, flowers, and natural treasures such as driftwood and attractive stones for visual appeal when the fireplace is not in use.

CHIMINEAS AND FIRE PITS

Chimineas, a portable fire source, resemble potbelly stoves. These kiln-fired ceramic pieces, which originated in Mexico, spread first through the southwestern United States and have become increasingly popular in other regions. A chiminea holds a fire in its rounded base, which has an opening for feeding logs (and showing flames). It has a chimney tapering upward from the base. Usually chimineas sit on a metal stand to prevent overheating any underlying paving or decking.

These decorative fireplaces add comfort with their heat and provide the sound and scent of burning logs. But they are not designed for cooking. Store them indoors when temperatures fall below freezing. If moisture held by the porous surface of the terra-cotta freezes and expands, the chiminea can crack, flake, or begin deteriorating.

Other styles of freestanding gas and wood-burning fire pits are also now widely available. Classic, in-ground fire pits are open to the sky. Lined with firebricks and surrounded by a wide, fire-resistant coping, such as stone, their open flames resemble campfires. What's more fun than gathering around an inviting fire to toast marshmallows or even cook a meal?

Plan carefully before constructing a fire pit. Provide plenty of floor space on all sides of the pit to keep people a safe distance from the flames. Provide seating nearby so you and your guests can gather for conversation in the firelight and warmth.

Like other fireplaces, fire pits require common sense. Make safety a priority; instruct every family member what to do if a fire grows out of control, and keep an extinguisher handy. Have a cover for clamping over the pit to smother flames should they grow too large. The cover also helps contain sparks, which could blow out of the pit after the party is over.

SOFT LIGHT

Don't despair if fires are not allowed in your community or your space is too small. Even the tiniest outdoor area has room for candles, no matter where you live. Their glimmer transforms the plainest spot into a magical world. Lighting groups of candles gives you the satisfaction of settling into your own little retreat. Candlelight sets an intimate mood for dinner under the stars. Candles also complement a low-voltage lighting system and offer just the right touch for nighttime outdoor entertaining.

WATER FEATURES

For a natural look, edge a pond with materials native to your region. Keep edges irregularly shaped, as if the water had cut a channel through the soil or the stones over time. Set water plants around the edges and stock with fish for movement.

a hole for a pond next to your patio and form the base of the pond with a flexible liner.

All water features must follow one basic guideline: The water should be aerated. Stagnant water breeds mosquitoes, anaerobic—smelly—bacteria, and algae. It also collects silt and debris. Water spilling over the edge of a waterfall or splashing out of a fountain picks up air, which helps it stay fresh.

To keep water moving install a submersible pump that recirculates the water, sending it to the top of a waterfall, out of a fountainhead, or back and forth in the pond. You must also keep intake filters clean so that debris doesn't clog the pump. Liners, submersible pumps, and fountainheads are readily available at home centers, aquatic shops, and nurseries. Ask an employee to help you select the right materials for your water garden.

Want your landscape to really sparkle? Let the sound of moving water do the job. Even if you don't need to subdue distracting sounds from beyond your yard, the gentle splashes and trickles will make your outdoor room seem a world apart.

Still water in a shallow reflecting pond, with its glassy surface, acts as a natural mirror and creates a contemplative, calm setting. Moving water plays with light, catching it, refracting it, and casting it about. Fountainheads spurt water in several basic patterns: glassy mushrooms, multilevel tiers, gurgling bubbles, and streams from a spitter. Some fountainheads offer several patterns in one.

INSTALLATION OPTIONS

Putting in a water feature can be as easy as setting up a small pond using a preformed, rigid liner. Leave room in the paving for excavating, and set the liner either in or on top of the patio surface, camouflaging it with landscape timbers or rocks. Alternatively dig

The sound of splashing water soothes and cheers us. Moving water also muffles the noise of an air-conditioner, traffic, and other common annoying sounds.

MAKING PLANS

When including a water feature in the construction of a paved patio, plan for the installation of a pair of 2-inch schedule-40 PVC pipes across the patio site. Draw them in your plans so they run like tunnels under the paving—from one end of the patio to the other. Always run power and water lines through separate sleeves.

STORAGE

Any utilitarian items you plan to use in your landscape—garbage cans, firewood, furniture covers, pet supplies, garden tools, or barbecue utensils—need a spot to call home. Finding places to put such items—and keeping the living space from looking like a giant storage box—takes a little creative thinking.

NIFTY STORAGE PLACES

■ When adding a privacy wall, build it with space for firewood.

■ Paint a child's toy box with weatherproof exterior paint and use it as an outdoor coffee table with built-in storage.

■ Keep pet supplies and birdseed in watertight galvanized bins, which protect them from weather and pesky critters looking for food.

■ Buy an extra mailbox or decorative bin to provide a dry place for storing small hand tools and garden gloves.

■ Place a baker's rack against a blank wall to store empty flowerpots, harvest baskets, and watering cans.

■ Use everyday yard tools as outdoor art. Mount hooks or handle holders on walls for hanging shovels, rakes, and hoes. The back or side of a garage, where the roof overhangs, provides a protected place. If you have a wall but no eaves, mount a shallow awning overhead to shelter the tools from weather and help prevent rusting.

■ Buy freestanding benches with lids—or build them into the perimeter of your deck.

■ Prefabricated fence sections or lattice panels mounted on posts conceal garbage cans as well as heating and cooling units without obstructing airflow.

■ Mount a trellis to support vines on the side of your home to hide exterior conduit and wires. If a utility meter spoils the look of your outdoor room, build a box around it with a hinged door for the meter reader to open. (Contact your utility company first; some have rules against this.)

Overhanging eaves protect outdoor closets full of yard and garden tools. Hung above the ground and under the roof, such cabinets are simple and secure.

Unused space beneath a built-in bench offers a dry niche for storing firewood conveniently close to a fire pit.

Old shutters create functional as well as stylish screens.

ASSESSING THE SITE

Look out at the vast wilderness of your yard. In that space lie both numerous limitations and countless possibilities. You'll want to know exactly what these are before you begin constructing any outdoor structure.

The features of your landscape can affect both where you put your project and how you design it. Now is the time to assess your site to determine any modifications it will require.

Terrain is perhaps the most important feature. Although no site is perfectly level, a basically flat yard will keep your job uncomplicated. A slope, especially one that falls off sharply, might call for grading the soil and installing a retaining wall to hold back the remaining soil. A steep slope might mean locating your project at another spot.

Drainage, existing vegetation, views, and climate should be considered. After a rain, is there a newly carved canyon or a sparkling lake marking your lawn? Are your trees providing shade or just blocking a view, or is the view undesirable anyway? How about street noise and privacy?

Many of these features, of course, are beyond your control, but ignoring them can result in an unused and unattractive area. If you design your outdoor living space with them in mind, you can minimize their effects. The key is working with nature and not against it.

Steps make a slope easier to climb. They also break the contours of the slope and add interest to the course of the walk.

This Victorian gazebo provides shade from the midday sun and shelter from the rain. Outdoor structures should take into account local climate as well as family recreational needs.

A deck can make practical use of terrain that might otherwise prove impractical. Here the ground-level platforms break the slope into tiers, a solution that minimizes extensive grading.

ON-SITE PHOTOS

Take pictures of your yard when assessing your site. The camera is less forgiving than your eye. It's easy for you to overlook things you see every day. You'll be surprised how much the photos call attention to details you may have missed.

Perhaps you forgot that the neighbors can see right into your window. Or you may not have noticed how unattractive your shed is.

Photos allow you to bring landscaping problems indoors to your kitchen table, giving you an objective tool to help you plan.

Digital cameras and accompanying computer software programs can make your picture planning even more fun. Take photos from one end of your property to the other and let the computer create a panoramic view. Other programs allow you to add trees and architectural elements to your photos so you can preview potential landscape changes.

CLIMATES AND MICROCLIMATES

Your outdoor room should offer more than privacy, protection, and plenty of seating. It should take advantage of the natural surroundings, such as cooling breezes, warm sun, shade, and subtle garden fragrances. Paying attention to weather patterns and

designing your project for maximum comfort in a variety of conditions can extend its usefulness.

OFF THE AXIS

Many homes are not situated on a true north–south, east–west axis, and an outdoor room on such sites will get a mixture of sun and shade. For example, a patio on the southeast side of a house will get sun much of the day but escape the hot late-afternoon sun.

To get an idea of how your site will be affected, make a rough sketch of your home. Experiment with different locations for your new outdoor structure, shading in the shadow patterns illustrated on these pages.

SUN AND SHADE

As the sun travels overhead throughout the day and year, it sends down varying amounts of warmth and light. Shadows cast by trees, walls, and rooflines will also shift with the sun's movement. Plan your outdoor room so this natural effect corresponds to the times of the day and the seasons when you'll use it.

Take an inventory of how much sun and shade your yard receives during the day, especially during the warm months. Keep track of shifting shade patterns with stakes driven in the ground. Note the patterns on paper. Refer to your notes when you begin to draw your plans.

If your proposed site is already shaded during the times you'll use it, then locating it is not a problem. However, if you are limited on where your patio can go and shade is what you desire, consider these options:
■ Trees and other plants provide shade to a site that gets too much afternoon sun.

Most north-side locations will be in almost constant shade and will probably be cool on all but the hottest days. If you're planning a north-side patio or deck, you may want to build it some distance from the house or large enough to reach beyond the shadow line of the house. That would provide both shady and sunny areas in the summer. This site would work well in a climate that is hot year-round.

Southern sites get sun all day and may need added shade from trees or an overhead structure. Although the south side of the house receives sun most of the day, it does so from different angles, depending on the season. A summer sun arcs high in the sky, but a winter sun arcs low. A south-facing patio or deck with a lattice-covered pergola would have filtered sun in summer and full sun in winter. Outdoor space on the south side will have the best chance of getting winter sun in mild-winter climates.

■ A pergola helps filter hot sunlight, and so can a roll-out awning, which also can be retracted when it's not needed.

■ Let roses or vines climb up an arbor to create a private shaded spot that doesn't block cooling summer breezes.

■ Vines climbing up a lattice wall can cool off a site that gets hot in the late afternoon.

■ Or you could find a location that features both partial shade and partial sunlight during the hours of greatest use.

If you can't find the perfect patio spot that gets both sunlight and shade, create separate areas for each. As shown here, an open table and shaded lounge chair would allow you to sit in the sun on cool days and move to a shady spot when it's hot.

For breakfast in the early light or a cool spot for evening meals, an east-facing site is ideal. The eastern sun warms the cool morning air, but an east-side site will also be shaded sooner than any other location. For example, by 5 p.m. an east-side location will be shaded for several feet, and by 7:30 p.m., even in the summer, it will be engulfed in shade. Depending upon your climate, such early shade can be an asset to your outdoor room or restrict its hours of use.

A west-facing site will get the hot afternoon sun and without natural or added shade may become unbearably hot in the afternoon. The west side starts the day in shade but gets the hot sun from early afternoon until sunset, and surfaces will radiate heat long after dusk. To create an outdoor room that's enjoyable from early afternoon to evening, you may want to consider a wraparound style that takes advantage of both western and northern exposures.

CLIMATES AND MICROCLIMATES
continued

Trellises invite climbing plants to form screens that provide beauty and privacy without blocking breezes.

TREES, PLANTS, AND MICROCLIMATES

Unless you're building a brand-new house, your choice of outdoor living sites will be affected by your landscape: Your yard will be either hilly or flat, sunny or shaded. And although you have little control over the terrain, you can moderate temperature extremes around your outdoor room by carefully planting trees and shrubs.

Trees can add welcome shade and break up harsh winds. Deciduous trees—oaks, maples, and walnuts—are quite bushy in the summer, providing cooling shade, but lose their leaves in the winter, warming the area by letting the sun shine through. That makes

them a practical investment in moderate-climate areas where a patio, deck, or gazebo is in use most of the year.

No matter where you live, your yard will have prevailing winds—most often coming from different directions in the summer and winter. Plant to take advantage of the wind. In summer you'll want to channel the wind toward the site; in winter you'll want to block it.

As you design your space, minimize the variety of trees and bushes to unify the design, and don't plant deep-rooted trees or bushes too near the house or patio; their roots can undermine the foundation or the surface.

WIND

The wind will affect your outdoor comfort as much as the sun. A pleasant breeze may bring welcome relief on a hot day, but gusting winds can make it impossible to enjoy the space.

Study the wind patterns in your yard, and learn to make a distinction between prevailing winds (the general direction of wind currents) and seasonal breezes (those localized to a time of day or season).

If possible locate your outdoor living space in a spot that's sheltered from the effect of strong prevailing winds. If your site is exposed, a slatted fence or windbreak (trees or hedges) can transform a strong wind into a breeze that flows across a deck or patio, cooling and freshening the air.

RAIN AND SNOW

Rain doesn't need to inhibit your outdoor fun. A solid roof over a part of your patio or deck can keep you dry outdoors in wet weather. So can a gazebo or retractable awning.

If you live in an area with harsh winters, construct overhead roofs so they won't be vulnerable to snow buildup or ice dams. And be sure to retract the awning before the first snow. Rain will also affect the relationship of your outdoor floor to the indoor floor. Build your patio or deck about an inch lower than the floor inside to keep rain from seeping in.

In snowy climates you'll want to keep the snow from becoming an uninvited guest in your family room or kitchen. Build the surface 3 or 4 inches below the interior floor. Heavy snowfalls might mean dropping the outdoor floor to about 8 inches below the inside room, but you can ease this drop with an outdoor landing.

CREATING A MICROCLIMATE

Did you ever notice that the air on a patio feels a bit different from that a few feet away? That's because the materials create what's called a microclimate.

Different paving materials absorb different amounts of heat and light from the sun each day. For example, a light-colored concrete slab in full sun reflects a lot of heat. Although its surface may remain comfortable, it can reflect harsh, glaring sunlight. By contrast a dark brick surface won't reflect the brilliance of sunlight but will absorb a tremendous amount of heat. This can make a patio uncomfortable underfoot during the day, but the stored heat radiates during the cool of the evening, prolonging the daytime warmth.

Likewise a hilltop site will feel warmer on a calm day than one at the base of a hill because cooler air flows downhill. What's more, if you trap the cold air at the bottom of a hill with a retaining wall, a fence, or a house wall, you might make your space quite cool in the evening.

The construction of a wall or fence can also create a microclimate. Don't expect a solid structure to help reduce winds. Wind-control research shows that solid fences create low-pressure pockets that pull the wind down into the very area you want protected. The wind swirls over the top and drops back down at a distance roughly equal to the height of the fence.

This means that if your quiet site is "protected" by a solid 6-foot wall, the force of the wind on your patio at about 6 feet from the wall is roughly the same as on the other side. Build louvered fences or walls with open areas on top to filter the wind and let it through instead of causing it to vault over the top and come down with a vengeance.

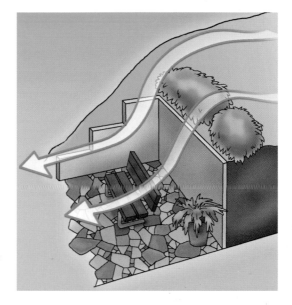

Because cool air is heavier than warm air, it will flow downhill, making a deck or patio site at the bottom of a slope cooler than one at the same elevation but on level ground.

FROST AND FOUNDATIONS

In climates that experience frequent freeze-thaw cycles, a mortared surface will require excavation and concrete footings. Without this extra support, the frost will heave and crack the surface.

WINDSCREEN/FENCE HEIGHTS

Wind protection drops off at a distance approximately equal to the height of the fence.

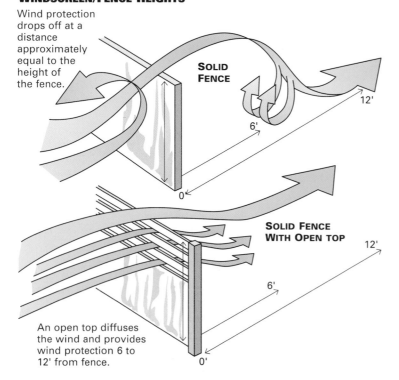

SOLID FENCE

12'

6'

0'

SOLID FENCE WITH OPEN TOP

12'

6'

0'

An open top diffuses the wind and provides wind protection 6 to 12' from fence.

This fence was built for privacy and to reduce prevailing winds. Although it is tall, topping it with lattice admits sunlight, controls the view, and tames the winds into gentle breezes.

SLOPES, SOIL, AND DRAINAGE

Raised decks put living space where you want it. This curving bench doubles as a safety rail. Before building a deck around existing trees, check whether the trees are healthy and a long-lived species.

Sloping sites, such as hillsides, banks, ravines, and drainage swales, often pose problems, but they may offer more opportunities than you think. If you ignored a slope when developing your design concept, take a second look.

Land sloping away from a high spot offers a view to the area below. Land that slants uphill generally creates privacy and shelter from harsh winds. A seemingly problematic area might turn out to be the best spot for a new landscape structure. Where there's a slope, there's usually a way to grade it level.

LEVELING THE SOIL

To level a slope, cut into its side to remove soil and form a flat area, or fill in a low point, or do both.

Cutting or filling will create a level surface suitable for a patio, but fill dirt is not stable and will settle unevenly, causing your patio to crack. You'll need to tamp and firm the loose surface of a filled area before paving it. If you plan a paving project that requires more than 6 inches of fill, consider spanning the slope with a deck instead.

If soil sloughs off when you cut into a slope,

you should build a retaining wall to hold it in place. Even if a retaining wall isn't necessary, building one will give you a cozy site nestled into a hillside.

DRAINAGE

Improper drainage can damage hard scape and plantings. It can cause concrete surfaces to become slick with mud, wash out flower beds, cause seepage into basements, and crack foundations.

Where will the runoff go? You need to answer that question before beginning any grading. Fortunately, you can rescue almost any area in your yard from the threat of bad drainage.

POSITIVE DRAINAGE: Paved surfaces should slope slightly away from foundations and toward lower ground. Slope patio and concrete surfaces toward their edges so water doesn't puddle on the patio. A slope of about 1 inch every 4 feet is adequate to move runoff.

SWALES: Intercept water and direct it around objects with these gentle surface ditches. A swale must slope continuously and can be tiled or planted with grass. Water from

Cutting into a slope created a level area for this snug patio. The brick retaining wall holds back the higher soil and radiates stored heat, which can extend the use of the space into cooler evening hours.

Use a trench drain to catch and redirect water that would otherwise collect where horizontal and vertical hard surfaces meet—such as on stone steps.

a swale should empty on an open lawn—but never into the neighbors' yard. It is usually illegal and certainly inconsiderate to divert water so it flows onto adjacent properties.

TRENCH AND CURTAIN DRAINS: Easy to install, these are trenches with perforated pipe set in gravel to carry water away from structures or low spots (see above).

DRY WELLS: These gravel-filled holes serve as outlets for water from other trenches. Typically 2 to 4 feet wide and 3 feet deep (check with local codes), they must be placed at least 10 feet from the house and covered with a concrete slab and planted soil. They are especially useful in places where water cannot be diverted to a storm sewer.

CATCH BASINS: These underground receptacles hold water from surface drains and direct it through underground pipes to storm sewers or other outlets. You can purchase precast units at your materials outlet store.

TREES, ROCKS, AND OTHER OBSTACLES

Many existing features of your landscape, such as flower beds, foundation plantings, fences, walls, and walkways, will affect the location of your project. If you can't part with these things, integrate them into your design. The same goes for trees, rocks, and other obstacles. Incorporating trees into your design, however, calls for some careful planning.

ENCLOSING A TREE: A deck or patio built around a tree can appear as if nature put it there. The tree's height and mass will balance the horizontal expanse of the surface. But take care to avoid damage to the root system. The tree can be the life of your patio or deck. Don't let your structure be the death of the tree.

Sand-set patios let rain enter and reach roots. Build an edging of 6×6 timbers around the tree base, well away from any exposed roots. Secure the timbers with 2-foot rebar driven into the soil.

Don't hem in trees too tightly with decking. Allow room for trunks to grow or you'll end up cutting planks.

Build grade-level decks above a gravel bed using lumber rated for ground contact. Keeping the end grain of wood dry by extending the gravel strip beyond the deck intercepts runoff and looks tidy.

DESIGNING WITH MATERIALS

Perhaps no other aspect of your project—with the possible exception of standing back and admiring your completed handiwork—will prove as rewarding as choosing which materials to use.

The right choice of materials, more than any other design element, will help harmonize your project with the overall architecture of your yard.

You may be surprised—or even overwhelmed at first—at the range of options available. If you stay flexible about your design, you will discover materials that have the qualities—shape, size, color, and texture—to give your structure the look and feel you want.

LOOKS AREN'T EVERYTHING

Don't choose a material for your landscape project just because you like the way it looks. Ask questions about how much maintenance it requires, how long it will last, and how suitable it is for your climate. The chart below lists several things you should consider when choosing materials and ranks them on a scale of 1 (least or shortest) to 5 (most or longest).

Material	Cost	Maintenance	Durability	Skill Level Required
Flagstone				
In sand	2	1	5	3
Mortared	5	2	5	5
Brick				
In sand	3	3	4	4
Mortared	5	1	5	5
Precast pavers	3	1	5	4
Concrete				
Natural	2	1	5	4
Tinted				
Integral	3	1	5	4
Stained	3	1	5	4
Stamped	4	1	5	5
Loose Material	1	4	2	1
Tile	5	1	5	4
Wood				
Redwood	5	1	5	4
Cedar	4	1	4	4
Pressure-treated pine	2	4	3	4
Composite wood	3	1	5	4

HIDDEN COSTS

Remember that your project costs will include surface materials as well as foundation, fillers, and shipping and delivery fees. Choose the look you want first, then make adjustments to your materials selection if your initial design proves too expensive.

Materials make the difference. The varied hues and shapes in this stone patio present an interesting contrast to the stark white and rigid balluster pattern of the the decks.

All materials possess color, texture, line, and form. How these attributes interact will affect the style of your project. Make sure your choices match your design needs.

COLOR

Color can link your project with your landscape and help set the mood. Reds, beiges, rusts, browns, yellows, and oranges generally appear warm and complement traditional settings. Blues, grays, or blacks appear cool and enhance contemporary designs. Remember that paving fillers—mortar, sand, and moss or other plants—add color too. So does wood. Scale also affects color: Color recedes in small quantities but can be overpowering in large areas.

TEXTURE

Textures can affect the appearance of a structure. Decking patterns and baluster styles, for example, establish a visual texture. Textures can also affect function.

SMOOTH OR ROUGH: Smooth surfaces are great for dancing and also are less absorbent than rough materials, so they resist stains. However, smooth materials such as glazed tile, polished stone, smoothly troweled concrete, even wood, are slick when wet. Polished surfaces can assault you with glare in direct sunlight. The surface variation in natural stone will give your patio a natural or old-fashioned look. Poured concrete offers the flattest, least varied surface, but even concrete can be textured.

HARD OR SOFT: Brick, tile, and concrete surfaces are hard; alternatives such as gravel, rock beds, wood chips, and bark offer softer, more comfortable options that give when you walk on them. They make rustic complements to woodland or informal designs.

Attributes are often mixed in designs. Board-and-batten siding has the straight lines of a formal style, but the boards are often rough-textured, giving the siding a less formal look. While intricate Victorian gingerbread trim is often composed of curved lines, has a smooth surface, and is painted, the overall effect is usually formal.

BRICK

The bricks in this expansive patio complement the clapboard siding, cedar shakes, and rough stone wall. Traditional materials often are used to blend with an older home, but brick works well in contemporary designs too.

If you're looking for a warm, earthy material that lends an old-world formality to your landscape, brick is the perfect choice.

Most distributors stock many choices of sizes, colors, styles, and densities. And if you purchase a modular style—one with dimensions that are proportional—design becomes virtually goof-proof.

When shopping for paving materials, avoid common brick, face brick, and firebrick. These varieties are made for purposes other than paving. The following types are good choices:

■ Paving brick resists moisture and wear. Some types have rounded or chamfered edges, a feature that makes sand-laid installation easier.

■ Brick salvaged from old buildings or streets may come with the mortar left on, which many designers feel adds to the charm of a cottage-style patio.

Depending on its original use, used brick may be softer than paving brick and may not wear as well. Many homeowners find that its worn appearance enhances its rustic look. You can approximate a used-brick look with manufactured salvage brick.

■ Adobe pavers, impregnated with asphalt, resist water almost as well as clay brick. They are not fired at high temperatures, however, so they won't stand up to hard use. Install them in sand in dry, nonfreezing climates.

ADVANTAGES

Brick has a range of appealing qualities, including durability, variety of color and texture, and adaptability.

■ Hardness: Brick is graded for hardness. The SX grade withstands the most severe weather conditions and costs more. If you live in northern climates, the extra cost may be worthwhile. In milder climates, the MX grade holds up to light frosts. Your supplier will be able to guide you in your selection.

■ Color: Colors range from white and light yellow to reds and dark browns.

■ Texture: Paving is slightly rough but the

BUYING BRICK

■ Purchase brick from brickyards, lumberyards, or garden and home centers. Most suppliers will deliver for a small fee.

■ Some specialty-brick suppliers maintain websites.

■ Brick is sold individually or by the square yard. Order on pallets to reduce breakage.

■ Prices vary considerably with size, type, and color.

Pavers

Manufactured "salvage" brick

Common brick

Used brick

effect of texture depends more on the pattern and installation method than on the brick.

■ Siting: Most common in formal landscapes, brick can be cut and laid in gentle or dramatic shapes. Its modular dimensions fit almost any design.

■ Modular bricks are easy to lay in sand, requiring only basic skills and a little time. Mortared patios and paths are more difficult.

■ Brick conforms to minor terrain variations.

■ It fits an array of designs, mixes well with other materials, and is excellent for edging.

■ Mortared walkways need virtually no maintenance.

■ New pavers stand up to hard use.

DISADVANTAGES

■ Salvage brick may crack in winter and gradually crumble in any season.

■ It can become a haven for moss.

■ Smooth brick surfaces get slick when wet, a danger on even moderate slopes.

■ Brick set in sand may require periodic weeding, resetting, and leveling.

■ Most brick will stand up to weather if properly bedded, but some porous brick may absorb water and crack when it freezes.

ESTIMATING QUANTITIES

■ Determine the area of your installation in square feet.

■ Multiply the area by 5. (About five standard 2×4×8-inch bricks cover 1 square foot.) Order 5 to 10 percent extra to allow for cutting and breakage. For other brick sizes divide the surface area by the face area of one brick.

DESIGN TIPS

Add interest to your brick design with alternating colors. Slight contrasts, a red-brown interspersed with dark red bricks, for example, look more pleasing than sharply contrasting colors. Bricks set on edge offer unusual design possibilities, but the smaller-edge surface will require more bricks and a larger budget.

Consider safety, too, when shopping for brick. Avoid material with slick surfaces.

Basket weave

45° herringbone

90° herringbone

Running bond

Offset bond, bricks on edge

Diagonal bond

HOW TO INSTALL BRICK

■ Remove existing sod and excavate. Install edging and landscape fabric. Pour and level base. Install paving. Mortared installations require a concrete slab and a mortar bed. (See installation instructions on pages 132–134.)

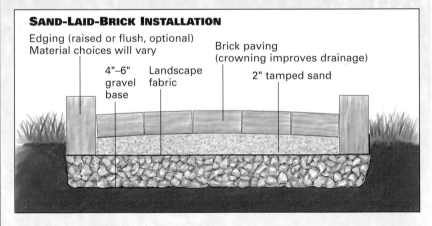
SAND-LAID-BRICK INSTALLATION
Edging (raised or flush, optional) Material choices will vary
Brick paving (crowning improves drainage)
4"–6" gravel base
Landscape fabric
2" tamped sand

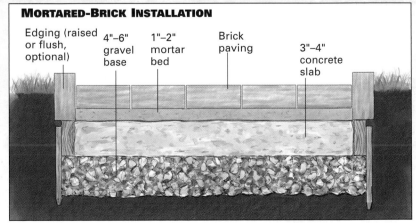
MORTARED-BRICK INSTALLATION
Edging (raised or flush, optional)
4"–6" gravel base
1"–2" mortar bed
Brick paving
3"–4" concrete slab

FLAGSTONE

By using fewer and larger flagstones, the owner of this patio created a bit of drama in an unassuming corner of the yard. The size, color, and layout of the stone make the small patio inviting and attractive.

CUT STONE

Cut stone originates from the same natural rock as flagstone. The difference between the two is in their shapes. Flagstone edges are natural and irregular. Cut stone is uniform, with straight edges and square corners. Cut stone ranges in size from about 1 foot to 4 feet and comes in different thicknesses. Get paving at least 2 inches thick to avoid breakage under traffic.

Cut stone lends itself to the same kind of installation as flagstone—as stepping-stone or stone-carpet surfaces in soil, in sand, or mortared to concrete.

The general term flagstone refers to rock fractured or cleft into flat slabs 2 or more inches thick and used for paving. Flagstone most commonly used for patios and pathways includes bluestone, limestone, redstone, sandstone, granite, and slate. Its irregular shapes make it ideal for both free-form and geometric patterns—in an individual stepping-stone design or in stone surfaces set in sand or installed over concrete with mortar.

DESIGN EFFECT/SITING

■ Color and texture: Flagstone offers an array of colors and textures. Colors range from blue-gray (bluestone) to various hues of tans and reds (limestone, granite, redstone, and sandstone) to deep, sometimes slightly iridescent, black (slate). Textures vary from generally smooth to moderately rough.
■ Siting: Adaptable to both formal and informal styles; the final effect depends on the contours of the patio. Stepping-stone installations almost always look casual. Sand-laid and mortared installations can enhance both informal and formal styles, depending on their contours.
■ Random shapes and varied surface contours bring a sense of rough-hewn permanence to the landscape.

ADVANTAGES

■ Dry-set flagstone is among the easiest of hard-surface materials to install and requires no specialized skills. Mortared surfaces are more difficult.
■ Flagstone conforms moderately well to minor variations in terrain, working well on gentle slopes.
■ It adapts to an unlimited number of design variations.
■ Properly prepared, a flagstone surface is not subject to heaving in freeze-thaw cycles and is virtually permanent.

Slate

Limestone

Marble

Granite

Sandstone

Bluestone

DESIGN TIPS

To increase the formality of a design, keep straight edges to the outside of the installation or use geometric edging, such as brick. Use large stones to pave large expanses of landscape, smaller units in smaller yards.

Lay the general contour out on paper and then carry the plans to the landscape to verify the practicality and aesthetics of your design. Unlike designing with materials that have regular shapes, design your flagstone project on-site, laying the stones in a pleasing arrangement and experimenting with patterns at the site of the excavation.

DISADVANTAGES

■ Large stones can be heavy and thus difficult to move and place.
■ A well-laid design will take time, especially if you're planning a stone surface set in sand or over concrete. Stepping-stone layouts require less precision.
■ Flagstone is more costly than loose stone.
■ It has pores that can collect water and become slick when frozen. Slate is slick when wet.

DURABILITY AND MAINTENANCE

■ Most varieties will stand up to hard use, continuous traffic, and wheeled garden equipment. Sandstone wears with use.
■ Stepping-stone surfaces may require periodic weeding, resetting, and leveling. Sand-laid stone may need resetting from time to time.

BUYING FLAGSTONE

■ Flagstone is generally sold by the ton or square yard.
■ Garden and home centers, landscape outlets, and building-supply retailers may carry individual pieces for small projects.
■ A bulk purchase from a local quarry or stone yard will save you money on a large project. Order bulk on pallets to reduce breakage. Hand-picking your stone increases costs considerably.
■ Prices vary with the size and type of stone. Stone native to your area will cost less.

Mortared walks need little maintenance.
■ Climate conditions have little effect on most flagstone varieties—they endure the harshest of conditions. Some porous rock, like sandstone, may absorb water and crack in freezing temperatures.

INSTALLATION

■ Determine the square footage of your project. Your supplier may convert this amount to tonnage. One ton covers about 120 square feet.
■ Remove sod and then excavate consistent with drainage needs and material thickness. Install edging (optional) and landscape fabric; pour and level base and sand bed. Lay out the trial pattern; install paving. Mortared installations require pouring a concrete slab and laying a mortar bed. (See illustrations and installation instructions on pages 136–138.)
■ Large stone will cover a surface more quickly than smaller stone but may prove harder to move, cut, and design.

SAND-LAID-FLAGSTONE INSTALLATION

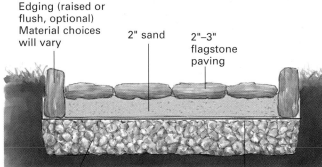

Edging (raised or flush, optional) Material choices will vary

2" sand

2"–3" flagstone paving

4"–6" crushed stone or gravel (optional for increased drainage)

Landscape fabric (put landscape fabric on top of gravel if not using crushed-stone base)

MORTARED-FLAGSTONE INSTALLATION

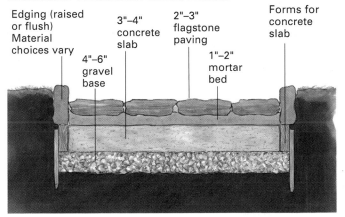

Edging (raised or flush) Material choices vary

3"–4" concrete slab

2"–3" flagstone paving

Forms for concrete slab

4"–6" gravel base

1"–2" mortar bed

CONCRETE PAVERS

Using only three shapes specifically designed for this purpose, the concrete pavers in this patio form an elegant circle. Notice the crown in the surface that tapers down from the center of the patio to its perimeter, allowing quick drainage in all directions.

Concrete pavers resemble brick in their versatility and installation. Once made only as gray squares, they are now manufactured in a variety of shapes and colors. In fact, rectangular pavers have taken a back seat in popularity to other shapes—circles, chamfered squares, diamonds, hexagons, octagons, crescents, and more.

Unlike brick, which is made of fired clay, concrete pavers are manufactured from dense, pressure-formed cast concrete.

SIZES, SHAPES, AND TYPES

Concrete pavers are as durable as brick but lighter in weight and less costly. Many are thinner too, running from 1½ inches to 2½ inches (the size of a brick) and larger. You'll find large rectangles measuring about 4×6 (and up to about 9 inches), geometrics about 2×4, and keyed varieties that you can lay in circles and fans.

Concrete pavers come in different categories, based on method of installation.

■ **INTERLOCKING PAVERS** resist lateral movement because their sides—contoured, numbering more than four, S-shaped, or crescent-shaped—fit together and keep the units stable. They stay in place even under heavy use and dramatic weather changes. Manufactured corners and end pieces finish off the edges and don't need cutting.

■ **STANDARD PAVERS** are rectangular and not as stable as the interlocking variety. They may shift over time, especially if your patio gets hard use or is set in poorly draining soil.

SKIN DEEP

Look carefully at the depth of the color and avoid pavers with shallow color. Colors applied to the surface only can wear off quickly, exposing bare concrete. Buy pavers that have pigment impregnated throughout their thickness.

DESIGN TIPS

Because of their regularity, many concrete pavers look best in formal design schemes. The paver itself creates the pattern.

Pay close attention to scale when you make your dimensioned plan. A small paver can make any site look busy. Large pavers take less time to set because each unit covers more area, but their size can overwhelm your installation.

In the planning stages, if you sense that your design will end up looking too busy, enlarge the size of the paver or consider setting it with wider spacing. Planting ground covers in the gaps can minimize the busy look.

BUYING PRECAST PAVERS

Building-supply centers, concrete suppliers, landscape centers, and home and garden centers sell concrete pavers individually, by the square foot, or in banded cubes (enough for about 16 linear feet).

MAKE YOUR OWN

You can make your own pavers with premixed concrete and homemade or commercial forms. Making them yourself might limit you to rectangular shapes. Commercial forms, available at garden and home centers, come in various shapes and sizes. (See page 141 for more information.)

■ **TURF BLOCKS** have an open design with holes designed for planting. They are even strong enough to be used in driveways.

All varieties are weatherproof and extremely durable.

DESIGN CONSIDERATIONS

■ Color and texture: Colors come in a narrow range, typically reminiscent of brick—reds, browns, and earth tones—but also in black, grays, and off-whites. Textures also abound, from smooth to stamped to aggregate surfaces. Some pavers look remarkably like brick, stone, adobe, marble, or cobblestone.
■ Siting: Pavers are adaptable to both formal and informal styles. Although the regularity of their shapes tends to suit this material to formal designs, the final effect depends on the contours of the installation.

ADVANTAGES AND DISADVANTAGES

■ Pavers are modular and easy to lay in sand, requiring only basic skills and a little time. Mortared pavers are less common because pavers are manufactured for dry-set installations.
■ They conform well to minor terrain variations.
■ They fit an endless array of designs and mix well with other materials.
■ Standard pavers must be cut to fit geometric designs.

DURABILITY AND MAINTENANCE

■ Pavers stand up to hard use, continuous traffic, and wheeled garden equipment.

■ Although not common because of their tightly fitting design, pavers may require periodic weeding, resetting, and leveling.
■ Most paver surfaces will stand up to harsh weather if properly bedded.

INSTALLATION

Compute the area of your site and divide it by the coverage for your particular paver style as determined by the manufacturer or distributor.

Install concrete pavers using the same techniques as you would for brick. Sand-bed installations are more common, and some pavers are molded with built-in tabs that give consistent spacing in sand-laid installations. (Installation instructions are on pages 136–139).

SAND-LAID-PAVER INSTALLATION

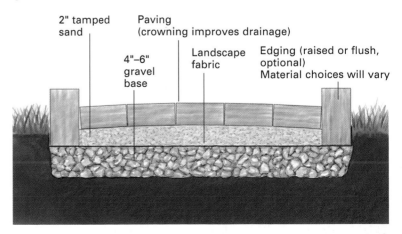

2" tamped sand

Paving (crowning improves drainage)

4"–6" gravel base

Landscape fabric

Edging (raised or flush, optional)
Material choices will vary

POURED CONCRETE

Concrete can be an attractive surface. Four poured slabs divided by single lines of brick make this landing a place to pause on the way in and out of the house. A carefully applied texture blends the concrete with the stone wall and wooden deck.

Because concrete goes in wet and cures to a hard, durable solid, it adapts easily to almost any design. You can pour it in gentle, meandering curves or in straight, formal configurations. Modern concrete techniques, such as stamping, coloring, texturing, and embedding with aggregates, can create a dazzling landscape surface.

DESIGN CONSIDERATIONS

■ Color: Gray in its natural state, but coloring options make design possibilities almost endless.

■ Texture: Smooth or moderately rough when unfinished. Stamping, aggregates, and texturing create unusual likenesses to other materials.
■ Siting: It can be sited anywhere and in any design scheme.

ADVANTAGES

■ Poured concrete has unlimited design potential in both formal and informal installations.
■ It requires little maintenance.

WHAT'S IN CONCRETE?

■ 1 part portland cement (a fine mixture of clay and limestone)
■ $2\frac{1}{4}$ to $2\frac{1}{2}$ parts clean construction sand
■ $2\frac{1}{2}$ to 3 parts coarse aggregate (gravel or rock)
■ $\frac{1}{2}$ part clean water

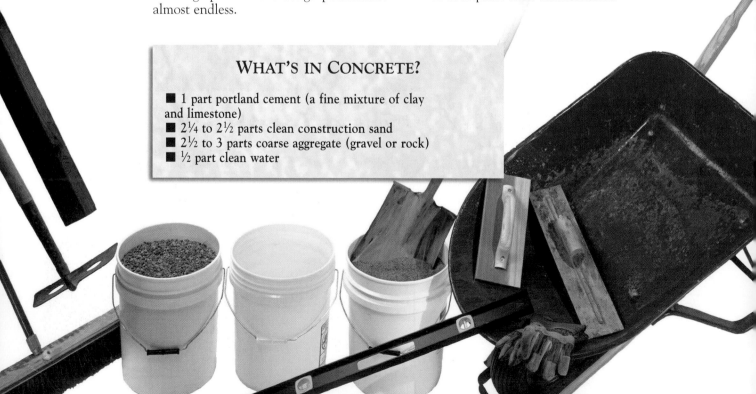

MIXING OPTIONS

BULK DRY INGREDIENTS: Refer to "What's in Concrete" on the opposite page. You can buy the first three ingredients separately and mix them with water by hand in a mortar box or wheelbarrow or mix them in a rented concrete mixer. Mixing concrete is a heavy job that requires a strong hoe and stamina, but for small jobs it's economical.

PRE-MIX: An easier but somewhat more costly alternative is to buy concrete in bags with the dry ingredients mixed in the correct proportions. You just add water, mix, and pour. Pre-mix takes the guesswork out of mixing—but not the effort. It makes jobs under a cubic yard manageable (you'll need 40 to 50 bags for a cubic yard, depending on the weight of the bags), but for anything larger than that, order ready-mix.

READY-MIX: Ready-mix relieves you of the mixing process but requires a hardy and experienced work crew. Your site must be accessible to a large truck and be ready for the pour as soon as the truck arrives. Ready-mix has additives that will make it workable in a variety of weather conditions.

DISADVANTAGES

■ It must be mixed to specifications or it will weaken or disintegrate over time.
■ A very smooth finish can make concrete dangerously slippery when wet.
■ Concrete surfaces are not as resistant to cracking as stone, brick, tile, or pavers.
■ Large expanses of concrete reflect heat and can make your site uncomfortable.
■ It requires careful planning and, on large projects, some heavy equipment.
■ Installation is hard work and can be exacting. Large projects require helpers.
■ Concrete has to be worked within specified time limits. It is unforgiving of mistakes.

DURABILITY AND MAINTENANCE

■ It stands up to all climatic conditions.
■ It resists damage from freeze-thaw cycles if properly installed.
■ If necessary, order additives in the mix to accommodate hot or cold temperatures during the curing process.
■ It is extremely durable if properly mixed and poured.

ADDED INGREDIENTS

If your climate treats you to wide variations in temperature and strong or frequent freeze-thaw cycles, you'll need to add ingredients to your mix that will allow the concrete to expand and contract without cracking. Ask your vendor to recommend additives for use in your climate.

INSTALLATION

■ Determine the volume of your excavated site and add 5 percent to the total.
■ A 40-pound bag of pre-mix makes ⅓ cubic foot; a 60-pound bag, ½ cubic foot; and an 80-pound bag, ⅔ cubic foot. A 4×20-foot walk, 4 inches deep, requires 26⅔ cubic feet of concrete—about 1 cubic yard (27 cubic feet).
■ Remove sod and excavate. Install staked forms and tamp the gravel base. Lay in reinforcing wire mesh (optional). Pour and finish. (See pages 140–143 for specific installation instructions.)

BUYING CONCRETE

■ Buy pre-mix at hardware stores, home centers, lumberyards, or building-supply centers.
■ Order bulk concrete from a ready-mix concrete company.
■ Buy dry ingredients (portland cement, sand, and aggregate) at any of the above outlets.

INSTALLING A POURED-CONCRETE SLAB

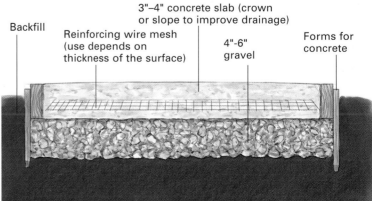

Backfill

3"–4" concrete slab (crown or slope to improve drainage)

Reinforcing wire mesh (use depends on thickness of the surface)

4"-6" gravel

Forms for concrete

DRESSING UP CONCRETE

Who says concrete must be stark and unimaginative? Even if you have an old, discolored slab, don't reach for the sledgehammer just yet. You can dress up both old and new slabs with amazingly attractive effects.

COLOR

You can color concrete paving with one of several techniques, but the following are the most common.

EXISTING SLABS: Staing concrete provides the biggest change and the quickest facelift.

■ Use darker colors to make defects less noticeable. Natural browns, grays, and greens create an attractive surface that blends well with the landscape.

■ Apply the first coat evenly, then unevenly dab on subsequent coats, overlapping areas as in sponge painting.

■ Use stencils to create patterns of contrasting colors.

NEW CONCRETE:

■ Spread colored dyes over a slab after it's poured. This method produces quick color, but it's only skin deep, and if the surface chips, you'll see gray beneath it.

■ Mix pigment into the wet concrete before you pour the slab. Because this method distributes color throughout the concrete, hues tend to have a uniform appearance even if the surface of the slab chips.

A CONCRETE FRAME-UP

Another method of dressing up existing concrete uses stain to frame the perimeter of the patio surface.

Transform a plain concrete slab into an attractive outdoor floor by saw-cutting concrete lines into a pattern. Lines should be straight, not curved, and made by someone experienced with a wet saw.

Colored concrete is a good choice for outdoor flooring. Have new concrete poured with the color mixed in, or apply stain to existing concrete.

■ First, stain the entire patio. When the first coat of stain dries, measure in 6 to 10 inches from the outside edge of the concrete and apply duct tape to this area.

■ Apply subsequent coats of the same color stain to the untaped area, letting it dry between coats until you reach the desired intensity of color. When the final coat dries, remove the tape and you'll have an understated border.

PATTERNS

To completely alter the look of an existing slab, saw-cut lines into its surface. Measure your site, sketch it to scale on graph paper, then design a simple pattern. Think big— plan 1- to 3-foot squares. Or have lines scored on a diagonal to form diamonds.

Freshly poured concrete—plain or colored—can be stamped with a pattern. Stamps create patterns that resemble brick, cobblestones, cut stone, irregular stone, or precast pavers. Open-mold stamps outline the shapes; closed-mold stamps add surface texture as well, creating realistic-looking brick, cobblestone, slate, and paver patterns.

Ask your contractor to use a concrete stamp with a closed top when you want the textured look of stone.

Open-top stamps impress shape but not texture to concrete. Combine any stamp pattern with your choice of color.

These hexagonal shapes are newly stamped in tinted concrete. Other shapes mimic cobblestone, brick, cut stone, or pavers.

Aggregate concrete has a gravellike texture. Use it alone or combine it with other materials, as shown here.

Rock-salt-finished concrete appears aged. The pitted surface is unsuitable for cold regions with freezing weather.

TEXTURED FINISHES

The cheapest, easiest way to pattern new concrete involves tooling, or creating various surface effects by manipulating the wet concrete.

While stamps and cut designs may require professionals or the use of expensive concrete saws, the finishes featured on this page are ones you can achieve yourself with simple, inexpensive hand tools.

Of course there's no reason you can't combine the textures mentioned below with stains, patterns, or other materials set into the concrete for a unique look.

There are several textures you can use. Try experimenting with the following four textures—offered in sequence from coarsest to smoothest—to see which you like the best. Remember, more than one texture on a project adds visual interest.

TROWELED: Swirls made with a finishing trowel add interest to large expanses of flat concrete, giving them the hand-tooled look of an old-world material. An added bonus: The swirls increase traction for a more surefooted feel when the surface becomes wet. A troweled finish isn't recommended for surfaces that freeze, however, as the texture can become icy and be difficult to clear completely of snow.

BROOMED: A damp, stiff, coarse-bristled push broom of the type often used to clean garages can be pulled in long, even strokes across the concrete surface when it's still wet. The result is a patterned, slip-resistant surface that's still easy to clean. An added benefit: It prevents the glare that a smooth-finished slab can exhibit.

SEMISMOOTH: Dragging a wood float across a wet slab produces a surface that's a bit smoother than a broomed surface, but one that still provides an attractive matte look and good skid resistance.

SMOOTH: Finishing the surface with a metal trowel creates a marble-smooth finish. Such a surface is slippery when wet but is good for dance parties. An added benefit: It's the easiest finish to sweep clean.

TILE

For this house with a clay tile roof and a colored stucco exterior, ceramic tile is the obvious choice for the patio. Beds and pots of flowers add contrasting shape and color.

With regular geometric shapes and distinct edges, ceramic and stone tiles make excellent paving materials. Their beauty and tactile appeal make them unique. Made from thin panels of high-fired clay, ceramic tiles are durable and offer more variety in colors, shapes, and sizes than any other material.

TYPES OF CERAMIC TILE

Four types of tile are made for outdoor use:

PATIO OR TERRA-COTTA: Fired ceramic tile with earthen colors and irregular surfaces creates pleasant, unobtrusive moods.

QUARRY TILES: Machine-made and formed from dense clay pressed tightly into molds, quarry tile is hard and is made with rounded or sharp edges and corners. Ask your dealer to show you how to judge quality. Its appearance varies from one brand and firing to another—even within the same firing. Make sure all the tiles you buy have the same lot number—your best insurance for getting consistent tiles.

TILE PAVERS: These molded tiles are larger than other tiles and are made to cover larger areas. Some are designed to retain the deliberately imperfect look of a handcrafted item. Mexican pavers, for example, are grainy and unglazed and have rough edges. The earthy colors work well outdoors. Others are regular and modern. Tile pavers are usually more expensive than quarry tiles.

GLAZED TILE

Glazed tile is for decorative uses only and is dangerously slippery when wet. However, its glossy look and bold colors make fine accents for edges and trim, raised beds, or wall decorations.

SEALING TILES

Ask your dealer if your tiles have been pretreated with a sealer at the factory. If they haven't been, you'll need to apply a good sealant after they've been set. Repeat this process periodically to protect the tiles from scratches and to keep them from absorbing water. Quality sealants are easy to apply, won't discolor tile, and provide an even, effective barrier against stains and soiling.

SYNTHETIC STONE TILES: As the name suggests, this type of tile is made of stained clay bodies that look very much like stone surfaces such as granite or sandstone. Synthetic tiles are thinner, flatter, lighter, smoother, and more regularly shaped than natural stone and measure either 6 or 12 inches across. They offer a clever alternative for homeowners who want the practical qualities of a synthetic material yet prefer the look of stone.

No matter what type of tile you use, you will need to set it in mortar on a 4-inch concrete slab over a 4-inch gravel base. Make sure the base is absolutely smooth and level.

DESIGN CONSIDERATIONS

■ Color: Tile comes in a nearly endless array of colors. Many varieties for outdoor use are available in earth tones, subtle tans, reds, and browns.
■ Texture: Tile for outdoor use is manufactured with a slightly roughened surface, but the effect of texture depends more on the pattern than on the tile itself.
■ Siting: It is excellent in formal landscape designs and can be cut and laid in gentle or dramatic shapes. Its modular dimensions fit almost any design scheme.

ADVANTAGES

■ Tile absorbs very little water and resists cracking in changing temperatures. Once restricted to warm climates, newer varieties make tile extremely practical in colder climates as well.
■ Unglazed tile is less likely than glazed tile to get slick when it's wet, which means a patio surface of unglazed tile will be safer after it rains. For best results use unglazed, textured tile made specifically for outdoor paving.
■ Its high density will support heavy loads

and constant use (but only when properly bedded).

DISADVANTAGES

■ Tile is more expensive than other materials (although with diligent hunting, you can find lower-quality tile on sale for as low as $1.50 per square foot, but beware of bargains).
■ Because it's square, it is more difficult to lay in bricklike patterns.
■ It's thin and susceptible to cracking on uneven surfaces. Repairing cracked tiles means chiseling them out.

DURABILITY AND MAINTENANCE

■ Tile stands up to hard use, continued traffic, and wheeled garden equipment.
■ Most tile will endure all kinds of weather, but some porous varieties may absorb water and crack when it freezes.
■ Set properly on a mortared slab, tile needs virtually no maintenance.

INSTALLATION

■ Compute the area of your site in square feet and add 10 percent for waste, mistakes, and cutting. Order cartons that have the coverage equivalent to the surface area.
■ Excavate and pour slab as you would for mortared brick or flagstone. Spread thin-set mortar on slab sections. Set tile, then grout and clean. (See page 135 for specific installation instructions.)

BUYING TILE

■ Purchase tile at tile retailers, ceramic suppliers, home centers, and floor covering outlets. National retailing franchises specialize in tile.
■ Certain retailers may sell individual tiles, but most will sell it in cartons by the square foot or in boxes of large quantities.

TILE INSTALLATION

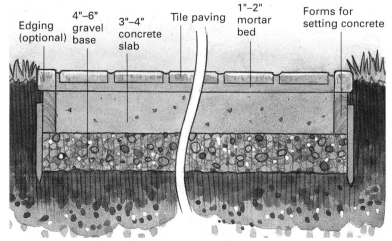

Edging (optional) · 4"–6" gravel base · 3"–4" concrete slab · Tile paving · 1"–2" mortar bed · Forms for setting concrete

Railway tie

Redwood decking

Treated 2×6 decking

Treated 4×4 landscape timber

WOOD

WOOD FOR PATHS AND PATIOS

With a few weekends of work and a modest supply of redwood, the homeowners transformed this shady spot into a wooded hideaway.

Wood brings a warmth to the landscape unmatched by any other material. Its appealing, organic look offers numerous design options. You can set it directly in the soil, in a sand bed, or in anchored frames.

Treated landscape timbers, wide wooden rounds, and end-grain blocks that look like brick are found in patios and paths set in a woodland atmosphere. You can install wood decking squares (they look like parquet) in rectangular beds or use wood rounds in free-form layouts set within larger areas of loose materials.

Insects, rot, and mildew attack most wood. Redwood, cypress, and cedar, however, contain natural resins that resist insects and the elements. Use only the heartwood of these species; the sapwood is not resistant. Tropical hardwoods are durable, and their high cost can repay itself with years of freedom from maintenance. Make sure your tropical wood comes from sustainable-forestry sources.

Buy treated lumber rated for ground contact. Look for a "Ground Contact" or "LP25" stamp (or both) on the surface of the wood. Read the safety label attached to the lumber and follow the instructions. See "Buying Lumber," pages 68–71, for more information on choosing the species for your project, lumber grading, and choosing material that is structurally sound.

DESIGN EFFECT/SITING

■ Color: Its natural colors range from light (cypress) to purple-red (cedar) to deep reddish-brown (redwood). The green cast of treated lumber turns gray in time. Stains, paints, and finishes will alter colors to suit your tastes.
■ Texture: Wood is generally smooth but its texture, especially in decking and balusters, is conveyed more by pattern and design than by the material itself.
■ Siting: Wood will almost always look informal in the landscape but is suitable for formal, rectangular designs, especially as an edging and in modular patterns.

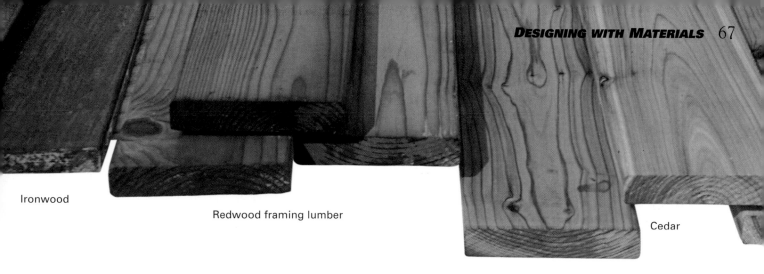

Ironwood

Redwood framing lumber

Cedar

ADVANTAGES

■ Wood is less expensive than brick, flagstone, and cut stone (though for paths and horizontal surfaces, it's more expensive than loose stone and organic materials).

■ Ease of installation depends on complexity of design, but wood generally requires only basic carpentry skills.

■ It mixes well with other materials.

DISADVANTAGES

■ It can become moss covered when damp and slippery when wet, which can be especially dangerous on slopes and steps.

■ It does not conform as well to terrain variations as smaller materials. Changes in slope will require posts or the installation of small sections.

DURABILITY AND MAINTENANCE

■ You may have to replace worn or damaged sections and periodically reapply finishes and preservatives, even in mild-weather climates.

ESTIMATING QUANTITIES

■ Determine square footage and structural requirements. Take your dimensioned plan to your supplier for assistance.

HOW TO INSTALL

■ Remove sod and excavate. Install wood rounds or sections. For boardwalks, set posts or sleepers; then install decking. (See illustration below. Installation instructions are on page 152.)

■ Embed wood rounds and blocks directly in the soil or in a 2-inch sand base in places where better drainage is needed.

INSTALLING DECKING ON SLEEPERS

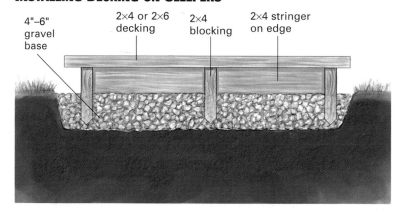

4"–6" gravel base

2×4 or 2×6 decking

2×4 blocking

2×4 stringer on edge

DESIGN TIPS

Wood can go almost anywhere but is especially suited to woodland-setting patio installations with boardwalks and footbridges.

Cut your own wood rounds with a chain saw. Embed them or lay 3- to 4-inch lengths of timber set on edge in loose stone or sand. Plant variety into the spaces with groundcovers, or fill the gaps with bark or loose stone.

BUYING WOOD

■ Purchase wood from lumberyards or home centers.

■ Wood is sold by the piece or by the board foot. Prices vary with size and species.

BUYING LUMBER

Pound for pound, wood is almost as strong as steel. Its warm, natural beauty and remarkable workability make it ideal for any outdoor structure. Not all woods are alike, however. Select wood for your project based on appearance, cost, and durability.

SPECIES

Several species resist decay and insects, making them ideal for outdoor structures. Here's a brief summary of their characteristics:
REDWOOD, CEDAR, AND CYPRESS: Unmatched for their beauty, these species are naturally resistant to weathering, warping, cupping, shrinkage, and insect damage, but they carry a higher price tag than other woods (redwood is the most costly). Untreated, they weather to a silvery gray, or if you prefer, you can easily color them with stain. Cedar tends to split easily, and cypress may be hard to find outside its natural growth areas.

Only the heartwood is naturally resistant to decay. Use heartwood for posts and structural members fastened close to the ground; use sapwood treated with a sealer for rails, studs, and boards that will be visible.
FIR AND PINE: These species are strong, lightweight, widely available, and less expensive than naturally resistant woods. They are available in two forms: untreated lumber and pressure-treated lumber.
UNTREATED LUMBER: This stock is susceptible to outdoor weathering and decay if left unfinished. Not suitable for posts, it can be used for nonstructural members if painted.
PRESSURE-TREATED LUMBER: Pine and fir that have been treated with chemicals under pressure are extremely rot-resistant. They are a less-expensive substitute for redwood, cedar, and cypress.

Both chromated copper arsenate (CCA)—identifiable by its green tinge—and ammoniacal copper arsenate (ACA) have been used widely, but wood treated with these and other arsenic compounds will not be available for residential use after December 2003. Ammoniacal copper quaternary ammonia (ACQ), a newer preservative, will remain available. Grade stamps tell which chemical has been used. They also tell how much preservative the lumber holds. Posts and boards that contact or are close to the ground (skids, joists, and skirts) should have

Redwood

Cedar

Green treated

Brown treated

SHEET GOODS

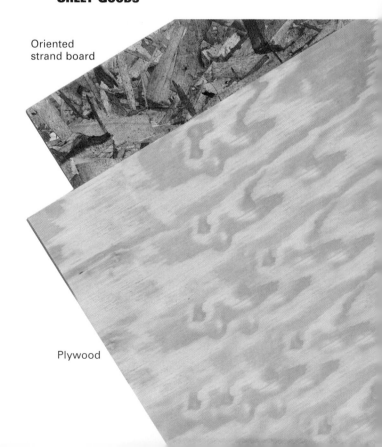

Oriented strand board

Plywood

a retention level of 0.60 or higher. Lumber treated to 0.40 works sufficiently for other components. Look for a markings that specify suitability for "Ground Contact."

LUMBER GRADES

Lumber is divided into categories according to its thickness. *Boards* are less than 2 inches thick, and *dimension lumber* is 2 to 4 inches thick. Lumber is graded for its strength and appearance in accordance with standards established by independent agencies.

BOARDS: Fir and pine boards are graded in two categories: select and common.

SELECT: This is the best grade, with few or no knots or blemishes. Select grades are labeled A–D.
■ A: contains no knots
■ B: has only small blemishes
■ C: has some minor defects
■ D: has larger blemishes that can be concealed with paint

COMMON: Utility board grades are ranked from 1 to 5 in descending quality. A middle grade, such as number 3, is a good choice for most projects.

COMPOSITION DECKING

Made of wood byproducts, wood and plastic, or 100 percent plastic, composition materials offer long life and extreme rot resistance. They cost more initially but require less maintenance over time. Some varieties snap together, making installation easy.

One disadvantage of synthetic material is that it can't be used for structural framing. Another is that it doesn't really look like wood. Some synthetics will weather into a silvery gray color, mimicking cedar.

DIMENSION LUMBER: There are three grades of fir and pine dimension lumber.
■ Construction Grade: strongest, fewest defects.
■ Standard Grade: almost as good as construction grade and less expensive.
■ Utility Grade: unsuitable for framing.
Pressure-treated lumber is also graded.

Buy at least standard-grade dimension lumber and common-grade number 3 boards for the projects in this book. Buy better grades where appearance is critical.

GRADE STAMPS: WHAT THEY MEAN

Manufacturers stamp their wood products to provide customers with information about the species, prevalence of defects, grade, and moisture content. A grade stamp may also carry a number or the name of the mill that produced it and a certification symbol that shows the lumber association whose grading standards are used.

Pressure-treated lumber carries a grade stamp that shows the year it was treated, the chemical used as a preservative, exposure condition (whether it can be used above ground or is rated for ground contact), and the amount of chemical treatment it received.

Plywood grade stamps also show whether the wood is suitable for ground contact or only for aboveground use and whether it can be used as sheathing. The stamp also specifies the thickness of the sheet and the distance it can span between rafters and joists. If the plywood is made to withstand exposure to the weather, such as siding for a shed, it is marked as exterior-grade.

Many projects fail because the lumber used wasn't suited to a specific application. Grade stamps help you choose lumber that meets your project's requirements.

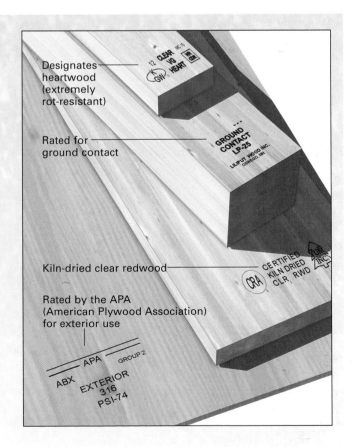

Designates heartwood (extremely rot-resistant)

Rated for ground contact

Kiln-dried clear redwood

Rated by the APA (American Plywood Association) for exterior use

BUYING LUMBER
continued

SEASONING

Most wood is either air dried or kiln dried. Marks specify the moisture content of wood: S-GRN (green lumber), over 19 percent moisture content; S-DRY, up to 19 percent; MC 15, up to 15 percent.

For framing and rough work, air-dried lumber is adequate, but S-DRY or MC 15 lumber is better. Dry stock warps less, works more easily, holds fasteners more tightly, and finishes better. Always use dry for finish work.

NOMINAL VERSUS ACTUAL

The dimensions that describe the size of lumber, such as 1×4, 2×4, or 2×6, are nominal, not actual, dimensions. They indicate the size of the stock when it was cut from the log, before drying and milling reduced its size. Actual dimensions of nominal lumber sizes are shown in "What Size Is It, Really?" on the opposite page.

Shrinkage is generally consistent from one kind of lumber to another, although pressure-treated boards may vary slightly from untreated boards. If exact size is significant to your design, measure the actual dimensions. For example, when planning a gazebo deck made of 1×6 decking, you'll want to know exactly how many boards will fit across the span of the floor, so measure the stock before fastening it.

PLYWOOD

Manufacturers produce plywood in a variety of sizes, thicknesses, textures, species, and grades. Plywood used for outdoor construction must be an exterior-grade material made with glue that does not deteriorate when exposed to moisture.

Purchase AA exterior grade for sheathing that you will stain or paint. Lesser grades work well for flooring, roof sheathing, or sheathing covered with siding, but they have blemishes that show through paint or stain. Grade stamps give you most of the information you need in buying plywood.

LOOK BEFORE BUYING

No lumber is perfect. To get good materials for your project, walk around the lumberyard. Take your project plans with you. Look at different species and grades to compare their colors, grain patterns, and quality. Compare pressure-treated with untreated products.

Ask a salesperson to recommend project materials. The retailer also can give you an idea of relative costs for various materials.

Shop around to compare both material

COMMON LUMBER FLAWS

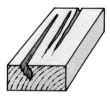

CHECKS: Splits that run perpendicular to the grain are called checks, a cosmetic—not a structural—flaw.

SHAKES: Splits following the grain will probably grow larger. Do not use boards with splits that extend halfway or more.

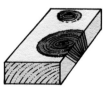

KNOTS: Use these rules when using boards with knots for joists and rafters.
1. Tight knots are OK in the top third of the board.
2. Missing knots are OK in the middle third.
3. No knots larger than an inch in the bottom third. Loose knots usually fall out in time.

WANE: Boards with a wane can still be very strong but may not provide enough nailing surface for sheathing joints.

CUP: Cupped wood is strong but unsightly. If the cup is severe, the board may crack when you fasten it.

TWIST: If you use a twisted board, one or more corners will stick out. Eliminate minor twists by installing blocking and strategic fastening.

BOW: Bowed lumber is usually not a problem unless very pronounced. Straighten bowed studs or joists with blocking.

CROWN: The high part in the middle of a board is the crown. Face all the crowns the same way on a wall frame. On joists or rafters, put the crown up. Avoid badly crowned lumber or cut it into shorter pieces.

costs and service. You might find a higher-grade stock costs less at one yard than lower-grade materials at another. If you can't get the material to the site yourself, add delivery charges to the cost of your material.

As you shop for lumber, check each board for defects. Common lumber flaws are shown opposite. Sight down the length of the board on both the face and the edge. Perfect lumber is rare, so look for the straightest, flattest boards you can find. Check for knots—small or tight ones are acceptable, but avoid boards with large, loose ones. Look for checks and splits. If the wood hasn't been kiln dried, more checks and splits will develop as the lumber seasons.

ESTIMATING, ORDERING, AND STORING

You can get a quick idea of project cost from your lumberyard visits, but ordering material requires more detail. Make a materials list that designates the species, quantity, and size of each stock. Be ready to tell the dealer what kind of footings you'll be using and how you will finish the structure. You may be able to negotiate a better price for materials if you place the full order with one supplier.

When the materials arrive, protect them from direct sunlight and moisture. If the lumber has not been kiln dried, let it dry for several weeks. Stack boards flat and evenly weighted, inserting spacers (called stickers) between them. Store them under a cover or in the shade. Kiln-dried lumber is ready to use right away; protect it from direct sunlight before you begin construction.

WHAT SIZE IS IT, REALLY?

After it is cut, lumber is dried, planed, and smoothed, all of which reduce its thickness and width. The nominal size of a board (for example, 1×4) refers to the size before drying and planing; actual size means the size you actually get.

Nominal Size	Actual Size
1×2	¾" × 1½"
1×3	¾" × 2½"
1×4	¾" × 3½"
1×6	¾" × 5½"
1×8	¾" × 7¼"
1×10	¾" × 9¼"
1×12	¾" × 11¼"
2×2	1½" × 1½"
2×4	1½" × 3½"
2×6	1½" × 5½"
2×8	1½" × 7¼"
2×10	1½" × 9¼"
2×12	1½" × 11¼"
4×4	3½" × 3½"

When figuring board feet, make your calculations using the nominal size.

To figure board feet, multiply the thickness of the piece in inches times the width of the piece in inches. Multiply that number times the length of the piece in feet, then divide by 12. (Or multiply times the length in inches, then divide by 144.) For example, a 2×4 that's 8 feet long contains 5⅓ board feet: 2×4=8, 8×8 (length in feet)=64, 64/12=5⅓.

OSB

Oriented strand board (OSB) is a sheet material of compressed wood strands arranged in layers at right angles to each other. The strands are bonded with phenol-formaldehyde adhesive. The strength and ability of OSB to hold fasteners make it an ideal—and less costly—alternative to plywood for sheathing and underlayment.

HOW FAR CAN JOISTS SPAN?

This table shows the lengths (feet-inches) that various species can safely span when joists are set 16 inches on center.

SPECIES	GRADE	2×6	2×8	2×10
California Redwood	Const. Heart or Const. Common	7-3	10-9	13-6
Western Cedar	Sel. Struct.	8-10	11-8	14-11
	No. 1	8-7	11-1	13-6
	No. 2	8-4	11-0	13-6
Douglas Fir	Sel. Struct.	13-7	17-4	21-1
	No. 1	13-1	16-5	19-1
	No. 2	12-7	15-5	17-10
Southern Pine	Sel. Struct.	13-4	17-0	20-9
	No. 1	13-1	16-9	20-4
	No. 2	12-10	16-1	18-10

Spans shown are for 40-pound live load, the standard required for residential floors.

LOOSE MATERIALS

Loose materials offer an alternative to hard pavements. Used by themselves or in combination with other hard scape, they offer an environmentally friendly means (many products are recycled materials) of creating a patio or path. Loose materials are generally available at low cost, and most require only moderate maintenance.

■ Unlike harder paving surfaces, loose materials will shift beneath your feet to enhance your walking comfort and to give your patio the feeling of a pleasant park or a spot in the woods.

■ The most popular loose materials for patio surfaces are easy to install and maintain and offer many appealing design possibilities.

■ Loose materials provide better drainage than any other surfaces. They help prevent erosion and, except for wood products, make any site easy to use after a rainfall.

Here are some of the more popular loose paving materials:

PEA GRAVEL: This material consists of medium-size stones that have been naturally smoothed by river or lake water. River rock is available in many colors, and it shifts easily underfoot. It also has a visually soft look and can be raked in interesting furrows and lines.

CRUSHED STONE: This is quarried rock that has been mechanically crushed and then graded so that most of the stones are of a similar size, with varying shapes and colors.

WOOD BARK, CHIPS, NUGGETS, AND SHREDS: Several types of wood—including redwood, cedar, cypress, and pine—are available in chipped and shredded forms. Redwood, cedar, and cypress are naturally resistant to the effects of weather and insects. Wood chips can serve a variety of landscaping purposes, particularly as mulch around plants, shrubs, and trees. They also are useful for cushioning surfaces under children's play equipment.

However, wood chips and other loose materials that are relatively light can be pushed out of place by footsteps. Add edging such as railroad ties, brick, pavers, or stone.

HOW TO ORDER

Redwood or cedar bark and chips are available in bags from your neighborhood home center, lumberyards, building supply centers, landscape suppliers, and patio supply stores. Or you may be able to get them from your local parks department—for free. Local parks often recycle wood chips from the trees they remove, and you might be able to have them for the hauling. Crushed stone and pea gravel can be bought by the ton from quarries, stone suppliers, or patio supply stores. See the Yellow Pages for "Lumber," "Building Materials," "Landscaping," "Quarries," or "Stone."

MAKING A LOOSE STONE PATIO

Backfill if forms are kept in place

2"–3" loose stone

Landscape fabric

4"–6" gravel base (optional where increased drainage is needed)

Form to contain material

Brick or other edging

FOUNDATIONS

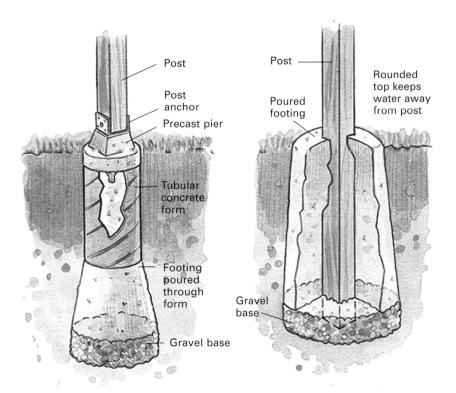

Post

Post anchor

Precast pier

Tubular concrete form

Footing poured through form

Gravel base

Post

Poured footing

Rounded top keeps water away from post

Gravel base

Decks and overheads require a foundation for each load-bearing post. The type and dimensions of the foundation you'll need will depend on the height of the structure, the types of materials you plan to use, how deep the ground freezes, and the load-bearing capacity of the soil.

Because they support wood posts or beams that deteriorate with ground contact, post supports typically extend above grade. They are usually cylinders or blocks at least 8 inches across, with straight or beveled sides.

Footings are typically 18 inches square and at least 6 inches thick. You should dig the holes for them to a depth prescribed by local building codes—anywhere from 1 foot to 6 feet or more, depending on the local depth of the frost and the stability of the soils in your area.

FOOTINGS AND PIERS

When it comes to supporting the posts for your deck or overhead, you have several options:

PRECAST PIERS: A precast pier generally looks like a pyramid with its top cut off. You can purchase precast piers at your local materials supplier in sizes that are appropriate to your installation. The better piers have post anchors already embedded and are ready-made for setting in a poured footing while the concrete is still wet.

POURED-IN-PLACE PIERS: These are piers that you make yourself, molding them in a form and pouring them at the same time you pour the footings.

You can buy prefabricated forms (usually they are large cylinders that you place in the footing hole) or make your own configurations with wooden forms. Poured-in-place piers offer decorative options that precast varieties do not.

POST ANCHORS: Some post anchors are designed to be set in the footings or piers while the concrete is still wet; others can be added later by drilling through the concrete, but these tend to be less stable.

PRE-MIX FOR FOOTINGS

Mixing concrete for post holes is usually easier with pre-mixed bags—you just add water and provide the muscle power to mix it. Using pre-mix is slightly more costly than mixing your own concrete from dry materials, but the expense is more than offset by the convenience.

Holes for 4×4 posts (3 feet deep) require only a little more than 2 cubic feet each—two 60-pound sacks per posthole. You can fill about three postholes with four 90-pound sacks of pre-mix. Make sure to buy extra. Concrete isn't expensive, and you won't want to come up short in the middle of pouring.

FASTENERS

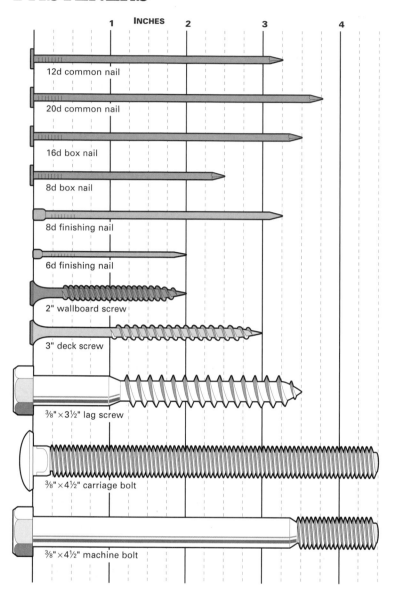

INCHES

12d common nail

20d common nail

16d box nail

8d box nail

8d finishing nail

6d finishing nail

2" wallboard screw

3" deck screw

⅜" × 3½" lag screw

⅜" × 4½" carriage bolt

⅜" × 4½" machine bolt

Don't scrimp on the quality or quantity of fasteners in your project—after all, it's the fasteners that hold all your hard work together. Framing fasteners come in a variety of forms—nails, screws, lag screws, bolts, and metal framing connectors. You may need masonry fasteners if you build your shed or gazebo on a slab or otherwise attach it to a concrete surface.

NAILS

Nails hold things together by the friction they generate against wood fibers. The size of a nail is determined by its length expressed as pennyweight, abbreviated as *d* (which stands for *denarius*, an ancient coin; it referred to the cost of 100 nails of a given size).

■ **COMMON NAILS,** used for general construction, have large heads and thick shanks. They hold well but are hard to drive and may split the wood.

■ **BOX NAILS,** narrower than their common cousins, reduce splitting in ¾-inch or thinner stock.

■ **RING-SHANKED AND SPIRAL-SHANKED NAILS** grip the wood fibers better than common or box nails and don't easily work their way out. They are very difficult to remove.

■ **FINISHING NAILS** have slender shanks and small, barrel-shaped heads that can be countersunk. Use them for trim work and wherever you don't want the heads to show.

■ **CASING NAILS** are hefty versions of finishing nails and provide more holding power.

■ **BRADS** are miniature finishing nails, used for attaching thin, fragile pieces.

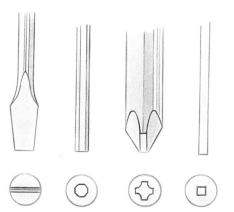

PREDRILLING FASTENERS

Once a board is split by a nail or screw, not only is the board unsightly, but the fastener has lost almost all its holding power. Small splits will almost certainly grow in time. Save time and disappointment by drilling pilot holes wherever there is a possibility of splitting—especially close to the end of a board.

For nails, drill a pilot hole using a drill bit slightly smaller than the nail. Test by drilling a hole and driving the nail. It should be snug enough so it takes some hammering to drive it in.

Try this trick for attaching softwood trim: Insert the finishing nail in the chuck of your drill. Drive the nail with the drill till it contacts the framing. Finish driving the nail with a hammer.

Use the chart below for predrilling pilot holes for screws. Drill through the top piece and into the bottom piece to a depth equal to the screw length. Clamp or hold the parts together as you drive in the screw.

Screw Diameter	Pilot Hole Diameter
4	$1/16$"
6	$3/32$"
0	$7/64$"
10	$1/8$"
12	$9/64$"
14	$5/32$"

■ **DUPLEX NAILS** come in handy as temporary fasteners. They have a double head, which makes them easy to pull out when you strip away framing braces, for example.

The metal used to fabricate a nail makes a difference. Some nails rust readily, and others won't ever rust.

■ **GALVANIZED NAILS** are the most common type. Hot-dipped galvanized (HDG) are more reliable than electro-galvanized (EG). But no galvanized nail provides insurance against rust; the coating often flakes off.

■ **ALUMINUM NAILS** won't rust, although they aren't quite as strong as HDG nails and can be very difficult to drive (they bend), especially in hardwoods.

■ **STAINLESS STEEL NAILS** won't rust, but they are very expensive, and not all suppliers stock them. They're a good choice and worth their expense for projects built near salt water.

SCREWS

Screws hold better than nails, don't pop out of the wood, and are easier to remove. They also come in a bewildering array of styles. You're looking for decking screws—generally in $2\frac{1}{2}$- to $3\frac{1}{2}$-inch lengths. Decking screws are coated for resistance to the elements and are sharp, tapered, and self sinking. With a cordless drill you can drive them about as fast as nails.

Regardless of what size you use, predrill them (see chart, *above*) when driving them within 2 inches of the end of a board. Predrilling keeps the wood from splitting.

Be sure to match your screwdriver bit to the type of screw head (or vice versa). Straight-slot screws are available only as round-headed wood screws. You won't use straight-slot or hex-head screws in your outdoor structure. Decking screws generally are machined with a Phillips or square head or a combination head.

Many types of combination heads will not hold a Phillips-tip securely against the torque of a cordless drill, especially when fastening 2× framing. If you're stripping your combination-head screws when you go to sink them, switch to a square tip.

LAG SCREWS

A lag screw is a bolt in a screw's clothing—its large size will attach heavy framing members and hardware. Lag screws have a hex head (square heads are available but uncommon). Tighten them with a wrench.

BOLTS

Bolts, nuts, and washers provide a solid connection with excellent load-bearing strength. They hold parts together by compressing their surfaces, and their size is designated by their shank diameter (under the head) and their length. Use only those with a hot-dipped galvanized finish and pre-drill them with a drill bit of the same diameter.

WHAT SIZE FASTENER?

The longer and thicker a nail is, the better it holds. However, if a nail is too thick for the stock, it will split the wood and have almost no holding power at all.

Although it might seem that building a deck calls for a wide selection of fasteners, those listed below will get you through most projects.

■ Common, spiral, or ring-shanked nails (10d or 16d) for framing in 2× or thicker stock
■ Box or ring-shanked nails (8d or 10d) in 1× or thinner stock
■ Finish nails (8d or 10d) for trim
■ Decking screws—#10, in appropriate lengths

FASTENERS
continued

■ **MACHINE BOLTS** have a hex or square head.

■ **CARRIAGE BOLTS** have a rounded head for a decorative or finished appearance.

Tighten machine bolts with two wrenches (putting washers under the head and nut). Carriage bolts have a square shank under the head, which pulls into the wood and keeps the bolt from turning. Tighten both fasteners until they are just snug, making the slightest indentation in the surface of the wood.

MASONRY FASTENERS

Masonry fasteners are similar to nails or screws. Some are made of hardened steel, and others rely on expansion and friction to grip masonry. Refer to the illustrations on this page for installation methods.

MASONRY ANCHORS

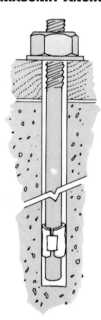

Anchor bolts expand against the concrete when the bolt is tightened. Drill a hole of the same diameter and at least ½" longer than the bolt. Blow the dust from the hole and drive the bolt in with the nut turned just to the top of the threads. Make sure the bolt doesn't turn when tightening.

GET A GRIP

Whether you assemble your deck with nails or screws, make sure that two-thirds of the fastener shank is in the lower (usually the thicker) member of the joint. Where possible, and to get the best holding power, drive the fasteners at an angle, toward or away from each other.

FRAMING CONNECTORS

Framing connectors are designed for a number of special purposes. Those available from your distributor may not look exactly like the styles illustrated here, but their general shape should be the same.

Most manufacturers supply nails (usually blunted to reduce splitting) for framing connectors, but you can use common nails of the closest size, cinching the nail if it's longer than the framing.

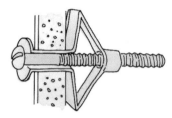

Hollow wall anchors can be used to fasten lumber between the recesses of concrete block. Drill a hole of the same diameter, insert the anchor, and tighten the screw to draw the flanges against the rear of the recess. Remove the screw, insert it through the material to be fastened, and retighten the screw in the anchor.

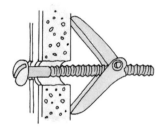

Toggle bolts have wings that expand against the rear of a concrete surface and can also be used to fasten material to concrete block. Drill a hole of the same diameter; insert the wings through the material to be fastened and into the block. Tighten the bolt to draw the wings snug.

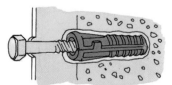

Expansion shields are made of soft metal or plastic whose sides expand as a screw or lag screw is tightened.

Drill a hole of the same diameter and length, set the shield in the hole, and tighten the screw.

FRAMING CONNECTORS

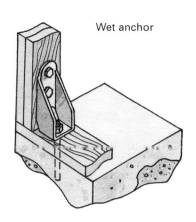

Wet anchor

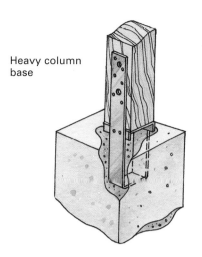

Heavy column base

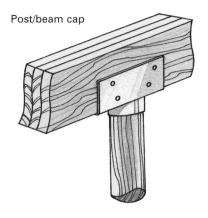

Post/beam cap

WET ANCHORS are a form of post connector inserted into a concrete foundation, slab, or post footing while the concrete is still wet.

HEAVY COLUMN BASES are also a form of post anchor inserted into wet concrete.

POST/BEAM CAPS tie a beam to a post of equal size.

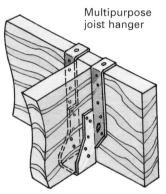

Multipurpose joist hanger

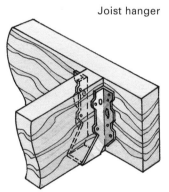

Joist hanger

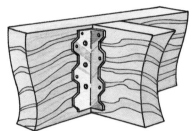

Angle bracket

JOIST HANGERS butt joists to beams or headers. Single and double sizes are available.

ANGLE BRACKETS strengthen perpendicular joints—at rim joists and stair stringers, for example.

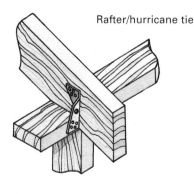

Rafter/hurricane tie

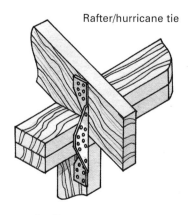

Rafter/hurricane tie

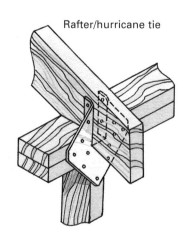

Rafter/hurricane tie

RAFTER/HURRICANE TIES connect rafters to top plates.

FINISHES

WOOD FINISHES

Whitewashed

Natural

Wood
preservative

Clear stain

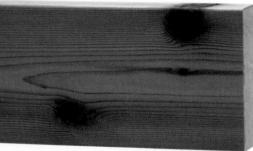

Tinted
stains

Paints

If it weren't for the weather, you wouldn't have to worry much about the durability of your deck or other outdoor structure. But wind, rain, snow, ice, and sun exact a heavy toll on wood. The right finish can help protect your project and enhance its look.

You can finish a structure in a variety of ways, depending on the type of lumber, your preference of color, and the environment of the deck. Here are some guidelines you can use in selecting a finish and applying it.

CHOOSING THE FINISH

Ask yourself how you want your structure to look. Do you want to paint it, stain it, or let it weather? With a clear finish, redwood and cedar show off their natural color. They also look good when left to weather. Some designs seem made for paint. Others, especially those in woodland settings, might look better weathered. What about your design?

■ First consider the style of the project and its setting, including colors on your home.
■ Turn your attention to what color, tone, and surface sheen (flat or glossy) complement the overall landscape design theme.
■ Finally research the durability and ease of application of various products.

If you mix finishes, make sure they're compatible. Your supplier may be able to help you choose the right combination.

SEALERS

Sealers, also called water repellents, seal wood against water penetration and present you with two basic options—clear or pigmented. Both protect the wood without changing its appearance appreciably.

A wide range of additives increases the effectiveness of sealers.

■ Fungicides and insect repellents ward off mildew, insects, and fungi.
■ Ultraviolet blockers diminish the effect of the sun's rays and help maintain the natural color of the wood.

THE BEAD TEST

To see if your deck is ready for a finish, sprinkle some water on the wood. If the water soaks into the surface, the wood is dry enough to take a finish. If it beads up in droplets, put the finish away, wait for a few weeks, and test it again.

All-purpose sealers usually contain water repellents, preservative, and ultraviolet blockers.

A clear sealer has the least effect on the wood's natural color. It may slow the graying of wood but won't stop it. Pigmented sealers provide the same protection but change the color of the wood slightly. You can apply sealers over or under stains and under primer and paint for extra protection.

STAINS

Stains change the look of a surface, but most are not designed to protect the wood. Stains are somewhat less expensive than paints, and application goes faster than painting because stains don't require an undercoat. They go on easily over rough or smooth surfaces.

Stains fall roughly into two categories based on the concentration of pigment:

■**SEMITRANSPARENT STAINS** allow the wood grain to show through, but they wear away more quickly. They are particularly suitable for highlighting the beauty of wood grains.

HEAVY-BODIED stains contain more pigments and tend to obscure the grain more.

No matter what their pigment level, stains don't offer much variation in sheen. They tend to retain the wood's low-luster, natural look.

Both kinds of stain come as oil-based or water-based products. In general, oil-based stains are more durable than their water-based counterparts. But new chemical techniques are producing water-based products that rival oil-based stains. Ask your retailer for recommendations, but on redwood and red cedar, apply oil-based stains.

Even if you've decided on a full-bodied stain for the frame of your deck, consider a light-bodied product for the decking. The inevitable wear won't be as noticeable on a light color, and the slight difference in tone can often produce a pleasing contrast with the rest of the deck. Periodic restaining will give you a more even color.

In any case, make sure you apply a nonchalking stain or sealer-stain to eliminate the possibility of tracking a powdery film into the house.

PAINTS

Painting a deck, shed, or gazebo creates an elegant, refined look. Unlike stain, an opaque film of paint can mask some of the defects in the wood, making paint an ideal finish for lower grades of lumber.

Paint offers an unlimited choice of colors and will look the same on all species. Paint takes more time to apply, however, is more expensive, and is harder to maintain than other finishes. All of this inconvenience is balanced by the fact that it offers the most complete protection. But once you have painted a deck, you can't change your mind and apply any other finish.

If you're painting, apply primer first. Painted finishes tend to last longer and look better on smooth surfaces than on rough ones. And, of course, they can be recoated.

Here again you have choices:

EXTERIOR ALKYDS (oil-based products) are costly, require solvents for cleanup, and dry slowly.

WATER-BASED LATEX PAINTS don't cost as much as alkyds, clean up easily with water, and dry quickly.

Both kinds come in a range of sheens (gloss, semigloss, flat, or matte).

Oil-based primers provide better protection on raw wood than water-based primers. Add stain blockers to stop bleed-through from redwood and cedar. A good-quality acrylic-latex top coat applied over an alkyd primer is a durable and protective finish.

When painting the decking itself, choose a product specified for outdoor decks or porches so it will withstand heavy wear. Like painted porches and steps, a painted deck surface can be slippery when wet. As an extra safety precaution, especially around doorways and stairs, you can mix a handful or so of clean sand (play sand for kids' sandboxes) with the paint used for the final coat to add traction.

FINISHES AND PRESSURE TREATMENTS

Most pressure-treated wood is kiln-dried before getting the preservative. This means that a great many boards are still soaked when they get to the lumberyard—and when you bring them home. Wet wood will cause a finish to blister and peel. Some boards may be dry to the touch but still contain enough moist chemicals to resist finishing. You can build your deck with freshly treated lumber, but you'll have to let it dry—sometimes several weeks—before applying a finish. Try "The Bead Test," opposite.

FINALIZING COSTS

Getting help with your project will save you time and money. It's best, however, to find friends who have some construction or carpentry experience. Don't hesitate to "assign" those with less experience to tasks requiring less skill. Your work will proceed more smoothly and will be safer for all.

Once your design has been approved by everyone who needs to review it, you're ready to start gathering bids. Get bids from at least two or three major suppliers, and ask friends and relatives for recommendations.

You can divide your costs into several parts; here are a few suggestions:

■ **YOUR TIME:** How much do you want to do yourself, and can you afford that much time? Of course you can put a value on your time based on what you earn, but you won't simply be "spending" your time. You will get some exercise, learn new skills, stay in control of the project, and benefit from the results of your work and the sense of accomplishment.

■ **CONTRACT COSTS:** You can get a fairly accurate estimate of contractor costs without seeking bids. Double your material costs for any section of the project (or the whole thing). The result will be in the ballpark.

■ **SITE PREP:** Include building permits, excavation, drainage, and landscaping. Site preparation costs may not apply to your project, but if your lot needs considerable grading, that expense should be included as part of the cost of your deck.

■ **MATERIAL:** Concrete, lumber, hardware, equipment rentals, other building supplies—

the cost adds up at computer speed. Fortunately material costs are the easiest to compare. You can create a materials list, then give copies to several suppliers, asking for prices and a package price.

WHAT'S YOUR TIME WORTH?

The time you spend building a deck probably isn't time taken from your job. It's weekends, evenings, or vacation days that you could be spending with your family or friends. How do you put a value on that?

The best approach to this question is to focus on satisfaction and not dollars. Set aside briefly the prospect of saving money by doing the work yourself. Save that as a tie-breaker. Here's the real issue: If you want to give yourself a challenge, enjoy working with your hands, or just want to call your deck your own in every way possible, the time you spend on it won't be lost. Instead it will be an investment in personal accomplishment and pride of ownership. The only question remaining about your time is whether you have enough.

SITE PREPARATION

You may not have thought much about preparing the site, but that little pond that forms in your yard after a rain can be real trouble if it's located right where you plan to put a deck post. You may have to grade your site to improve drainage.

If you need grading, get estimates from landscape contractors. Their equipment can make short work of jobs that would wear you out. Also, their speed means you can schedule site preparation to take place just before you start building.

SAVE YOURSELF A TRIP

When you get bids for materials, ask each lumberyard or building supply center about its return policy. Look for a business that will exchange defective goods and accept returns. Then buy more of each bulk item—such as fasteners and decking boards—than your plan requires. It's easier to return the extras after the project is finished than to make a separate trip each time you run short of materials.

SHOULD YOU HIRE A CONTRACTOR?

DOING IT YOURSELF

The explosive growth of the do-it-yourself industry shows that many homeowners can handle all but the most extensive landscape projects. When you're deciding whether to do the work yourself or hire it out, consider these points:

■ **DON'T KID YOURSELF:** Weigh your skill level and experience against the scope of the project. You can do minor excavating with a post-hole digger or shovel. Patios and driveway slabs require heavy equipment. If your carpentry skills are weak, buy precut kits for sheds, gazebos, and privacy fencing.

■ **WILL FRIENDS HELP?** Many construction projects require at least two sets of hands when setting deck joists, lifting framing lumber into position on an overhead, or pouring and leveling concrete slabs.

■ **EMPOWERMENT:** Power tools save time. So does proper planning. Buy a power screwdriver if you don't have one. It will be a valuable addition to your tool kit. Rent a power miter box for corner cuts and a reciprocating saw for cutting posts or timbers. Don't build fences until the major projects are completed, and have materials dropped next to the project. Anything you can do to reduce your labor will make the job more enjoyable.

■ **ADD IT UP:** What will your total costs be? Make sure your materials list is complete, and get prices for everything. Add subcontractor bids for any work you will definitely contract—excavation or electrical wiring, for example. Include the cost of tools you'll have to buy or rent, as well as the fees for waste removal, permits, and inspections. Add these costs together and compare them with a general contractor's bid.

Are the savings large enough to warrant taking the project on? Even if the savings are small, remember that doing it yourself can be an enjoyable and rewarding experience.

CONTRACTING THE JOB

Now that you've decided what projects to contract, how do you find a contractor? Friends and neighbors are good for references. So are local garden shops. Don't work with any contractor whose references you have not checked.

You may also need to enlist the services of landscape professionals such as:

■ **LANDSCAPE ARCHITECTS:** They completely design and plan your landscape, producing detailed drawings, plans, and written work descriptions. They will also supervise the construction.

■ **LANDSCAPE DESIGNERS:** They will assist you with the design of your project and will provide drawings for its general design, but not those showing construction details.

■ **LANDSCAPE CONTRACTORS:** These builders have particular expertise in landscape construction.

Some firms describe themselves as "Designers and Builders." Such firms have professional architects, designers, and builders on their staff.

The best way to find a reputable design professional is through the references of satisfied friends and family. Ask at work or parties; anyone who has a new landscape will be happy to talk about it and the professionals who made it happen.

■ **REFERENCES:** Once you've selected a group of contractors, ask each one for job references and check them. Visit one of their job sites and inspect the quality of the work.

■ **BIDS:** Get several bids and be wary of any that are significantly higher or lower than the average. The bids of reputable contractors bidding for the same work with the same materials should be close.

■ **CONTRACTS AND DOCUMENTS:** Get everything in writing—everything. Read the contract carefully and insert any information that you feel is needed. If you have any uncertainty, have your lawyer review the documents before you sign. The contract should specify:

■ The work to be done.
■ Materials to be used.
■ A start date and completion schedule.
■ Procedure for making changes.
■ Stipulations that the contractor will obtain building permits and lien waivers.
■ Methods for resolving disputes.

Often required by local laws, your contractor should provide evidence of:

■ Licensing: showing he or she has met government standards to do the work.
■ Bonding: evidence that if the contractor fails to perform the work, a bonding company will pay another contractor to finish the job.
■ Insurance: liability for nonworkers, worker's compensation for employees injured on the job.

FINAL PAYMENT

Before you make final payment, obtain signed lien waivers from the contractor for every subcontractor and supplier. You'll avoid liability in case the contractor fails to pay them.

When the job is completed, inspect it carefully. If anything looks questionable, make a note of it. Ask the contractor to do a walk-through with you so you can point out problems; then both of you can see firsthand what needs to be corrected. The contractor should either correct any problems or explain why they really aren't problems.

Many cities provide recourse for resolution of future problems—usually for a year. Check with your local building department. If problems arise, appeal first to the contractors involved and allow a reasonable time for repairs. Then appeal to the professional associations to which they belong, or consult a lawyer.

PUTTING YOUR PLANS ON PAPER

You've pondered the function of your project and its style. You've chosen the materials you'll use. Now you're ready for construction. Before you bring out the shovels and levels, however, you should refine your plan.

This is the time for you to put your plans on paper. Detailing all the elements now will save you time in the long run, to say nothing of money and frustration. Paper plans also will help keep you on schedule throughout the construction process.

Drawing a plan keeps you from having to make hurried decisions in the field. It allows you to experiment with the location of the structure, its contours, and its materials.

Paper plans also can give you a bird's-eye view of the landscape, helping you discover design ideas you might not otherwise have pictured. Even if you intend to contract all or part of the construction to a pro, a detailed plan will give you a basis for securing bids and will help your contractor build the patio or deck exactly as you envision it.

On the following pages you'll find planning tips as well as illustrations that demonstrate how professionals develop a complete landscape plan. If your project is small, you may not need to invest time in such an elaborate undertaking. Large or small, any patio project will profit from including each step of the design process.

DECK FRAMING PLAN

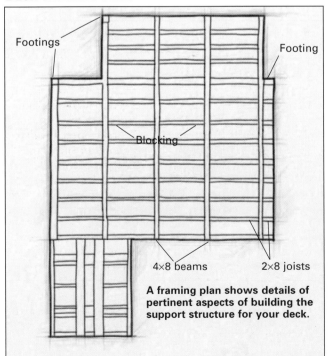

A framing plan shows details of pertinent aspects of building the support structure for your deck.

Footings

Footing

Blocking

4×8 beams

2×8 joists

SKETCHES AND PLANS

Planning framed structures requires more detail than planning other landscaping projects because of the complexity of their construction. In addition to the plans illustrated in this chapter, you'll need construction drawings, such as framing plans and elevations, to keep you or your contractor on target.

ELEVATION

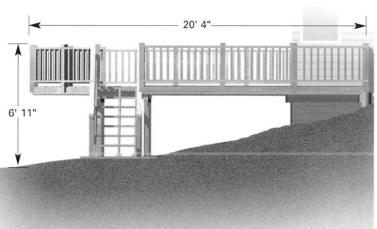

CONSTRUCTION DETAILS

FOOTINGS

4x8

4x4

POST/BEAM CONNECTION

Construction details help you keep track of methods you will use when building your outdoor structure.

An elevation shows the deck from one side—and others, if they are different. Show how far above the ground the structure will be built, and indicate any grading or other ground-level changes.

DRAFTING TOOLBOX

Here's what you'll need to get your paper plans on their way.
- An engineer's scale
- A roll or sheets of tracing paper
- 2 circle templates ranging from ¼" to 3½" in diameter
- Thick and thin black felt-tipped pens
- Rulers (6" and 12")
- Pencils with erasers
- Drafting or masking tape (drafting tape comes off surfaces more easily and doesn't leave marks)
- T-square
- Pencil sharpener

PLOTTING A BASE MAP

As with any decisionmaking process, you'll simplify the task (and reduce your confusion) by taking the planning process one step at a time. The first step is to draw a base map of your property.

START WITH A SKETCH

Begin by walking around the outside of your house with a clipboard and a 100-foot steel measuring tape. You'll be measuring and sketching in the outlines of structures and plantings and other major details. Later you will transfer these sketches more exactly to a graph paper map. Even though you're familiar with your own house and lot, don't take anything for granted.

BOUNDARIES FIRST: Starting with the exact location of your property lines (look for metal markers or use a metal detector to find them), sketch in the outline of your yard and house, noting its distance from all property lines. Take accurate measurements from all property lines. Measure and record the dimensions of each wall of your house and the sizes of other structures, such as detached garages or sheds. Your sketch should include how far structures are from one another.

LOOK AT SMALLER ELEMENTS: Include the little things on your sketch. They will matter when you build your patio. Here's a sample list of items to watch for:

■ Location of doors and windows, including width, height, distance from the ground, and what rooms they lead from.

■ Extension of roof eaves beyond the exterior walls of the house.

■ Location of downspouts and direction of runoff.

■ Where existing trees, shrubs, and gardens are planted.

■ Location of outdoor walls, fences, steps, walks, and driveways.

DRAWING A DETAILED MAP

Once your sketch is complete, transfer it to graph paper (24×36 inches is a good size, with a scale of ¼ inch = 1 foot). Include all the elements on your sketch, and note all the dimensions you've recorded.

Be sure to include the locations of windows, doors, hose bibs, and electrical outlets. Use dotted lines for any buried cable.

This is the time for precision. If you're in doubt about any measurement, go measure again. Doing so can save you hours of actual construction time. When you're done you'll have an accurate drawn-to-scale map of your property.

BASE-MAP SHORTCUTS

You may be able to shorten the base-map process by using existing maps of your property. Start with the existing legal maps and description of your house and lot. These documents—called deed maps, house plans, plat plans, or contour plans—are typically available from your title company, bank, mortgage lender, city hall, or county recorder's office. You may even have a copy filed in your records along with the other papers you received when you bought the house. Plot maps do not, however, show every measurement. You'll still have to measure the dimensions of your house and the elements outlined on the opposite page.

Another, though more costly, option is to have your property surveyed (a necessity if your plan includes extensive grading), but expect to pay several hundred dollars.

HIGH-TECH HELP

Computerized landscape-design programs take the pencil (and eraser) out of planning. They're easy to use, flexible, and can speed your progress from base plan to final design. One of a computer's more appealing features is deletion—an electronic eraser that allows you to change your design without redrawing it.

The features are slick: Programs calculate dimensions of each of your proposed structures and areas of use. Most programs have a number of symbols for trees and shrubs, as well as elements such as furniture, pools, and patios. Some will even create side elevations and three-dimensional views of your plan. Others can prepare material lists and cost estimates.

Check your home improvement center too. Many offer computer design services. If you're not familiar with computers, you can take your rough drawings (including dimensions) and the store's staff will computerize your project and produce a materials list and cost estimates. Ask for extra copies—your local government building department will need them when you apply for permits.

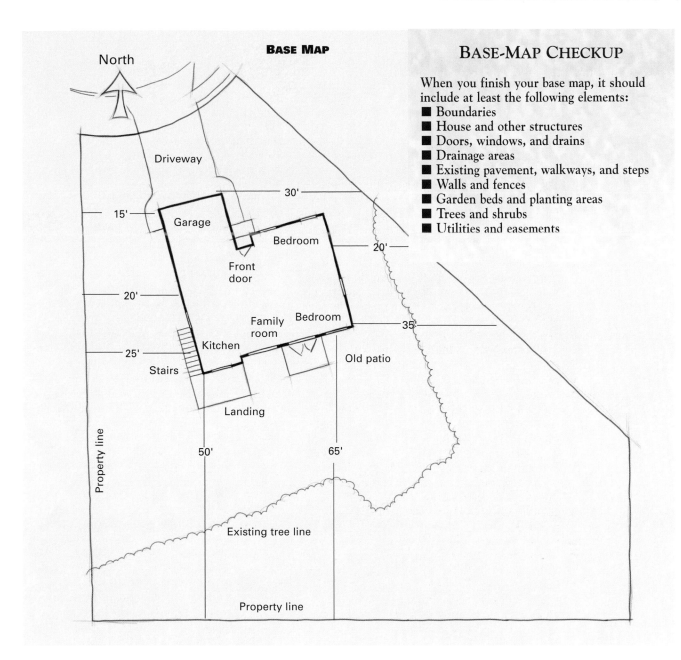

BASE MAP

North

Driveway

30'

15'

Garage

Bedroom

20'

Front door

20'

Family room

Bedroom

35'

Kitchen

25'

Old patio

Stairs

Landing

Property line

50'

65'

Existing tree line

Property line

BASE-MAP CHECKUP

When you finish your base map, it should include at least the following elements:
- Boundaries
- House and other structures
- Doors, windows, and drains
- Drainage areas
- Existing pavement, walkways, and steps
- Walls and fences
- Garden beds and planting areas
- Trees and shrubs
- Utilities and easements

WHEN IT'S TIME FOR A CHANGE

Did you inherit a dysfunctional patio or deck when you bought your house? Perhaps you built one years ago when your family's needs were different. When it's time for a change, here are some ideas for retrofitting a worn-out or out-of-date design.

■ Is your patio larger than you need? Consider building raised planters to divide it into smaller spaces. Or cut through the paving and plant trees.

■ Do you entertain on a regular basis but your patio is too small to hold all your guests? Convert a flower bed near the patio into lawn, where you can easily set up tents or party tables. Build a second patio and link the old and new spaces with a boardwalk or path so guests can move between the areas. Enlarge the space by

installing a brick patio at the foot of a deck. Extend a stone patio by pouring textured concrete at its edge and laying a border of stone that matches the existing one.

■ Make the patio seem larger by removing hedges, fencing, or obstructions that are merely decorative. This will open up the view and make the space seem larger. Be careful not to take out plantings or structures that were put there to increase privacy.

■ Improve the view. Bring compost bins, garbage cans, yard tools, and heating and cooling equipment into a single service area rather than leaving them scattered throughout the yard. Then hide them all behind an attractive screen.

ANALYZING YOUR SITE

A base map gives you a picture of the outline of your property and its contents just as they are. A site analysis takes that picture one step further.

A site analysis will enable you to view the components of your yard as if you were hovering overhead. It is primarily a tool that helps you evaluate the relationships among your landscape elements and to record what you consider to be your property's assets (the things you like and that work well with your lifestyle) and its liabilities (the things that don't).

CONDUCTING A SITE ANALYSIS

Take your sketch (not the base map) out in your yard and step back so you can evaluate its assets and liabilities (use the checklist on the next page as a guide). Ask yourself the following questions:

- What works well?
- What do I want to change?
- Is the route to the site pleasant?
- Is the site easily accessible, or will I have to take a circuitous route to reach it?
- Is the best part of the yard visible from the seating on the proposed patio space?
- Is this site private enough to feel comfortable when I relax?

Go through the checklist item by item and judge how each of these features of your yard will either enhance or detract from your comfort and convenience.

Make notes about your evaluation on your landscape sketch and include the following concerns:

- How does the distance from your proposed project to streets, alleys, and sidewalks affect your need for quiet and privacy?
- Will streetlights and light from neighboring properties affect your use of the site in the evening?
- What views do you want to keep?
- What views do you want to block?
- Are there sources of noise nearby, day or night? Are there drainage problems you need to correct? Are there neighbors' trees or bushes that overhang your yard?

Set your sketch and notes aside while you trace your base map on a piece of tracing paper. Label this first tracing "Site Analysis" and transfer your notes to it. When you're done, it should look something like the site analysis shown left.

SITE ANALYSIS

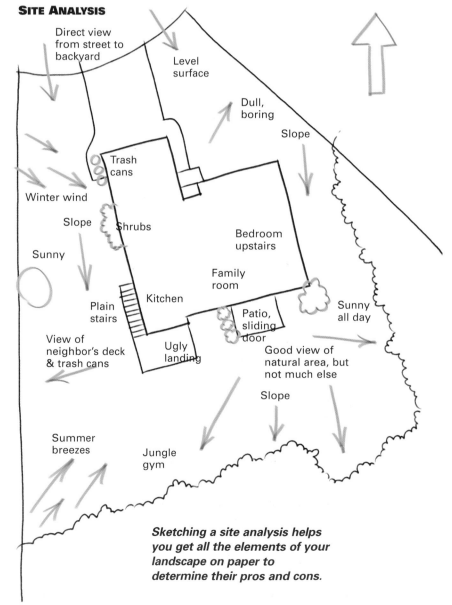

Direct view from street to backyard
Level surface
Dull, boring
Slope
Trash cans
Winter wind
Slope
Shrubs
Sunny
Bedroom upstairs
Family room
Plain stairs
Kitchen
Patio, sliding door
Sunny all day
View of neighbor's deck & trash cans
Ugly landing
Good view of natural area, but not much else
Slope
Summer breezes
Jungle gym

Sketching a site analysis helps you get all the elements of your landscape on paper to determine their pros and cons.

Notes for Site Analysis
✓ Too much sun on patio space
✓ Don't block view to woods
✓ Yard slopes steeply at rear
✓ Deck will shade patio
✓ Neighbor has too much view of patio (screen view)
✓ Improve visual access
✓ Good view from kitchen window

LOOK FOR UTILITY LINES

No matter where you build, consider utilities carefully. Verify with the local utilities where their gas, water, sewer, electrical, or communication lines are located. Make sure construction won't cut into them and that you won't cover them with paving.

Even if safety isn't an issue, you don't want your deck or patio to prevent future access. Rights of access by utility companies are called easements, and easements apply even if you don't receive the service of a particular utility. For example, even if you use a satellite dish for television, you need to find out if the cable company uses underground lines. Note all easements on your base map or site analysis.

CHECKLIST FOR SITE ANALYSIS

Effective landscape planning means more than drawing a plan and laying a slab or paving materials. A good plan should take into account the details of the total environment. When you sketch your plans, it's easy to overlook details you may later find important. Here's a checklist for the elements to include while you sketch your patio site. Use the list as a guide. Many items may not apply, and you may add other items not listed that are specific to your needs.

STRUCTURES
- Dimensions of house, garage, and any other permanent buildings
- Roof overhangs
- Walls, fences, and trellises
- Columns
- Built-in furnishings and appliances (benches, tables, grills, and counters)

PAVED SURFACES
- Existing and proposed patio pavings
- Driveways
- Walks and paths
- Steps
- Edgings

AMENITIES (DECORATIVE AND FUNCTIONAL)
- Freestanding furniture and grills
- Lighting
- Play areas
- Poolside areas
- Birdhouses
- Wind chimes
- Sculpture and decorative elements

ACCESS
- Foot-traffic patterns
- Doors and windows

DRAINAGE
- Spouts
- Gutters
- Current runoff areas and patterns

SLOPES OR STEEP GRADES
- Dips in ground
- Slope direction
- Steep grades that may need retaining walls
- Stairs and steps

PLACEMENT OF UTILITIES
- Electrical supply lines, overhead or underground
- Telephone lines, overhead or underground
- Television cable
- Natural-gas supply lines
- Water supply pipes
- Wastewater pipes
- Hose bibs
- Sewage pipes and catch basins
- Septic tanks
- Utility easements (access for utilities)

PRIVACY AND VIEW
- Open and closed areas within your property
- Views to preserve
- Views to block
- Privacy walls, fences, and plants

PLANTS (EXISTING AND PROPOSED)
- Trees
- Shrubs and bushes
- Groundcover
- Ground-level flower beds
- Raised flower beds
- Vegetable or herb gardens
- Edgings

WATER AND ROCK
- Erosion
- Natural ponds
- Streams
- Constructed pools and fountains
- Boulders or rock outcroppings

CLIMATE AND MICROCLIMATE
- Prevailing winds
- Precipitation
- Sun and shade
- Heating and cooling

CREATING A BUBBLE PLAN

Your site analysis is a snapshot of the existing landscape with all its attributes and drawbacks. The next step—bubble diagrams—will reflect how things could be.

MAKING THE DIAGRAM

Making bubble diagrams means using more tracing paper. Lay a fresh sheet over your site analysis and retrace the basic outlines of your property, including the house, fence, property lines, and driveway.

BUBBLE DIAGRAM 1

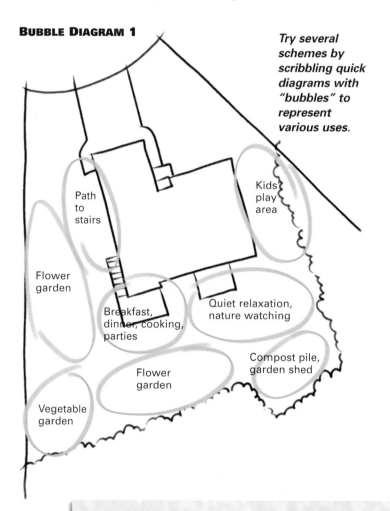

Try several schemes by scribbling quick diagrams with "bubbles" to represent various uses.

Path to stairs

Kids' play area

Flower garden

Breakfast, dinner, cooking, parties

Quiet relaxation, nature watching

Compost pile, garden shed

Flower garden

Vegetable garden

Next draw circles, or bubbles, on the tracing paper to represent various areas in your yard and how you want to use them. Label each bubble with a brief description of its intended use. If you don't like your first design, make another one. Repeat the process, overlaying the site analysis with new sheets of tracing paper to rearrange the bubbles. Try different schemes. Draw as many bubble diagrams as it takes to find one that works for you.

You don't have to be an artist to draw bubble diagrams. They are simply a tool to help you organize your ideas and get you going in the right direction.

BRAINSTORMING WITH BUBBLES

Using bubble diagrams as a design tool works like brainstorming. Many of your initial ideas may seem extreme, but in the end you'll find a creative solution that contains practical and affordable elements.

Move bubbles from place to place to explore different configurations. Set aside budget limitations at this stage. Some ideas—such as moving the lawn—may require more effort or expense than you want to expend. Don't worry about that now; just let the ideas flow.

By allowing yourself to dream and scheme at this point, you might find other ways to achieve your goals. Perhaps you can't tear down an old patio and rebuild it in a new location, even if the new site is *the* ideal spot. But you might be able to put in an inexpensive sitting area.

Here's another possibility. Your existing patio opens to the lawn, but you want a more intimate space. Use bubble diagrams to find a way to separate the patio from the activities on the lawn and to open views. Perhaps you could leave the lawn and the patio where they are and draw a bubble to represent a privacy planting between the two. Or you could move the patio bubble to another part of the diagram or move the lawn to a different spot. Or how about adding a fence and planting along the outer edge of the lawn to give the entire yard more privacy?

REALITY CHECK

As you sketch bubble diagrams, watch for one that stands out as the most appealing and appropriate to your needs. Take time to study this "final" diagram thoroughly. Look at your site analysis and transfer the notes on it to your bubble diagram. Compare the proposed

BUBBLES FOR AN OLD STRUCTURE

Sketching bubble diagrams is equally valuable when reevaluating an existing landscape structure. You might want to change adjacent areas to complement your present space. For example, if you want flowers nearby when you relax or entertain outdoors, sketch a flower garden bubble next to the deck. Rough out several schemes before selecting the sketch that illustrates the ideas that work best for your home.

BUBBLE DIAGRAM 2

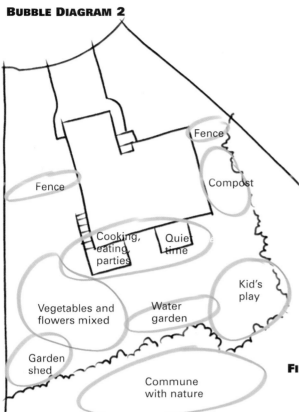

foliage to screen the parking area. And another solution comes to mind: building a plant-covered arbor over the parking area.

While you may not use all of your ideas, your efforts won't be wasted. The process usually leads to as many ideas as you'll need.

Notice the changes from Diagram 1 to Diagram 2. The areas for cooking, dining, and quiet relaxation are left pretty much unchanged—accessible to compatible indoor rooms. But the children's playground is now moved to the corner of the yard, allowing easy supervision from the house and relaxation area. Other areas have been rearranged for both functional and aesthetic reasons. Even this diagram may not be the final plan. Note the differences between it and the Final Diagram, below.

FINAL BUBBLE DIAGRAM

use of each bubble to the physical description of its location. Are they compatible?

For example, you may have picked the ideal spot for a new patio. You like the connection between indoors and out, the view from the area, and the size of the space. However, your site analysis reveals that this location slopes too steeply for a patio.

If you abandon this scheme for a flatter, otherwise less desirable, area, you might not use the area as much as you would like. Looking at site conditions before deciding on a final plan allows you to find a solution that works with existing assets or liabilities. In this case the process could be as simple as building a deck, instead of a patio, over the slope.

Evaluate your entire scheme, bubble by bubble, considering the assets and limitations for each part of the site. Rearranging the bubbles may inspire a new strategy. For example, you might want to move a parking area because the cars ruin the view from a balcony. When you combine the notes from the site analysis with the bubble diagram, however, you realize that you'll have to cut down several lovely mature trees. In this case the bubble diagram was a good start, but the site analysis reveals that it's back to the drawing board. Thinking about the trees, however, could lead you to consider using

Sketch as many bubble diagrams as you want before selecting the one that combines the best ideas for an attractive and practical landscape that works with your home and your life.

DRAWING YOUR MASTER PLAN

Now that you're sure where everything in your new landscape will be, it's time to get a little more specific.

THE DESIGN CONCEPT

A design concept includes every decision you've made about your landscape—for example, where you intend to add shade, wind protection, privacy, or overhead shelter. In one way it is the final bubble diagram with instructions, and these instructions will be the key to drawing your master plan.

Note the differences between a concept diagram and a bubble plan. The design concept tells you specifically what you need to build or add to accomplish the goals you've set out in earlier plans. To make a concept, trace your house and property on a fresh sheet of tracing paper and write descriptions of plantings and construction.

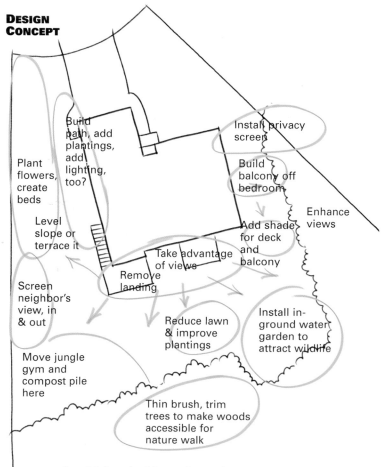

DESIGN CONCEPT

Build path, add plantings, add lighting, too?

Install privacy screen

Build balcony off bedroom

Plant flowers, create beds

Enhance views

Level slope or terrace it

Add shade for deck and balcony

Take advantage of views

Remove landing

Screen neighbor's view, in & out

Reduce lawn & improve plantings

Install in-ground water garden to attract wildlife

Move jungle gym and compost pile here

Thin brush, trim trees to make woods accessible for nature walk

Combining the ideas of your favorite bubble plan with the realities shown on your site analysis will yield a design concept—a diagram of your landscape with instructions about what you plan to build, plant, or add to your site.

THE MASTER PLAN

Lay a piece of tracing paper over your base map and trace the outlines of your house and other existing features. Then make rough drawings of the new structures you will build, using your bubble diagrams to help you decide where everything will go.

STRUCTURES FIRST: Start with the patio and other structural elements, including decks, parking areas, landings, and pathways. Designers call this hard scape. Play with different shapes and lines but keep the basic configurations to scale.

There's still time to explore some ideas freely. If a square-cornered patio now doesn't look just right—or if it won't quite fit the space—round the corner. This is still a time for experimentation, and things are easier to change on paper.

PLANTS AND TREES: Once you draw in the hard scape, add lawn and planting areas with their bedlines. Because they are used as separations, bedlines shape two adjacent spaces at one time. Make them formal and geometric or curve them with a flowing informality.

Next sketch circles to represent any trees you plan to plant, referring to your design concept to remind you of any view you want to frame or areas that need privacy or shade.

Finally label your renderings and label the interior rooms of your home. Make one last check on the relationships each area has with the interior of your home. You may have forgotten that you had planned to remove a tree to open up a view or add high shrubbery to make an interior room more private.

DO A WALK-THROUGH

Now take your plan outside and walk its perimeters on your property. Make sure you haven't forgotten anything.
- Are all the access routes to your patio workable?
- Have you accounted for screening?
- Do the axis lines call attention to the right focal points?
- Can you move a structure within your plan to a spot where you won't have to excavate, without botching the rest of your design?

Even if you intend to build your landscape in stages over a period of years, the master plan will keep your design unified, both now and in the future.

Small ornamental trees

Lawn

Driveway

Lawn

Colorful planting

Fruit tree

Vegetables

Fruit tree

Fruit tree

Fruit tree

Walkway

Groundcover

Boardwalk

House

Front door

Vegetables

Vegetables and herbs

Arbor

Deck

Rapid-growing tree

New deck

Lawn

Walkway

Bench

Pond

Lower deck

Lawn

Stepping-stones

Perimeter planting

Buffer planting

Lawn

Accent planting

Wildlife feeding station

Bench

Mulch path

Your master plan incorporates all of the decisions you've made about your new landscape and renders them in a two-dimensional outline. Use your templates to make this drawing easier.

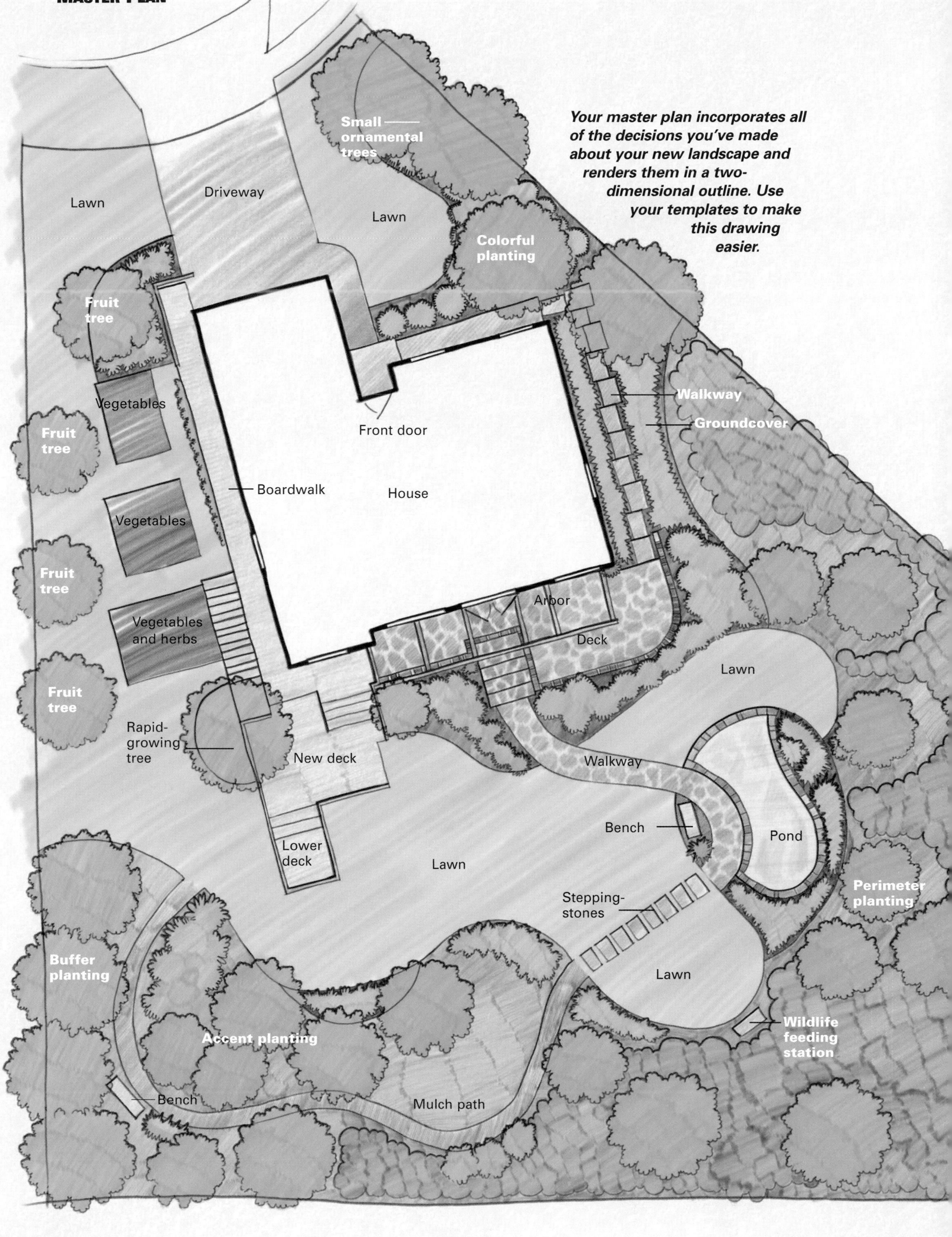

Careful preparation saves time, effort, and money. By having the site ready and all your tools and materials on hand, you get started right—and you avoid repeat trips to the lumberyard or hardware store.

RENTAL TOOLS: YOU'LL NEED THESE—BUT NOT FOREVER

For some homeowners part of the enjoyment of making home improvements is buying new tools. But there are some tools you won't use after you've built your deck. If you need a tool only once, renting it makes more sense.

Here are some of the tools you may need to rent for the construction of your deck:

■ Excavation equipment to clear the site.
■ Hammer drill to install masonry anchors in a brick or stucco wall.
■ Power auger to dig holes for footings.

■ Power cement mixer to prepare concrete for footings and piers.
■ Reciprocating saw to make cuts where a circular saw can't reach.
■ Hydraulic jacks to hold framing in place during construction.
■ Framing nailer to make assembly of framing members proceed quickly and with less effort.

Rent the tools you'll use infrequently. Have the work ready when you rent the tool so you're not paying for idle time.

BUILDING BASICS

Basic construction techniques and practices apply to almost all landscape structures. In this chapter you'll learn everything you need to know to build the projects illustrated in this book. Even if you consider yourself an old hand at building, you'll find a tip or two that will make the job go more smoothly. You'll find information and advice on everything from laying out a site and mixing concrete to methods for installing roofing and siding. Use this chapter as a reference for the projects in this book and other projects.

Before you begin construction, inventory both your tools and your skills. Follow the guidelines, below right, if you need to buy tools. If you run into an aspect of the work that's unfamiliar or that you're uncomfortable with, ask a contractor or a knowledgeable friend. A contractor might charge you for time spent answering your questions, but you'll save time and money in the long run. In some cases you may decide it's better to hire a professional to do a portion of the work. The information in this section can help you make that decision.

Construction projects are noisy, hectic, and wearing. Minimize the effect of inevitable snags by organizing your work in a logical sequence and by allowing enough time to complete each portion. Wear a tool belt or use a bucket with a tool apron to keep your tools organized and out of the way. When you're done with a tool, return it to the same place every time so you won't waste time looking for it. Keep materials organized. Stack lumber to minimize warping and damage. Make a separate pile for scrap wood. Cover materials to protect them from weather. Keep the work site tidy.

SAFETY FIRST

Building a shed or gazebo can be great fun, as long as you make safety a top priority. You wouldn't want to mar an otherwise enjoyable experience with injuries.
■ Wear safety glasses or goggles when using power tools or striking tools. Get the kind of goggles that have side protectors.
■ Wear a dust mask when sawing.
■ Don't use power tools in the rain or in wet locations. Always unplug them before making adjustments, and make sure the switch is off before plugging them in.
■ Wear clothing that fits snugly. Loose sleeves or jewelry can get caught in power tools or even on the work.
■ Make sure ladders are supported on level surfaces before climbing them. Set them close enough to the work so you don't have to overreach. Don't set tools on a stepladder where you can't see them.
■ Use roof jacks when you are roofing.

RULES FOR TOOLS

If you have any experience with home maintenance or basic construction, you may already own many of the tools you need to build your shed or gazebo. If you need to add to your tool chest, consider these suggestions:
■ Buy the best tools you can afford. Cheap tools wear out quickly, can be dangerous, and cost more in the long run.
■ Add a 100-foot drop cord, rated for outdoor use, to your tool inventory.

■ Buy power tools with double insulation for safety. When you will use a tool frequently or for other projects—a circular saw or drill, for example—buy a heavy-duty model with better bearings and a more powerful motor for greater durability.
■ Garage sales and flea markets might be good sources for bargain hand tools. When you're buying power tools, get new ones and stick with respected brands.

GRADING AND DRAINAGE

If your yard has only a minor slope that will interfere with the location of your structure, constructing a swale may be a sufficient remedy. Large-scale drainage problems, however, may require a full-fledged drainage plan such as the one shown here—and probably the help of a landscape professional. Arrows on the plan show the direction of water flow.

Slope

Sod

Pipe in trench

No matter what your landscape construction plans, the first step is to prepare the site. The amount of site preparation will vary from landscape to landscape and from project to project, and generally includes removal of the following:

■ Debris
■ Weeds and other unwanted vegetation
■ Trees
■ Structures, such as old paving, posts, trellises, buildings, and walls.

Your site preparation may also include altering the contours of the landscape with grading.

GRADING

Making changes to the grade is often the first—and sometimes the only—step in preparing the site for a landscape project. If your deck or patio site abuts a slope, you may have to remove some—or all—of it to make the deck level. Even a perfectly flat site can often benefit from alteration of contours to the land.

Begin all the rough grading before laying out the site, and minimize the amount of soil you have to move by filling in low spots with the cut soil. This is the work that calls for heavy equipment. Let the finish grading go until last; you can do it with a garden rake.

After the rough grading is done, lay conduit sleeves that lie outside the site. Continue their run in the site itself after you've excavated it.

Making minor changes often can be accomplished by eyeballing the grade, but for greater precision, stake out the site to mark changes in the grade, making sure the slope you leave runs downhill slightly—¼ inch per linear foot.

SITE SAFETY

Site preparation can leave an area temporarily hazardous. Take the following precautions.

■ **PROTECT YOUR TREES:** Use flagging tape to mark trees you want to keep. Siltation fences keep displaced soil from covering root zones.

■ **LIMIT ACCESS:** Designate and mark heavy equipment access points. Barricade driveways against heavy equipment, which can crack the concrete.

■ **KEEP IT SAFE:** Barricade holes (even shallow excavations) and make sure tools are removed at the end of each workday.

CALL IN THE PROS

Although you can do finish grading and many small excavations yourself, rough grading and major excavation call for earth-moving equipment.

Even if you can do the work by hand, it may be more efficient to spend $500 to have it done all at once than to spend four weekends at hard labor. You'll free your time to work on other aspects of the project you can easily do yourself.

Costs include an hourly equipment fee plus an operator expense—another reason for scheduling grading and excavation for the same time.

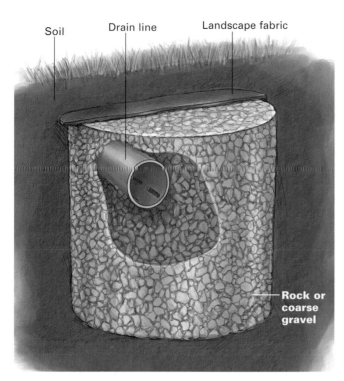

Soil   Drain line   Landscape fabric

Rock or coarse gravel

DRAINAGE TRENCH: *A typical drainage trench is 12 inches wide and as deep as needed to maintain a uniform slope of ¼ inch per foot. Fill half of the trench with gravel, install perforated drainpipe (holes down), and add more gravel. Cover the gravel with landscape fabric, soil, and sod.*

DRY WELL: *A dry well is a large, gravel-filled hole located at a spot lower than the structure (but above the water table) and removed from the deck site. A dry well collects water and lets it slowly disperse into the surrounding soil. It must be connected to the site by drainpipe sloped 1 inch every 4 feet. Dig a hole 3 feet deep and 2 to 4 feet wide. Fill it with coarse gravel, cover the gravel with landscape fabric, then topsoil and sod. Landscape fabric keeps soil from washing into the gravel.*

WEED CONTROL

Ground-level decks and other low-lying surfaces need some weed control. Otherwise you will have vegetation crashing your parties. Prepare the site as described below, either immediately before or after setting posts—certainly before building the frame. The same goes for any structure built over soil without a concrete foundation—a deck whose lower frame will be enclosed with latticework, for example.

Remove the sod in rolls and use it elsewhere in your landscape. Store it out of the sun and keep it moist if you're not ready to use it right away. Then lay down landscape fabric, which blocks sunlight but allows water to flow through. Cover the fabric with loose gravel.

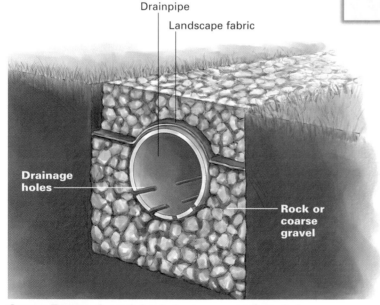

Drainpipe

Landscape fabric

Drainage holes

Rock or coarse gravel

CATCH BASIN: *A catch basin is an open surface drain with a receptacle that holds water and disperses it through piping when it reaches a certain level. Install a catch basin to collect water from terrain that is too low to drain elsewhere. Concrete catch basins are sold ready to install. The drainpipe can empty into a distant dry well or—if local codes allow—into the storm sewer system.*

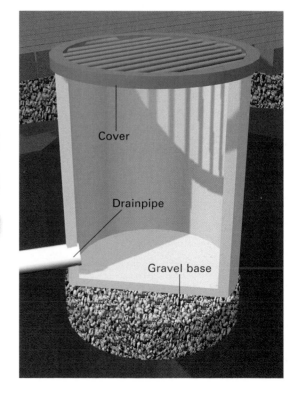

Cover

Drainpipe

Gravel base

LAYING OUT THE SITE

The first step in laying out the site is to mark the perimeter edges. For small jobs you might be able to get by using an uncut sheet of plywood. Moderate size projects will lay out nicely with the frame layout illustrated, *opposite*. For larger sites you'll need batter boards and mason's line.

SETTING BATTER BOARDS

Batter boards are a homemade tool that will make layout and excavation more precise.

To make a set of batter boards (you'll need two for each corner, except where a structure abuts the house), cut scrap 2×4 lumber to 2-foot lengths and point the ends so you can drive them into the ground.

■ Fasten a 15- to 18-inch 1×4 crosspiece to the legs a couple of inches below the tops of the 2×4 legs. The crosspiece will let you adjust the position of the mason's lines.

■ Set temporary corner stakes. Drive the batter boards at right angles to each other, 2 to 4 feet beyond the proposed patio corners. Don't worry if they're not level; that comes later.

RUNNING MASON'S LINES

Tie a mason's line to the crosspiece or to a nail driven in the center of the crosspiece, then run the line to the opposite corner and

fasten it. Repeat the installation of the lines between the remaining batter boards. These lines represent the outside edge of the layout—the perimeter of a patio, for instance. If your plans call for wide timbers or concrete, for example, a parallel set of lines inside the first set will help you mark the excavation width for the edging.

■ Hang a line level in the middle of one of the mason's lines and adjust the height of the line until the bubble in the level is centered between its marks.

■ Adjust the height of the line by repositioning the mason's line on the nail you drove in the crosspiece.

■ Once you're confident that the first line is level, tighten it so it won't slip.

■ Repeat this procedure until you have all lines level.

To get the right slope for drainage (about 2 percent will do), lower the lines at the outside corners by 1 inch for every 4 running feet. That may seem like undoing what you've already done, but the lines need to be level first so you have a point from which to start.

USING A FRAME LAYOUT

The frame layout described here is quicker and easier than setting up batter boards and lines. Use 14-foot 2×6s to lay out any size structure up to 12×12; use shorter or longer pieces if necessary. When you're done laying out the site, cut the frame—use the boards for

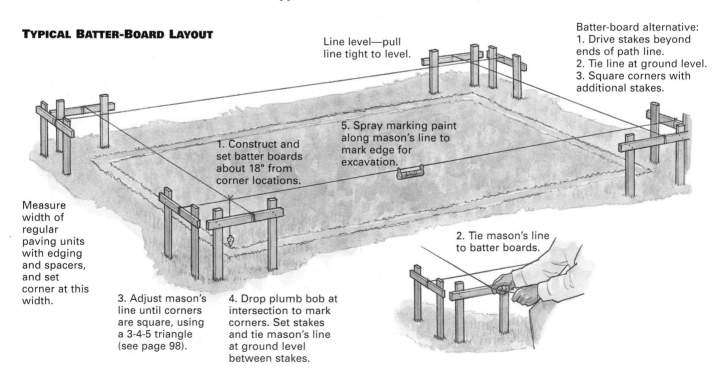

TYPICAL BATTER-BOARD LAYOUT

Line level—pull line tight to level.

Batter-board alternative:
1. Drive stakes beyond ends of path line.
2. Tie line at ground level.
3. Square corners with additional stakes.

1. Construct and set batter boards about 18" from corner locations.

5. Spray marking paint along mason's line to mark edge for excavation.

Measure width of regular paving units with edging and spacers, and set corner at this width.

3. Adjust mason's line until corners are square, using a 3-4-5 triangle (see page 98).

4. Drop plumb bob at intersection to mark corners. Set stakes and tie mason's line at ground level between stakes.

2. Tie mason's line to batter boards.

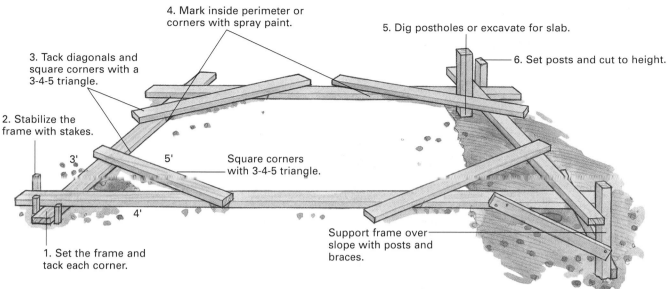

4. Mark inside perimeter or corners with spray paint.

5. Dig postholes or excavate for slab.

3. Tack diagonals and square corners with a 3-4-5 triangle.

6. Set posts and cut to height.

2. Stabilize the frame with stakes.

Square corners with 3-4-5 triangle.

1. Set the frame and tack each corner.

Support frame over slope with posts and braces.

joists or rafters. Here's how to lay out the site.
■ Overlap four 14-foot 2×6s to make a frame with interior dimensions the size of your structure. Tack each corner with one screw. Stabilize the frame with stakes.
■ Lay diagonal braces across the corners. Tack each on one end.
■ Square the corners with a 3-4-5 triangle (see page 98). Tack diagonals in place.
■ For a foundation excavation, mark the perimeter on the ground with spray paint.

Remove the frame and excavate. For posts or piers, mark the corners on the ground and leave the frame in place.
■ Dig postholes to the depth required by local codes. Pour 6 inches of dry concrete mix into each hole and tamp.
■ Set the posts and tamp the soil around them with a 2×4. Plumb each post on two adjoining sides. Remove the frame and cut the posts with a reciprocating saw.

LONG-DISTANCE LEVELING

When leveling objects that stand about 6 feet apart, you can use a line level and tightly stretched mason's cord. But even over short distances (especially on a windy day) a line level won't always give you accurate results. A water level offers a foolproof, low-cost way to level over any distance.

Operating on the principle that water seeks its own level in a closed system, the level consists of two clear plastic tubes that attach to each end of a garden hose. Fill the level with water, place the ends on the objects to be leveled, and mark them, as shown at right. Some water levels sound a tone to indicate level. Water levels are available at hardware stores, home centers, and lumberyards.

Another option is to rent a surveyor's transit or a builder's level. Home centers and tool-rental dealers usually have them available. Some use a laser to mark a point, others employ small telescopes mounted on tripods. Both levels are designed to help you mark a spot on a pole. Renting this survey equipment usually costs more than buying a simple water level.

Water level here will be the same here.

LAYING OUT THE SITE
continued

SQUARING THE CORNERS

The four lines of your layout (or three sides and the house) should create a rectangle with square (90-degree) corners. There's a handy method for squaring layout corners called the 3-4-5 method. It's based on the geometric principle that when one side of a right triangle is 3 feet and the other side is 4, the longest side will be 5 feet exactly. Here's how to use the 3-4-5 method to check for square.

■ At the intersection of the lines on one corner, measure out 3 feet along one mason's line and mark it with a piece of tape.

■ Along the other line, tape a point exactly 4 feet from the intersection.

■ Now measure the distance between the two pieces of tape. If it is exactly 5 feet, the corner forms a 90-degree angle. If not, readjust the lines until the two markers are exactly 5 feet apart. For large jobs, use multiples of 3, 4, and 5 feet, such as 9-12-15.

When you're confident that the layout is square, cut notches in the crosspieces to mark the final location of the lines. That way you can take the lines down and retie them at the same point later.

MARKING THE EDGES

Drive stake and tie mason's lines between the corners at ground level. Check plumb with a plumb bob.

To mark the corners and edges of the site so you'll know exactly where to dig, suspend a plumb bob so that its cord just touches the intersection of the layout lines. The point on the ground below the intersection of those lines will become the corner of the excavation.

■ Lower the plumb bob to the ground and have a helper mark the spot with a stake. If you're laying out the site yourself, let the plumb bob settle to the ground and let go of the line. Mark the point with a stake.

■ Plumb and stake each corner and tie a line at ground level tightly between them.

■ Repeat the procedure for the second set of lines

(for the edging) if you've installed them.

■ Then mark the line on the ground with spray paint (get upside-down paint at your hardware store—it sprays when the can is inverted) or with powdered chalk from a squeeze bottle. The chalk comes in colors, so find one that stands out from the ground color. With the painted or chalked line on the ground, you have a clean edge along which to start your excavation.

BREAKING GROUND

Excavating the soil requires more than brute strength. There is some science to it. First remove the mason's lines from the batter boards to get them out of your way. If you're not installing forms, begin your excavation along the edges of the painted line. Forms will require some additional elbowroom, so if you're using them, you'll have to dig out about a foot beyond the painted line.

■ Using a square shovel or spade, cut the sod along the painted outline This chore becomes easier if you first cut the sod into strips about a foot wide.

■ Dig down 2 inches to preserve the roots and push the shovel handle under the roots sharply to dislodge them. Roll the sod away

To outline a curved contour, lay a rope or hose in the shape of the contour and mark it with paint or chalk. Once you pull the hose up, you'll have a clear digging line.

EXCAVATING A PATIO SITE

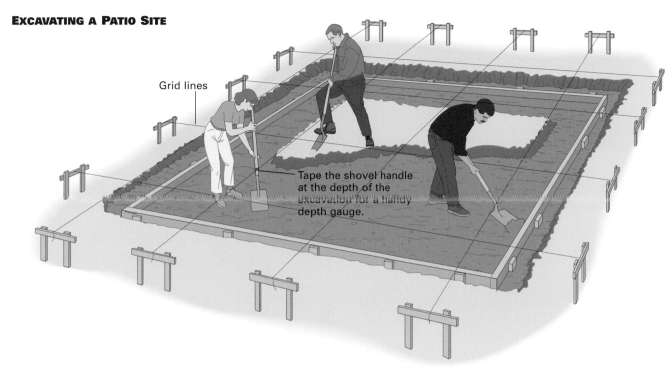

Grid lines

Tape the shovel handle at the depth of the excavation for a handy depth gauge.

from you as you go to keep a fresh edge continuously exposed. When you have the sod strip out, store it in the shade if you're not going to use it right away.

■ Use a rotary cultivator set to the depth of the patio materials (see "Excavation Depths," *below*) to loosen the soil. Then excavate the trench for your edging so it will be at the height of the finished patio surface.

■ If you're using grid lines to help maintain your slope and depth, tie them now as shown, *above*. Otherwise use a round-nose shovel to dig out the entire width between the painted lines, working from the center to the perimeter.

■ Dig out the soil to the depth equal to the combined thickness of all the patio materials, holding the shovel at a low angle to avoid digging too deep, and removing the surface

in small amounts. The excavation doesn't have to be perfect; bedding materials will even out any variations.

Once you've excavated the site, you'll need to compact the soil to keep it from settling and to make a firm base for the bedding materials. Moisten the soil before tamping. Rent a power tamper for any area larger than 10 square feet; hand tamping is strenuous and produces inconsistent results on large areas.

EDGING

If you pour concrete, now is the time to install forms. However, vertical brick edging goes in after excavation. For other materials it's usually easier to install the edging now. It will help you guide the screeding (leveling) of the base.

EXCAVATION DEPTHS

The depth of an excavation will depend on the materials you use.
BRICK OR STONE IN SAND: 8 to 9 inches (4 inches of gravel base, 2 inches of sand, and 2 to 3 inches of brick or stone).
POURED CONCRETE: 8 to 10 inches (4 inches of gravel, an optional 2 inches of sand, and 4 inches of concrete).
MORTARED BRICK OR STONE: 10½ to 12 inches (8 inches of gravel and concrete base, ½- to 1-inch mortar bed, and 2 to 3 inches of brick or stone).
LOOSE MATERIALS: 6 inches (2 inches of sand plus 4 inches of material).

STAKING STRAIGHT EDGING OR FORMS

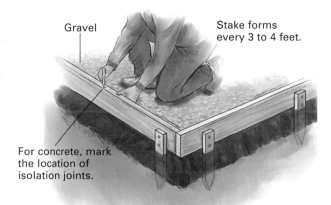

Gravel

Stake forms every 3 to 4 feet.

For concrete, mark the location of isolation joints.

LAYING OUT THE SITE
continued

STAKING CURVED FORMS

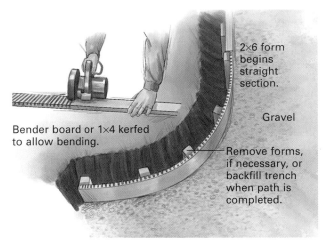

2×6 form begins straight section.

Gravel

Bender board or 1×4 kerfed to allow bending.

Remove forms, if necessary, or backfill trench when path is completed.

INSTALLING PREFORMED EDGING

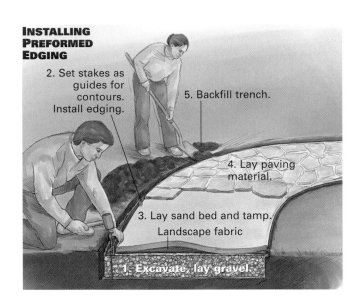

2. Set stakes as guides for contours. Install edging.

5. Backfill trench.

4. Lay paving material.

3. Lay sand bed and tamp.

Landscape fabric

1. Excavate, lay gravel.

INSTALLING TIMBER EDGING

5. Set sand and pavement.

4. Drive in rebar.

2. Predrill timbers for ½" rebar.

3. Set timbers at edge of excavation.

Landscape fabric

1. Excavate for paving and gravel.

INSTALLING BRICK EDGING

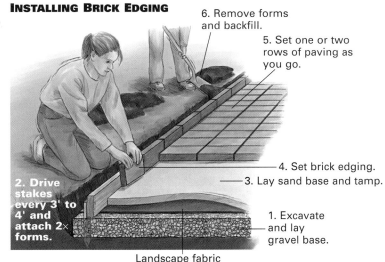

6. Remove forms and backfill.

5. Set one or two rows of paving as you go.

2. Drive stakes every 3' to 4' and attach 2× forms.

4. Set brick edging.

3. Lay sand base and tamp.

1. Excavate and lay gravel base.

Landscape fabric

INSTALLING A CONCRETE CURB

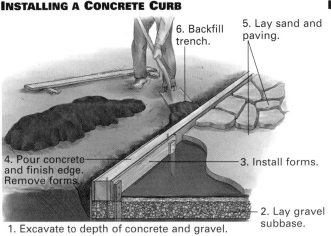

6. Backfill trench.

5. Lay sand and paving.

4. Pour concrete and finish edge. Remove forms.

3. Install forms.

2. Lay gravel subbase.

1. Excavate to depth of concrete and gravel.

INSTALLING FLAGSTONE EDGING

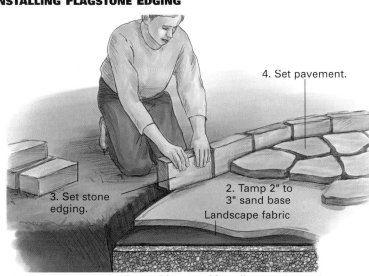

4. Set pavement.

3. Set stone edging.

2. Tamp 2" to 3" sand base

Landscape fabric

1. Excavate to depth of gravel base and install tamped gravel.

POURING A SLAB

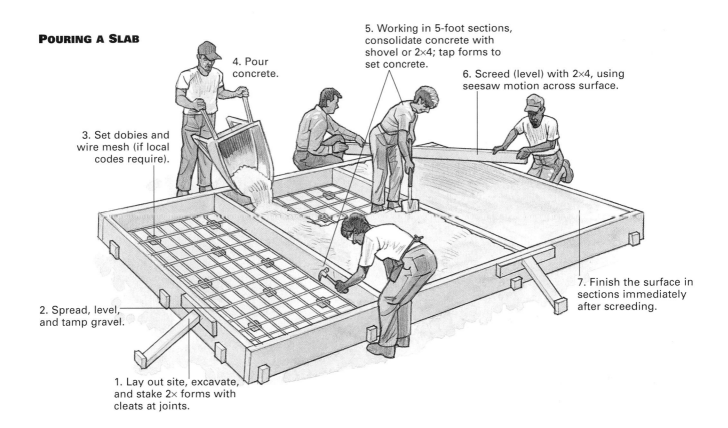

5. Working in 5-foot sections, consolidate concrete with shovel or 2×4; tap forms to set concrete.

4. Pour concrete.

6. Screed (level) with 2×4, using seesaw motion across surface.

3. Set dobies and wire mesh (if local codes require).

7. Finish the surface in sections immediately after screeding.

2. Spread, level, and tamp gravel.

1. Lay out site, excavate, and stake 2× forms with cleats at joints.

BUILDING FOUNDATIONS

When building a floor for an outdoor framed structure, you have two choices: a wood frame floor supported on posts or piers, or a concrete slab foundation. Check your building codes to ensure your foundation meets local requirements. Refer to the illustrations on these pages for installation methods and keep the following tips in mind:

■ For posts or piers, pre-mixed concrete is the most economical. For slabs smaller than 10×12 feet, consider mixing your own concrete in a rented power mixer. For larger slabs, ready-mix is most cost-effective.

■ When pouring concrete, work from the far end of the forms toward the mixing site or ready-mix truck. If you're pouring ready-mix concrete, enlist a crew of two or three helpers.

■ Excavate for slabs to a depth that accommodates a 4- to 6-inch gravel base and 3 inches of concrete.

■ Make the slab forms the same height as the finished slab so the forms can serve as guides for screeding.

■ For posts use naturally resistant woods or treated lumber that's rated for ground contact.

■ Using your scaled plans, mark one post at the correct height, cut it with a reciprocating saw, and use a line or water level to mark and cut the remaining posts.

POST FOUNDATIONS

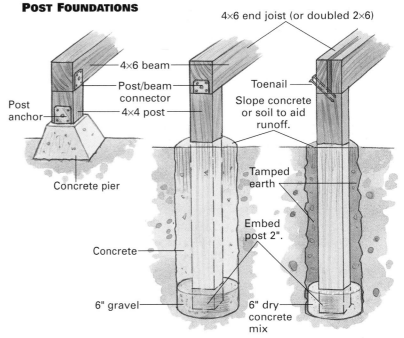

4×6 end joist (or doubled 2×6)

4×6 beam

Post/beam connector

Post anchor

4×4 post

Concrete pier

Toenail

Slope concrete or soil to aid runoff.

Tamped earth

Embed post 2".

Concrete

6" gravel

6" dry concrete mix

FRAMING A FLOOR

Framing the floor of an outdoor structure is relatively easy. Marking, cutting, squaring, and leveling the assembly creates a solid base for the walls and the roof. If the floor frame proves solid, strong, rigid, and square, the rest of the structure goes up with ease. Most floors are built either on piers or on a slab base as illustrated on these pages.

TERMINOLOGY

All floors have the same basic structural members.

JOISTS: Horizontal flooring members set on edge to support the floor. Generally they run parallel to the short dimension of a structure, set either 16 or 24 inches on center. Such spacing allows the edges of standard 4×8 flooring to be centered on the joists.

HEADER: A member at the end of shortened joists to keep them vertical.

END JOISTS: Joists attached to the headers at each end of the floor.

BEAM: A header on the long dimension of the frame.

FLOORING (or decking): Fastened to the joists. (Called subflooring when used to support finished flooring.)

BLOCKING: 2× stock fastened within and perpendicular to the joists to keep them from twisting. Not usually necessary in small outdoor structures.

MUDSILL: Attached to a concrete slab with J bolts or other anchors, it provides a nailing surface for framing on a slab.

FLOOR FRAMING TIPS

To frame a floor, refer to the illustrations on these pages and follow the steps shown. Here are a few additional tips to help you keep everything straight.

■ Mark both headers at once to ensure that the joists run parallel to each other. If the distance between posts or the length of one side of the slab is longer than the other, make allowances and mark the headers together.

■ Measure all similar distances before cutting. Lumber, an imperfect product, will

TYPICAL FLOOR FRAMING

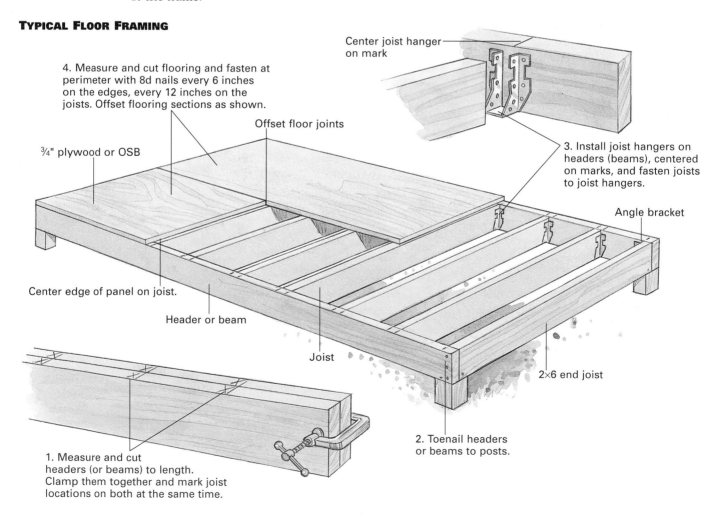

4. Measure and cut flooring and fasten at perimeter with 8d nails every 6 inches on the edges, every 12 inches on the joists. Offset flooring sections as shown.

Center joist hanger on mark

Offset floor joints

¾" plywood or OSB

3. Install joist hangers on headers (beams), centered on marks, and fasten joists to joist hangers.

Angle bracket

Center edge of panel on joist.

Header or beam

Joist

2×6 end joist

1. Measure and cut headers (or beams) to length. Clamp them together and mark joist locations on both at the same time.

2. Toenail headers or beams to posts.

exhibit variances despite your best intentions. For example, measure the length of all joists before cutting the first one and write the result on the top of the header. If the measurements are the same, cut them all at one time. If each measurement is different, cut and attach them one at a time.

■ Center J bolts on the mudsill or position them 1¾ inches from the edge of a slab. They often end up, however, more or less removed from the edge. After scribing the sides of the bolt on the sill, mark their positions from the edge before drilling the sill.

■ Use full-length boards where possible. Structural splicing should not be necessary for small outdoor structures.

■ Use pressure-treated lumber for all floor framing members, and plywood or OSB-rated lumber for flooring and exterior use (⅝ inch or ¾ inch stock is typical).

■ If building a structure larger than the dimensions in this book, install a central beam supported by a center post, or consult span tables and adjust the size of the joists (see "How Far Can Joists Span?" on page 71).

■ Check all corners for square with a framing square and adjust framing as you fasten it.

■ Snap chalk lines on the flooring at 16- or 24-inch intervals to keep the nails centered in the joists.

■ Though plywood and OSB expand very little, leave a ⅛-inch space between sheets to avoid compression buckling. Use an 8d nail to get the right spacing.

DECKING PATTERNS

The framing methods shown at right accommodate both parallel and diagonal decking patterns. Other decking patterns require additional support, which can be added to the basic parallel-joist construction. Whatever pattern you choose, plan the framing before you start, making sure it is adequately supported at the ends.

FRAMING A FLOOR ON A SLAB

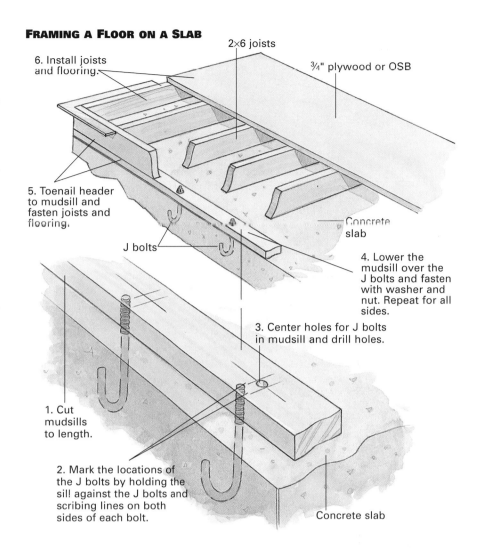

2×6 joists

¾" plywood or OSB

6. Install joists and flooring.

5. Toenail header to mudsill and fasten joists and flooring.

J bolts

Concrete slab

4. Lower the mudsill over the J bolts and fasten with washer and nut. Repeat for all sides.

3. Center holes for J bolts in mudsill and drill holes.

1. Cut mudsills to length.

2. Mark the locations of the J bolts by holding the sill against the J bolts and scribing lines on both sides of each bolt.

Concrete slab

DECKING PATTERNS

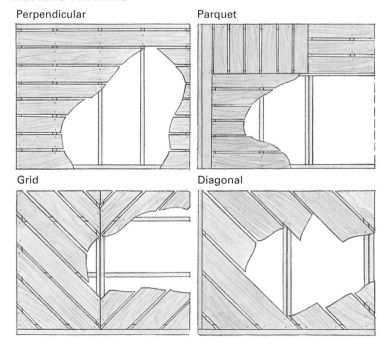

Perpendicular

Parquet

Grid

Diagonal

FRAMING A WALL

TYPICAL WALL FRAMING PLAN

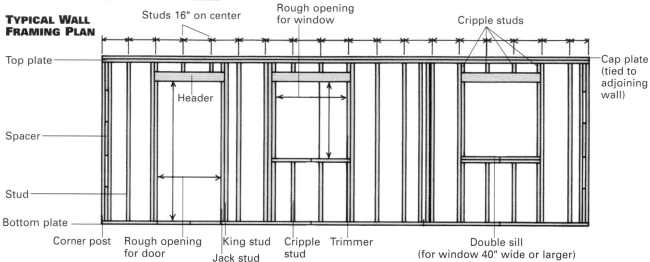

- Studs 16" on center
- Rough opening for window
- Cripple studs
- Top plate
- Header
- Spacer
- Stud
- Bottom plate
- Corner post
- Rough opening for door
- King stud
- Jack stud
- Cripple stud
- Trimmer
- Double sill (for window 40" wide or larger)
- Cap plate (tied to adjoining wall)

All frame walls consist of the same elements arranged in the same fashion. Differences arise primarily in the location of window and door openings.

ANATOMY OF A WALL

Before building your walls, familiarize yourself with their components.

STUDS: 2×4s spaced every 16 or 24 inches on center and fastened between top and bottom plates. Cut the studs 3 inches shorter than the height of the ceiling to account for the thickness of the top and bottom plates. Studs for an 8-foot (96-inch) unfinished ceiling would therefore be cut at 93 inches. When estimating, figure one stud for every lineal foot of wall. You'll cut up the extras for blocking and cripple studs. Use standard framing lumber for the framing; kiln-dried stock for door and window openings.

PLATES: Dimension lumber the same size as the studs that support the bottoms of the studs and span their tops. An overlapping cap plate on top ties the walls together (see the illustration above).

OPENINGS: Doors and windows are framed with a **header** (doubled 2× stock) across the top, supported by **jack studs** (also called shoulder studs) that run to the floor. Support the jack stud with a full-length **king stud** at its side. **Cripple studs** fill in the opening at the top of doors and at the top and bottom of windows. Make sure the rough openings are about 1 inch wider than the frame of your window or door. Have these units on-site so you can measure them before framing the walls.

LAYING OUT A WALL

Lay out the longest walls first, marking stud locations as shown in the illustration on the opposite page. Clamp together the top and bottom plates of each wall and mark the stud locations as well as the locations for framing members for door and window openings.

If you're working in inches on center, begin at the end of the plates. If your marks represent the edges of the studs, tack a ¾-inch scrap on the end of the plates and measure from the inside of the scrap. This makes the first mark 14¼ inches from the end of the plates. Measure 16 inches thereafter.

ASSEMBLING A WALL

Assemble each wall as a separate unit, using the floor as a work surface. Build the corner posts first, face-nailing blocking between two studs. Assemble door and window openings with a header, king studs, trimmers, and sill, if needed. Lay these assemblies on the floor between the top and bottom plates and nail them through the plates at the marks with two 16d nails. Then face-nail the cripple studs from the plate and toenail them into the header.

WALL LAYOUT (TOP VIEW)

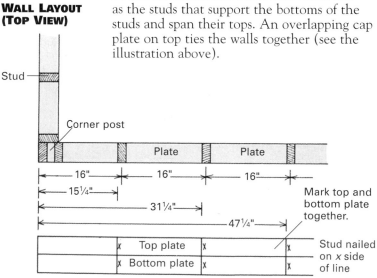

- Stud
- Corner post
- Plate
- Plate
- 16"
- 15¼"
- 31¼"
- 47¼"
- Mark top and bottom plate together.
- Top plate
- Bottom plate
- Stud nailed on *x* side of line

RAISING THE WALLS

Snap chalk lines on the floor to mark the inside edge of the bottom plates. Then with the aid of a helper, lift the wall in place and nail it to the floor at every stud. Plumb the wall in both directions and brace it temporarily to the deck with 2×4s. Assemble, erect, and brace the adjoining wall. Measure and cut the cap plates and clamp the longest pair together, offsetting them by 3½ inches. Mark the locations of the rafters and nail the plates to the top plates, overlapping them at the corners to tie the walls together. Finish by installing sheathing.

PREASSEMBLING A WALL

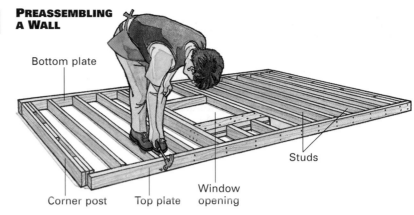

Bottom plate

Studs

Corner post

Top plate

Window opening

TYPICAL WALL FRAMING

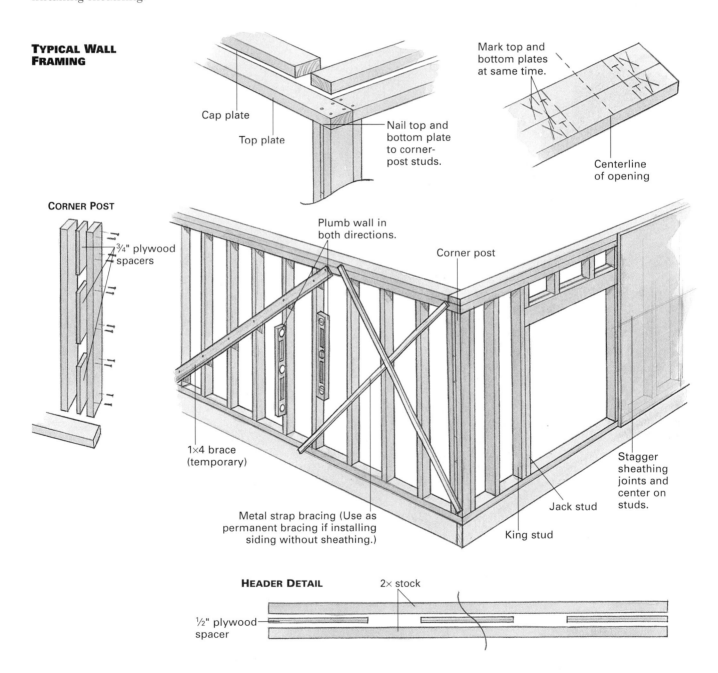

Cap plate

Top plate

Nail top and bottom plate to corner-post studs.

Mark top and bottom plates at same time.

Centerline of opening

CORNER POST

¾" plywood spacers

Plumb wall in both directions.

Corner post

1×4 brace (temporary)

Metal strap bracing (Use as permanent bracing if installing siding without sheathing.)

King stud

Jack stud

Stagger sheathing joints and center on studs.

HEADER DETAIL

2× stock

½" plywood spacer

ROOF FRAMING

The way in which you frame the roof of your garden shed contributes more to the style of the structure than any other aspect of its construction. Although there are many different roof-framing styles, the three illustrated on these pages are easily adapted to almost any garden shed.

TYPICAL GABLE-ROOF FRAMING

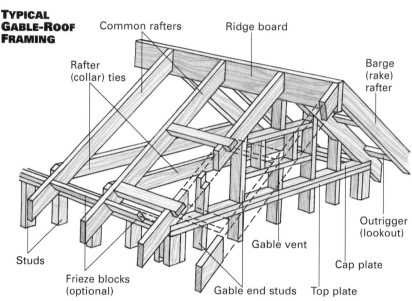

Common rafters
Ridge board
Rafter (collar) ties
Barge (rake) rafter
Outrigger (lookout)
Studs
Gable vent
Cap plate
Frieze blocks (optional)
Gable end studs
Top plate

TYPICAL HIPPED-ROOF FRAMING

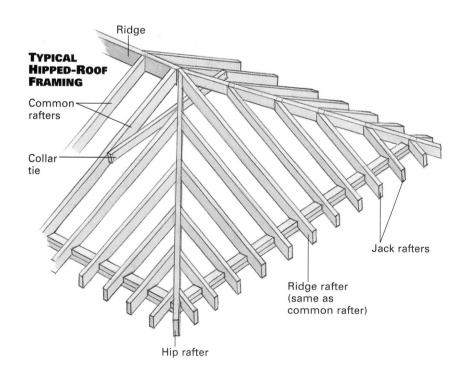

Ridge
Common rafters
Collar tie
Jack rafters
Ridge rafter (same as common rafter)
Hip rafter

ANATOMY OF A ROOF

For the average do-it-yourselfer, roof framing is often accompanied by a fair amount of anxiety. It doesn't need to be. Like any other task, it pays to start by familiarizing yourself with the basic anatomies of each style. Each of them has the same common elements.

RIDGE BOARDS: stiffen the entire roof and provide a nailing surface for the rafters.

RAFTERS: the main support for the finished roof materials, rafters have different names depending on their positions.

■ **COMMON RAFTERS** extend from the ridge to the wall.

■ **BARGE RAFTERS** (also called rake rafters or verge rafters) extend beyond the wall and overhang the rakes.

■ **OUTRIGGERS** (or lookouts) are 2×4s notched into the last two common rafters on the rake to support the barge rafters.

■ **HIP RAFTERS** (on a hipped roof) extend from the ridge to the corners of the wall.

■ **JACK RAFTERS** extend from hip rafters to the wall.

■ **VALLEY RAFTERS** attach an extended roof to the main roof.

RAFTER TIES (also called collar ties): span the shorter dimension of a structure and keep the weight of the roof from pushing out on the walls.

Notice that the framing beneath the rake (called the gable wall) is actually an extension of the lower wall and is framed with studs and a rough opening for the gable vent. Frame the gable wall after the roof is up, cutting and notching each stud to fit.

VOCABULARY OF RAFTERS

Each rafter is cut from a single board, but each cut has its own name and function.

RIDGE CUT (or plumb cut): Determines the pitch of the roof and fastens to the ridge board.

BIRD'S MOUTH: Allows the rafter to fit squarely on the cap plate. Its **PLUMB CUT** is made at the same angle as the ridge cut. The **SEAT CUT**, at right angles to the plumb cut, rests on the cap plate.

RAFTER TAIL: Extends beyond the wall and ends in a **TAIL CUT** made at the same angle as the ridge cut.

RISE, RUN, AND PITCH

Roofs need to slope in order to shed rain or snow, but the pitch of a roof (how much it slopes) also contributes greatly to its appearance. How you pitch the roof is largely a matter of aesthetics, but steeper roofs are more difficult to work on and require longer rafters and more roofing material. As a starting point, you may want to match the pitch of the roof on your house, especially if the shed lies close to the house.

Here's what you need to know before you lay out your rafters.

RISE: The distance from the top plate (or seat cut) to the center point on the ridge.

RUN: The distance from the outside edge of the wall (the edge of the cap plate or rafter plumb cut) to the midpoint of the ridge.

SPAN: The total distance from the outside edge of one wall (the cap plate) to the opposite wall.

SLOPE: How much the rafter rises for each foot of its run. Thus a roof with 6/12 pitch rises 6 inches for every foot of run.

TYPICAL GABLE-ROOF EXTENSION

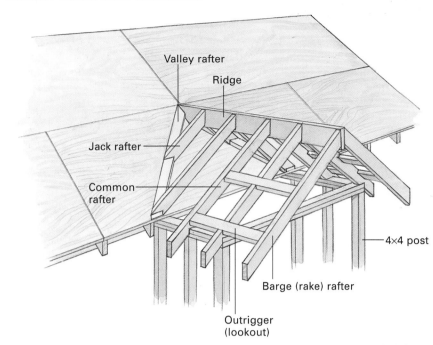

Valley rafter
Ridge
Jack rafter
Common rafter
4×4 post
Barge (rake) rafter
Outrigger (lookout)

ROOF PITCH

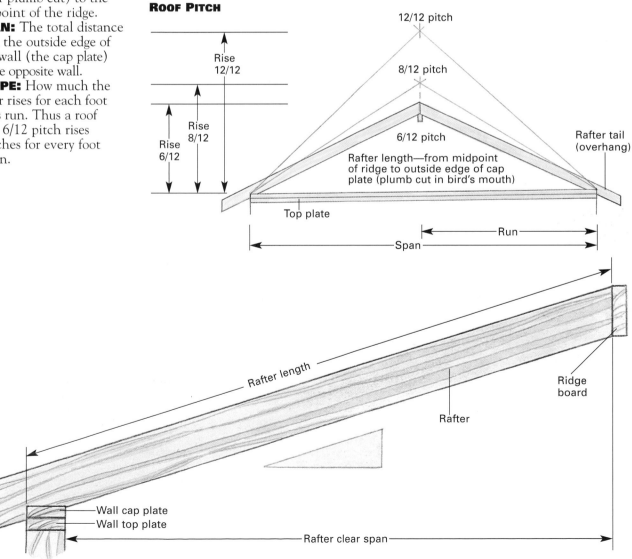

Rise 12/12
Rise 8/12
Rise 6/12

12/12 pitch
8/12 pitch
6/12 pitch

Rafter length—from midpoint of ridge to outside edge of cap plate (plumb cut in bird's mouth)

Rafter tail (overhang)

Top plate
Run
Span

Rafter length
Ridge board
Rafter
Wall cap plate
Wall top plate
Rafter clear span

ROOF FRAMING
continued

PITCH AND ANGLE	
Pitch	**Angle**
12/12	45.0°
10/12	39.75°
8/12	33.75°
7/12	30.25°
6/12	26.5°
5/12	22.5°
4/12	18.5°

USING A FRAMING SQUARE

A framing square is a remarkable tool that combines a squaring tool and a calculator. With it you can mark consistently perpendicular lines and also make other calculations critical to rafter layout.

Before you begin using the square, remember that the length of a rafter is the distance from the center of the ridge to the plumb cut of the bird's mouth—not the distance to the rafter tail.

The rafter scales are six rows of numbers along the middle of the square's body. The top shows the length of a common rafter per 12 inches of run. The inch marks above the rafter tables correspond to pitch. For example, the 6 represents a 6/12 pitch. The number in

the first row below the 6 is 13.42. This means that for a 6/12 pitch, each common rafter is 13.42 inches long for every 12 inches of run; 67.1 (67⅛) inches for a 5-foot run, for example.

At the same pitch a hip rafter (the second line on the scale) would be 18 inches long for every foot of run. This is because a hip rafter slopes in two directions.

LAYING OUT RAFTERS

No matter what kind of roof you're constructing, lay out rafters in this order:
■ Position the framing square with the rise and run intersecting the bottom of the rafter.
■ Mark all plumb cuts: ridge cut, bird's mouth, and tail.
■ Mark the seat cut 3½ inches long at a right angle to the bird's-mouth plumb cut.
■ Reposition the square at the same numbers back one-half the thickness of the ridge from the first line and mark the ridge cut.

CUTTING RAFTERS

Keep these tips in mind when cutting rafters:
■ Make all cuts for common rafters 90 degrees to the face of the board.
■ Hip and jack rafters extend two directions from the ridge, so the ridge cut is a compound miter. Refer to the illustration, *opposite*, and make these cuts with a compound miter saw.

RAFTER SCALES

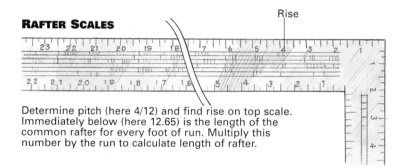

Rise

Determine pitch (here 4/12) and find rise on top scale. Immediately below (here 12.65) is the length of the common rafter for every foot of run. Multiply this number by the run to calculate length of rafter.

CUTTING COMMON RAFTERS

1. Place square on rafter so the rise (here 4") and the run (12" for common rafters) intersect with the bottom of the rafter. Mark the ridge cut line.

2. Determine rafter length from framing square and mark it on the top of the board. Extend the mark to the bottom of the board.

3. Reposition the square on the mark and scribe bird's-mouth plumb cut.

4. Position the blade perpendicular to the bird's-mouth plumb cut until the tongue is 3½" from the bottom of the board. Mark the seat cut.

5. Measure from the bottom of the bird's mouth to the length of the rafter tail (overhang) and mark the tail cut.

6. Mark a line parallel to the ridge cut and half the thickness of the ridge board. Cut here and at all other lines.

CUTTING RAFTERS

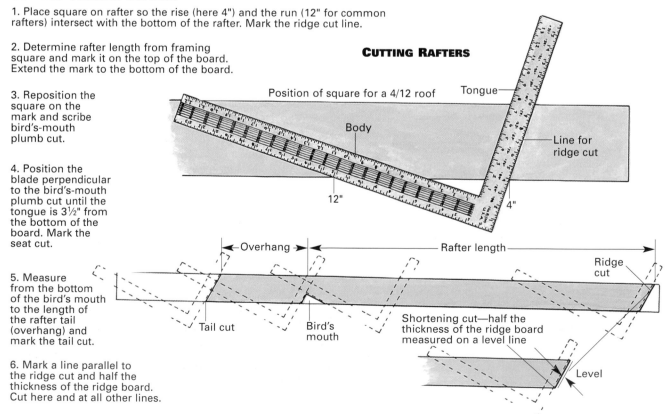

Position of square for a 4/12 roof

Tongue

Body

Line for ridge cut

12"

4"

Overhang — Rafter length — Ridge cut

Tail cut   Bird's mouth   Shortening cut—half the thickness of the ridge board measured on a level line

Level

CUTTING HIP RAFTERS

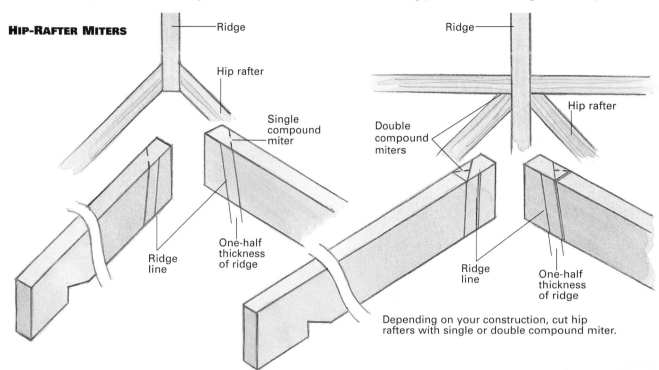

1. Position framing square with rise (here 4 inches) and run (17 for hip rafters) intersecting the bottom of the board.

2. Mark and make all cuts as you would a common rafter, shortening plumb cut and cutting it as a compound miter.

HIP-RAFTER MITERS

Depending on your construction, cut hip rafters with single or double compound miter.

■ Each succeeding jack rafter is shorter than the previous one, working down the hip rafter. This difference is consistent with the pitch of the roof. The third scale on the framing square shows how much shorter each rafter is.

Jack rafters are cut with left and right miters, depending on which side of the hip rafter they are on. Mark each one before you cut it.

INSTALLING RAFTERS

Mark the ridge board for the locations of the rafters. Cut the ridge to length and raise it into place with temporary bracing. After you've cut the first common rafter, test-fit it and make adjustments. Then cut the remaining common rafters to the same dimensions. Fasten the common rafters at the marks on the ridge and cap plates. Then install hip and jack rafters on a hipped roof. Fasten collar ties at each rafter, if necessary.

CUTTING JACK RAFTERS

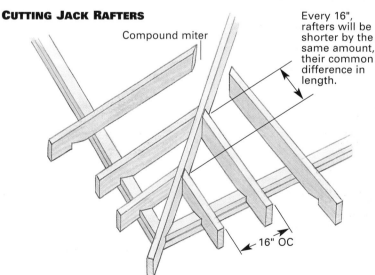

1. Using roof pitch from your dimensioned plan (here 4/12) and third scale on framing square, determine how much shorter each succeeding jack rafter will be (here 16.87") with rafters set 16" on center.

2. Lay out each jack rafter with the same methods used for a common rafter, shortening each rafter by the common difference.

3. Cut each rafter to length, keeping those with left and right compound miters separate.

INSTALLING COMPOSITION SHINGLES

Composition shingles come in many colors to match or complement your outdoor structure. Some even look like wood shingles and slate.

All composition shingles have strips of roofing cement just above the tabs. When the shingles are installed, the sun heats the cement and bonds the shingles together, making them extremely unlikely to blow off.

SHINGLING A GABLE ROOF

Shingling a roof begins with fastening the decking—¾-inch exterior-grade plywood or OSB—to the rafters. It's much like laying flooring at an angle. Sheathing a roof, however, is best done with a helper.

INSTALL SHEATHING: Start with a full panel and slide it up the ladder and on the roof. On roofs with shallow pitches, the decking might stay in place, but it's wise to have one person hold it temporarily with a notched 2×4. Position the panel flush with the outside edge of the rake rafters and square to the top of the rafter tails, and nail it with 8d nails every 12 inches on the perimeter, 8 inches on the rafters. Cut the remaining pieces and install them, offsetting the joints and spacing them at ⅛ inch.

EDGE THE EAVES: Drip edging keeps rain off the edges of the sheathing and helps prevent rot. Nail P-shaped drip edging to the eaves (not the rakes) with steel or aluminum nails, the same metal as the drip edge.

INSTALL UNDERLAYMENT: Underlayment is asphalt-impregnated paper (often called roofing felt) that provides a second layer of protection. Use 15-pound underlayment for composition shingles. Fasten the first row of underlayment with five or six staples squared to one of the bottom corners of the roof. Unroll the paper to the other side, pull tight, cut it flush with the rake, and staple it. Keep the paper straight along the eave.

Staple the second and succeeding courses in the same fashion, overlapping each one by 6 inches. Lay paper across the top of the ridge and staple it after laying the underlayment on the other side. At valleys and hips, and on gazebo roofs, carry the paper at least 18 inches past the joint.

FLASH THE VALLEYS: (Do this only on roofs with dormers or extensions.) Center a sheet of underlayment on the valley and staple it as illustrated at the bottom of the facing page.

EDGE THE RAKES: Nail drip edge to the rakes.

INSTALL THE STARTER STRIP: Like other courses, the starter strip needs to provide an adhesive for the next course. You can install shingles with the tabs pointing up or use starter roll made for this purpose (it's faster and less expensive). Overhang the starter strip on the drip edge by ¼ inch.

INSTALL THE FIRST COURSE: Snap a chalk line along the length of the roof at the depth of the shingle, minus ¼ inch. Line up a full shingle on the chalk line, flush with the rake edge. Nail it just below the adhesive strip with two nails per inch from each end and one above each tab.

Fasten shingles as far as you can reach, keeping them lined up on the chalk line.

If you installed upside-down shingles for a starter course, put a dab of roofing cement under each corner of the shingles. Then start the second course.

INSTALL THE REMAINING COURSES: After the first course is laid, offset the next course by 4, 5, or 6 inches. The illustration at the top of page 111 shows a 5-inch offset, a pattern very forgiving of discrepancies.

To run a 5-inch offset quickly, align the first shingle of the second course on the preceding row, offsetting it with a 5-inch piece of ¼-inch plywood lined up with the edge of the first corner shingle.

INSTALLING COMPOSITION SHINGLES

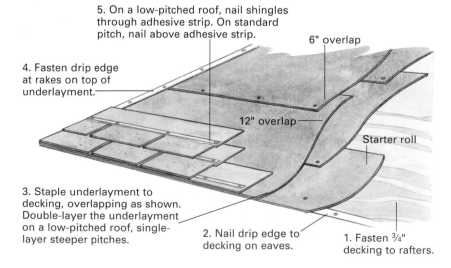

5. On a low-pitched roof, nail shingles through adhesive strip. On standard pitch, nail above adhesive strip.

6" overlap

4. Fasten drip edge at rakes on top of underlayment.

12" overlap

Starter roll

3. Staple underlayment to decking, overlapping as shown. Double-layer the underlayment on a low-pitched roof, single-layer steeper pitches.

2. Nail drip edge to decking on eaves.

1. Fasten ¾" decking to rafters.

Keeping the alignment straight, cut the shingle flush with the rake drip edge with a hooked roofer's utility knife, and nail it. Use the same procedure to offset each successive course until you have laid the seven courses.

Start the eighth course with a full shingle and continue to the ridge. Always start at the rake with an uncut shingle. Work in sections as far as you can comfortably reach, then move across the roof. If you're right-handed you'll probably find it more comfortable to start from the lower left-hand corner and work up and to the right.

At the ridge, cut the shingles so they don't overlap the other side.

INSTALL THE RIDGE SHINGLES: Make ridge shingles by cutting the tabs off a full shingle. Starting at the end of the ridge that faces the direction of the prevailing winds, nail down the first ridge shingle, overlap and nail the next one, and continue to the other end of the ridge.

SHINGLING A DORMER OR ROOF EXTENSION

As you shingle the main roof, carry the courses toward the ridge and the dormer or extension. If you have a dormer, extend the courses below it from one side to the other.

When you reach the rear of the eave of the dormer or extension, shingle the extended roof with the same offset and exposure as the main roof, letting alternate courses extend a foot across the valley. Then bring over the next courses of the main roof and finish the valley, letting alternate courses extend by a foot.

Before you carry the main roof shingles above the dormer ridge, shingle the dormer ridge, starting from the outer edge and working toward the main roof.

When you get to the main roof, split the top of the last shingle and carry it at least 4 inches up the main roof. Lap the shingles coming across on the main roof over the last shingle of the extension ridge. Neatly trim the main roof shingles around the dormer ridge shingles.

Carry the course immediately in line with the top of the dormer roof

at least 10 feet beyond the right side. Nail only the tops of these shingles. You will later slip the preceding course under this one.

Continue roofing above this line to the ridge. Now using the cutouts above and below the course you extended to the right of the dormer, snap a chalk line from the ridge to the eave near the right edge of the dormer. Snap succeeding lines at 3-foot intervals (the length of a shingle). Then finish shingling the main roof, sliding the last course under the top one.

LAYING A 5-INCH OFFSET PATTERN

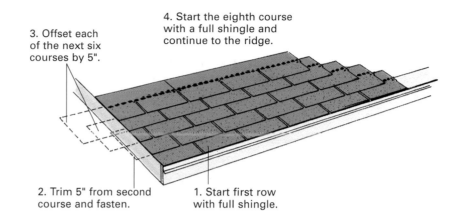

3. Offset each of the next six courses by 5".

4. Start the eighth course with a full shingle and continue to the ridge.

2. Trim 5" from second course and fasten.

1. Start first row with full shingle.

SHINGLING A DORMER OR ROOF EXTENSION

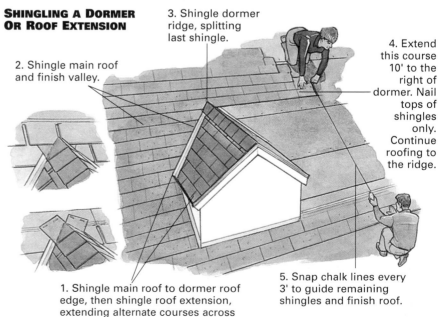

3. Shingle dormer ridge, splitting last shingle.

2. Shingle main roof and finish valley.

4. Extend this course 10' to the right of dormer. Nail tops of shingles only. Continue roofing to the ridge.

1. Shingle main roof to dormer roof edge, then shingle roof extension, extending alternate courses across the valley.

5. Snap chalk lines every 3' to guide remaining shingles and finish roof.

INSTALLING WOOD SHINGLES AND SHAKES

Wood shakes and shingles are installed in much the same way, but each has its own look. Shakes look more rugged; shingles, more orderly.

CHARACTERISTICS OF SHAKES AND SHINGLES

Wood shingles are sawn on both sides. Shakes may be split (taper-split), sawn (taper-sawn), or split on one side and sawn on the other (hand-split and resawn).

Shingles and shakes are sold in bundles, with four to seven bundles per square (100 square feet). They are cut in 15-inch lengths for the starter course and in 16-, 18-, and 24-inch lengths for finished courses. Each length has a maximum exposure—the amount of shingle showing: For a different look, install them with shorter exposures.

GENERAL GUIDELINES

Wood shakes and shingles are installed like composition shingles, with these differences:
■ Install untreated shingles and shakes over spaced 1×4s to allow air to circulate. Shakes and treated shingles can be installed over plywood sheathing, but shakes require underlayment between the rows, no matter what the sheathing. In areas with wind-driven snow, use solid sheathing and treated stock.
■ Metal drip edges are not used with wooden shingles and shakes. Instead overhang the first course by 1½ inches.
■ Use galvanized nails or aluminum staples with a minimum 7/16-inch crown in a pneumatic stapler. Put one fastener about an inch in from each edge and about 2 inches above the exposure. With a 5-inch exposure, for instance, you would nail about 7 inches up from the bottom edge of the shingle. See the chart on page 74 for fastener lengths.

INSTALLING SHEATHING

■ Install open sheathing for sawn shingles to allow air circulation. Use a short piece of scrap wood as a spacer when nailing 1×4s to keep them spaced consistently.
■ Sheath the top 18 inches of the roof solidly so you can adjust the exposure to make the last course come out even at the ridge.
■ Install sheet sheathing, spacing the sheets ⅛ inch and offsetting the joints.

INSTALLING UNDERLAYMENT

■ Use 30-pound felt paper.
■ When installing shakes, put an 18-inch-wide layer of felt paper between the courses as you go. Nail the top edge of the underlayment just enough to hold it straight; the subsequent courses will secure it.

If you can't buy 18-inch-wide felt in your area, cut a roll in half by cutting around it with a

SHEATHING THE ROOF (SPACED SHEATHING FOR SHINGLES)

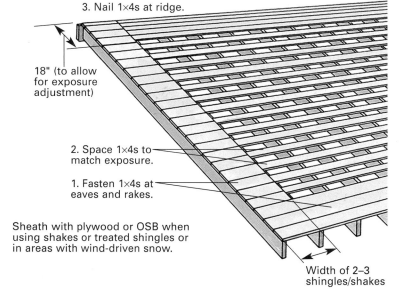

3. Nail 1×4s at ridge.

18" (to allow for exposure adjustment)

2. Space 1×4s to match exposure.

1. Fasten 1×4s at eaves and rakes.

Sheath with plywood or OSB when using shakes or treated shingles or in areas with wind-driven snow.

Width of 2–3 shingles/shakes

LAYING UNDERLAYMENT AND STARTER COURSE

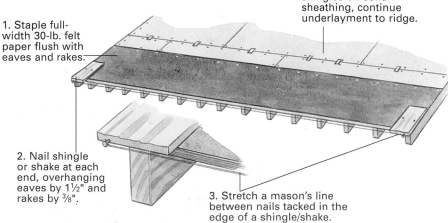

1. Staple full-width 30-lb. felt paper flush with eaves and rakes.

For shakes and treated shingles on solid sheathing, continue underlayment to ridge.

2. Nail shingle or shake at each end, overhanging eaves by 1½" and rakes by ⅜".

3. Stretch a mason's line between nails tacked in the edge of a shingle/shake.

circular saw with an old blade. You may have to finish the cut with a handsaw.

■ On hipped roofs and gazebos, overlap the underlayment by at least 18 inches, weaving alternate layers from one side to the other.

LAYING THE COURSES

■ Place shingles with straight, smooth edges at the rake.

■ Apply the first course directly over the starter course.

■ Maintain a consistent exposure for each course. Use a roofer's hatchet or cut a piece of ¼-inch plywood to the length of your exposure and use it to space the courses.

■ To ensure that your courses remain straight, measure up from the butts of the shakes at each end of the roof—every three or four courses up—and snap a chalk line as a guideline for the next course.

■ Maintain a ¼-inch spacing between each shingle or shake to allow for expansion. Offset the spacing 1½ inches from shingles in the preceding course. In addition make sure no joint is directly above another joint two courses below.

■ Shingles and shakes are not uniform in width—minimize trimming by trying different shingles instead of cutting.

■ If a shingle or shake splits as you nail it, consider it two shakes and put a nail on each side of the split.

■ Cut shingles and shakes with a jigsaw around obstacles, a circular saw at valleys.

VALLEYS

To cut valley shingles in advance, find several wide shingles. Lay one under the 1×4 spacer, score it, and cut it. Use it as a template for cutting the remaining shakes and shingles.

As you approach the valley, put a precut shingle up against the 1×4, then find one or more shakes or shingles that will fit. You may have to split one of the fill-in shakes or shingles to get it to fit just right, but that's usually easier than cutting all the valley shingles individually.

SHINGLING RIDGES

Shakes and shingles for ridges are factory-made to form a "V." Each one has a seam in its crown; the seams must alternate going up the hip or across the ridge for maximum protection.

■ Nail ridge shingles and shakes with nails long enough to penetrate the deck at least ½ inch—usually ½ inch longer than the nails used for the rest of the roof.

INSTALLING WOOD SHINGLES/SHAKES

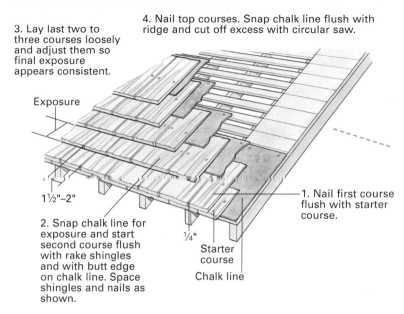

3. Lay last two to three courses loosely and adjust them so final exposure appears consistent.

4. Nail top courses. Snap chalk line flush with ridge and cut off excess with circular saw.

Exposure

1½"–2"

2. Snap chalk line for exposure and start second course flush with rake shingles and with butt edge on chalk line. Space shingles and nails as shown.

¼"

1. Nail first course flush with starter course.

Starter course

Chalk line

SHINGLING A VALLEY

1. Flash valley with 20-inch W metal flashing.

2. Lay 1×4 flush with valley ridge.

3. On the left side of the valley, select two shingles to fill space between 1×4. Nail the first one in place and slip the second under the 1×4. Scribe a line on the shingle, cut it, and nail.

4. On the right side of the valley, scribe and cut the first shingle with the 1×4 and use it as a template to cut the other valley shingles.

INSTALLING WOOD SHINGLES AND SHAKES ON A RIDGE

1. Nail ridge shakes at both ends of the ridge and snap a chalk line between them.

3. Continue nailing across the ridge.

2. Starting at the end of the ridge that is away from prevailing winds, nail a shingle/shake over the first one.

4. Remove the shingle used for the chalk line and nail final shingle.

INSTALLING SIDING

Siding comes in many choices of materials.

WOOD SIDING

PANEL SIDING: Plywood panel siding is durable and extremely strong. Available in 4×8, 4×9, and 4×10 sheets with redwood, cedar, and less expensive veneers, its styles include smooth and rough finishes and grooved patterns that imitate board siding.

Use ⅜-inch (smooth) or ⅝-inch (grooved) exterior-grade siding and paint or stain it. Install structurally rated siding directly on studs.

SOLID WOOD: Milled from lumber, board siding often comes with special edges or profiles. If made from cedar or redwood or treated with a preservative, solid wood siding can last 50 years or longer. Redwood, cedar, and cypress weather to a silver-gray if untreated. They can be stained and finished to a rich array of colors.

ORIENTED STRAND BOARD (OSB): OSB is not as strong or durable as plywood, but it has the advantage of being molded to look like clapboard siding. It ordinarily comes factory-primed, and you must reprime and paint it after installation.

SHINGLES AND SHAKES: The relatively high cost of cedar shakes and shingles is offset by several factors. You can install them yourself, they're attractive, they don't need painting or staining (although you can do either), and they last for many years. Both are sold unfinished or preprimed. Also available are 4×8-foot panels with wood shingles already attached. These panels are installed like panel siding but look like regular shingles. Buy No. 2 shingles and, if untreated, apply preservative yourself.

OTHER SIDING

You can side an outdoor structure with any of the same siding used on houses—fiber cement panels, metal and vinyl sidings, stucco, and any number of masonry surfaces. Some of these materials are made to approximate the appearance of wood products. All will provide long-lasting results. Choose your siding with design features and maintenance requirements in mind.

SHIPLAP AND TONGUE-AND-GROOVE SIDING: BOTTOM TREATMENTS

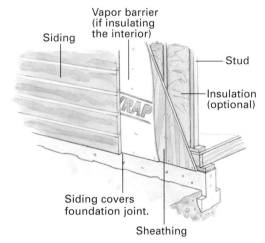

Siding

Vapor barrier (if insulating the interior)

Stud

Insulation (optional)

Siding covers foundation joint.

Sheathing

HORIZONTAL WOOD SIDING: CORNER TREATMENTS

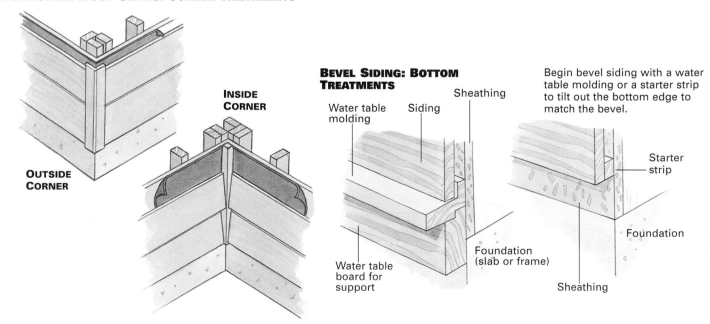

OUTSIDE CORNER

INSIDE CORNER

BEVEL SIDING: BOTTOM TREATMENTS

Water table molding

Siding

Sheathing

Water table board for support

Foundation (slab or frame)

Begin bevel siding with a water table molding or a starter strip to tilt out the bottom edge to match the bevel.

Starter strip

Foundation

Sheathing

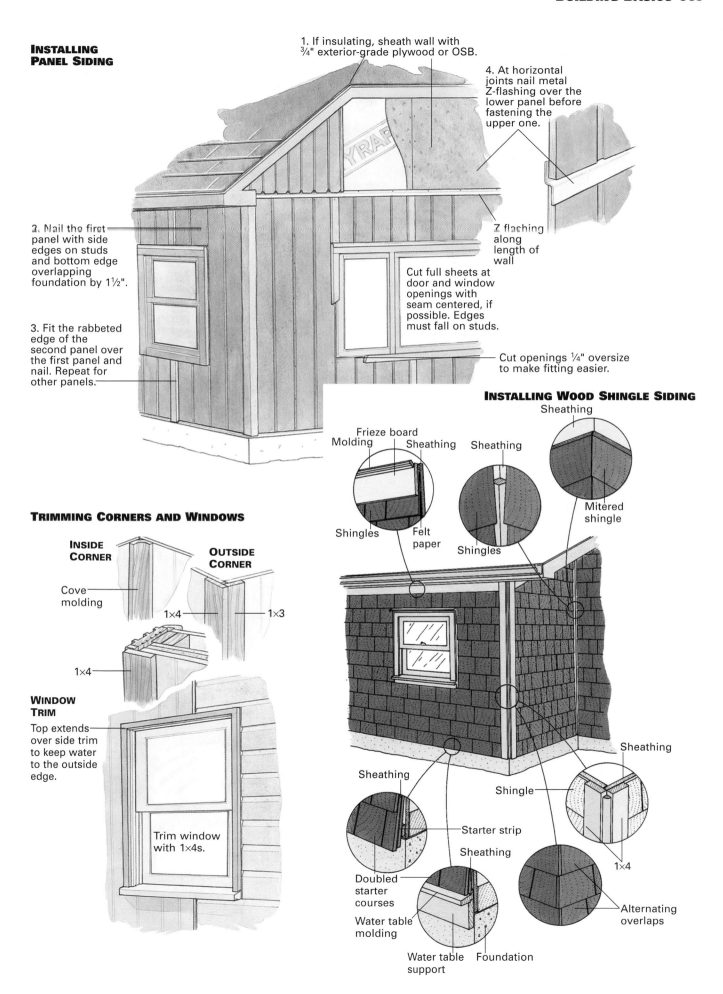

INSTALLING PANEL SIDING

1. If insulating, sheath wall with ¾" exterior-grade plywood or OSB.

4. At horizontal joints nail metal Z-flashing over the lower panel before fastening the upper one.

2. Nail the first panel with side edges on studs and bottom edge overlapping foundation by 1½".

3. Fit the rabbeted edge of the second panel over the first panel and nail. Repeat for other panels.

Z flashing along length of wall

Cut full sheets at door and window openings with seam centered, if possible. Edges must fall on studs.

Cut openings ¼" oversize to make fitting easier.

INSTALLING WOOD SHINGLE SIDING

Sheathing

Frieze board

Molding

Sheathing

Sheathing

Shingles

Felt paper

Shingles

Mitered shingle

TRIMMING CORNERS AND WINDOWS

INSIDE CORNER

OUTSIDE CORNER

Cove molding

1×4

1×3

1×4

WINDOW TRIM

Top extends over side trim to keep water to the outside edge.

Trim window with 1×4s.

Sheathing

Shingle

Sheathing

Starter strip

Doubled starter courses

1×4

Alternating overlaps

Sheathing

Water table molding

Water table support

Foundation

HANGING A DOOR

The door to any outdoor structure has a number of purposes. It encloses the structure, provides security, and adds to the structure's style. Its contribution to the design of your structure is second only to the style of the roof.

CHOOSING THE RIGHT DOOR

The first consideration in choosing a door is how you intend to use the structure. A simple potting shed or enclosed gazebo probably won't need extensive security, so any prehung single exterior door or even an all-weather storm door might be adequate. A garden shed where you'll park a riding mower and other motorized garden equipment, on the other hand, needs double doors wide enough to get the equipment through and substantial enough to resist intrusion. An outdoor workshop also needs secure double doors. For these installations you can build your own door.

PREHUNG OR DIY?

Prehung doors come complete with door, casing, and hardware already installed. The height, generally 80 to 82 inches, can be cut down. Most commercial exterior doors are 32 or 36 inches wide. Follow the manufacturer's instructions and the illustrations below to install a prehung door.

Do-it-yourself shed doors are built on a Z or X frame made of 2× stock with 1× or 2× facing, as shown on the opposite page. You can also make doors from ¾-inch plywood reinforced with battens. Determine the finished size of a door before building the framing so you can make the right size rough opening.

HANGING A DOOR

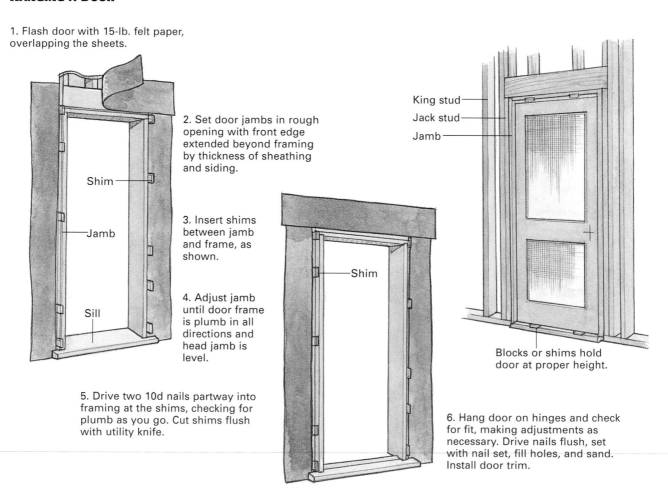

1. Flash door with 15-lb. felt paper, overlapping the sheets.

Shim

Jamb

Sill

2. Set door jambs in rough opening with front edge extended beyond framing by thickness of sheathing and siding.

3. Insert shims between jamb and frame, as shown.

Shim

4. Adjust jamb until door frame is plumb in all directions and head jamb is level.

5. Drive two 10d nails partway into framing at the shims, checking for plumb as you go. Cut shims flush with utility knife.

King stud
Jack stud
Jamb

Blocks or shims hold door at proper height.

6. Hang door on hinges and check for fit, making adjustments as necessary. Drive nails flush, set with nail set, fill holes, and sand. Install door trim.

DESIGNING YOUR OWN DOORS

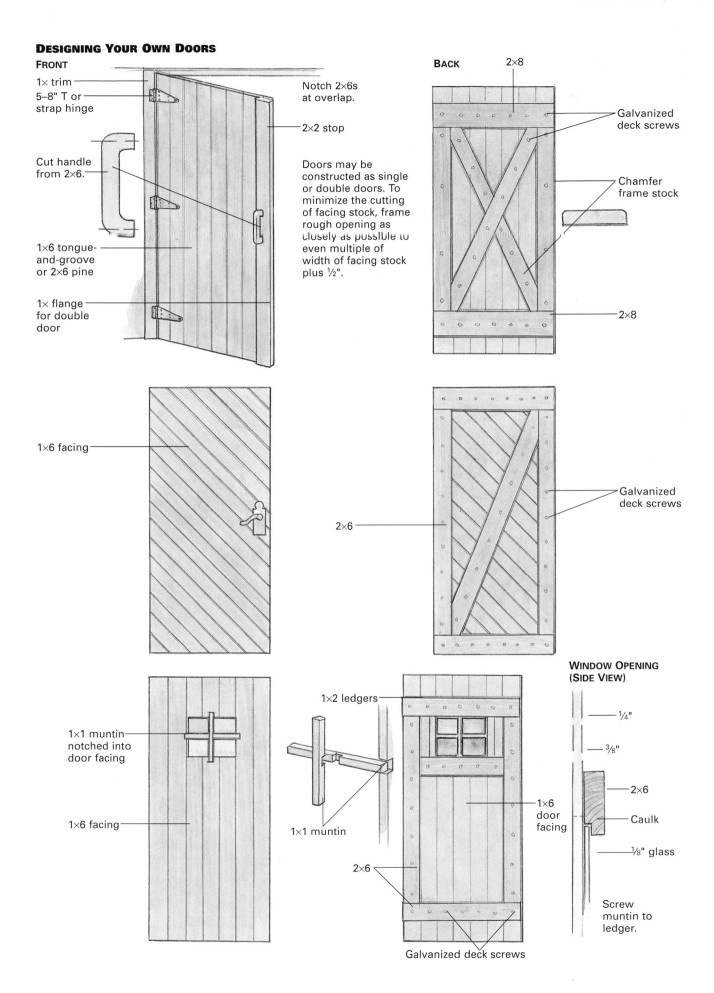

FRONT

1× trim

5–8" T or strap hinge

Cut handle from 2×6.

1×6 tongue-and-groove or 2×6 pine

1× flange for double door

Notch 2×6s at overlap.

2×2 stop

Doors may be constructed as single or double doors. To minimize the cutting of facing stock, frame rough opening as closely as possible to even multiple of width of facing stock plus ½".

BACK

2×8

Galvanized deck screws

Chamfer frame stock

2×8

1×6 facing

Galvanized deck screws

2×6

1×1 muntin notched into door facing

1×6 facing

1×2 ledgers

1×1 muntin

1×6 door facing

2×6

Galvanized deck screws

WINDOW OPENING (SIDE VIEW)

¼"

⅜"

2×6

Caulk

⅛" glass

Screw muntin to ledger.

INSTALLING WINDOWS

FLASHING A WINDOW

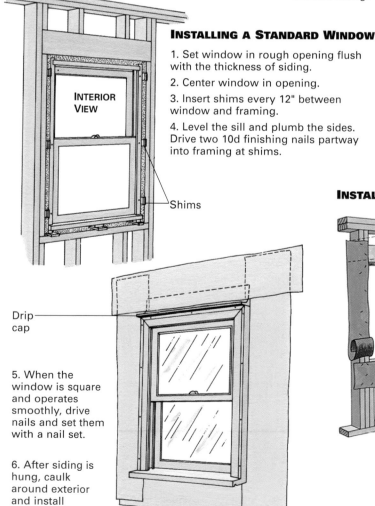

Ready-made unit with exterior casing

1. If necessary trim sheathing flush with interior of the opening. For windows with brick mold, trim back sheathing to exterior dimensions of brick mold.

2. Staple 15-lb. felt paper to bottom, sides, and top of window, overlapping the pieces.

3. Cut Z-flashing to width of window plus 1 inch and fasten it to sheathing or slide it under siding.

INSTALLING A STANDARD WINDOW

1. Set window in rough opening flush with the thickness of siding.

2. Center window in opening.

3. Insert shims every 12" between window and framing.

4. Level the sill and plumb the sides. Drive two 10d finishing nails partway into framing at shims.

INTERIOR VIEW

Shims

Drip cap

5. When the window is square and operates smoothly, drive nails and set them with a nail set.

6. After siding is hung, caulk around exterior and install hardware.

unting for a garden tool in the dark can be frustrating. In most cases windows will provide ample light and a cheery environment in your shed, or run electricity to the structure.

WINDOW STYLES

Almost any window made for a house can be installed in a shed. Start by looking at a home center. Retailers usually have a variety of styles—double-hung (both sashes slide up and down to open), casement (open on one side), hoppers (hinge at the bottom), and even bay windows.

Most commercial windows come complete with casings, sill, and hardware. If it's compatible with your design and you want to avoid delivery delays, order a standard size and design your rough opening to the manufacturer's specifications.

Local salvage yards are an excellent source for windows that can add unique accents to your shed. If you find a metal or flanged window you like, inspect it carefully. It's hard to remove these windows without damaging them, and most damage is impossible to repair. Wood windows are a better bet. You can even take apart double-hung units and use each sash separately.

INSTALLATION

Most windows are installed by nailing through the casing or a nailing flange. Directions for each style are illustrated on this page.

INSTALLING A WINDOW WITH A NAILING FLANGE

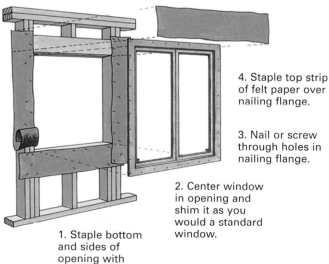

4. Staple top strip of felt paper over nailing flange.

3. Nail or screw through holes in nailing flange.

2. Center window in opening and shim it as you would a standard window.

1. Staple bottom and sides of opening with 15-lb. felt paper.

ALTERNATE WINDOW DESIGNS

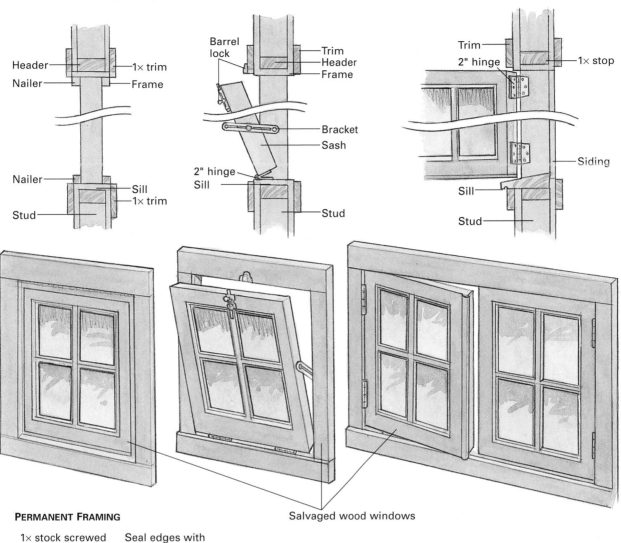

Header — 1× trim
Nailer — Frame
Nailer — Sill
Stud — 1× trim

Barrel lock
Trim
Header
Frame
Bracket
Sash
2" hinge
Sill
Stud

Trim
2" hinge — 1× stop
Siding
Sill
Stud

Salvaged wood windows

PERMANENT FRAMING

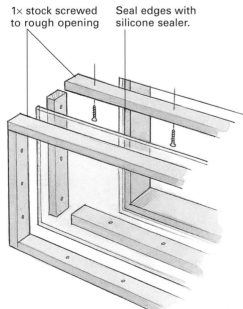

1× stock screwed to rough opening

Seal edges with silicone sealer.

COMMERCIAL BAY, GREENHOUSE, OR BOW WINDOW UNIT

WORKING WITH CONCRETE

Concrete, a mixture of sand, gravel, portland cement, and water, is the most versatile material you can use to build a path. You can form it into almost any contour or shape and use it either as the base for mortared materials or the finished surface itself. Modern finishing techniques can make concrete surfaces look remarkably like flagstone, brick, old stone pavers, and other hard materials. The chief drawback of concrete is that mistakes are not easy to correct.

PLANNING THE JOB

Unless you mix it yourself, concrete is the one material you shouldn't lay in stages. Even when you mix your own, it's better to pour all the concrete the same day—when all the materials, tools, and helpers are on-site and arranged. So if you're planning concrete or mortared walks both in front and in back of the house, make sure both sites are ready at the same time—excavations completed, forms made, and reinforcements in place.

Should you mix your own or call for a ready-mix truck? Generally it's cost-effective to mix your own if your project doesn't need more than a ¼ yard of concrete. You can do this easily using pre-mixed bags or combining the dry-mix ingredients yourself in a wheelbarrow or power mixer.

You should order ready-mix for projects of a yard or more. For those amounts in between, you may also want to have the material delivered. To mix ⅔ yard of concrete, enough to cover an 18×4-foot walk, you'll have to shovel and mix about 370 pounds of cement, 900 pounds of sand, 1,300 pounds of gravel, and 180 pounds of water.

BUILDING THE FORMS

If you pour a slab for a small structure, you may be tempted to skip building forms and pour directly into the excavation. You'll get more precise results with forms, however. If the concrete will serve as the finished surface, you must use forms.

Refer to the illustrations on the opposite page. Keep these tips in mind when building concrete forms:
■ Align the inside edges of the forms with the layout lines.
■ Brace all forms securely: Set diagonal kickers every 6 feet to keep the weight of the material from bowing the forms.
■ Drive stakes into the ground at least a foot deep so the forms won't float on the concrete.
■ Fasten the forms to the stakes, keeping the forms level throughout. Use a 4-foot level, and tap down any errant boards.
■ Keep the top of the stakes below the form, or saw the stakes off flush so you will have a smooth surface to pull the screed along.
■ When creating slopes measure the slope carefully. Drive the lower form deeper into the ground by the amount of the slope.
■ Lubricate the inside faces of the forms with oil (used oil is fine) for easier removal.
■ Set fiber or mechanical expansion strips every 10 feet.

If your forms will remain as edging:
■ Use naturally resistant species or pressure-treated wood rated for ground contact (see page 69).
■ Before pouring the concrete, tape the exposed edge of permanent wood edging to keep the liquid concrete from staining it.
■ Drive 16d galvanized nails through the edging into the concrete to keep the edges

WHAT'S IN A YARD?

Concrete is sold by the cubic yard, which is often just called a yard. A cubic yard is 3 feet long, wide, and deep, so it contains 27 cubic feet. A slab path 10 feet long, 4 feet wide, and 3 inches thick (.25 ft.) has a volume of a little over ⅓ cubic yard (10×4×.25=10/27=.37).

A DRY-MIX RECIPE

If you're mixing your own batch from scratch, use this handy recipe:
 1 part portland cement
 2 parts sand
 3 parts gravel
 ½ part water
Mix all the dry ingredients together in a wheelbarrow or power mixer, then add water a little at a time. Correctly mixed, concrete should have the consistency of a thick malt.

CONCRETE ADDITIVES

Plain concrete will work just fine in moderate weather conditions. Extreme temperatures, however, both hot and cold, may make the mix unworkable and can cause it to cure improperly, crack, or even powder.

Engineers and chemists have developed additives that allow concrete to be poured in imperfect weather.
■ Air bubbles in the concrete (entrainment) help keep concrete from freezing when pouring in extreme cold.
■ Accelerators help concrete set up faster in cold weather.
■ Retardants slow down the curing when the weather gets hot.
■ Water reducers make the mix more workable, reducing time and labor on large jobs.

of the form locked against the sides of the slab.

Once you have set the forms, shovel in a washed-gravel base, level it, and tamp it to a depth of 4 inches.

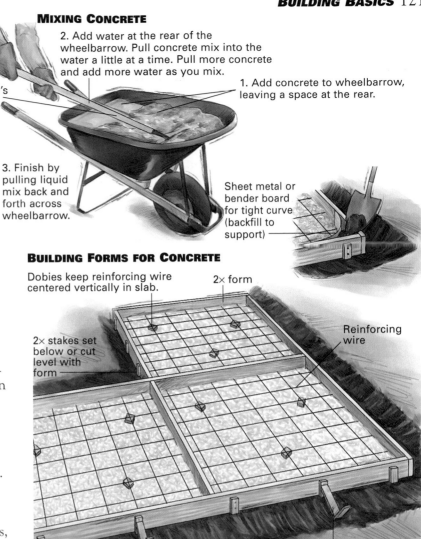

MIXING CONCRETE

2. Add water at the rear of the wheelbarrow. Pull concrete mix into the water a little at a time. Pull more concrete and add more water as you mix.

1. Add concrete to wheelbarrow, leaving a space at the rear.

Mason's hoe

3. Finish by pulling liquid mix back and forth across wheelbarrow.

Sheet metal or bender board for tight curve (backfill to support)

BUILDING FORMS FOR CONCRETE

Dobies keep reinforcing wire centered vertically in slab.

2× form

2× stakes set below or cut level with form

Reinforcing wire

Kicker brace

BRINGING IN REINFORCEMENTS

Concrete has terrific compression strength, meaning it will withstand great, crushing forces. It has little tensile strength, however, and needs internal reinforcements to keep it from cracking. Once you have built the forms, bring in the reinforcements.

■ Set *dobies*—3-inch blocks used to keep reinforcing wire centered in the concrete— every 3 to 4 feet on the gravel base. You can use concrete paver pieces as dobies. Dobies available from building supply dealers have a tie wire attached.

■ Lay down reinforcing mesh and tie it to the dobies. Use 10-gauge 6×6 mesh, which comes in rolls or flats, generally 5 feet wide. Rolled mesh costs less, but it's springy and can be hard to work with. Precut flats of mesh are worth the slight extra expense.

Using fencing pliers or heavy wire cutters, cut the mesh 4 inches shorter than the width of your path. Center the mesh between the forms, leaving 2 inches on each side.

MAKING THE POUR

If you mix your own concrete, get two wheelbarrows—put one at the mixing site, use the other for pouring.

However you bring the concrete to the site, these tips will make the job go smoothly:

■ Dampen the gravel bed and forms to keep them from drawing moisture out of the mix.

■ Pour the farthest corners first, then work toward the truck or mixing area.

■ If a ready-mix truck can not get within 20 feet of the site, have the concrete pumped through a hose—it's worth the extra cost.

■ Fill depressions in the mix with shovelfuls; don't throw the mix. Throwing can cause the aggregate to settle, weakening the surface.

■ Work shovels or 2×4s up and down in the concrete across the path to let out the air. Tap the forms on the side with a hammer about every 3 feet or so to help the concrete settle into any recesses.

■ Tamp the surface with a hoe to even it out. Don't overtamp or you'll bring too much water to the top.

POURING CONCRETE

2×10 ramp

Start your pour at far corners of site.

Mason's hoe

Use a round-nosed shovel and mason's hoe to spread concrete evenly.

Tap form to settle concrete along perimeter.

WORKING WITH CONCRETE

continued

SCREEDING THE CONCRETE

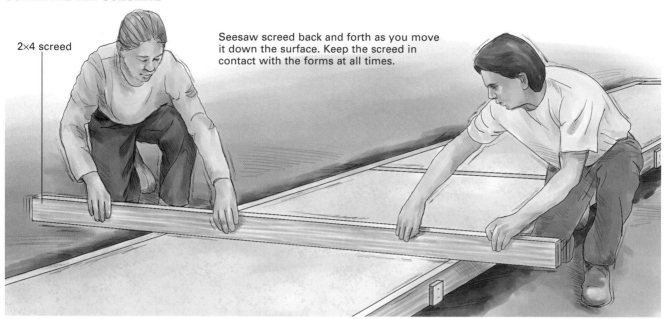

2×4 screed

Seesaw screed back and forth as you move it down the surface. Keep the screed in contact with the forms at all times.

SCREEDING

Screeding or striking off the surface of the concrete levels it with the forms and provides a preliminary smoothing. It's a job best done by two people. Use a 2×4 about 1 foot longer than the width of the poured walk. Set the edge of the screed on the forms and draw the screed back and forth across the surface.

The first pass might leave humps or depressions. Fill in low spots and make a second pass, repeating the process until the surface is uniform.

FLOATING THE SURFACE

Floating is the second smoothing, the one that pushes the aggregate below the surface. If you can reach the entire area from both sides, float it with a hand float or darby, as shown on the opposite page. Larger areas are easier to work with a bull float.

To use a float push it away from you with the leading edge raised slightly off the surface. Pull the float back toward you, again with the leading edge raised. Move the float in arcs (but work a bull float back and forth). Overlap each pass until you have covered the area.

If you plan to lay tiles, pavers, or other materials in mortar on the slab, floating will leave the surface smooth enough. When it stiffens, push and pull a stiff-bristled driveway broom across the surface, applying slight pressure. This will give it a slight tooth so the mortar will adhere better.

If the concrete will be a path surface, finish it as shown on page 153.

CUTTING EDGES

Wait for the water sheen to evaporate from the surface, and when it's gone, work a pointed trowel down about 1 inch between

COLORING CONCRETE

Although you can color concrete by sprinkling stain on it or by painting the surface, surface colorants will eventually (sometimes quickly) wear off. Adding coloring agents to the mix before you pour it is more effective. Coloring agents tint the entire thickness of the slab and won't wear off. Save money by pouring uncolored concrete to within 2 inches of its final height, then pour a 2-inch colored layer.

Pigments are made in a wide range of colors and can be combined to make tints. You'll find pigments at your building supply center in 5-, 25-, and 50-pound bags.

FLOATING THE SURFACE

Hand float

Darby

Bull float

the concrete and the forms. This will make the forms easier to pull away later.

Then run an edging tool back and forth along the inside of the forms. Edging rounds the concrete edge so it will resist cracking and chipping. Just as you did when floating, keep the tool's leading edge slightly raised.

LAYING A MORTAR BASE

Brick, tile, flagstone, and cut stone will make a permanent, almost maintenance-free path if mortared to a concrete slab. Excavations for such installations will need to be deeper than for other paths. You're actually pouring a concrete walk—a pad below the materials to be mortared.

Pour the pad and let the concrete cure for three days to a week. Then with a mason's trowel and a flat trowel, spread on a layer of mortar—about ½ inch for brick and tile, 1 inch for flagstone. Set the paving materials in the mortar with a slight twist and level them. Let the mortar cure overnight. Grout the joints with a mortar bag. See pages 148–150 for more information on mortared paths.

MAKING CONTROL JOINTS

Control joints are grooves in the concrete designed to control where it cracks. By cutting the surface of the concrete slightly with a jointing tool, you give the slab a place to crack underneath without marring the surface. In general you should space control joints approximately 8 to 10 feet apart in a pathway slab.

CURING

Concrete will harden rather rapidly. It will support your weight within a few hours. It does not reach full strength, however, for three to five days, depending on weather conditions.

The key to curing concrete is to keep moisture in it during the process. Either spray the surface lightly at periodic intervals or cover it with plastic, burlap, or roofing felt. Whatever material you use, tape or weight the covering against the sides of the slabs.

In extremely cold temperatures you must keep the concrete from freezing for at least two days after you've poured it. Cover the surface with straw or blankets. Concrete gives off low-level heat when curing, and the straw or blankets will help hold the heat in and prevent the concrete from freezing.

After two days remove the forms.

DESIGNING STEPS AND STAIRS

Transitional stairways or steps are sometimes needed in a patio project. A stairway between two patio levels carved into a hillside can lie on a natural slope. Stairs that will bridge abrupt level changes, such as a patio floor to a doorway in the house, need to be built up from a level surface. Design your steps as an integral part of the patio and pick materials that complement its style.

EASY ASCENT

Most landscape steps should be gradual—short risers with deep treads are preferred. (*Tread* refers to the part of the step on which you place your feet. A *riser* separates one tread from another.) To climb extremely steep slopes—10 percent or more—construct a series of steps with landings at least 30 inches deep. If you slope each landing a little, the climb will feel gentle and you may be able to reduce the overall number of steps. Let each tread overhang the riser below by about 1 inch. This overhang is the architectural detail that signals that a step is ahead.

RISE AND RUN

Whether you build steps into a hillside or against a vertical surface, you need to calculate the total run—the horizontal length from the front edge of the bottom step to the back edge of the top step, not including any landings. Also measure the total rise—the perpendicular distance from the base of the stairway to the top step. This exercise results in dimensions for the tread and risers.

MEASURING THE RISE AND RUN (LONG SLOPE)

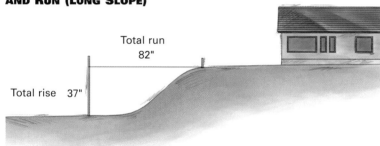

Total run 82"

Total rise 37"

MEASURING THE RISE AND RUN (SHORT SLOPE)

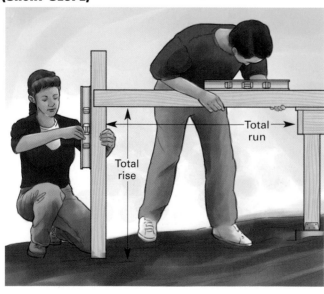

Total run

Total rise

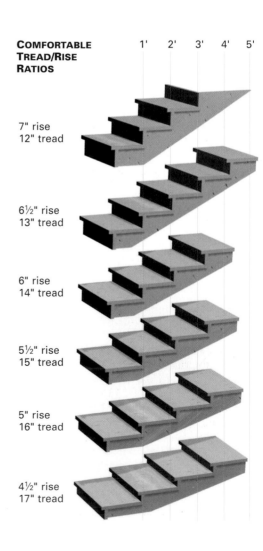

COMFORTABLE TREAD/RISE RATIOS

1' 2' 3' 4' 5'

7" rise
12" tread

6½" rise
13" tread

6" rise
14" tread

5½" rise
15" tread

5" rise
16" tread

4½" rise
17" tread

Here's how to compute them:

■ Drive stakes at the top and bottom of the slope. Tie mason's line to the top stake at ground level and to the bottom stake, keeping the line level across the span.

■ Measure the horizontal distance between the stakes. This is the total *run* of the steps.

■ Measure the distance from the ground to the line on the bottom stake. This is the total *rise*.

■ Calculate the unit rise. Divide the total rise by 6 inches—the standard comfortable height for outdoor steps. Round up the result to the nearest whole number. This is the number of 6-inch risers needed for the slope.

In the example, divide the total 37-inch rise by 6, which results in 6.2 risers. Round that up to 7.

Now divide the total rise again by the number of steps (7), which in this example results in a riser height of approximately 5¼ inches—a little lower than the ideal 6 inches. (It's better for risers to be a little lower than too high.)

■ Calculate the unit run next. To figure the unit run, divide the total run by the number of steps from the first calculation.

In the example, divide the total 82-inch run by 7, resulting in a tread of about 11¾ inches. You can adjust both figures slightly to assure a comfortable climb (see "Trip-Proof Steps," below).

In the example you could safely install 6-inch risers and 13-inch treads or 5-inch risers with 15-inch treads, making small adjustments in the path to keep the steps equal and at the correct height.

TYPICAL STEP CONSTRUCTION

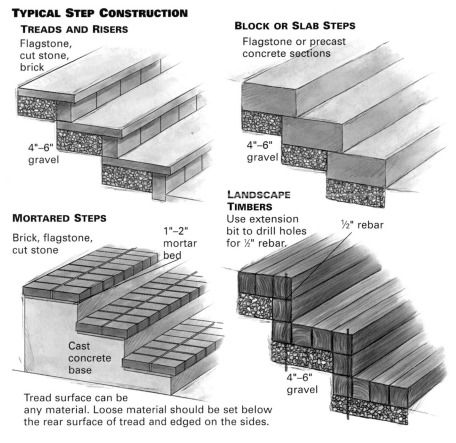

TREADS AND RISERS
Flagstone, cut stone, brick
4"–6" gravel

BLOCK OR SLAB STEPS
Flagstone or precast concrete sections
4"–6" gravel

MORTARED STEPS
Brick, flagstone, cut stone
1"–2" mortar bed
Cast concrete base

Tread surface can be any material. Loose material should be set below the rear surface of tread and edged on the sides.

LANDSCAPE TIMBERS
Use extension bit to drill holes for ½" rebar.
½" rebar
4"–6" gravel

BUILDING THE STEPS

Building steps in your landscape will require the same general methods used in construction of the patio—layout, excavation, and installation of the base materials.

All step materials require a stable gravel base for support and drainage. Mortared steps call for a concrete base, which in turn means you have to build forms. For detailed instructions on how to build steps, see the specific sections on pages 126–129.

TRIP-PROOF STEPS

Outdoor steps will be comfortable to climb if twice the riser height plus the tread depth equals a number from 25 to 27. That works out to a tread depth of 13 to 15 inches for a standard 6-inch rise. (2x6=12; 12+13=25, 12+15=27.) After you complete your preliminary calculations, adjust the rise and run of your stairs to comply with the formula. Using this formula guarantees safe and comfortable landscape stairs.

SELECTING STONES FOR STEPS

If you build flagstone steps, use stones from 2 to 4 inches thick. Flagstones are considerably heavy. To make stair-building efforts less strenuous, have these large stones delivered at the top of the site, not the bottom.

Begin installing them at the bottom. Sliding them down the slope will prove much easier than hauling them to the top.

Avoid tearing up the turf by laying an 8-foot sheet of plywood next to the site and pushing or pulling the stones in place.

BUILDING WOOD STAIRS

Stairs let you connect different parts of your landscape with one another. A simple flight of steps can help you expand the useful area of any landscape structure, provide additional places for guests to sit, and act as a decorative extension of your design.

PRESCRIPTION FOR STAIRWAYS

At any place in your landscape where you have more than a 1-foot rise from one surface to another, build stairs. Most stairs should be a minimum of 36 inches wide, and the tread depth and rise will depend on its location (see "Rise and Run," page 124). Wider stairs require a center stringer.

If your stairway will rise more than 8 feet, add a landing. Two short flights of steps add visual interest and provide an easier climb than one long flight. Whether you build one short flight or multiple stairways, all stairs should have the same unit rise and run. (See page 125 for calculating the rise and run.)

All wooden stairs are composed of the following parts:

TREAD: The part you walk on.
STRINGER: The part that supports the treads. Stringers can be closed (with treads set on stair cleats inside the stringers) or open (with treads set on cutout notches).
RISER: An optional enclosure for the back of each step.

Unless you are constructing wood steps from one level of a deck to another or steps that terminate on a deck, you will need to install a landing pad at the bottom.

CHOOSING LUMBER

Choose clear, straight boards for the stringers, at least 2 feet longer than the total run of the stairs; this allows you to cut the ends where they attach at the top and at the landing. Stringers for one or two steps can be 2×10s; for all others, use 2×12s.

MARKING STRINGERS

The procedure for marking closed and open stringers is the same.
■ Take out your carpenter's square and, using tape or stair gauges, mark the unit rise on the short arm of a carpenter's square and the unit run on the long arm (see opposite page).
■ Set the carpenter's square on the top of the stringer with the crown side up, and draw light pencil lines for the unit rise and run.
■ Move the square down for each step. Mark the bottom step 1½ inches shorter than the others to allow for the thickness of the tread.

CUTTING AN OPEN STRINGER: To make an open stringer (with treads resting on the top of cutout notches):
■ Cut on your marks with a circular saw, stopping just short of the corners.
■ Then finish each cut with a handsaw to keep the stringer from becoming weak at the corners.
■ Test your stringer by holding it in place, then use the first stringer as a template for marking the other.
■ Apply sealer to all of the newly cut surfaces.

MAKING A CLOSED STRINGER: To make a closed stringer (with treads supported by cleats on the inside):

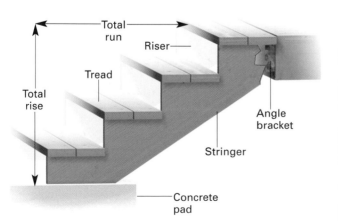

Total run / Riser / Tread / Total rise / Angle bracket / Stringer / Concrete pad

MAKING A LANDING

When you calculate the total rise and run for your stairway, include the height of your landing. A landing can be a poured concrete slab, densely packed gravel, or footings under the stringers. Local building codes may affect your choice of materials, so check before you build.

The landing doesn't need to extend below the frost line, but it must support the stringers and keep them off the ground. Pour the landing slab along with the deck footings or after the deck is finished.

■ Cut the top and bottom only.
■ At the lines attach stair cleats with 1¼-inch decking screws driven through pilot holes.
■ If you plan to use straight stringers on the sides and a notched stringer in the middle of your stairway, cut the middle one first and use it to mark the locations for the cleats on the two side stringers.

BUILD THE LANDING PAD

The bottom of the stairway should rest on a firm, slightly sloped concrete or masonry surface about an inch above grade.

To make a concrete pad, first mark its location.
■ Set the stringers in place and mark the ground where the stringers rest.
■ Mark a perimeter about 2 inches wider than the foot of the stringer.
■ Dig out 8 inches of soil and install 2×8 forms staked with 2×4s.
■ Add 4 inches of gravel, tamp it, lay in reinforcing mesh, and pour the concrete.
■ Drag a straight board over the forms to level the concrete.
■ Trowel it smooth and let it cure.

You also can set bricks or pavers in sand or tamp gravel or stone inside timber edgings.

ASSEMBLE THE STAIRS

Before you assemble the stairs, you must install posts if you're using them to support a handrail.
■ Tack the stringers at the top and mark the ground for the posthole locations.
■ Take the stringers down and dig holes at least 3 feet deep—or to the level specified by local codes.
■ Attach the stringers to the framing.

Follow the next steps regardless of whether you've installed posts:
■ Square the stringers.
■ Plumb and attach the posts.
■ Measure the distance between the stringers and cut treads to fit.
■ Attach the treads (notched around the posts, if necessary), and fill any postholes with concrete.
■ Fasten treads to the notches or stair cleats with galvanized ring- or spiral-shank nails or with decking screws.

EASY SPEED AND ACCURACY

Stair gauges can speed up your measuring and marking jobs. Stair gauges, available at building supply stores, are small, hexagonal brass blocks with set screws. They fasten on the sides of a carpenter's square to provide consistent measurements from one step to the next.

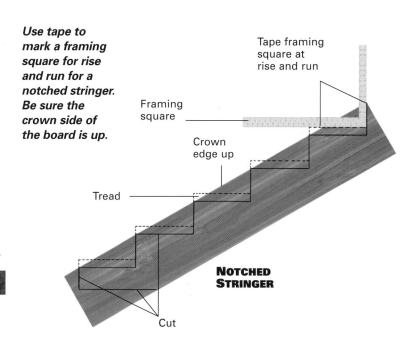

Use tape to mark a framing square for rise and run for a notched stringer. Be sure the crown side of the board is up.

Tape framing square at rise and run

Framing square

Crown edge up

Tread

NOTCHED STRINGER

Cut

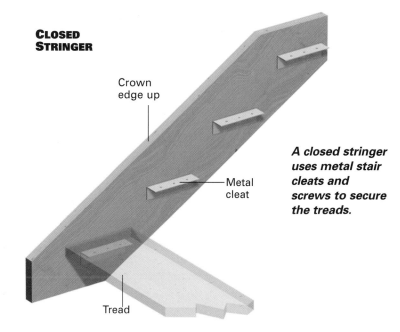

CLOSED STRINGER

Crown edge up

Metal cleat

A closed stringer uses metal stair cleats and screws to secure the treads.

Tread

POURING CONCRETE STEPS

Concrete steps provide one of the easiest solutions to changes in grade. You can buy precast steps—generally with 6- to 7¼-inch risers and 11- to 60-inch runs—but building your own is more fun. Here's how. Design their dimensions as you would any steps or stairs (see pages 124–125).

BUILDING FORMS

For steps between fixed heights, cut the form from a sheet of ¾-inch plywood. (You may need two sheets for a large stairway.)

■ Using a framing square and the techniques discussed on page 127, draw the steps on the plywood, sloping the upper landing so that water drains away from the structure. If the steps will be paved with a mortared surface, subtract the thickness of both the paving and bedding material from the height of the first riser only. *Note: All of the other steps should be the height you computed earlier. Keep in mind that the finished surface of the steps will be higher than the tread line on the form.*

■ Draw light lines for each step. Then draw darker lines, angling the risers back 1 inch and raising the backs of the treads ¼ inch per foot.

■ Cut the plywood sheet and set it in place to make sure you drew the layout correctly. If it's OK, use this form as a template to mark and cut a sheet for the other side of the stairs. Set the two forms in place and support them with stakes and braces made of 2×4s (see the

HILLSIDE STAIR FOOTINGS

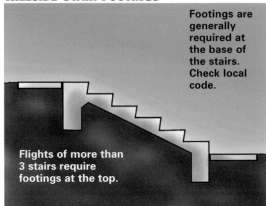

Footings are generally required at the base of the stairs. Check local code.

Flights of more than 3 stairs require footings at the top.

illustrations on the facing page). Check for square and plumb as you assemble the form.

■ To make risers, rip-cut 2×8s to the calculated riser height and bevel their bottom edge at 30 degrees to leave a space so you can slip a trowel under the form as you finish the step below.

EXCAVATE THE SITE

Excavate the site 6 inches below grade and a foot wider and longer than the finished steps. If drainage is poor, excavate an additional 4 inches and add a gravel base.

HILLSIDE STAIRS:

■ Prop the side forms in place and roughly square them up.

■ Drive 24-inch 2×4 stakes every 2 or 3 feet along one side board.

■ After plumbing the board and checking the slope of the treads (¼-inch drop per foot),

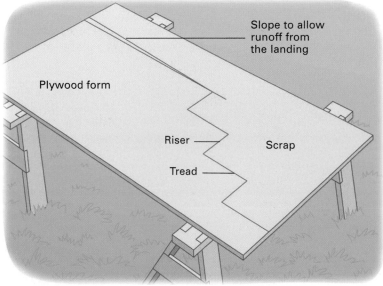

Slope to allow runoff from the landing

Plywood form

Riser

Scrap

Tread

Carefully plan your stair layout. You may need fewer or more steps than you had anticipated; if so, measure again and refigure the dimensions.

STEPS FOR A SLOPING YARD

For landscape steps, use this technique: Dig two 3- to 4-inch-deep trenches in the slope, as far apart as the width of the steps. Set 2×12s on edge in the trenches. Ensure that they are parallel, then stake them in place.

Excavate a series of stepped platforms between the forms. These don't have to conform to the finished steps; they provide a place for a 4-inch layer of concrete.

Use plywood for the forms. First, mark the point where the steps and the finished surface of the walk leading up to them will meet. Next, using a level, draw the risers and treads, starting at this bottom step and working up. Make light, erasable lines and experiment before coming up with identical, easy-to-climb steps.

fasten the side to the stakes with double-headed nails or drywall screws.

■ Position the other side of the form and stake it in place.

■ Attach boards to the top and bottom of the side forms and stake them in place.

■ Place riser boards with the beveled edge facing down and out and nail them to the side boards.

■ Brace the center of the risers with a long 2×6 set on edge. Attach it to the risers with 2×4 cleats angled so they won't interfere with the treads.

■ Stake the bottom of this brace firmly.

■ If the stairway is long, stake the top too.

STAIRS AGAINST A STRUCTURE:

■ Before setting it in place, assemble the form by attaching the risers to the sides. Do not put a back on this form. Set the form against the wall.

■ Square and plumb the form, making sure it's level from side to side and has a ¼-inch drop per foot on the treads and the landing.

■ There will be tremendous pressure on this form from the weight of the concrete. Stake it all around with 2×4s attached with two-headed nails, and brace the stakes. The bigger and taller the stairway, the greater the number of stakes and braces.

■ Make sure there is no space where the form meets the wall. Use silicone caulk or isolation joint material to help close small gaps.

■ Brace the center of the risers with a 2×4 or 2×6 set on edge and attached to the risers with angled 2×4 cleats. Firmly stake the bottom of this brace.

■ Paint the wall inside the form with mastic to serve as an isolation joint.

POURING AND FINISHING

■ Coat the forms with a release agent.

■ Pack gravel into the base of the form. To cut down on the amount of concrete needed, fill the forms with rubble, such as broken pieces of concrete. Leave enough room for the concrete to be at least 4 inches thick at all points.

■ Reinforce the steps with wire mesh.

■ If the steps attach to a house, drill holes in the foundation and insert rebar.

■ Starting at the bottom step and working up, spade concrete around the edges first and then fill the center.

■ Pour the concrete flush with the tops of the forms, screed it level with the treads, smooth with a float, and broom-texture the surface.

■ After the concrete sets, you can remove the forms.

■ Use a step trowel to finish inside corners and an edger and a steel trowel for the rest.

HILLSIDE STAIR FRAMEWORK

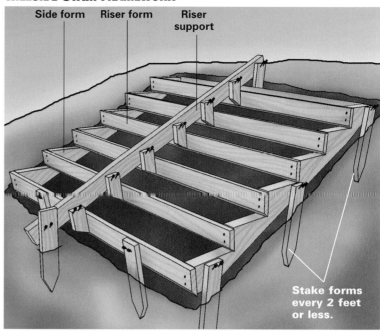

Side form   Riser form   Riser support

Stake forms every 2 feet or less.

BUILDING STEPS AGAINST A STRUCTURE

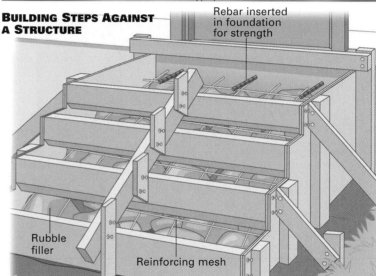

Rebar inserted in foundation for strength

Rubble filler

Reinforcing mesh

Keep forms upright and plumb with 2×4 stakes and braces. Attach the riser forms to both of the side forms and to step braces to prevent the concrete from warping the forms.

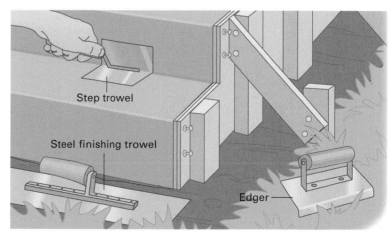

Step trowel

Steel finishing trowel

Edger

Finish the inside corner of the step with a step trowel. Rounding the outside edges of the step with an edger prevents chipping.

BUILDING PATIOS

In this chapter are instructions that show you how to build almost any kind of patio with almost any kind of material. Step-by-step information will guide you through each phase of the building process, from layout and ground breaking to laying the finished paving.

Before you start, schedule your material delivery. Arrange the delivery date so you have plenty of time to complete the preparation of the site beforehand. That way you can have the materials dropped close to the work area itself, eliminating the need to store them on your driveway and move them to the construction zone later.

Consider the size of the project and recruit a crew of helpers, if possible. This is especially important when pouring ready-mix concrete. Although you can take your time with any concrete you mix yourself, ready-mix won't wait. Once the truck arrives, you have to get the concrete into the forms quickly.

Building a patio, even a small one, is a big job—and it gets even bigger with ambitious designs. If you have any doubts about your ability to construct the patio yourself, find a contractor who's willing to let you carry out some of the work. You'll get a reduced price, access to top-quality tools, and advice. In addition you'll learn new skills and will still be able to put your personal mark on your project.

All patios begin with the proper site preparation and layout. Make sure the site is as level as possible, grading it if necessary, and remove any trash and debris. Once the site is properly prepared, you're ready for the layout.

LAYING OUT THE SITE

Using the procedures outlined on pages 96–97, set temporary stakes at the proposed corners of your patio and use one of the layout methods to lay out the site. A 4×8 plywood sheet makes a handy layout tool for small sites or additions to an existing patio. Moderate sites will lay out quickly with the frame layout shown on page 97, but for anything larger than about 16 feet, you'll need batter boards and mason's lines. Set them up, square the corners with a 3-4-5 triangle, and mark the excavation line with spray paint. Then excavate the site to the depth that your materials will require.

EASY MOWING

All patio surfaces should be about an inch above grade to permit rain to flow off the surface. Subtract that amount from the depths of the material thickness and your patio surface will be slightly above soil level. A patio raised by this amount will also allow you to mow the edges without having to trim them separately.

GRID LINES

Grid lines help keep the slope of the excavation consistent across its surface. Set additional stakes or batter boards at 4- to 5-foot intervals outside the excavation line. Tie lines across the area at the same height above the forms. The grid lines will now follow the slope you've set on the forms. If you are working on a small site, you can probably get by with the slope gauge, but using grid lines is more accurate, especially on patios larger than 10×10 feet.

Chalk line

If your patio will abut the house, snap a chalk line under the door to indicate the height of the surface on the foundation.

BATTER-BOARD LAYOUT

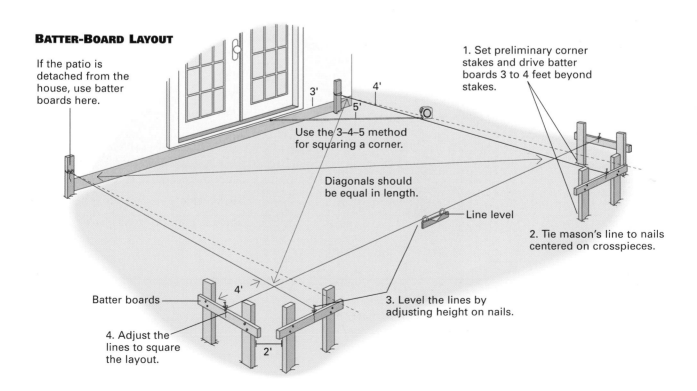

If the patio is detached from the house, use batter boards here.

Use the 3–4–5 method for squaring a corner.

Diagonals should be equal in length.

Line level

Batter boards

4. Adjust the lines to square the layout.

1. Set preliminary corner stakes and drive batter boards 3 to 4 feet beyond stakes.

2. Tie mason's line to nails centered on crosspieces.

3. Level the lines by adjusting height on nails.

BRICK PATIO

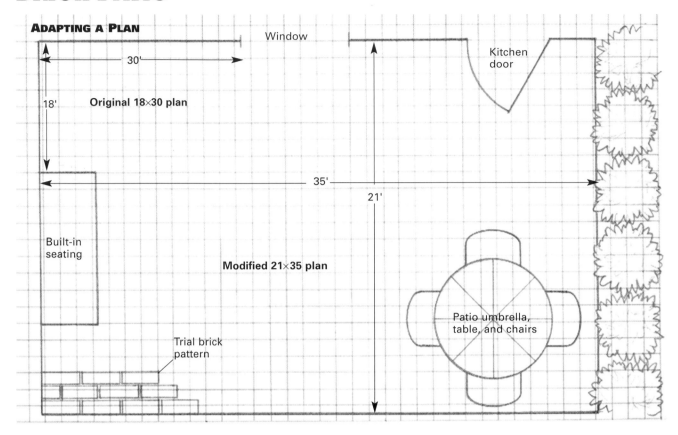

ADAPTING A PLAN

Window

30'

18'　Original 18×30 plan

Kitchen door

35'

21'

Built-in seating

Modified 21×35 plan

Patio umbrella, table, and chairs

Trial brick pattern

L aying brick in a bed of sand is a fairly quick and easy way to install a patio. It allows you to work in stages, leaving the job and picking it up later. Mortared brick patios will require your attention from start to finish. The key to success for both styles is a well defined layout.

Pave a large sand-set patio in sections. Install the pavers for the first section, using mason's line stretched between the edging and the temporary screed to keep them level.

String pulled taut

LAYOUT AND EXCAVATION

Before you lay out the site, finalize its dimensions so it will accommodate an even number of whole bricks, if possible. That way you minimize the number of bricks you have to cut.

Then, using the methods discussed on page 98, lay out and excavate the site deep enough for the materials you've chosen. Allow for slope and mowing height, moisten the soil, and tamp it with a power tamper.

INSTALLING THE EDGING

If you're pouring concrete, now's the time to install forms. However, vertical brick edging goes in after excavation. For other materials, it's also usually easier to install the edging now. It will help you guide the screeding (leveling) of the base materials. Installation techniques for edging vary with the kind of edge you want to create. Refer to page 99 to get the details about installing your edging.

BUILDING A SAND-SET PATIO

Order the gravel and schedule its delivery so it can be dumped directly into the patio area.

Follow these steps to build a sand-set brick patio:

INSTALLING THE GRAVEL BASE: Set stakes at various locations in the bed, driving them in so the tops are 4 inches above the surface.
- Shovel in the gravel even with the stakes and use a garden rake to roughly level it.
- Smooth the base with a straight 2×4.
- Compact the gravel with a tamper.
- Install landscaping fabric.

INSTALLING THE SAND BASE:
- Shovel 2 inches of unwashed coarse sand into the site and spread it evenly with a garden rake.
- Screed the entire surface of the sand base.
- Soak the sand and tamp it.

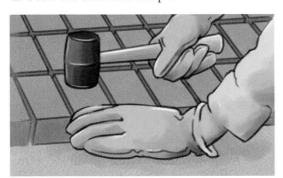

Set and level the brick with a rubber mallet. Fill joints with sand to stabilize the brick. Then wet and tamp the surface.

SETTING BRICKS:
Start in the corners and set the pattern in all directions outward from the corners.
- Set bricks by pushing straight down—don't slide them.
- Tap the brick in place with a rubber mallet.
- Every three or four rows, level the surface with a carpenter's level and sloping jig, raising low brick by adding sand and tapping raised pavers with the mallet.

FILLING THE GAPS:
Use fine sand in the joints. It will compact and keep the bricks tightly in place.
- Sprinkle sand over the entire surface and sweep it back and forth into the joints with a push broom.
- When the joints are full, sweep the excess to one side and settle the sand with a fine mist from the garden hose.
- Continue sweeping sand and settling the surface until the joints are full.
- Wet the surface with a fine spray and tamp it with a power tamper.

Set the width of a brick patio to include any permanent edging. That way you'll minimize cutting brick. Use a mason's line as a guide to level the bricks as you set them.

LAYOUT PATTERNS

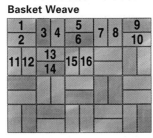

Jack-on-Jack

Running Bond

Half Basket Weave

Basket Weave

Ladder Weave

Herringbone

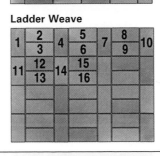

When choosing brick patterns (also called their *bond*), consider aesthetic effects and how many bricks you'll have to cut.

The jack-on-jack pattern is the simplest to lay but is the least interesting. A running bond will hide small variations in the sizes of the brick. Herringbone looks best when it can spread out. Basket weave and its half-weave cousin are best set with modular brick.

BRICK PATIO
continued

Use a mortar bag to fill the joints. Keep tip in contact with brick.

GROUTING MORTARED BRICK

BUILDING A MORTARED BRICK PATIO

Brick on mortar packs a double dose of patio building: You build one "patio"—the concrete slab—then add another—the brick surface.

BUILDING THE SLAB BASE: If possible, make the dimensions of the slab equal to an even multiple of your brick pattern, including grout.

■ Lay out, excavate, and pour gravel using the techniques described on page 98.
■ Set forms and pour the slab.

LAYING THE BRICK: Reinstall mason's lines at the finished surface level of the patio.

■ Spread mortar in a ½-inch bed.
■ Starting in a corner, push each brick straight down with a firm motion and tap it in place with a rubber mallet.
■ As you finish each section, pull out low pavers, remortar, and reset the brick. Tap down pavers that are high.

SETTING BRICK IN A MORTAR BED

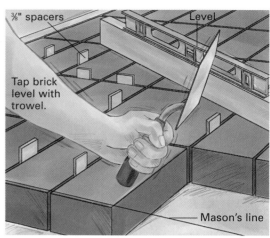

Use the trowel handle to tap bricks level into the mortar bed. Make sure the top of the surface is consistent—use a a carpenter's level to check it every 6 to 8 square feet.

■ When you have laid the entire surface, let the mortar cure for 3 days.
■ Pack the joints with mortar.
■ Clean spilled mortar with a wet sponge and finish joints with a jointing tool.
■ Keep the surface moist for 3 or 4 days so it cures slowly.

SETTING A MORTARED BRICK PATIO

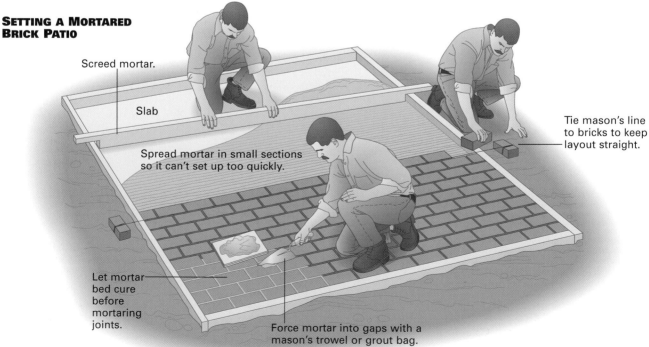

Screed mortar.

Slab

Spread mortar in small sections so it can't set up too quickly.

Tie mason's line to bricks to keep layout straight.

Let mortar bed cure before mortaring joints.

Force mortar into gaps with a mason's trowel or grout bag.

TILE PATIO

Depending on your choice of material, tile can look rugged or refined, and it will last for years if you install it properly on a level concrete slab. Lay out and pour the slab base using the techniques on page 99. Then take a trial run with your tile pattern.

TESTING THE LAYOUT

Test the layout before you start setting the tile. In general, you'll want as many full tiles as possible in the central part of the site (called the "field") and as few cut tiles as possible on the edges.

Set tiles in place across the slab without any mortar, following these procedures:

■ Mark the center of the patio by snapping diagonal chalk lines from the corners.

■ Snap chalk lines also between the midpoints of each side.

■ Starting at the center point, lay tiles and spacers on both the horizontal and vertical axes, extending the tiles to all sides of the slab.

■ If one side ends with a full tile and the opposite side has only part of a tile, move the center point so both sides will have tiles of the same size (cut or uncut). Adjust the tiles on both axes.

■ When the layout best fits the dimensions of the slab, snap parallel reference lines every 2 feet. These lines will help keep the tile straight when you lay it.

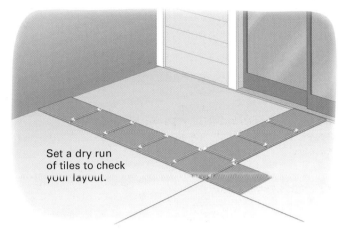

Set a dry run of tiles to check your layout.

■ Mark the locations of the control joints—you'll need to know where they are when you're setting the tile because you won't apply mortar over them.

SETTING THE TILE

Start with enough mortar for a section you can complete in 10 minutes.

■ Spread a thin coat of mortar with the flat side of a notched trowel.

■ Rake the mortar at a 45-degree angle with the notched side of the trowel.

■ Drop each tile in place with a slight twist and tap it with a mallet or beater block.

■ After completing each section, check your work. If a tile is too low, pull it up and apply mortar to the back, then reset it. If a tile is too high, scrape off excess mortar and reset.

■ Once you have set all the tiles, remove the spacers. Let the mortar set for at least a day.

■ Using a grout float, fill the joints with grout. Remove the haze with a damp sponge.

Draw perpendicular layout lines in the center of the slab and set the tiles in a dry run—complete with spacers—to make sure you will not end up with slivers or a row of cut tile that tapers along its length.

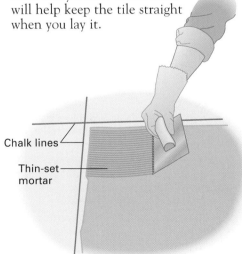

Chalk lines

Thin-set mortar

Using a notched trowel, spread thin-set mortar over a small area so that you will have time to lay all the tiles before the thin-set sets up.

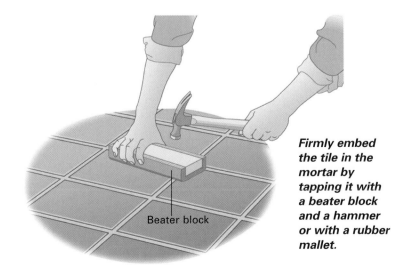

Beater block

Firmly embed the tile in the mortar by tapping it with a beater block and a hammer or with a rubber mallet.

FLAGSTONE PATIO

**BUILDING A
SAND-SET
STONE PATIO**

Sand-set or mortared, rough-hewn flagstone has a rustic charm that bring a timeless appeal to any landscape.
Installation techniques are substantially the same for both sand-set and mortared patios, but because flagstone is irregular, you can't predict the pattern until you have the stone on site. So after you prepare and excavate the site, using the techniques outlined on page 99, set the pattern in a dry run (see "Taking a Test Drive," *below*).

MAKING A DRY-SET BED

GRAVEL BASE: Drive stakes every 4 to 6 square feet so the tops are 4 inches from the excavation surface. Shovel the gravel level with the stakes. Even it with a garden rake or level it with a 2×4. Fill in low spots and tamp with a power tamper. Lay landscape fabric to keep the weeds down.

SAND BED: Shovel sand into the site and spread it with a garden rake. Check for a 2-inch thickness and screed with a 2×6 long enough to span the site or screed it in sections. Cut out the ends of the screed so they ride on the edging or screed guides at a depth that will level the sand at 2 inches. Work the screed back and forth, moisten the sand, and tamp it. Add sand, moisten, and tamp until the bed is uniform.

TAKING A TEST DRIVE

No two flagstones are the same (not even those cut in rectangles), so you'll need to experiment with the pattern. This may take some time, but you'll be more satisfied with the results if you don't rush the process. You can do this before you excavate, but your dry run will be easier after excavation. Set stones on the surrounding ground so you can see the shapes and sizes. Then lay out the pieces in the bed, using the suggestions in "Size, Shape, and Color" on page 138. *Note: If you're working on a sand base, support your weight with 3×3 plywood platforms to keep from indenting and dislodging the sand.*

■ Don't treat the stones as individual pieces; see how they look in pairs and

threes. Visualize sections, not puzzle pieces. Don't worry about getting the contours to match exactly; flagstones can be cut to fit. Use small stones as corner fillers.

■ Vary the size, shape, and color as you go. Variety is not only the spice of life—it can liven up your patio too.

■ Keep the spacing as uniform as possible— ½ to ¾ of an inch for both dry-set and mortared surfaces. Use wider, consistent spacing for turf or planted joints.

■ Once the pattern is laid, stand back and look at it from different perspectives. Rearrange it if you don't like it, then leave the stones in place for the final bedding.

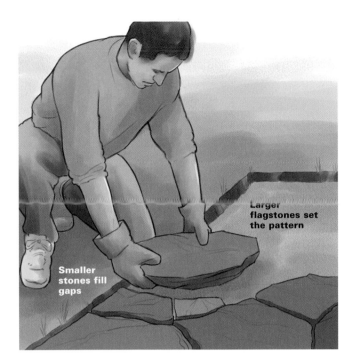

Larger flagstones set the pattern

Smaller stones fill gaps

this easier) and pour it to a 4-inch depth. Work a shovel up and down in the poured mix to get it into recesses and remove air. Span the site with a 2×4 laid on the forms and work the board back and forth to level the concrete. Roughen the surface with a stiff broom (see page 122) or notched trowel and let the concrete cure for 3 to 7 days.

MAKING THE MORTAR BED

To retain the pattern from your trial run, lift the stones out in 3×3-foot sections—the size of an area you can finish in 10 to 15 minutes. Lay them on the grass next to the site in the same pattern. Mix enough type M mortar (it's for outdoor use) for the section and use a trowel to spread it 1 inch thick on the surface of the concrete slab.

Take the stones up from the surrounding grass and reset each one in the mortar bed, being careful to keep the joints at the original spacing. Push the stones down; don't slide them in place. Tap them with a rubber mallet. As you complete each section, lay a 2×4 across it. You are certain to have high and low stones. Fix them now—you won't be able to later. Pull out stones that are low, add mortar, and reset them. Tap down the high stones and, if necessary, lift them and scoop just enough mortar out to make them level again. Then clean off any spills with a wet broom and set the next and succeeding

SETTING STONES IN SAND

Before adding sand to the joints, place a long 2×4 at several angles across the surface, checking for high and low stones. Use a carpenter's level to check the slope. Pull up high stones, dig out sand to conform to the bottom of the stone, and reset. Add sand and adjust low stones. Then walk the surface and correct stones that "rock."

Sprinkle washed sand across the entire surface and sweep it into the joints with a push broom. When the joints are full, collect the excess and wet the sand with a fine mist. Continue adding sand and wetting it until the joints are full. Then sweep the surface clean.

MAKING A CONCRETE BASE

GRAVEL BED: Using the methods described on page 133, level a 4-inch gravel base and tamp it even with the tops of 4-inch stakes.
REINFORCEMENT: Lay in reinforcing wire mesh (ask for 6×6 10/10). The mesh will help keep the concrete slab from cracking. Overlap the joints in the mesh by 4 inches and tie at the joints. Support the mesh and tie it to dobies (small 3-inch concrete block that will center the mesh in the slab).
POURING THE SLAB: If your site is 10×10 or smaller, mix your own concrete from dry ingredients (see page 121). For larger sites order ready-mix. Carry it to the site in wheelbarrow loads (a 2×10 runway will make

BUILDING A MORTARED STONE PATIO

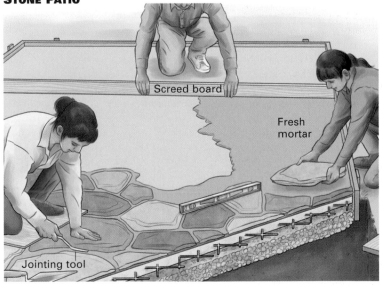

Screed board

Fresh mortar

Jointing tool

FLAGSTONE PATIO
continued

sections. Let the mortar cure three to four days, remove any temporary forms, and then fill the joints.

MORTARING STONE JOINTS

Mix mortar in a mortar box and fill the joints using a pointed trowel or mortar bag. The bag has a spout through which the mortar is squeezed into the joints—it's less messy and will reduce cleanup chores. Clean spilled mortar right away with a wet sponge. Wait until the mortar will hold a thumbprint and then finish the joints with a jointing tool. Cover the surface with plastic or burlap (you'll need to keep it wet) and let it cure for three to four days. Then install edging if you have not already done so.

CUTTING FLAGSTONE

1. Place an adjoining stone on top and trace a cut line.

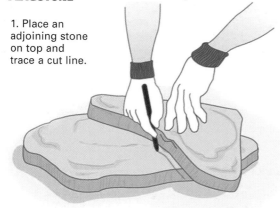

2. Score the cut line with a hammer and brickset. Tap repeatedly, moving the brickset a bit at a time along the line between each tap.

3. Set the stone on a pipe, place the brickset on the score, then break the stone with a single strong blow.

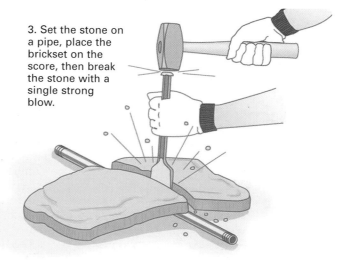

SIZE, SHAPE, AND COLOR

Variety, a design strength of flagstone, also can be a weakness. Because flagstones range in size from skipping stones to carports, you need to plan for sizes that will best fit the scale of your patio project. A variety of sizes will also add versatility to your design.

Shape is another factor that can work in your favor, depending on the amount of time you're willing to spend finding stones that fit together well. In a carelessly chosen grouping the stones will look as if they were placed by accident.

Finally, flagstones are available in several colors, sometimes within a single shipment from one supplier. If your design already uses variations in shape and texture, you may not want to add more contrast using color.

PRECAST PAVER PATIO

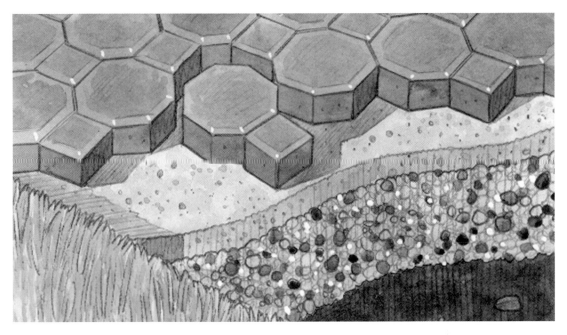

Concrete pavers are available in several designs and colors. One of the most popular combines squares and octagons for a pattern of alternating shapes. Most pavers are cast with lugs on the sides to create a small gap between each pair of adjoining units.

Precast concrete pavers combine the design versatility of tile with the easy installation of brick. They are made of cast concrete in sizes and patterns to fit any style or space and are designed to be set in a sand bed over a gravel base. Most pavers come with molded lugs to keep them properly spaced. If your pavers don't have lugs, use ⅛-inch plywood to space them.

Because precast pavers are made specifically for setting in a sand bed, installation techniques are the same as for a brick-in-sand patio. Follow the preparation and layout steps for a brick patio as shown on pages 132–134, but before you build the patio, spend a little extra time planning your layout. You'll be rewarded by a professional-looking installation.

PLANNING THE LAYOUT

To make accurate estimates of how much material you will need, draw a trial layout on graph paper with ¼-inch increments.

Start with the outline of an approximate patio size and draw it to a scale of ¼ inch = 1 foot. Then draw in your pattern to scale. Most patterns will lend themselves to sectioning—figure how much area one section covers and the number of sections of the same size your patio dimensions will accommodate.

Adjust the final patio size so your patterns will be complete with a minimum of cutting. Then count the number of pavers in each section and multiply by the number of even sections to estimate material quantities.

Most suppliers will allow you to return unused materials, so buy 10 to 15 percent more than you expect to need. A leisurely return trip is more pleasant than interrupting your work because you ran out of materials.

SETTING PRECAST PAVERS

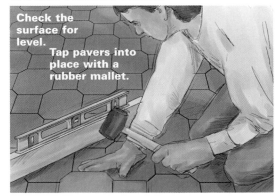

Check the surface for level. Tap pavers into place with a rubber mallet.

Set cut pavers at the edges as you install the field pattern. If you set the edges last, the paver may not fit the recess.

FINISHING THE SURFACE

Sweep sand into joints from all directions.

CONCRETE PATIO

Concrete is one of the most versatile construction materials. When it's wet it can assume almost any shape. When it's cured it will stand up to hard use and extreme weather conditions. It accepts color and texture treatments and costs less than many other building materials.

Working with it requires strength and stamina, however; once you start a pour, you must finish it within a couple of hours. (Get helpers, especially for any patio larger than 10×10.) The key to successful concrete work is careful preparation.

PLANNING

How thick to make the slab, as well as the amount and type of reinforcement to use, depends on its function. For sidewalks and patios, a 3-inch slab with no reinforcement is fine—although 3½ to 4 inches reinforced with 6-inch mesh is preferable. Let your building codes be your guide.

Plan for drainage, sloping the slab 1 inch every 4 feet. Let the runoff pour into a mulched border or dig a trench around the slab and fill it with gravel. For seriously wet

MAKING CURVED FORMS

Here's how to create curved forms:
KERFED WOOD: Make ½-inch cuts (at 1-inch intervals) in 8-inch-high pieces of ¾-inch stock. The board will bend at the kerfs (the cutouts) but will not break on gentle curves. See page 100.
PLYWOOD: Cut strips of ¼-inch plywood.
SHEET METAL: Use 16-gauge sheet metal cut to 8-inch widths.

Drive stakes along the curve—inside and out—and fasten the forms to the exterior stakes. Remove the interior stakes before pouring.

sites embed a perforated drainpipe in the trench (see page 95). Crown the surface (make it a little higher in the center) so water flows away from the center and off to both sides.

PREPARING THE SITE

After you have decided where to locate the patio, lay out and excavate the site with the techniques shown on pages 96–97. If you are installing wide edging (timbers, concrete forms, or perpendicular flat brick), attach

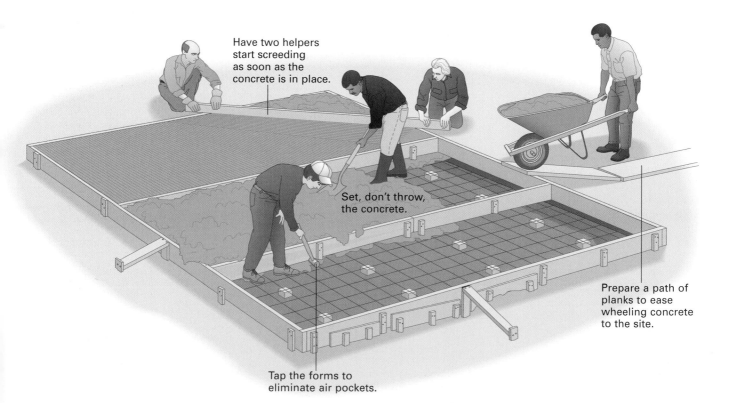

Have two helpers start screeding as soon as the concrete is in place.

Set, don't throw, the concrete.

Prepare a path of planks to ease wheeling concrete to the site.

Tap the forms to eliminate air pockets.

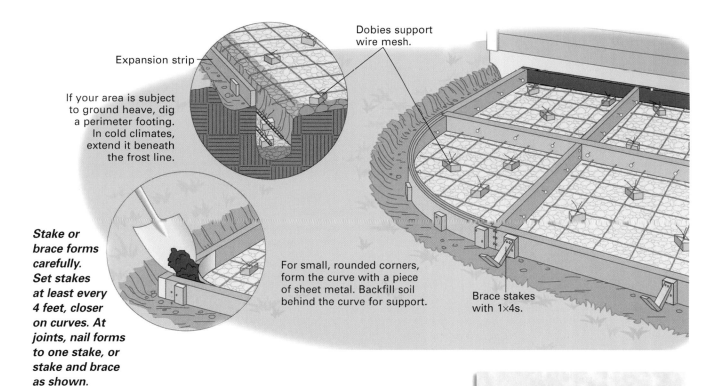

Expansion strip

Dobies support wire mesh.

If your area is subject to ground heave, dig a perimeter footing. In cold climates, extend it beneath the frost line.

Stake or brace forms carefully. Set stakes at least every 4 feet, closer on curves. At joints, nail forms to one stake, or stake and brace as shown.

For small, rounded corners, form the curve with a piece of sheet metal. Backfill soil behind the curve for support.

Brace stakes with 1×4s.

a second set of lines parallel to the first and separated by the width of the edging. Skip this step for narrow edging and remember that the mason's lines represent the outside edge of the patio, including the edging.

BUILDING FORMS

Wet concrete must be contained by forms. You can assemble the forms in the excavated site, but it's easier to do as much assembly as possible on the ground.
■ Use deck screws to attach 2×4 stakes to the corners and at 2- to 4-foot intervals.
■ Make sure the forms follow the correct slope as you install them. Measure down from your grid lines or use a slope gauge.
■ If the forms are temporary, coat the inside edges with a commercial

COLD JOINTS

Avoid pouring new concrete against concrete that has already set up. This creates a cold joint, which fractures easily.

releasing agent so that you will be able to pull them away after the concrete has cured.

POURING THE SLAB

Prepare a gravel base and reinforce it as shown in the illustrations above, then pour, screed, and float the surface as discussed on page 101. Use an edger and a jointer before you apply any final finish.

APPLYING THE FINAL FINISH

Depending on weather conditions, you may have as little as an hour (in hot, dry weather) or as much as half a day (in cool, humid weather) to smooth the slab surface to its final finish. Consider hiring a professional concrete finisher to help on large jobs. Smaller jobs offer a better opportunity to learn this skill yourself.
   Finishing is performed with various tools and techniques, depending on the texture you want for the slab.

DIVIDER STRIPS

If your patio will be larger than 8×8, you will need divider strips—or you will need to cut control joints in the surface. Install divider strips every 8 feet in each direction, using 2× stock staked at 2-foot intervals.

CASTING YOUR OWN PAVERS

1. Pour concrete into mold (cut from large ice cream container or other container), level it, and let it set until firm.

2. Scribe outline of stencil with screwdriver or pointed dowel. Remove stencil and scribe additional lines. Let concrete cure.

3. Remove form and set paver in path.

CONCRETE PATIO
continued

TRAVERTINE

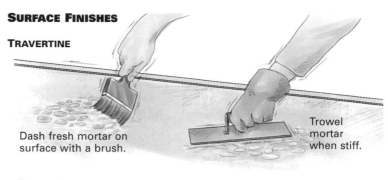

Dash fresh mortar on surface with a brush.

Trowel mortar when stiff.

ROCK SALT

Sprinkle rock salt on concrete.

Embed salt with trowel.

Hose slab when cured to dissolve salt, leaving rough surface.

■ For a slightly rough texture, refloat the surface with a wood float.

■ Steel troweling creates a slick surface, like that on basement floors. Although it's not the best finish for an outdoor slab, troweling is the first step when creating some types of rough finishes.

To achieve a smooth steel-trowel finish, hand-trowel the surface two or three times. The concrete should be hard enough to support your weight on knee boards but fresh enough to produce a moistened paste as you work. Keep track of the concrete's wetness. If it gets too dry, it becomes unworkable. Overworking it when it is very wet can cause the top layer to flake off later.

■ Start troweling from the edge of the slab. Get into a comfortable position so you won't have to overreach. Do as much as you can from the lawn, then use a knee board to work in the middle.

To make a professional-looking rounded edge on your concrete patio, separate the concrete from the form by cutting along their boundary with a mason's trowel. Then round the edge with an edger.

Use a guide to make a control joint. When using a jointer or edger, make one pass using short back-and-forth strokes, then follow up with long strokes.

Edger

Jointer

■ Hold the steel trowel almost flat, with the leading edge raised slightly. Use long, sweeping arcs. Don't press hard. Overlap each succeeding arc by half the tool's length.

One finish that you begin by steel-troweling is brooming. It creates a patterned nonslip surface. Trowel the concrete, then drag a dampened broom across it in straight lines, curves, or waves. Soft brooms designed for this purpose produce a shallow pattern. Stiff-bristled brooms cut deeper. After grooming the surface, you may need to touch up the edges and control joints.

CUSTOM FINISHES

Floating, troweling, and brooming are only three of the many ways to produce decorative concrete surfaces. Here are some others.

SEEDED-AGGREGATE FINISH:
Divide the project into manageable sections so the concrete mix doesn't harden before you can work in the stones. Pour the concrete so its surface is about ½ inch below the top of the forms; then screed, float, and finish it.

Sprinkle aggregate evenly over the slab. With a helper, press the aggregate into the concrete with long 2×6s or flat shovels. Embed the stones firmly so their tops are just visible. If necessary, go over them with a wood float to push them down more.

When the concrete has hardened enough to support your weight on knee boards, remove excess concrete around the stones with a stiff nylon brush or broom. Work carefully so you don't dislodge the stones. Remove the debris, spray a curing agent over the slab, then cover it with a plastic sheet.

After the concrete cures for 24 hours, repeat the brooming followed by a fine spray of water to expose about half of each stone. The spray should be strong enough to wash away the concrete loosened by the broom but not dislodge the stones. Let the aggregate dry for a couple of hours, then hose off any film that develops on the stones. Again, cover the area with plastic so it can cure slowly. After curing, remove any haze on the aggregate with muriatic acid.

HAND-PATTERNED FINISH: Float the slab, then make geometric or random lines in the finished concrete with a joint-strike tool. If you need to retrowel part of the surface, be sure to strike the lines again.

STAMPED FINISH: Use a steel or rubber stamping tool to produce patterns resembling brick, cobblestone, flagstone, and others. See page 63.

First, measure the base of the stamp and adjust spacing so the pattern comes out even. Increase efficiency by using two stamps side by side. Set both stamps in place. Stand on one, then step over to the other. The impressions should be about 1 inch deep. Smooth out the edges of the pattern with a joint-strike tool.

CURING CONCRETE

Although concrete will harden in a day, it doesn't reach full strength until it has cured for at least three to seven days. During this time it must be protected from drying out too quickly. Help your slab cure properly with any of the following methods.

COVER IT: To prevent evaporation, cover the concrete with plastic. If the temperature is cool, use black plastic because it absorbs heat from the sun. Weight the edges of the plastic and any seams with small stones or boards to trap as much moisture as possible. Let the concrete remain protected for at least three to seven days.

KEEP IT WET: If you are able to attend to your slab regularly, sprinkling it with water is better than covering it with plastic. Cover the slab with old blankets or burlap and wet them down often enough that they stay wet. You can also wet the concrete directly. To keep the water drops from pitting the surface, wait until the concrete is fairly hard before spraying it.

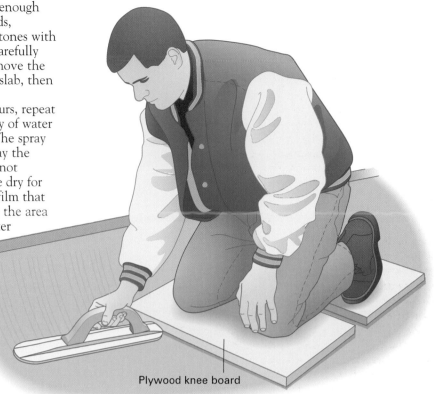

Plywood knee board

Keep your knees and toes from denting the wet concrete by supporting your weight on plywood sections. Use two boards, or one board large enough to accommodate both knees and toes. Have a second set of boards handy so you can move around without stopping.

STEPS FOR EMBEDDING

1. Spread aggregate. 2. Embed stones and settle with wood float. 3. Sweep off excess concrete. 4. Wash excess concrete with fine spray. Support weight on plywood when embedding internal patterns.

Make an aggregate finish when the concrete is still wet and workable. Work in sections right after the water sheen disappears, embedding stones so that only their upper surfaces show above the surface. Brush the surface when the concrete begins to set.

BUILDING PATHS AND WALKWAYS

With a little imagination, you can transform a featureless area in your lawn into the most idyllic garden path. Whether your path will be natural material, stone, brick, wood, or concrete, this chapter shows you how to build it.

A walkway is an easy amenity to build because you can reach its entire surface from outside the forms. The techniques for building a path or walk are the same as for a patio, but expect differences when laying out the walk and building forms.

Because they receive only foot traffic, concrete sidewalks are often just 3 inches thick. In areas without frost heave, you may be able to pour them directly on the ground without a gravel base, but check with your building department to see if local codes permit such installations.

LAYOUT

Layout procedures will vary slightly depending on whether your walk is straight or curved.

STRAIGHT WALK:
■ Stretch two parallel mason's lines between stakes driven into the ground, making sure the walk is square with the house or other predominant features in the landscape.

CURVED WALK:
■ Lay two hoses in the desired shape.
■ Measure between them every foot or so to ensure that each side conforms to the other.
■ Mark the location of the hoses with flour, sand, or chalk; then remove them.

BUILDING THE PATH

The surface of the walk should be slightly higher (½ to 1 inch) than ground level and slightly sloped so water won't puddle. Excavate the walk the same as you would for a patio of the same materials (see pages 136–137). Then construct the walk in the same order as you would a patio.
■ Set forms or edging. Some materials, such as flagstone, won't require edging.
■ Install subbase and base materials.
■ Install surface materials.

WHEELBARROW RUNWAYS

Storing materials away from the job site poses a problem—how to get them from the storage area to the path. Wheelbarrows are the frequent answer, but these one-wheeled assistants can really tear up your yard.

To reduce the damage and avoid having to repair the wheelbarrow path, lay 2×10 or 2×12 planks to form a runway from storage to work site.

LOOSE-STONE PATHS

You may be tempted to lay loose stone directly on well-drained soil. However, your path will feel more solid underfoot, require less maintenance, and last longer without drainage problems if you lay it on a prepared base.

BUILDING THE BASE

◼ Lay out the contours of your path using batter boards or garden hose as shown on page 98. Be sure to include the width of the edging materials and any forms used to keep the edging straight.

◼ Mark the lines with spray marking paint, remove the sod, and excavate. If your soil drains rapidly, you can build the path on a 4-inch gravel base. In poorly draining soil, you'll need 6 inches of gravel. In heavy clays, excavate deep enough to install a drainpipe.

◼ If you are using forms, set them now. Drive the stakes first and then screw the forms to them.

◼ Shovel in gravel for the base and spread it with a garden rake.

◼ Set the edging and lay in landscape fabric.

Loose stone crunches underfoot, making every stroll along it feel like a walk in the country. Aggregates are naturals in everything from rustic woodland settings to formal gardens.

TOPPING OFF THE PATH

Adding the top layer of loose stone will go more quickly than the base construction.

◼ Pour the stone from a wheelbarrow or shovel it in with a round-nosed shovel. Shovel the stone into low areas and level it with the back of a garden rake, pushing and pulling the gravel to a consistent surface.

◼ Dampen the surface with a fine spray and tamp it firmly. After tamping, add more stone, dampen it, and tamp again.

BUILDING A LOOSE-STONE PATH

1. Excavate.

2. Set edging.

3. Pour and tamp base material.

4. Pour and level surface material.

BRICK PATHS

If you're looking for a classic path design, brick is the natural choice. Edging helps hold unmortared bricks in place.

Brick paths often look complicated because of their patterns, but they are no more difficult to build than any other hard-surface path. Set up a mock section and measure it, allowing for mortar joints, edging, and the width of forms. Set your layout stakes exactly to this width.

SETTING BRICK IN SAND

Like other materials, sand-laid brick calls for a solid base and a level sand bed.
BUILD THE BASE: Lay out the path using the techniques shown on page 100 and excavate to a depth that will accommodate the materials. Add 4 to 6 inches of gravel, depending on drainage requirements for your soil, and level and tamp the gravel. Cut

landscape fabric and lay it on the gravel. Then set the edging on the fabric.
LAY THE SAND BED: Shovel in and spread about 2 inches of washed sand. Dampen the sand, screed it level, and tamp it.
SET THE BRICK: Tie a mason's line to the bricks (shown in the illustration below, left) to make the line easier to move.

■ Space the path bricks ⅛ inch apart and check each course with a straightedge before laying the next one.

■ Beginning in one corner, push each brick straight down into the sand. Continue until you have laid about a 4-foot section, supporting your weight on 2-foot plywood squares. Check the section in several directions with a 4-foot level. Pull up bricks if necessary, digging out or adding sand. Set each brick by tapping it with a rubber mallet.
FILL THE GAPS: Shovel sand into the joints and brush it with a push broom. When it nearly fills the joints, dampen it. Sweep in more sand from all directions, leaving the sand about ⅛ inch below the surface, or at the bottom of the chamfer for chamfered brick.

BUILDING A MORTARED-BRICK PATH

Mortared brick requires a concrete base.
BUILD THE BASE: Lay out the path. Excavate to a depth of 10 to 12 inches. Build forms and shovel in 4 to 6 inches of tamped gravel. Lay in reinforcing wire mesh.
POUR THE SLAB: Bring concrete to the site in wheelbarrows or by truck. Pour the concrete between the forms, spreading it with shovels and making sure it fills all recesses.
SCREED AND FLOAT THE SLAB: Pull a screed across the concrete to level it, repeating the screeding after filling in any

ALIGNING A BRICK SETTING

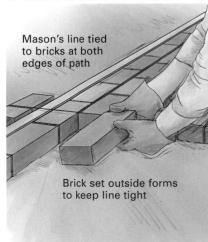

Mason's line tied to bricks at both edges of path

Brick set outside forms to keep line tight

LEVELING BRICK

Check for level and set brick with rubber mallet.

SWEEPING IN THE SAND

Sweep sand into joints from all directions.

LAYING BRICKS IN SAND

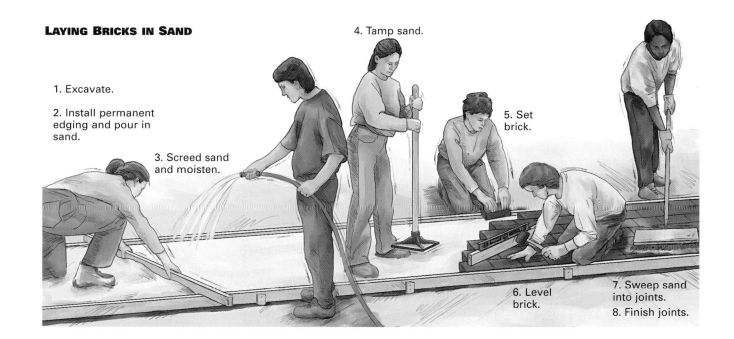

1. Excavate.

2. Install permanent edging and pour in sand.

3. Screed sand and moisten.

4. Tamp sand.

5. Set brick.

6. Level brick.

7. Sweep sand into joints.

8. Finish joints.

depressions. Float the surface (see page 143) and broom-finish it. Let the concrete cure for three days to a week.

SPREAD THE MORTAR BED: Mix enough type M mortar (for outdoor use) to cover a space you can set in about 30 minutes. Using a square trowel, spread a mortar bed about ½ inch thick. If you've installed 3-inch screed boards, screed each section with a 2×4 notched 2½ inches deep at both ends to spread the mortar evenly to ½ inch thick.

SET THE PAVING: Starting in a corner, push each brick straight down into the mortar. Then tap it with the handle of a trowel. Continue laying brick, moving the mason's line and checking the rows with a straightedge until you've covered the entire path. Let the mortar set up overnight.

MORTAR THE BRICKS: Mortar the joints with a mortar bag. Squeeze the bag to push the mortar into the joints, cleaning off any spillage immediately.

BUILDING A MORTARED-BRICK PATH

1. Build temporary edges for screeds.

Mason's line

5. Grout and smooth joints after mortar sets.

4. Lay brick.

3. Pour slab and let it cure.

2. Screed bed to 1".

FLAGSTONE PATHS

The varied textures and sizes of flagstone go well with almost any design scheme. The flat stones can be arranged as stepping-stones or laid as a solid surface.

You can set individual flagstones in the soil in a stepping-stone pattern or lay them in a solid surface, either in sand or mortared to a slab.

SETTING STEPPING-STONES

Stepping-stones do not require a gravel base unless bedded in a loose-stone path or set in soil subject to extreme frost. (In climates with severe winters, prepare a gravel and sand base as shown on pages 136–137, lay the stones, and backfill soil between them.)

Set stepping-stones directly on the soil, but adding 1 to 2 inches of sand under each one will help them drain and minimize settling. Outline the path with hose or stakes and lines as shown on page 98. Then follow the installation procedures shown at left.

STEPPING-STONE LAYOUT TIPS

Here are ideas for your stepping-stone design:
- Stepping-stones are usually a one-person path, so you can keep the scale small.
- To start and stop the path or signal changes of direction, use stones about 1½ times larger than average. Lay these junction stones first.
- Lay long stones across the path, not parallel with its direction.
- Stones with recesses will collect water, which can freeze, become dangerous, and split the stone. Select stones with flat surfaces.
- Stones equal in thickness will make installation much easier.

BUILDING A STEPPING-STONE PATH

4. Take up the stone and remove or add sand to make it level.

2. Use a round-nosed shovel to dig out the edges at the chalk. Remove the soil and shovel in 2" of sand.

3. Set the stone in the recess and check it for level.

1. Lay out the stones in the pattern of your choice. Outline each stone with chalk. Remove the stone and set it aside.

DESIGNING A STONE SURFACE

The infinite variety of natural flagstone lends itself to stunning layouts but can also leave you overwhelmed with design possibilities. For both dry-laid and mortared flagstone surfaces, make things easier by laying a trial pattern beside the site.

Sort the stones into piles according to size. Begin your trial pattern at the path edge, selecting larger stones with straight sides. Vary the sizes of these edge stones and leave some for the interior as well. Try to arrange the contours of the stones so they mirror each other, fitting the concave edge of one stone near the convex side of the other.

SETTING FLAGSTONE IN SAND

The naturally uneven edges of flagstone prohibit you from spacing them consistently on the path, but try to set them about ½ inch or less from each other. More sand will tend to work its way out of a wider gap.

BUILD THE BASE: Lay out the path using the techniques shown on the previous page. Excavate to a depth that will accommodate the materials and leave the paving about ½ inch above grade. Add 4 to 6 inches of gravel depending on drainage requirements. Level and tamp the base. Cut and lay landscape fabric on the gravel and set the edging, if you are using it.

LAY THE SAND BED: Shovel in and spread about 2 inches of washed sand. Dampen the sand, screed it level, and tamp it.

SET THE STONES: Begin with the edge stones first, transferring them from your trial layout. Fill in the gaps with smaller stones.

Push and rock the stones into the sand bed as you lay them. After you have set a 3- to 4-foot section, check it for level. Pull up stones that aren't level, removing or adding sand as necessary.

Set the stones by tapping them with a small sledge (protect the stone surface with a scrap of 2×4). Continue setting the stones in sections, making the surface of each section level with the previous one. Smooth stones will level easily. Check several sections at a time by placing the level on an 8-foot 2×4. Leveling rough stones by eye is usually adequate.

FILL THE GAPS: Shovel sand between the joints and sweep it across the surface with a push broom until it nearly fills the joint, then dampen it. Top off the joints by sweeping in sand from all directions. Repeat this process until the sand in the joints is ¼ to ⅛ inch below the surface of the stones. That small recess will reduce the amount of sand displaced—or tracked into the house.

SETTING FLAGSTONE IN SAND

7. Sweep sand into gaps.

6. Check each stone for level as you go.

5. Set stone by tapping in place.

4. Lay flagstone.

3. Spread sand, dampen, and tamp.

2. Pour and level gravel base.

1. Excavate to the depth required by the thickness of materials.

Set edging if desired.

CUTTING NATURAL STONE

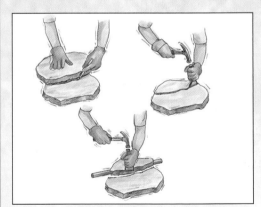

You can cut flagstone to fit your path or to conform to the edges of other stone when nature (or the stone yard) doesn't supply the right shapes.

■ First mark the stone to be cut. Use a carpenter's pencil or welder's chalk. Set an adjoining stone on top if cutting to match contours.

■ Next place a mason's chisel on the line and strike the chisel sharply with a small sledge.

■ Lay the stone on a pipe or another stone and strike the line again to break off the waste.

■ You may be able to trim the edges of thin flagstone by chipping the edge with a mason's hammer.

FLAGSTONE PATHS
continued

THE MORTARED-STONE PATH

Mortared flagstone requires a solid concrete base. Refer to the information on page 137 when building a mortared path. Joint spacing is a matter of preference, but ¾-inch joints look good and are easy to mortar.

BUILD THE BASE: Lay out the path. Excavate to a depth that will accommodate the gravel base, the concrete slab, and the thickness of your flagstone. Build forms for the slab and shovel in 4 to 6 inches of gravel. Level and tamp the gravel. Lay in reinforcing wire mesh supported on dobies.

POUR THE SLAB: Bring concrete to the site in wheelbarrows or by truck. Pour the concrete between the forms. Spread it with shovels and make sure it fills the forms.

SCREED AND FLOAT THE SLAB: Pull a screed board across the surface of the concrete to level it. Repeat the screeding after filling any depressions. Float the surface (see page 143) and broom-finish it. Let the concrete cure for three days to a week.

MAKE MORTAR SCREED BOARDS (OPTIONAL): You can spread mortar to its proper depth without screed boards, leveling the stones as you go, but screeding the mortar will make the bed depth more consistent. Fasten 2×4s to stakes (keep the tops of the stakes flush with the top edges of the 2×4s). Set these preassembled guides on top of the slab forms. Toenail the screed guides to the forms.

SPREAD THE MORTAR BED: Mix enough type M mortar (for outdoor use) to cover an area you can set in about 10 minutes. Using a square trowel, spread a 2-inch mortar bed. Then if you've installed screed guides, screed each section with a 2×4 notched 1½ inches deep at both ends. The notched 2×4 will spread the mortar evenly 2 inches deep.

SET THE PAVING: Bring each stone from the test site and push (don't slide) it gently into the mortar. Continue setting stones until you have finished the section, then lay a level on the section and adjust

SCREEDING MORTAR

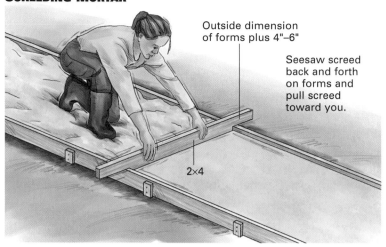

Outside dimension of forms plus 4"–6"

Seesaw screed back and forth on forms and pull screed toward you.

2×4

any stones that are too high or too low. Tap each stone with a small sledge and a 2×4. Continue setting stones until you've covered the entire path. Let the installation set up overnight.

MORTAR THE STONES: A mortar bag makes it easy to put the mortar in the joints, not on the stones. Squeeze the bag to push the mortar into the joints, cleaning off any spillage immediately. When the mortar will hold a thumbprint, smooth it with a pointing tool. Let the mortar cure.

INSTALLING A MORTARED FLAGSTONE PATH

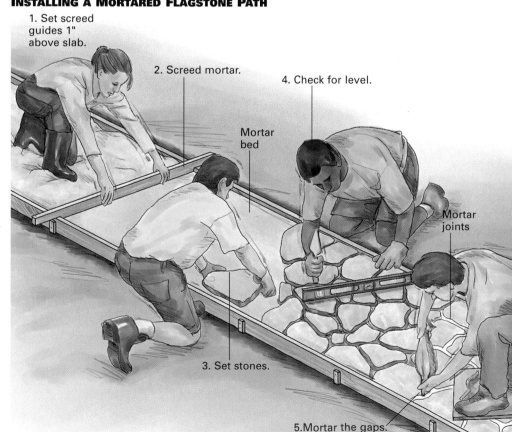

1. Set screed guides 1" above slab.

2. Screed mortar.

4. Check for level.

Mortar bed

Mortar joints

3. Set stones.

5. Mortar the gaps.

PRECAST PAVERS

Precast pavers are made for the do-it-yourselfer. Uniform shapes and repeating patterns make layout and design decisions easy.

BUILDING THE BASE

Like other materials, pavers need a well-drained base and a level sand bed.
■ Lay out the path and excavate to a depth that will accommodate the materials.
■ Add 4 to 6 inches of gravel, depending on how well your soil drains. Level and tamp the gravel.
■ Cut landscape fabric and lay it on the gravel.
■ Shovel in and spread about 2 inches of washed sand. Dampen the sand, screed it level, and tamp it.

Precast pavers are easy to install, but choose the pattern carefully. Make sure the scale of the pattern suits your landscape.

SETTING THE PAVERS

Pavers must be set precisely, and interlocking edges on many styles make this easy.
■ Starting in a corner, lay the first few pavers snugly against the edging.
■ Tap each block with a rubber mallet to set it firmly into the sand. As you lay the pavers, work in two directions to keep your design from shifting to either side.
■ Every few courses, lay a carpenter's level or a long, straight 2×4 across the surface to make sure the pavers have been set at a consistent height.
■ To adjust pavers, remove several from the area, remove or add sand as necessary, and reset the pavers. Pavers can be difficult to remove. To remove a stubborn paver, pry it from opposite sides at the same time with two straight screwdrivers gripping the sides about ¼ inch below the surface.
■ Fill joints in the path with sand. You can fill them in sections or wait until you complete the entire path.
■ Shovel sand between the joints, brushing it with a push broom. When it nearly fills the joint, dampen it.
■ Top off the joints by sweeping in more sand from all directions, leaving it about ⅛ inch below the surface or at the bottom of the chamfer on chamfered pavers.

BUILDING A PATH WITH PRECAST PAVERS

1. Excavate.

2. Install permanent edging.

3. Add sand and screed.

4. Dampen sand and tamp.

5. Lay pavers.

6. Sweep sand into joints.

WOOD PATHS

A boardwalk and a wood bridge look distinctive in this garden. Naturally resistant wood species or pressure-treated lumber are necessary in ground contact.

Basic carpentry skills and a few tools are all you need to install a small wood walk in a weekend. Longer walks might take more time, but most of your effort will be spent on the preparation of the base.

Decking sizes vary with individual designs, from 2×6s to 2×8s or wider. Wider boards will cover the walk more quickly, but be careful to maintain a pleasing scale.

BUILDING A WOOD WALK

The design shown here works well on generally flat ground. To accommodate small variations in grade, either alter the depth of the excavation or build small sections to avoid spanning changes in grade.

BUILD THE BASE: Lay out the path. Excavate to a depth that will leave the decking at least 1½ inches above the ground.

■ Drive stakes every 3 feet on both sides of the excavation. Make sure the stakes are the same height from the bottom of the excavation throughout.

■ Cut landscape fabric and lay it on the pathway.

■ Add 4 to 6 inches of gravel and level and tamp it.

INSTALL THE SLEEPERS: Cut 2×4s to lengths that will span each flat area on the path, and fasten them with 2½-inch treated deck screws driven through the stakes.

INSTALL THE DECKING: Cut the decking long enough to span the width of the walk so it overhangs the sleepers by 1½ to 2 inches on either side.

■ Using a cordless drill, fasten the decking to the sleepers with 3-inch treated deck screws, two screws into each sleeper.

APPLY THE FINISH: If you haven't done so already, spray or brush on the finish.

INSTALLING SLEEPERS

2×4

2" sand (optional)

4"–6" gravel

2×4

LAYING THE DECKING

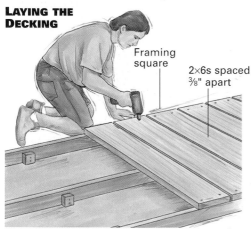

Framing square

2×6s spaced ³⁄₈" apart

BUILDING A DECKED WALK

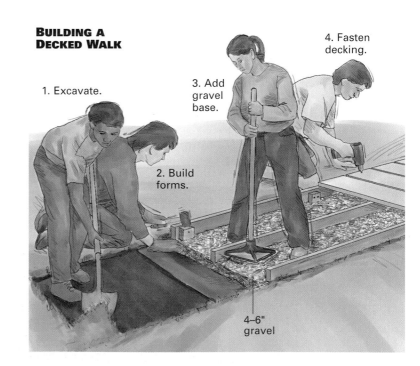

1. Excavate.

2. Build forms.

3. Add gravel base.

4. Fasten decking.

4–6" gravel

CONCRETE FOR PATHS

No matter what size the job, prepare the surrounding lawn to minimize damage caused by concrete work. Lay 2×10 ramps for hauling bags of mix or the concrete itself across the lawn in a wheelbarrow.

MAKING THE SLAB

■ Excavate to a depth that will accommodate the materials you will use.
■ Install 2× forms, referring to the information on page 120.
■ Spread, level, and tamp the gravel subbase and install reinforcing wire mesh.
■ Fill the forms with concrete, working from the far end of the path to the mixing site.
■ Consolidate the concrete by jabbing a shovel or 2×4 up and down in it.
■ Screed the surface.

FINISHING THE CONCRETE

Concrete finishing needs to start immediately after each section has been screeded. See page 123 for more information on floating and finishing.
■ Float and edge the surface.
■ Cut control joints at intervals equal to 1½ times the width of the walk (every 4½ feet for a 3-foot walk).

Colored and patterned concrete makes surfaces durable and attractive. Concrete paths and sidewalks can be finished the same way.

■ Apply custom finishes of your choice, as shown on pages 142–143.
■ Let the concrete cure for three days to a week.

BUILDING A CONCRETE WALK

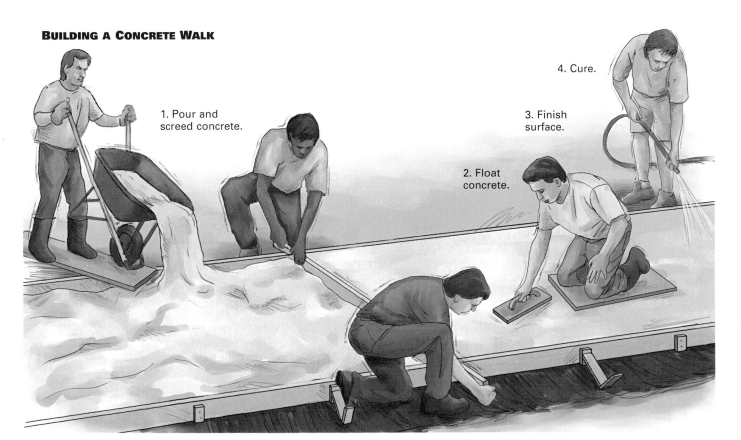

1. Pour and screed concrete.

2. Float concrete.

3. Finish surface.

4. Cure.

A well-planned deck is constructed in orderly steps. Here the site has been laid out and squared, postholes dug, footings poured, and framing for all sections completed. Decking for each section will be laid next, followed by railings, balusters, and steps.

DECK
CONSTRUCTION BASICS

You've decided on your deck design. You've selected the materials. You have all the permits and plans in hand. You know what you need to do and why. If your site is graded for drainage, your supplies have been delivered, and you have your friends lined up to help, it's time to start building.

Construction is different from planning in several key ways: Mistakes are more expensive, they can be dangerous, and they take longer to correct. So work carefully at an easy, steady pace, and use help from others whenever you can. The extra time you spend will pay off in reduced frustration and well-built results.

This chapter describes principles and techniques that can apply to any deck project. Instructions, though, do not account for every building site, all materials, or varied skill levels. Get more details or experienced help before taking on a task you don't understand.

WATCH WHERE YOU'RE GOING

By now you should have a complete construction schedule, which organizes the tasks you'll need to accomplish. If you haven't made one, do it now. Include every step of the project, from applying for your building permit to sending invitations to your first deck party. Then review the list, determine how much time each step will take, and add cost estimates and dates. Here's a sample to get you started:

- Order materials
- Grade building site for drainage
- Prepare outside of house
- Set up materials at work site
- Attach ledger board
- Set up batter boards
- Locate and pour footings and piers
- Set anchors and posts
- Install beams and joists
- Attach decking boards
- Install railings and balusters
- Build stairs
- Build additions such as benches
- Finish deck surface

Be sure to complete each task before starting the next one. Put everything away when you stop each day. Even if your neighborhood is secure and the weather won't harm materials left out overnight, keep the site orderly so you can start work again right away instead of hunting for materials buried under yesterday's scrap heap.

ANATOMY OF A DECK

The first step in building a deck is to familiarize yourself with some terms. Here's a quick deck-builder's dictionary:

BEAMS OR GIRDERS: Hefty framing members attached horizontally to the posts to support the upper deck structure.

DECKING BOARDS: 2× or ¾-inch stock attached to the joists to form the floor of the deck.

JOISTS: Horizontal framing members fastened on top of the beams or girders to support the decking. Joists can be either 16 or 24 inches *on center* (the distance between the centers of adjacent, parallel framing members in a series).

LATTICE: A grid-work of PVC or wood slats that conceals the base framing and keeps out windblown debris while permitting free airflow for ventilation. See page 166.

LEDGER: A horizontal support attached to the house to hold up one side of the deck.

PIERS: Masonry columns that support the posts and the structure above. Piers protect the posts from water and insect damage at ground level. On sites subject to frost heave, piers are supported by concrete footings poured to frost line. Consult your building department for frost line in your area. Where frost heave is not a factor, piers may be set on shallow bases, or footings.

POSTS: Timbers set on end (vertically) to support beams.

RISERS: Boards that enclose the vertical spaces between stairway treads—often omitted on deck and other exterior steps.

STAIR RAILS: Lumber that provides a safety barrier at the edges of the steps. Rails should be built so the handrail can be completely gripped by a person's hand and should be securely attached so they are strong enough to support a falling person's weight.

RAILINGS: Horizontal timbers that extend from one deck post to another to form a safety barrier at the perimeter of the structure. The term is often used to refer to the entire rail construction, including posts, top rails, and balusters/spindles. The balusters, the smallest vertical components, are positioned to fill the space between the top and bottom rails and between rail posts. Minimum baluster spacing for child safety is 4 inches.

SKIRT BOARDS: Finished lumber that covers and finishes the exposed face of rough perimeter joists.

STRINGERS: The long wood components that support the weight of the step load and to which the treads are attached.

TREADS: The horizontal stepping surfaces of a stairway.

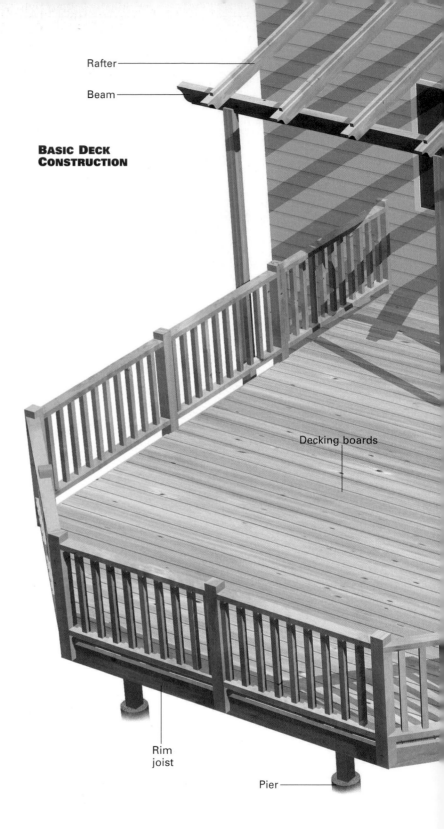

Rafter

Beam

BASIC DECK CONSTRUCTION

Decking boards

Rim joist

Pier

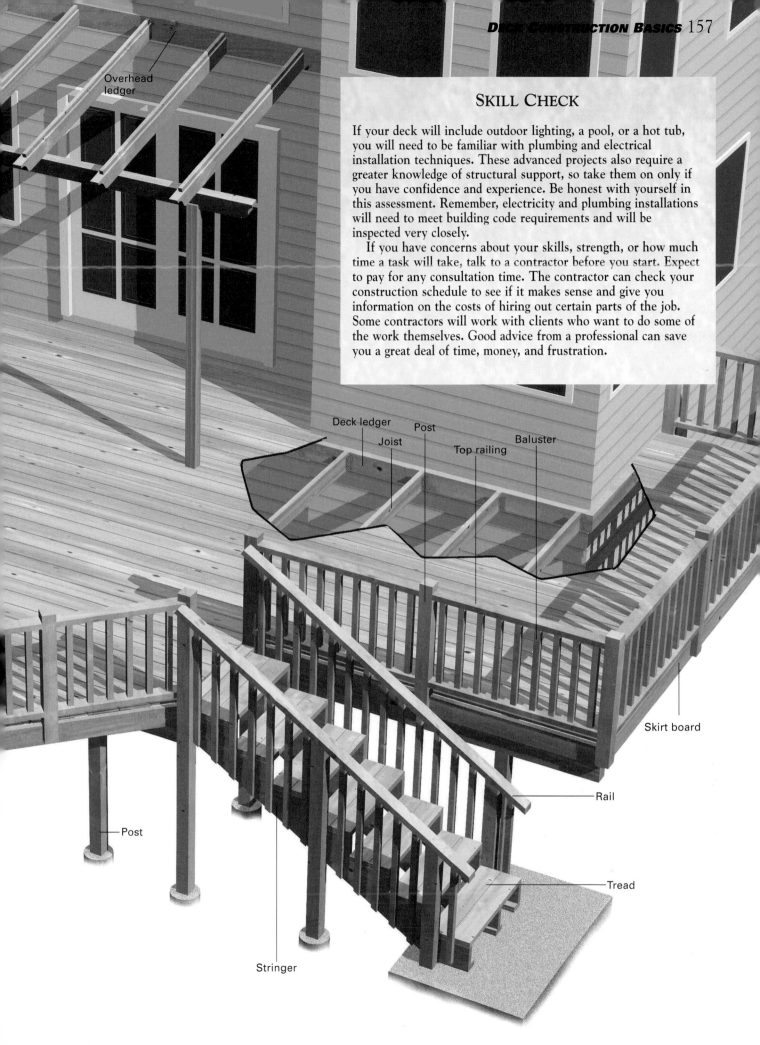

Overhead ledger

SKILL CHECK

If your deck will include outdoor lighting, a pool, or a hot tub, you will need to be familiar with plumbing and electrical installation techniques. These advanced projects also require a greater knowledge of structural support, so take them on only if you have confidence and experience. Be honest with yourself in this assessment. Remember, electricity and plumbing installations will need to meet building code requirements and will be inspected very closely.

If you have concerns about your skills, strength, or how much time a task will take, talk to a contractor before you start. Expect to pay for any consultation time. The contractor can check your construction schedule to see if it makes sense and give you information on the costs of hiring out certain parts of the job. Some contractors will work with clients who want to do some of the work themselves. Good advice from a professional can save you a great deal of time, money, and frustration.

Deck ledger

Post

Joist

Top railing

Baluster

Skirt board

Rail

Post

Tread

Stringer

INSTALLING THE LEDGER

The ledger attaches to a joist or joist header of the house and bears the weight of a deck. A poorly attached ledger can be a safety hazard.

Cut away siding in the area where the ledger will attach so you can fasten the ledger securely. Attach the ledger with bolts or lag screws. Lag screws must go through the sheathing and all the way into the joist or joist header, which sits on top of the sill on the house foundation. If you're attaching the ledger to a masonry wall, install the ledger flush with the surface with a Z-bar flashing or insert washers to provide airspace between the ledger and the house.

POSITIONING THE LEDGER

Place the ledger so the deck surface will be set below the door at the height your plans indicate (see page 131). Typically this means 1 inch to keep rain out, 3 inches to keep snow at bay. Be sure to allow for the thickness of the decking when setting the ledger.

POSITIONING THE LEDGER

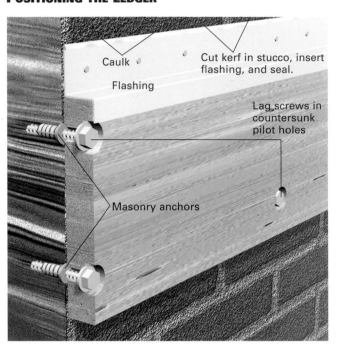

Caulk

Cut kerf in stucco, insert flashing, and seal.

Flashing

Lag screws in countersunk pilot holes

Masonry anchors

ATTACHING A LEDGER TO SIDING

REMOVING WOOD SIDING

Mark for ledger.

You can tack a 2×4 here as a guide to increase the accuracy of your cut.

LEDGER ON WOOD SIDING

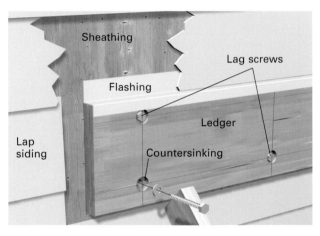

Sheathing

Lag screws

Flashing

Ledger

Lap siding

Countersinking

LEDGER WITH OVERHANGING SIDING

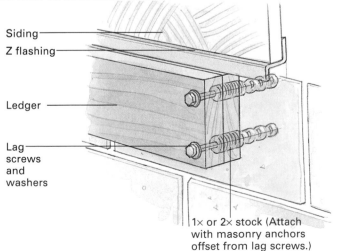

Siding

Z flashing

Ledger

Lag screws and washers

1× or 2× stock (Attach with masonry anchors offset from lag screws.)

LEDGER ON MASONRY

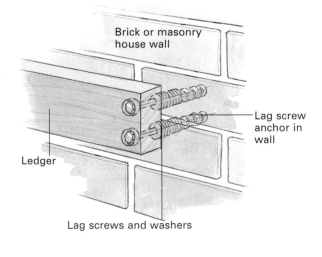

Brick or masonry house wall

Lag screw anchor in wall

Ledger

Lag screws and washers

LAYING OUT THE SITE

Whether you start the layout of your deck from a ledger or from a framing member of an existing deck, the next step is laying out the site for footings and post locations. Here's how to get things right.

THE STAKE-OUT

Drive temporary stakes at the corners of your layout. If you're building a cantilevered deck where the joist will extend beyond the beams, allow for the extension when you place the stakes.

TYPICAL DECK SITE LAYOUT

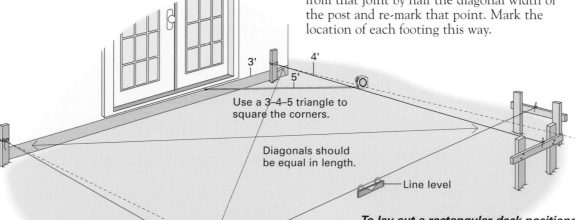

Use a 3-4-5 triangle to square the corners.

Diagonals should be equal in length.

Line level

Batter boards

SET BATTER BOARDS

Drive batter boards in the ground about 2 feet beyond the temporary stakes. Stretch mason's lines from the ledger (or a framing member, if you're expanding a deck) to the batter boards in all directions. Then tie a line between the other set of batter boards, across what will be the front edge of the deck. This line will be parallel to the ledger and will help you mark the footing locations. Don't worry if your angles aren't right on the money yet. That comes after you have all the lines tied.

Then square the corners with a 3-4-5 triangle (see right). Keep the lines level with a line level as you square them.

MARK THE POST LOCATIONS

When the mason's lines are square and level, you are ready to transfer the footing locations to the ground.

Depending on how you've drawn your plans, the intersection of the mason's lines represents one of two points—either the corner of your posts or their centers. It doesn't matter which, but you need to refer to your plan to make sure.

Drop a plumb bob at the intersection of the lines and mark the spot with a small stake. If this point represents the center of the posts, that's where you'll start digging footing holes. If the point is at the post corners, measure in from that joint by half the diagonal width of the post and re-mark that point. Mark the location of each footing this way.

To lay out a rectangular deck positioned against a house, use the ledger as your starting point and batter boards at the outside corners. Square the lines to the house using a 3-4-5 triangle. Then measure the diagonals.

SQUARING THE CORNERS: 3-4-5 TRIANGLE

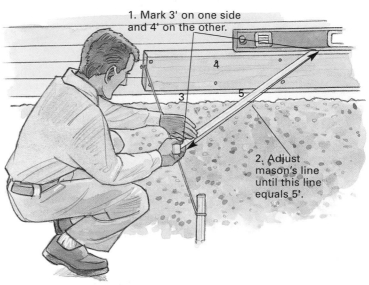

1. Mark 3' on one side and 4' on the other.

2. Adjust mason's line until this line equals 5'.

FOOTINGS AND PIERS

1. Set the post in the anchor and hold it in place with one or two nails or screws. Stake two braces in the ground and tack the other ends to the post.

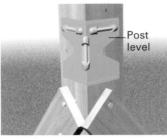

Post level

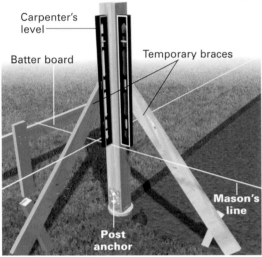

Carpenter's level

Batter board

Temporary braces

Post anchor

Mason's line

2. Using a carpenter's level or post level, check the post on two adjacent sides to make sure it is plumb in all directions. Adjust the braces as needed.

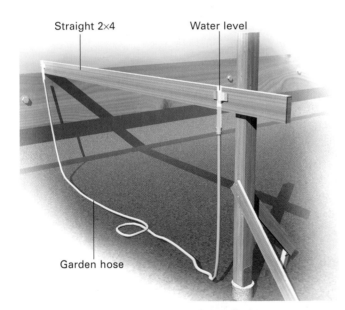

Straight 2×4

Water level

Garden hose

3. For any decks larger than 10×12 feet, checking for level between the ledger and a corner post can be a difficult job. One person can hardly hold both ends of the level, read it, and adjust it all at once. An inexpensive water level makes this task easy. For smaller decks use mason's line and a line level or a straight board and a carpenter's level.

The building codes in your area will have a lot to say about the kind of footings you need. In some localities posts set in concrete or tamped earth and gravel may be OK. Other municipalities will require above-grade posts set on piers and footings. In this case footings must reach below the frost line to keep them from heaving when the ground freezes.

To prevent moisture damage to the posts, set your finished footings and piers slightly above grade. If you plan to set post anchors directly in wet concrete without piers, use tube forms. If you plan to pour the footings first and add piers later, make sure your footings are high enough so the piers will keep the posts above ground level.

DIGGING THE HOLES

With a clamshell digger or auger, dig the footing holes. (See page 73 for typical footing dimensions.)

Pour 4 inches of loose gravel in the hole to help water drain away from the footings. If you are using prefabricated forms, attach them to a 2×4 frame so they are set at the correct level—the bottom of the form should be approximately 8 inches above the bottom of the hole.

If you're installing posts below grade, put them in and brace them as shown on page 169 before pouring the concrete or tamping in earth and gravel.

POURING FOOTINGS

No matter what kind of concrete you use—pre-mix bags or mix-your-own—it's best to mix it in batches, one hole at a time, unless you have a crew of helpers.

Shovel the mixed concrete carefully into the footing hole, pushing the mixture down with a scrap 2×2 to force out any air bubbles. Once the footing is filled, smooth it with a trowel and, if you haven't used tube forms, slope its surface to let water drain away. Install the post anchor or J-bolt. Once the footings and piers or anchors are in place, the concrete needs three days to a week to cure.

SETTING CORNER POSTS

Treat the bottom of each post with a protective sealer at least one day before you set the posts in the anchors. Pour the sealer in a shallow pan and soak each post for a few minutes before setting it up to dry.

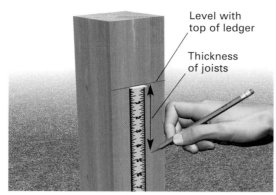

4. Mark the point on the post that is level with the top edge of the ledger. Measure down by the thickness of the joists, and mark the post.

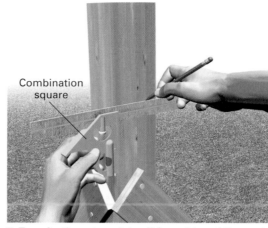

5. Transfer the cut mark to all four sides of the post using a combination square. Check the post height against the ledger for level one more time before cutting.

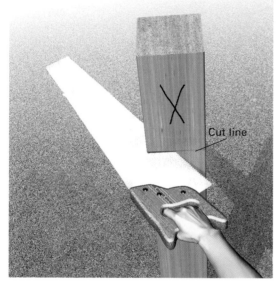

6. Cut through the post at the marks with a handsaw or reciprocating saw. Check the opposite side often to make sure the blade doesn't wander.

7. After marking and cutting the posts, and while the braces are still attached, fasten the post to the anchor with the hardware recommended by the manufacturer. In the absence of specific directions, ask your hardware retailer for information.

Set the corner posts first. That way you will have a benchmark from which to level all the posts with the ledger.
■ Place a corner post in an anchor; hold it temporarily with decking screws.
■ Brace the post with scrap 1×4 lumber angled to ground stakes.
■ Check the post on two adjacent sides for plumb with a post level or a carpenter's level.
■ Adjust the bracing as needed.

If you plan to cut the post in place, fasten its base securely with lag screws. If you are going to remove posts for cutting, don't fasten them securely. In either case, leave the braces in place as you continue.
■ Using a water level, a line level on a taut mason's line, or a 48-inch carpenter's level placed on a long, straight 2×4, mark the post level with the top edges of the ledger.

If your posts will extend above the deck, use this line as a reference when you install the beams and joists. If the posts won't extend above the deck, mark them as follows:
■ Measure down from the line by the depth of the joists and mark this point.
■ Use a combination square to make a line and to transfer the line to all four faces of the post. This is where you will cut.
■ Mark an X on one side of a line to indicate the waste portion.
■ Set and mark the remaining corner posts in the same way.
■ Cut the corner posts as illustrated above.

LEVEL THE REST

Once you have the corner posts cut, install the remaining posts and use the following method to mark them.
■ Stretch a chalk line between the tops of the corner posts and snap it on the uncut posts. This puts your cutting line level on all posts. Cut the posts as before.

INSTALLING BEAMS AND JOISTS

Once the ledger and posts are in place, install the beam(s) that support(s) the joists and decking. Beams run parallel to the ledger. They fasten to the posts, and the number of beams increases as the span away from the house increases.

MOUNTING

Mount the beams on the sides of the posts or on top, using the method that best suits the specific requirements of your design and construction details. Make certain that any joints fall directly over the center of a post so they get adequate support.

INSTALLING RIM JOISTS

Rim joists are the outer joists of the deck frame and typically define its edges.
■ End joists are attached to the ends of the ledger.
■ A header ties the ends of the joists together.

Use angle brackets to attach end joists to the ledger and the header to the end joists.

Brace each end joist against the ledger and the beam or corner post. Level it and fasten it with an angle bracket. Fasten the end joists to the beam or corner post with lag screws or bolts (see "Fasteners," page 74). Brace the header against the end joists and nail it.

INSTALLING INNER JOISTS

Inner joists will bear the weight of the decking and everything that goes on it.

MEASURE AND MARK: Measure from the outside edge of the end joist and, on the ledger, mark the location of center of the first joist hanger (use the spacing you derived from your span calculations—usually 16 inches). Then mark the center points for the remaining joists at the same interval.

Using a combination square, mark the ledger for the edges of the joist hangers.

TEST ALIGNMENT: Place a scrap piece in a joist hanger and line up the top edge flush with the ledger. Remove the scrap and nail one side of the hanger in place. Fit the scrap in the hanger again to make sure it has not spread, and nail the other side.

Then measure and mark the joist locations on the beam or header joist. Insert each inner joist in its hanger and nail the hangers to the joists.

LAPPING JOISTS: If your deck design requires joists longer than standard lengths,

DECK FRAMING

Attach beams to posts with beam/post hangers or seismic ties. After marking the joist ends, cut them and attach the header joist.

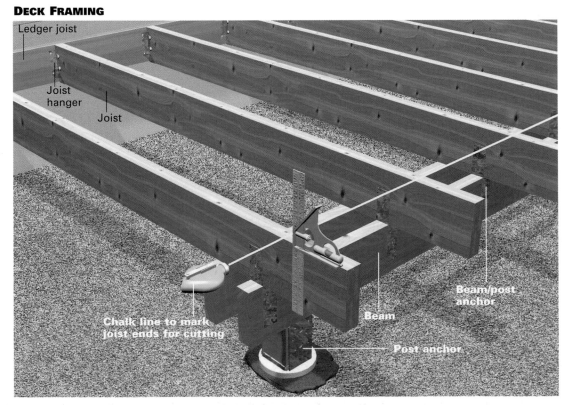

Ledger joist

Joist hanger

Joist

Chalk line to mark joist ends for cutting

Beam/post anchor

Beam

Post anchor

lap or splice two joists over a beam. To lap them allow each joist to extend 8 to 12 inches beyond the beam, nail them together from both sides, and anchor them with seismic ties. If you lap the joists, be sure you shift the markings on the header before installing the hangers.

To splice joists, butt the ends on the center of an interior beam. Nail cleats of the same stock to both sides of the butt joint.

DECKING PATTERNS

In the simplest and most straightforward decking pattern, the boards are laid perpendicular to the joists, but there are many ways to vary this layout.

Some variations won't require you to alter the subframing. Others will. Most diagonal patterns, for example, won't require framing modifications, but alternating diagonal modules will.

The key to making decking patterns safe is to recognize that offset patterns mean that deck boards have to span a longer distance than perpendicular decking. This may require closer joist spacing or stronger decking. If you want to change the direction of the pattern within the surface of the deck, or if you wish to lay out an elaborate design, you will have to plan the direction of the joists accordingly.

When planning unusual decking patterns, remember to design structural framing members carefully. The cut ends of each board must always be centered on a joist.

For simple patterns such as perpendiculars and diagonals, install the joists and scatter the butted ends of decking randomly across the surface.

For more complex styles such as basket weaves and herringbones, support each modular decking unit with framing. Typically this means installing blocking at regular intervals, with joists often doubled to receive the edge of the decking pattern.

FASTENERS

In general, hex-head or carriage bolts provide more strength to structural joints than lag screws—if you can get a wrench on one or both sides of the joint. If you can't, because a joist or bracket is in the way, use lag screws. Bolts give you the chance to tighten joints that loosen.

BUILDING A CANTILEVERED DECK

Not all decks have their edges neatly corresponding to the edges of the posts and beams. Cantilevered decks have joists that extend past their beams. The header joist, parallel to the ledger and tying together the ends of the extended joists, is not supported directly by the beams or posts (see illustration at right).

ADVANTAGES:
This design is often very attractive and can make it possible for you to build a larger deck than you could with a corner-post design.

For example, cantilevering can extend a deck out over a slope that is too steep or rocky to allow footings and posts at the corners. Such an extension creates space that otherwise might not be used.

Cantilevering creates a floating effect on a deck of any size. With footings inside the perimeter of the deck, the structure appears to hang in space.

PRIME RULE:
Local codes will govern the length of the overhang, but in general, no more than a third of the deck's total area should extend beyond the outer beam. The distance from the ledger to the beam should be at least twice the distance of the overhang.

The beam that supports a cantilevered deck can be a single board, a pair of boards mounted on either side of the posts, or a laminated beam of two or three boards fastened together. Such laminated beams can likewise rest in post caps or flank the posts.

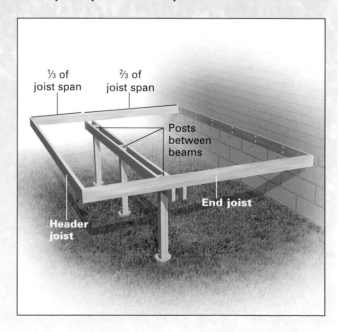

⅓ of joist span

⅔ of joist span

Posts between beams

End joist

Header joist

INSTALLING DECKING

Width of decking
board, plus gap

As you approach the ledger or header, check the remaining distance to make sure the last board will fit. Remember to include the gaps in your measurements. Adjust the gaps between the last few decking boards so everything fits. If the differences are too great to correct with small adjustments, rip the last board to fit.

Because decking provides the surface appearance of your deck, you may want to invest a little more for high-quality lumber—cedar or redwood. Even if you choose to use pressure-treated lumber for your decking, measure and install it with care.

STARTER BOARD

This is the first board laid either at the header joist or along the house. Starting at the header allows you to make minor adjustments to spacing next to the house, where it won't be as noticeable.

In either case, measure and cut the starter board to the exact length of the deck and fasten it in place.

THE REST OF THE DECK

Lay out the remaining decking with ends overhanging the joists—you will cut them off later. Before you start to fasten the decking, arrange it so joints are centered on joists and fall in a random pattern.

SPACE untreated lumber ⅛ inch apart (an 8d nail makes a handy spacer). Butt treated lumber together—it will shrink the first year.

FASTEN each board with nails or decking screws, drilling pilot holes at butt joints (or on all of the ends) to avoid splitting.

FIXING BOW & WARP

Pull back to
increase gap

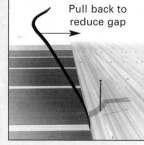

Pull back to
reduce gap

If some decking boards have slight bows (and they will), you can correct them during installation.

Fasten the bowed board at each end, then insert a flat pry bar along the bow.

For an inward bow, fit the pry bar between the last finished board and the bowed one, and pull back until the bowed board is straight. Fasten before you let go.

For an outward bow, drive the pry bar into the joist next to the bow, pull back on the bar to straighten the board, and nail or screw it in place.

As you approach the ledger (or the header, if you have started at the house), lay the boards exactly as you will fasten them and make adjustments in the spacing. (You may have to rip the final boards to fit.) Leave a ¼-inch space between the last board and the house to allow for expansion.

TRIM THE ENDS: When all the decking is fastened, snap a chalk line from the starter board to the ledger and trim the ends of the decking with a circular saw. Tack a 1×4 on the decking to keep the saw on the line. Set the saw to the exact depth of the decking to avoid scoring the face of the end joists.

OTHER PATTERNS

The instructions above describe the method for laying a standard decking pattern. When using a diagonal pattern, joists must typically be spaced 12 inches on center.

To lay your starter board, measure 3 feet from a corner on both the header and end joist. Start at this point and lay decking on either side of the starter board. Cut the boards to fit at the ledger and trim the excess as above. A herringbone pattern is a zigzag, which also requires joists on 12-inch centers. Double every other joist so the decking joints meet on them at right angles. Measure from a corner to the first double joist and mark this distance on the header. Lay the starter board at a 45-degree angle on this mark and the next board at 90 degrees to the first one.

Chalk line — Cut notches to thickness of post

If the posts in your deck design extend upward to support a canopy or railing, notch the decking to fit around the posts. Cut into the decking board by the thickness of the post, then chisel out the material between cuts.

JOINTS

Use full-length boards where possible. Make sure joints butt together over the center of the joists and nail 2×4 cleats to the joists under the decking. Staggering the joints will also increase their strength and will greatly improve the appearance of the deck.

To reduce squeaks and fastener pops, use a deck adhesive and spiral or ringshank nails or deck screws—two fasteners for 4-inch stock, three for 6-inch boards. Drive the fasteners at a slight angle toward each other.

Treated lumber is dense, so it may help to predrill it before putting in fasteners. If any wood is splitting, predrill it.

NAILING TIPS

Cordless tools are convenient, but a variable-speed corded drill won't stop you when batteries need charging. It will keep going as long as you do.

You can get a good idea where to drive nails or screws by watching the joist beyond the boards. But to line them up consistently, lay a carpenter's square against the decking and parallel to the joist.

If the nails you're using tend to split the decking boards and you can't always drill pilot holes, try blunting the tip of each nail before installing it. This prevents most minor splits.

After you've snapped a chalk line, use your circular saw to trim the edges of the decking. Set the saw to just the thickness of the decking.

TRIMMING DECK BOARDS

BUILDING RAILINGS

If you plan to extend the posts above the surface (right), fasten the end and header joists to the posts and add fascia boards for a finished appearance. Lattice panels (below) make inexpensive and attractive infill for railings.

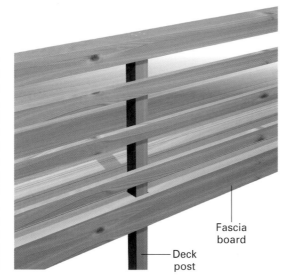

Fascia board

Deck post

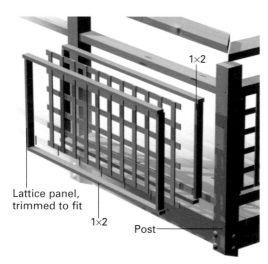

1×2

Lattice panel, trimmed to fit

1×2

Post

A simple spacing jig keeps balusters evenly spaced. Place each baluster tightly against the jig, then fasten the baluster to the rails with nails or screws.

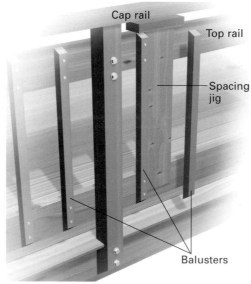

Cap rail

Top rail

Spacing jig

Balusters

For most railings, install the posts first, then the rails, then the balusters, and finally, any decorative trim. The balusters illustrated on these pages are cut from 2×2s, but you can use other styles as well—spindled, turned, and even 2x stock set edge-out.

ESSENTIALS

Most building codes require railings on decks built 18 inches or more above the ground—in some areas, even less than that.

Typical codes also set a minimum height for railings, usually 36 or 42 inches. Your local codes will also specify the distance between posts, the openings under the railings, and baluster spacing (usually no less than 4 inches and no more than 6 inches).

In a popular railing installation that is one of the easiest to build, posts are attached to the header and end joists. This system allows you to add the railings after installing the framing and decking. Because you'll be working along the outside edges of the deck, you'll have easy access to each post.

INSTALLING POSTS

If the posts don't already extend above the deck, add your new posts beginning at the house and corners. Attach 4×4 railing posts to the facing at least every 6 feet. Install posts at your stair location too.

Installation is the same no matter where you locate the posts. Here's what you do:
■ Mark each post location. Then cut the posts to length and predrill them for ⅜ hex-head bolts (offset and countersink the holes) or carriage bolts. If you can't get a bolt in, use lag screws. Then make any decorative cuts.
■ Set each post plumb and run the drill bit through the holes to mark the joist. Drill ⅜-inch holes through the joist (pilot holes for lag screws) and fasten the post in place with ⅜×7-inch fasteners.
■ When the corner posts are in place, divide the space between them equally and at a spacing that conforms to local codes. Snap a chalk line between the bottoms of the corner posts so their outside faces will lie in the same plane. Then mark, cut, and install the remaining posts, using the fasteners for which you predrilled the holes.

Use the same marking methods for top-mounted posts set in anchors on the decking.

INSTALLING RAILINGS

To set the railings first mark the rail locations on the posts and cut the rail stock to fit.
■ Attach the bottom rail first, about 3 inches above the decking.
■ Fasten the top rail from the underside or sides to hide the screw holes.
■ Hold side-mounted rails in position and cut the joints so they are centered on a post.

Predrill the rails and drive two 3-inch galvanized decking screws just through the other side. Place the rail at the mark and press the screw tip into the post, then drive one screw at one end and one at the other. Finish by driving all screws home.

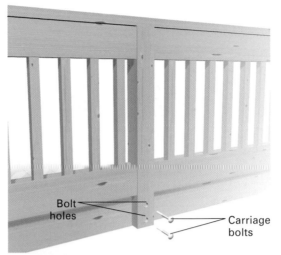

Bolt holes

Carriage bolts

Simplest of all methods, attach posts to the faces of end and header joists. Drill and countersink pilot holes in the posts, then fasten the posts to the joists with lag screws, hex-head bolts, or carriage bolts.

INSTALL THE CAP

Use a straight 2×6 or 2×8 that is low in moisture content and free of large knots. Buy the longest boards you can find and center any joints over posts. Bevel the joints and seal the cut ends to reduce moisture damage.
■ Position each piece so it overhangs the post and the top rail, and mark it for cutting.
■ Attach it with 12d finish nails or screws driven into the posts—and into the top rail if it is flush with the top of the post—driving a fastener every 8 inches.
■ Countersink the screw heads or use a nail set to drive the finish nails below the surface.
■ Fill the holes with putty, let them dry, and sand them smooth.

Miter the outside corners to keep them from separating, warping, or splitting. Attach the pieces by drilling pilot holes and driving screws.

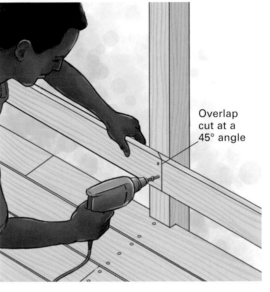

Overlap cut at a 45° angle

If you must splice the rails, cut the ends at 45-degree angles and join the boards in the middle of a post.

INSTALL THE BALUSTERS

Purchase ready-cut balusters or make your own from 2×2s. You may want to angle-cut one or both ends on the outside faces. Determine where you will drive the fasteners. Set a group of balusters side by side, use a framing square to mark fastener positions, then drill pilot holes.

Construct a jig to help maintain consistent spacing between the balusters.
■ Attach the balusters with 2½-inch fasteners, bottom first, flush with the bottom of the lower rail.
■ Install the first baluster plumb, then align the next few.
■ Check every five or six balusters to see that they are still plumb; reposition an errant baluster if necessary.

Rail

Pilot hole drilled at 45° angle

Work carefully when attaching flat-laid rails between posts. To avoid splintering, drill pilot holes at a 45-degree angle, then drive screws or nails.

A carefully chosen color scheme helps the structure complement the rest of your landscape to minimize or dramatize its presence.

Before you add a shed, decide whether you want to highlight it as a feature or downplay its appearance. Bright paint, flowers, weather vanes, and hanging relics make sheds stand out. Dark, neutral paints and stains, evergreen plantings, and less prominent placement can make your shed subordinate to the rest of your landscape.

Your landscape can meet specific needs just as rooms in your house do. A spot for firewood is an inexpensive yet valuable asset, and it's easy to add. Building this storage area against an existing wall cuts construction costs and keeps the wood stacked neatly. This design easily can be adapted from the first plan in this chapter for a lean-to shed.

BUILDING SHEDS

Over time, most people accumulate more tools, equipment, and supplies for outdoor maintenance than they can comfortably store on the patio or in a corner of the garage. That's when it's time to consider a shed.

When you build a shed think big from the start. In just a few years you'll probably outgrow a shed that seemed too big when you built it.

The designs in this chapter follow the same basic construction sequence and can be built to any size and with any design accents. Whether you're looking for a basic shed, a storage unit attached to the house, or a place for potting, you'll find a design here that meets your needs.

Each plan includes a materials list, with some of the quantities translated into linear feet or square feet to help you estimate costs. When you go to buy materials, take the plans with you. Study the plans to determine how many pieces of lap siding or sheets of vertical siding you need. The lumber salesperson can help you determine amounts.

All the designs in this chapter use the frame layout method illustrated below and on page 97. Use the instructions on pages 96–99 to lay out your site with this method, and remember that even though the plans on the following pages include dimensions, take measurements on-site before cutting any piece of lumber to ensure accuracy.

LAYING OUT THE SITE

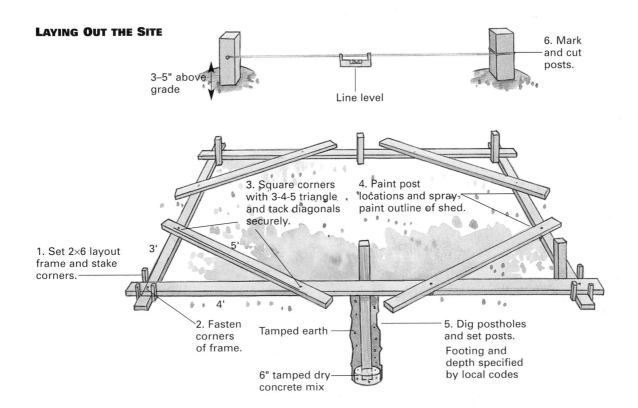

3–5" above grade

Line level

6. Mark and cut posts.

3. Square corners with 3-4-5 triangle and tack diagonals securely.

4. Paint post locations and spray-paint outline of shed.

1. Set 2×6 layout frame and stake corners.

3'

5'

2. Fasten corners of frame.

Tamped earth

4'

6" tamped dry concrete mix

5. Dig postholes and set posts.

Footing and depth specified by local codes

LEAN-TO SHED

If rakes, shovels, and other outdoor tools usually end up leaning against your house or are shoved into a corner of the garage, this medium-size lean-to shed is an easy way to corral them. You can build it in a weekend at little cost.

This easy-to-build shed hangs on a garage or house wall, so you could finish the exterior to match the house or garage siding. (If you prefer, build it as a freestanding shed by constructing a stud wall for the back with a top plate to support the joists. Install sheathing and siding on the back wall to complete the shed.)

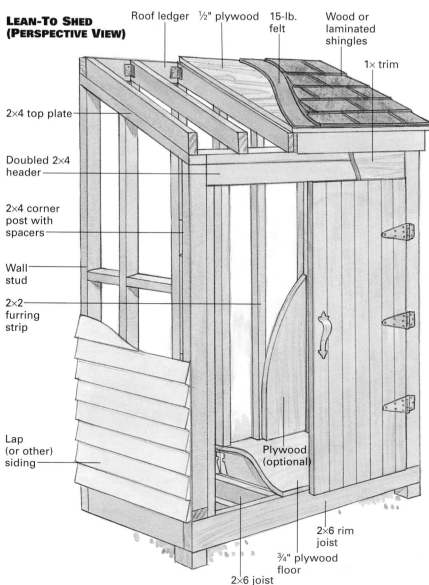

LEAN-TO SHED (PERSPECTIVE VIEW)

- Roof ledger
- ½" plywood
- 15-lb. felt
- Wood or laminated shingles
- 1× trim
- 2×4 top plate
- Doubled 2×4 header
- 2×4 corner post with spacers
- Wall stud
- 2×2 furring strip
- Lap (or other) siding
- Plywood (optional)
- 2×6 rim joist
- ¾" plywood floor
- 2×6 joist

If you like, add a worktable supported by diagonal 2×4s to make a potting shed. If you modify the design or dimensions of the structure, be sure to make a scale drawing of the unit before beginning its construction. Use naturally resistant woods or pressure-treated lumber rated for ground contact for the posts and floor framing. Use exterior-grade plywood for the floor. For more information on basic building techniques, refer to pages 102–116.

MARKING THE LOCATION

The shed attaches to an existing wall with two ledgers—a 2×4 for the roof and a 2×6 for the floor. Locate the shed so the roof ledger is centered on the studs of the house wall. Look for a nail line in the siding or use a stud finder to locate them. You can install either ledger first, but it is often easier to mark the location of the roof ledger and drop a plumb bob to mark the position of the floor ledger. If your house or garage has lap siding, plan the height of the roof ledger so the siding of the shed lines up with that on the house.

SETTING THE LEDGERS

Cut the roof ledger, the floor ledger, and the rim joist to length and clamp them together with their top edges flush. Starting at one end, mark the tops of the boards at 16-inch intervals. The marks on the 2×4 correspond to the rafters; those on the 2×6s indicate the locations for the centers of the joist hangers. Unclamp the boards and install the floor ledger as illustrated at right, with the bottom of the ledger about 3 inches above the ground. This height allows sufficient ventilation to prevent rot and mildew, yet isn't so high that it requires a step up into the shed. Install the roof ledger directly above the floor ledger.

FILLING IN THE GAPS

The floor ledger must be mounted on the same plane as the house siding, which is easy if the siding extends past the ledger location. But if the ledger attaches to the building foundation, install spacer boards behind it to bring the ledger flush. If the position of the roof ledger puts the floor ledger partly on the siding and partly on the foundation, install spacers under the lower section of the ledger. Then countersink the fasteners for the spacer boards so the ledger lies flat.

PREPARING THE GRADE

Once the ledger is in place, excavate the area 4 inches deep, extending about 4 feet from the wall. Cover the area with landscape fabric and cover the fabric with coarse crushed stone to discourage weeds and to provide good drainage.

SETTING THE POSTS

Mark the location of the supporting posts or piers. (Local codes may specify which type of foundation to use.) Square the locations with a 3-4-5 triangle, as shown on page 169. You may have to take down the mason's lines when you dig the postholes, but put them back up for guidance when you set the posts.

Whatever foundation you employ, leave about a foot of post standing above grade. Stretch a line from the bottom of the floor ledger to each post. Level the line with a line level and mark the posts. Cut them square at the mark with a reciprocating saw.

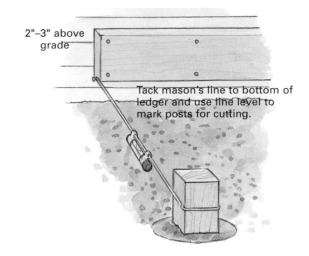

2"–3" above grade

Tack mason's line to bottom of ledger and use line level to mark posts for cutting.

FLOOR FRAMING PLAN

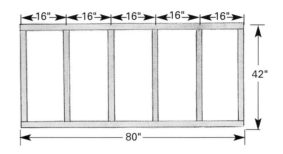

16" 16" 16" 16" 16"

42"

80"

BUILDING THE FLOOR

Center the joist hangers on the marks you made on the ledger and rim joist. Toenail the rim joist to the posts, then face-nail the end joists, reinforcing them with angle brackets. Then place the joists in the hangers. Fasten down the plywood floor with 10d nails spaced 6 inches apart on the perimeter and every 10 inches in the field.

MATERIALS LIST

FOUNDATION, FLOOR, AND WALLS
- Posts(check local codes)   4×4×8', 2
- Joists   2×6×8', 5
- Floor (¾" plywood)   4×8', 1
- Studs, plates, rafters, header   2×4×8', 23
     2×4×6', 6
- Siding   300 sq. ft.
- Trim   1×8×8', 7

ROOF
- Area   30 sq. ft.
- Shingles   ½ square
- Roof (½" plywood)   4×8', 1

LEAN-TO SHED
continued

CONSTRUCTING THE SIDEWALLS

Following the framing plan at right, preassemble the sidewall units. The blocking allows you to install any kind of siding on the shed, but you can leave it out for lap siding. Fasten the sidewalls to the floor and the house or garage wall. Toenail the roof ledger into the top plate to tie them together.

FURRING THE BACK WALL

You can leave the exterior house or garage wall that is exposed inside the shed as is, but installing 2×2 furring strips and sheathing allows more shelf and storage options. Place a furring strip adjacent to each sidewall to provide a nailing surface for the sheathing at both ends. If you add perforated hardboard, place 1× spacers between the hardboard and the sheathing to leave space to insert the hangers.

BUILDING THE FRONT WALL

As shown in the framing plan at right, the front wall consists of two jack studs, a header, and a top plate. The header is built from two 2×4s with ½-inch plywood spacers to make it 3½ inches thick. This particular design accommodates the double door shown on page 170 and other doors as well. To provide for a narrower door, add jack studs to the opening. Preassemble the wall, place it between the sidewall corner posts, and nail it in place.

ERECTING THE SIDEWALLS

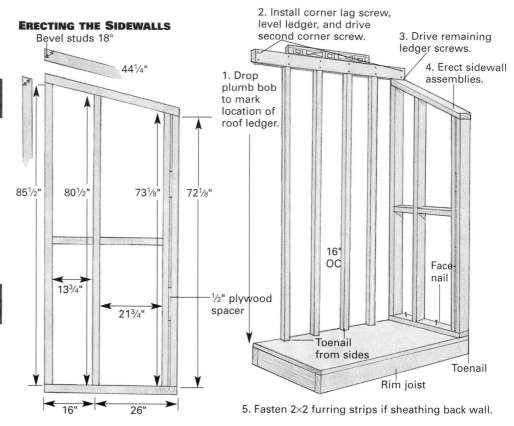

Bevel studs 18°

2. Install corner lag screw, level ledger, and drive second corner screw.

3. Drive remaining ledger screws.

1. Drop plumb bob to mark location of roof ledger.

4. Erect sidewall assemblies.

16" OC

Face-nail

Toenail from sides

Toenail

Rim joist

5. Fasten 2×2 furring strips if sheathing back wall.

INSTALLING THE FRONT WALL

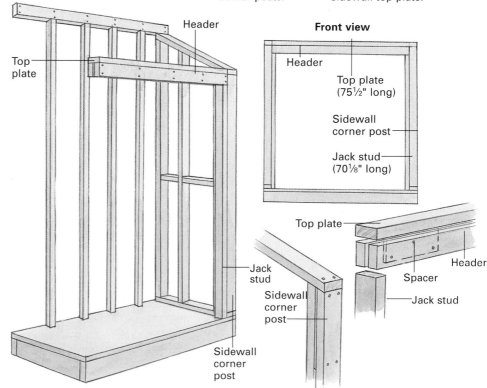

1. Measure and cut front-wall framing.

2. Nail jack studs to corner posts.

3. Toenail header to jack studs and corner posts.

4. Face-nail top plate to header and toenail to sidewall top plate.

Header

Top plate

Front view

Header

Top plate (75½" long)

Sidewall corner post

Jack stud (70⅛" long)

Top plate

Header

Spacer

Jack stud

Jack stud

Sidewall corner post

Sidewall corner post

FINISHING THE SHED

Install the siding before the roof for added strength and structural stability, but fasten the end rafters in place first so you can measure and attach the siding accurately. Attach the siding with rustproof nails.

Install the rafters and cut the roof sheathing from exterior-grade plywood ($46\frac{1}{2} \times 82$ inches for the shed shown). The rafters do not have a bird's-mouth cut because the short span and relatively small roof size do not require the added surface support. Refer to the illustration below and the instructions on pages 110–111, then cover the sheathing with 15-pound felt paper and laminated composition shingles, shakes, or treated wood shingles. Untreated wood shingles require open sheathing to permit adequate air circulation (see page 112). Install flashing where the shed roof meets the house or garage siding and install metal drip edges at the rakes

and eaves if you are installing composition shingles.

The width of the trim on the front wall varies depending on the kind of siding you use. A 1×6 might be sufficient with $\frac{1}{2}$-inch siding. In most cases, however, you'll have to measure the combined thickness of the jack stud, the sidewall, and the siding, then rip the trim from a 1×8.

ASSEMBLING THE DOORS

The doors are built with 2×4 box frames faced with 1×6 planking. For easy opening and closing, each door is $\frac{1}{4}$ inch shorter than the opening and $\frac{1}{4}$ inch narrower than half the width of the opening to allow a $\frac{1}{8}$-inch space on all sides. Door construction is shown below.

The planking extends 3 inches above and below the door frame so it covers both the header and most of the rim joist, which would otherwise be exposed. The header and rim joist also act as stops for the doors in this design.

Install the door with T- or strap hinges that will allow at least two screws to be driven into the door frame. Use 3-inch screws to attach the hinges to the door and through the trim into the jack stud.

ROOFING, SIDING, TRIM, AND DOORS

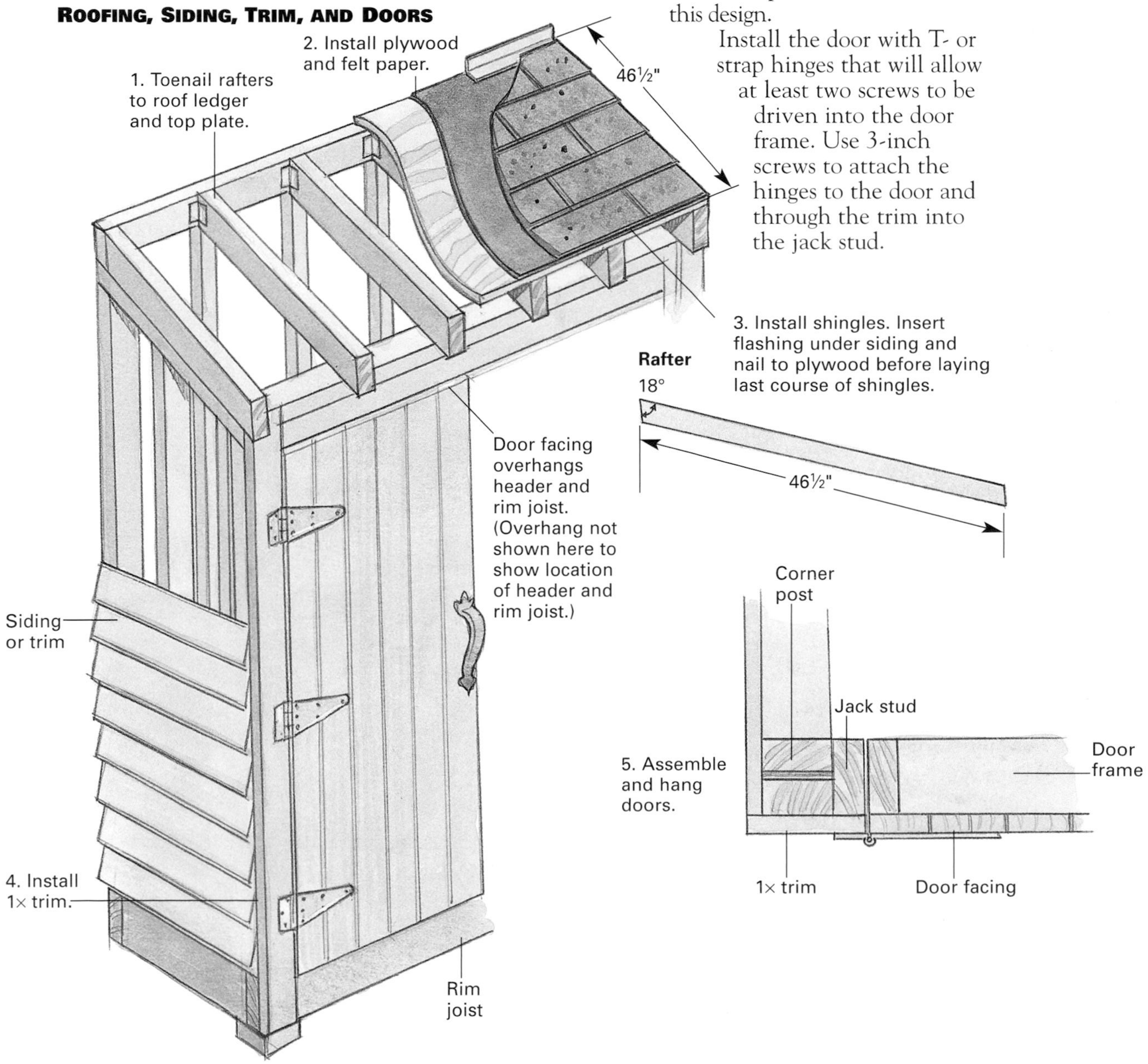

1. Toenail rafters to roof ledger and top plate.

2. Install plywood and felt paper.

$46\frac{1}{2}$"

3. Install shingles. Insert flashing under siding and nail to plywood before laying last course of shingles.

Rafter
18°

$46\frac{1}{2}$"

Door facing overhangs header and rim joist. (Overhang not shown here to show location of header and rim joist.)

Siding or trim

4. Install 1× trim.

Rim joist

Corner post

Jack stud

Door frame

5. Assemble and hang doors.

1× trim

Door facing

BASIC GARDEN SHED

Built on a 10×12-foot area, this versatile garden shed is both practical and stylish.

Whether you build exactly from the plans or modify the design, pay particular attention to the window opening. Before you assemble the window wall, determine the exact rough opening for the unit you will install. A 5×6-foot window may require a rough opening larger or smaller than 60×72 inches. If you plan to install a salvaged window, get the window first, then cut the rough opening ½ to 1 inch taller and wider than the window frame.

GARDEN SHED (PERSPECTIVE VIEW)

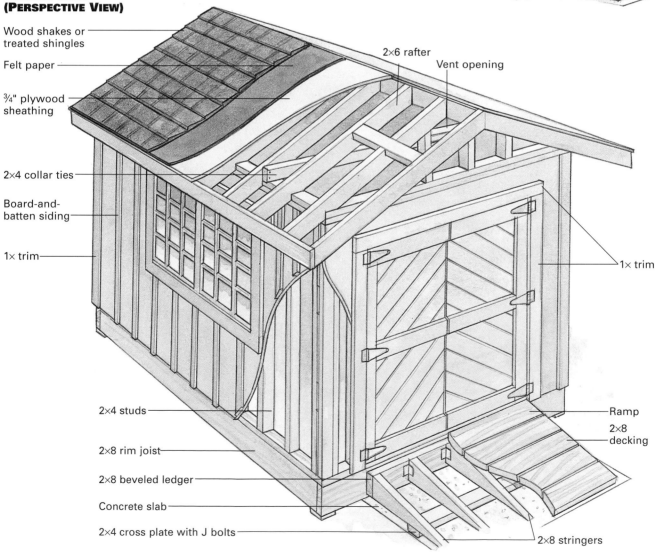

Wood shakes or treated shingles

Felt paper

¾" plywood sheathing

2×4 collar ties

Board-and-batten siding

1× trim

2×4 studs

2×8 rim joist

2×8 beveled ledger

Concrete slab

2×4 cross plate with J bolts

2×6 rafter

Vent opening

1× trim

Ramp

2×8 decking

2×8 stringers

PREPARE THE SITE

Lay out the site with the frame layout shown on page 101. Excavate 4 to 6 inches and fill the excavation with coarse crushed gravel. Cover it with landscape fabric. Cut the posts 2 to 3 inches above grade to allow air circulation. Then frame the floor.

FRAMING THE FLOOR

Using the techniques illustrated on pages 102–103, assemble the floor frame on the posts, marking the rim joists and installing joist hangers.

Tack the perimeter joists to the posts and recheck the frame for square by taking diagonal measurements. Cover the floor with ¾-inch exterior-grade plywood, starting with a full sheet set flush with a frame corner.

MATERIALS LIST

FOUNDATION, FLOOR, AND WALLS
- Posts (check local codes) 4×4×8', 4
- Joists, ramp stringers, ledger 2×8×10', 11
  2×8×12', 6
- Floor (¾" plywood) 4×8', 4
- Studs, plates, blocking 2×4×8', 48
  2×4×10', 10
  2×4×12', 6
- Header 2×10×12', 2
- Siding 325 sq. ft.
- Trim 1×4, 54'
  1×3, 32'
  1×6, 15'

ROOF
- Area 200 sq. ft.
- Shingles 2½ squares
- Rafters 2×6×14', 12
- Roof (½" plywood) 4×8', 8
- Fascia 1×8×14', 2

ERECTING THE WALLS

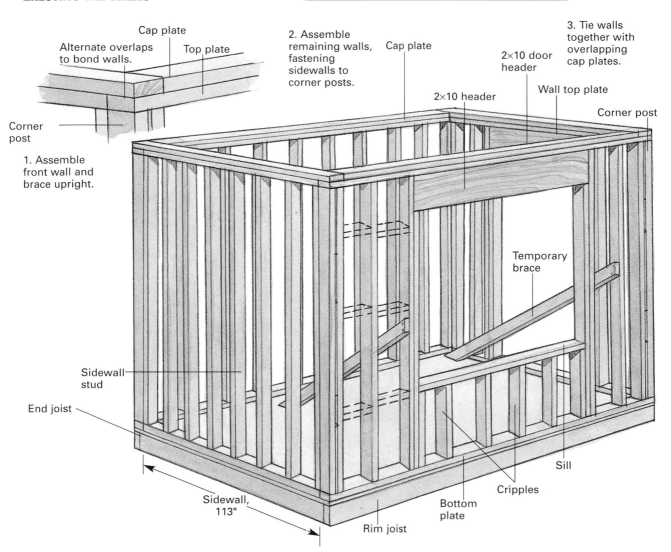

Cap plate

Alternate overlaps to bond walls.

Top plate

Corner post

1. Assemble front wall and brace upright.

2. Assemble remaining walls, fastening sidewalls to corner posts.

Cap plate

2×10 header

2×10 door header

3. Tie walls together with overlapping cap plates.

Wall top plate

Corner post

Temporary brace

Sidewall stud

End joist

Sidewall, 113"

Rim joist

Bottom plate

Cripples

Sill

BASIC GARDEN SHED
continued

FRONT WALL

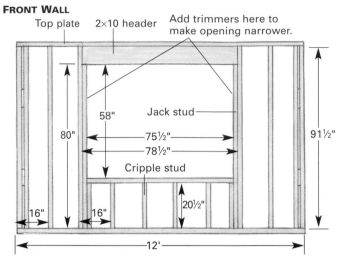

Top plate   2×10 header   Add trimmers here to make opening narrower.

58"   Jack stud
80"   75½"   91½"
78½"
Cripple stud
16"   16"   20½"
12'

Note: Rough opening will vary from one window to another. Add trimmer studs or alter stud spacing to adjust width and center the window. Change length of cripple studs to modify opening height.

DOOR WALL

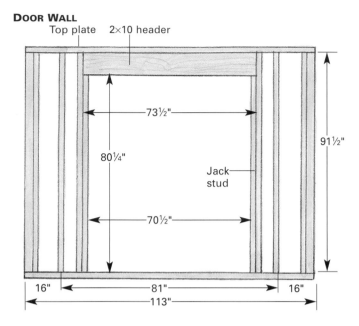

Top plate   2×10 header

73½"
80¼"   Jack stud
70½"
91½"
16"   81"   16"
113"

FRAMING THE WALLS

Following the framing plans on these two pages, cut the lumber for one wall at a time and assemble it. Build the walls on the floor, then raise them into place. Starting with the back wall, raise each one and brace it temporarily. Vertical siding requires 2×4 blocking between the studs, but you can install it later. (See pages 104–105 for more about walls.)

■ **MARK THE PLATES:** Align the top and bottom plates and mark them for each stud location, including king studs, jack studs, and cripple studs. Build each corner post as a unit and treat it as a single stud.

■ **RAISE THE BACK WALL:** When you stand the wall up, fasten it to the floor and brace it with 1×3 braces nailed to the studs and the floor, making sure it's plumb. Temporarily nail a 1×3 diagonally across the wall to keep it square.

■ **SETTING THE SIDEWALLS:** Assemble and attach the sidewall and door wall next, then complete the framing with the front wall. Brace each one plumb and square. Leave the braces in place until you install roofing or siding, whichever you do first.

■ **CENTERING A WINDOW:** If you are installing a window that's larger or smaller than the one specified, you probably will have to alter the stud layout to center the window. It's best to lay out window framing on paper before marking the plates.

To center a window, subtract the width of its rough opening (the length of the header) from the total length of the wall. Draw in

the jack studs, the header, and the king studs, centering them on the wall sketch. Then measure 16-inch intervals from each end until you reach the king stud that supports the window, keeping the space between any two studs at 16 inches or less. Transfer the dimensions to the top and bottom plates.

■ **TYING THE CORNERS:** Mark the rafter centers on the cap plates and install the cap plates. Lap the cap plates over the top plates

BUILDING A RAMP

A ramp makes getting a lawn mower or other wheeled equipment into the shed easier. When you prepare the site, pour a 4-inch-thick grade-level slab 6 feet wide (or a little wider than the doorway), extending 4 feet from the rim joist. Then build the ramp later. (See pages 120–123 for information on concrete slabs.)

To build the ramp, saw a 10-degree bevel on the top edge of a 6-foot-long 2×8. Lag-bolt the piece, bevel facing up and out, to the rim joist in front of the door opening. Cut five 2×8 stringers 41 inches long that taper from 7¼ inches wide at one end to a point at the other. (You can probably cut two from one 42-inch piece of 2×8.) Attach the stringers to the beveled 2×8 with angle brackets. Install 2×8 planking on the ramp. Bevel the leading edge of the first plank to reduce the bump onto the ramp.

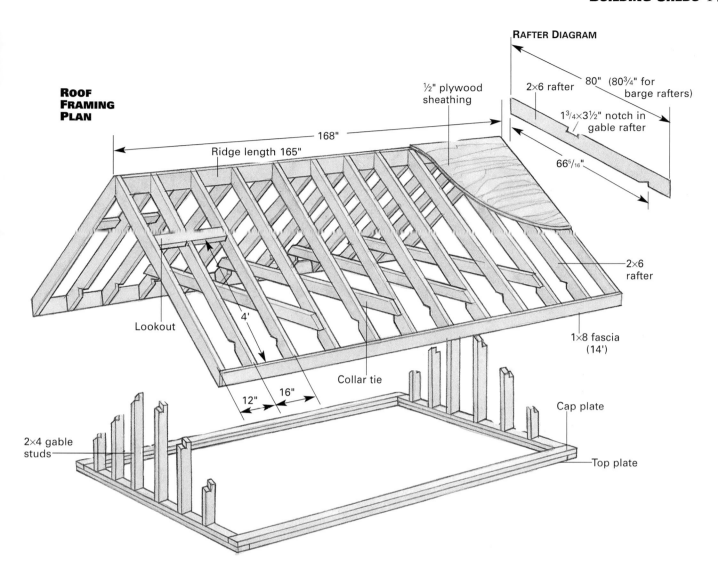

ROOF FRAMING PLAN

RAFTER DIAGRAM

½" plywood sheathing

2×6 rafter

80" (80¾" for barge rafters)

1¾×3½" notch in gable rafter

66⁵⁄₁₆"

168"

Ridge length 165"

Lookout

4'

Collar tie

12"   16"

2×6 rafter

1×8 fascia (14')

2×4 gable studs

Cap plate

Top plate

at the corners, as shown at right. Center the rafter ties on the cap plate at rafter locations.

FRAMING THE ROOF

The basic shed roofing plan follows home-construction practices and goes up easily if you approach it one step (and one piece) at a time.

■ **FRAMING INVENTORY:** The roof consists of 2×6 rafters supported by a 2×6 ridge at the top and the cap plates on the wall frame. This design incorporates barge (or verge) rafters, which overhang the gable ends, supported by 2×4 lookouts. A 1×8 fascia hides the exposed rafter tails, and 2×4 collar ties keep the weight of the roof from spreading apart the walls or rafter tails.

■ **SUPPORTING THE RIDGE:** Cut the ridge first and raise it into position with temporary 2×4 braces, as illustrated at the top of page 178. Make the supports long enough to place the top of the ridge at the height of the roof. Center the supports on the sidewall

and door wall. Make sure each support is straight and plumb, then tack it to both the top plate and the joist. Position the ridge on the support so it extends 10½ inches past the cap plates on both ends. Attach the ridge to the supports.

■ **CUTTING THE RAFTERS:** Cut the first pair of rafters according to the rafter diagram above and test-fit them. When the test rafters fit correctly, use them as templates to cut the remaining rafters. Make the barge rafters for each end ¾ inch longer than the common rafters to cover the end of the ridge board. (See pages 106–109 for more information about laying out and cutting rafters.)

■ **NOTCHING FOR LOOKOUTS:** Notch the four gable-end rafters, as shown in the rafter diagram. Place the notch 4 feet from the top of the rafter to provide sufficient nailing surface for the plywood sheathing.

WASTE NOT...

After installing both the floor and the roof of this 10-foot structure, you'll have some leftover plywood. Instead of throwing it away, cut the pieces into strips and use them for shelves or nailing ledgers for storage.

BASIC GARDEN SHED
continued

■ **INSTALLING THE RAFTERS:**
Set each bird's mouth in the rafter tie on the cap rail and nail it in place before nailing the rafter to the ridge. This makes it easier to position the rafter on the ridge. Use 16d nails to fasten the rafters to the ridge. Once you have the first pair up, the rest fall into place quickly. Install the main rafters in opposite pairs. Install the lookouts and barge rafters last. You can fasten the collar ties as you go or put them in after the rafters, whichever you find easier. Leave the 2×4 ridge supports in place until you have sheathed the roof.

■ **FINISHING THE ROOF:** Install the fascia on the tails of the rafters next; the edges of the sheathing fit flush with the front of the fascia. Bevel the top of the fascia to match the roof angle and attach it to the rafter tails with 10d nails. Then install the plywood sheathing, felt paper, and shingles. (See pages 110–113 for more information about roofing.)

INSTALLING THE MAIN ROOF RAFTERS

1. Measure and cut temporary ridge supports and tack to bottom and top plates on both sidewalls.

2. Tack ridge to supports.

3. Toenail notched gable rafters to top plate and fasten to ridge.

4. Fasten remaining rafters.

Notch for lookout

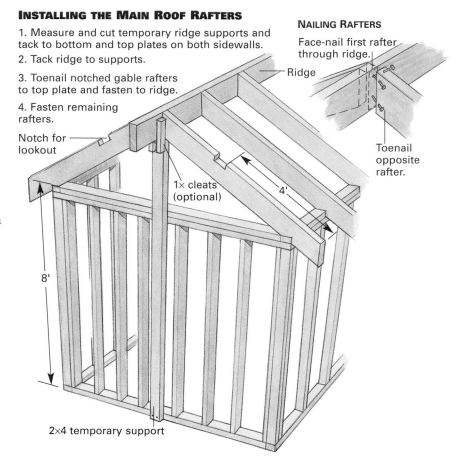

NAILING RAFTERS
Face-nail first rafter through ridge.

Ridge

Toenail opposite rafter.

Ridge

1× cleats (optional)

4'

8'

2×4 temporary support

INSTALLING THE BARGE RAFTERS

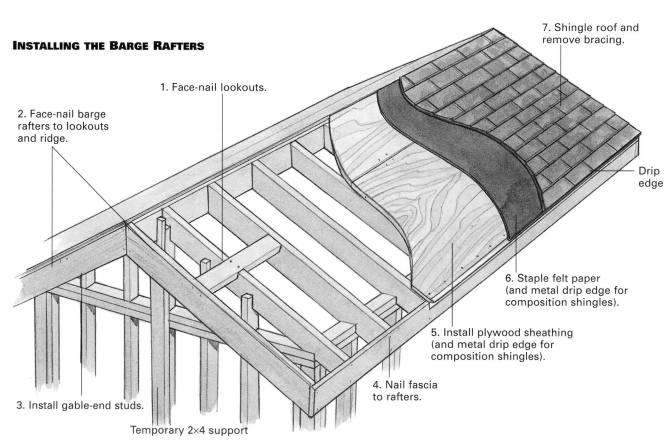

2. Face-nail barge rafters to lookouts and ridge.

1. Face-nail lookouts.

7. Shingle roof and remove bracing.

Drip edge

6. Staple felt paper (and metal drip edge for composition shingles).

5. Install plywood sheathing (and metal drip edge for composition shingles).

4. Nail fascia to rafters.

3. Install gable-end studs.

Temporary 2×4 support

TRIMMING THE WINDOW

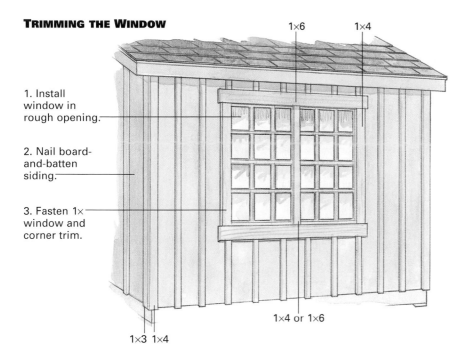

1×6   1×4

1. Install window in rough opening.

2. Nail board-and-batten siding.

3. Fasten 1× window and corner trim.

1×4 or 1×6

1×3 1×4

HANGING THE DOOR

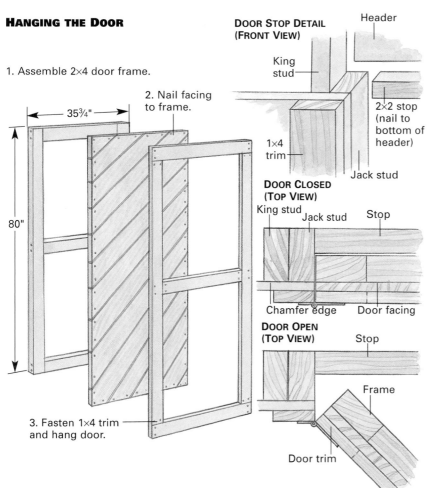

1. Assemble 2×4 door frame.

2. Nail facing to frame.

35¾"

80"

3. Fasten 1×4 trim and hang door.

DOOR STOP DETAIL (FRONT VIEW)

Header

King stud

1×4 trim

2×2 stop (nail to bottom of header)

Jack stud

DOOR CLOSED (TOP VIEW)

King stud

Jack stud

Stop

Chamfer edge

Door facing

DOOR OPEN (TOP VIEW)

Stop

Frame

Door trim

WINDOWS AND SIDING

Whether you install the window or the siding first depends on the type of window. Most windows that have a nailing flange go on before the siding. Cased wood windows are installed after the siding so the casing can be brought flush with the siding. Refer to pages 118–119 for information about windows.

■ **BLOCKING:** Board-and-batten and other vertical sidings require horizontal 2×4 blocking spaced 2 feet on center between the studs. Offset the blocks by 1½ inches so you can face-nail them through the studs. If you don't want to use blocking, you can install sheathing over the walls instead.

Start board-and-batten and other vertical or panel siding flush with the edge of the frame. Plumb the first board with a 4-foot level and check for plumb every three or four boards.

Start installing horizontal siding and shingles at the bottom. Sheathing must be installed for shingles. (See pages 114–115 for more about siding.)

HANGING THE DOOR AND TRIM

The door framing in this design accommodates both the flat-frame styles shown at left and the box-frame style shown on page 170. Flat-frame doors require the 2×2 stop nailed to the bottom of the header, as shown here. If you build a box-frame door and don't want it to be self-trimming, nail a 2×4 to the back of the header and jack studs to act as a stop. Without the stop the door will swing too far into the opening when closed, putting extra stress on the hinges and jack studs.

Trim the shed in the style shown here or install trim of your choice. Using 1×6 trim on tops of windows and doors and extending the horizontal trim beyond the side pieces are ways to add a touch of style to the shed.

POTTING SHED

This potting shed is similar to the work shed shown on pages 174–179, but it has a gable roof and a portico that extends over the entry. The 4×4 posts that support the portico, clean trim lines, and narrow windows create a classic look suitable for a formal landscape. It can also provide a pleasant contrast in an informal cottage garden.

POTTING SHED (PERSPECTIVE VIEW)

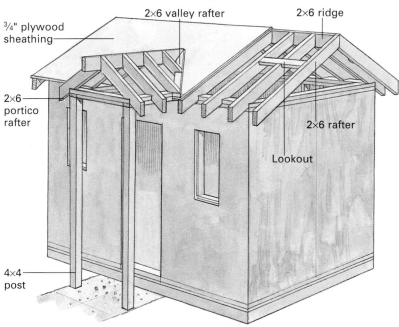

¾" plywood sheathing

2×6 valley rafter

2×6 ridge

2×6 portico rafter

2×6 rafter

Lookout

4×4 post

PORTICO PRELIMINARIES

Think of the portico as a small room without walls. The portico roof meets the main roof the way a dormer would. The shed in effect has two perpendicular gable roofs.

The addition of the portico makes laying out this shed a little trickier than a four-sided structure. Before you lay out the portico, use the layout frame on page 169 to prepare the site for an 8×12

MATERIALS LIST

FOUNDATION, FLOOR, AND WALLS
- Posts (check local codes)
  - 4×4×8', 4
  - 4×4×12', 2
- Joists   2×8×8', 10
  - 2×8×12', 2
- Floor (¾" plywood)
  - 4×8, 3
- Studs, plates   2×4×8', 66
  - 2×4×12', 6
- Header   2×12×8', 2
- Siding   350 sq. ft.
- Trim   1×3×8', 8
  - 1×4×8', 6
  - 1×6×8', 2

ROOF
- Area   300 sq. ft.
- Shingles   3½ squares
- Rafters   2×6×10', 4
  - 2×6×14', 13
- Roof (½" plywood)
  - 4×8, 10
- Fascia   1×8, 30'

LAYING OUT THE PORTICO

1. Assemble floor frame.

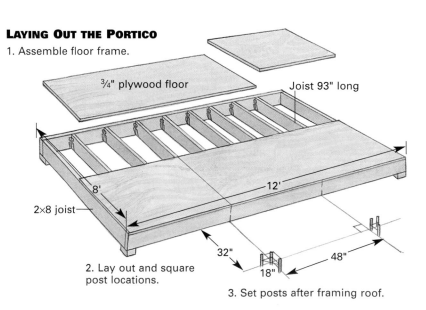

¾" plywood floor

Joist 93" long

2×8 joist

8'

12'

32"

18"

48"

2. Lay out and square post locations.

3. Set posts after framing roof.

structure. Set the posts, cut them, and build the floor frame complete with flooring. (See page 175 for more about floor framing.)

ADDING THE PORTICO

Start by marking the center at the front of the main floor. Tack mason's lines to the rim joist 24 inches from each side of the center.

■ **LOCATING THE POSTS:** Stretch the lines perpendicular to the rim joist to triangulated stakes about 3 feet from the rim joist. Because the dimensions of the portico are small, square the corners with a scaled-down version of the 3-4-5 triangle. Use 18, 24, and 30 inches as your marks and adjust the stakes to locate the posts where shown in the illustration at the bottom of page 180.

■ **SETTING THE POSTS:** Dig the postholes, pour 3 to 4 inches of dry concrete mix into the bottom, and insert the posts. Make sure the posts are more than 8 feet tall. If you removed the lines to dig the holes,

reset them and line up the edges of the post with the intersection. Don't cut the posts until the walls are up.

Build the walls, back wall first, then side walls, then the front wall. Tie the corners with cap plates and install rafter ties.

FRONT WALL FRAMING PLAN

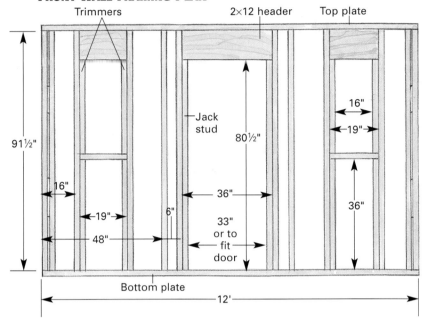

ERECTING THE WALLS

1. Set posts and assemble walls.

2. Toenail portico top rail to main top rail and face-nail to post.

3. Nail portico top rail and cap rail.

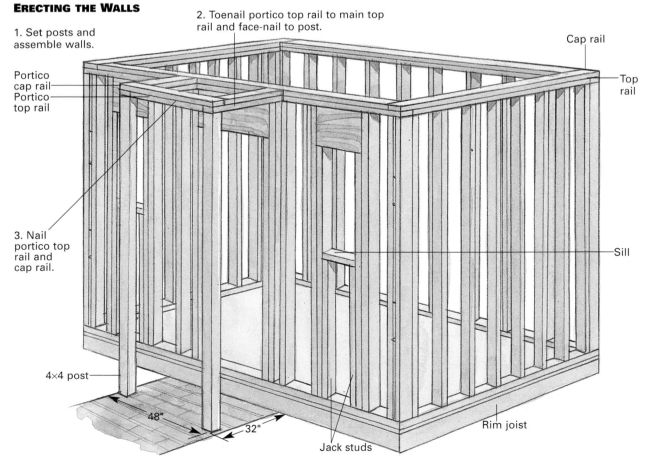

POTTING SHED
continued

ROOF FRAMING PLAN
RAFTER DIAGRAM

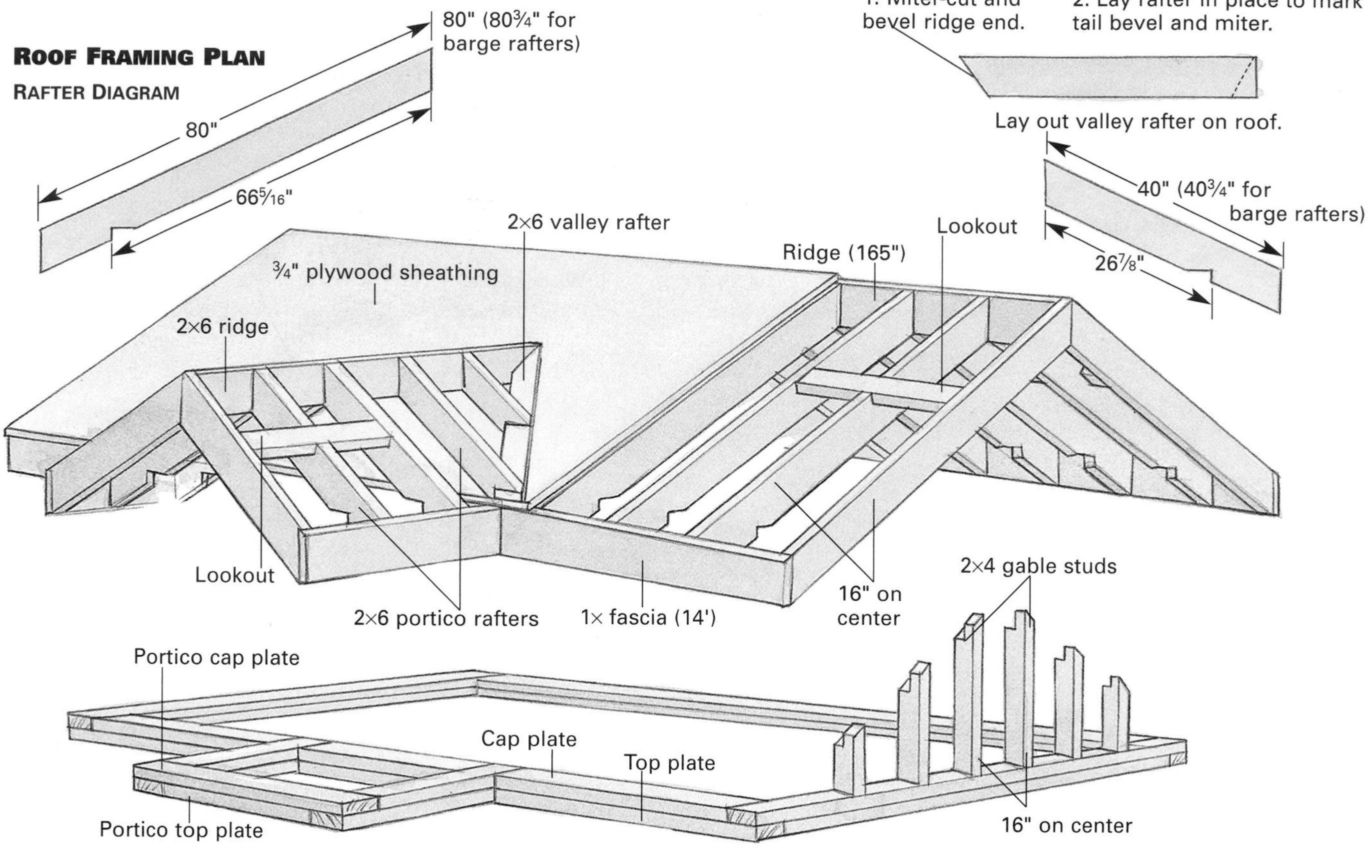

80" (80¾" for barge rafters)

80"

66⁵⁄₁₆"

¾" plywood sheathing

2×6 valley rafter

Ridge (165")

Lookout

2×6 ridge

1. Miter-cut and bevel ridge end.

2. Lay rafter in place to mark tail bevel and miter.

Lay out valley rafter on roof.

40" (40¾" for barge rafters)

26⁷⁄₈"

Lookout

2×6 portico rafters

1× fascia (14')

16" on center

2×4 gable studs

Portico cap plate

Cap plate

Top plate

Portico top plate

16" on center

FRAMING THE PORTICO ROOF

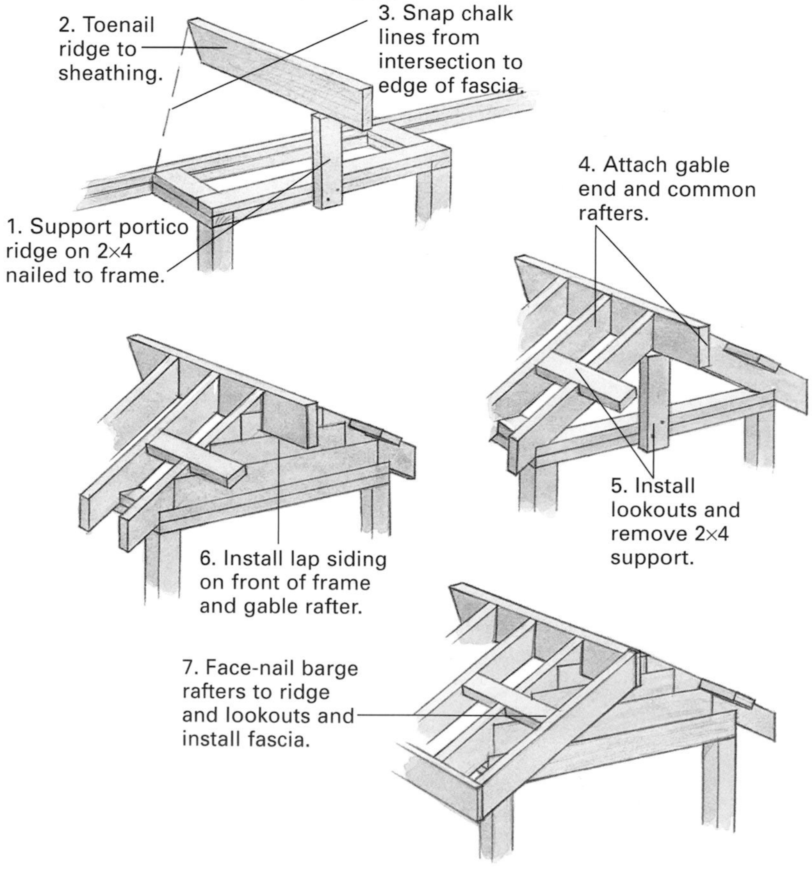

2. Toenail ridge to sheathing.

3. Snap chalk lines from intersection to edge of fascia.

1. Support portico ridge on 2×4 nailed to frame.

4. Attach gable end and common rafters.

5. Install lookouts and remove 2×4 support.

6. Install lap siding on front of frame and gable rafter.

7. Face-nail barge rafters to ridge and lookouts and install fascia.

■ LINING UP THE PORTICO PLATES:
To line up the portico plates exactly with the posts, first cut the posts level with the bottom of the top plate. Use a mason's line and line level to mark the post height and cut each one with a reciprocating saw.

■ PORTICO TOP PLATES:
Place a 2×4 on top of one post and square it to the main top plate with a framing square. Mark the main top plate at the intersection of the 2×4, cut it to length, and toenail it to the top plate. Face-nail the portico top plate to the top of the post and repeat the process on the other side. Measure the distance between the posts and toenail the front portico top plate level with the side plates.

■ PORTICO CAP PLATE:
Extend the portico top-plate lines to the front-wall cap plate. Cut out the 3½-inch section between the lines to allow the portico cap plate to lie on the front-wall top plate. Nail the portico cap plates, as shown above.

FRAMING THE ROOF

Build the main roof using the procedures described on pages 177–178. Bevel and install the fascias.

■ **INSTALLING THE FIRST PORTICO RAFTERS:** Cut the portico rafters and lookouts. Support the portico ridge and gable-end rafters with a 2×4 nailed to the portico plates. Nail the ridge to the sheathing, centered on the front wall. Snap chalk lines from the intersection of the ridge down to the intersection of the portico plates and the outer edge of the fascia. Lay out the valley rafters using the chalk lines.

■ **INSTALLING THE REMAINING RAFTERS:** Fasten the remaining portico rafters to the ridge and sheathing, keeping the rafter tails lined up on the chalk line. Nail the lookouts and install siding on the front of the portico. Then face-nail the portico barge rafters and fascia.

■ **FINISHING THE ROOF:** Shingle the roof following the procedures shown for shingling a dormer or roof extension on page 111. Start by sheathing the portico and stapling felt paper, creating a valley. Shingle the roof with composition shingles or the material of your choice. All roofing except untreated wood shingles can be installed over plywood.

INSTALLING THE SIDING

For horizontal lap siding, install a spacer or molding at the bottom of the first course, as shown on page 114. To properly space the siding, begin on the front wall and transfer the lines around the remainder of the building. If you start on one of the sidewalls, the lines probably won't correspond to the top and bottom of the doorway and windows. Nail the siding into the studs with 8d nails, then add trim.

HANGING THE DOOR

The rough opening and door frame is designed to accommodate a standard 32-inch prehung exterior door. (See page 116 for information about installing doors.)

You may not be able to find the exact door illustrated. Select a door with a center pane of glass to allow more light into the potting shed. Any full-view steel (or wood) door with a center pane of glass will work. Most models come with snap-in muntins that allow you to create the pattern of your choice.

If you install a solid door, consider electrifying the shed or installing additional windows or skylights. This is a decision you should make during the planning stage of your project. It's possible to add windows to existing walls but much easier to install them in framing that was designed for them.

TRIMMING DETAILS

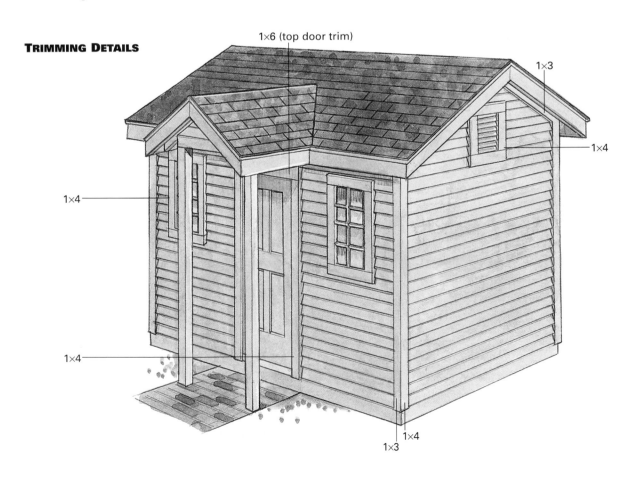

1×6 (top door trim)
1×3
1×4
1×4
1×4
1×4
1×3

THE ESSENTIAL GAZEBO

A gazebo looks complicated to build because it has more than four sides, but constructing this gazebo shouldn't be a challenge because the 2×6 layout frame dispenses with complicated geometry and computations. And since it's adjustable you can adapt it to any size.

This design employs 2×4 corner studs instead of posts, which minimizes angle cuts; allows you to install a variety of gussets, friezes, sidings, and enclosures; and provides wiring channels for lights, fans, and speakers. The design also allows you to test-fit the rafters at ground level, making construction significantly easier.

The basic frame shown on page 185 can be left open or enclosed. If you decide to build a screened gazebo, read the appropriate pages to familiarize yourself with the changes required. If you change the design, make scale drawings before you begin construction.

Use treated lumber rated for ground contact for the posts and floor frame and use redwood, cedar, or treated lumber for the rest of the structure. Small variations in dimensions often occur in carpentry projects, so verify measurements and test-fit parts before you cut multiple pieces.

Stains accentuate the tones of the wood and give you a choice of colors with which to complement nature's work. Protect stained surfaces with sealers or other finishes.

Consider the overall look and character of the neighborhood when planning any outdoor structure, especially if the building will be visible across property lines. Remember that your neighbors have to live with whatever you choose too.

PERSPECTIVE VIEW

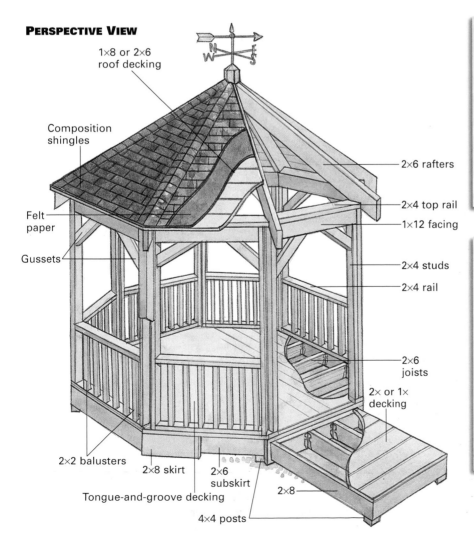

1×8 or 2×6
roof decking

Composition
shingles

Felt
paper

Gussets

2×2 balusters

2×8 skirt

2×6
subskirt

Tongue-and-groove decking

4×4 posts

2×8

2×6
joists

2× or 1×
decking

2×6 rafters

2×4 top rail

1×12 facing

2×4 studs

2×4 rail

MEASURE TWICE

The plans in this chapter include
specific dimensions, but be sure to
verify sizes and dimensions as you
work. Dimensioned lumber may
not be exact, so variations can
occur in all projects. Check each
measurement on site before
cutting any lumber.

DRESSING UP
THE EDGES

Square lumber edges look just fine
inside a garden shed. After all, the
interior of a shed is primarily
functional. Gazebos, however, are
all about style. Dress up the edges
of exposed framing and trim with
chamfered, rounded, or molded
edges made with a router bit.
This added touch enhances your
gazebo's custom-built look.

SITE LAYOUT AND POST SETTING

LAYOUT FRAME FOR GAZEBO

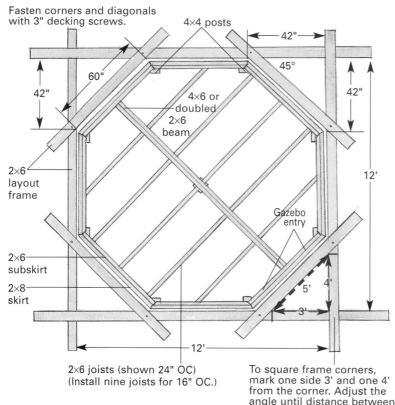

Fasten corners and diagonals with 3" decking screws.

4×4 posts

42"

60"

45°

42"

42"

4×6 or doubled 2×6 beam

12'

2×6 layout frame

Gazebo entry

2×6 subskirt

2×8 skirt

5'

4'

3'

12'

2×6 joists (shown 24" OC)
(Install nine joists for 16" OC.)

To square frame corners, mark one side 3' and one 4' from the corner. Adjust the angle until distance between marks (dotted red line) is 5'.

The integrity of any structure depends on its foundation. Lay out the site accurately and set the posts solidly to minimize difficulties during later construction. The layout frame shown at left ensures accurate post placement.

LAYING OUT THE SITE

Before you build the layout frame, level the site. Remove rocks, grade down high spots, and mow the grass to about 1 inch. Prop the frame on bricks or blocks where there are minor inconsistencies in the grade. If the ground falls away sharply, you'll have to build temporary supports.

The 12-foot floor plan shown has facets of about 60 inches. The facet length increases or decreases about 5 inches for every 1 foot change in gazebo diameter.

INSTALLING THE DIAGONALS

Square the corners using the 3-4-5 triangle method, as shown at left. Measure from the inside corner of the frame. Using an 8-foot board for each diagonal, mark a 5-foot length in the middle (18 inches from each end).

LAYING OUT THE SITE AND SETTING THE POSTS

1. Set 2x6 layout frame and stake corners.

2. Fasten corners of frame.

3. Square corners with 3-4-5 triangle and install diagonals securely.

4. Locate center post where midpoints of sides intersect.

5. Mark post locations.

6. Dig postholes.

7. Set posts with template.

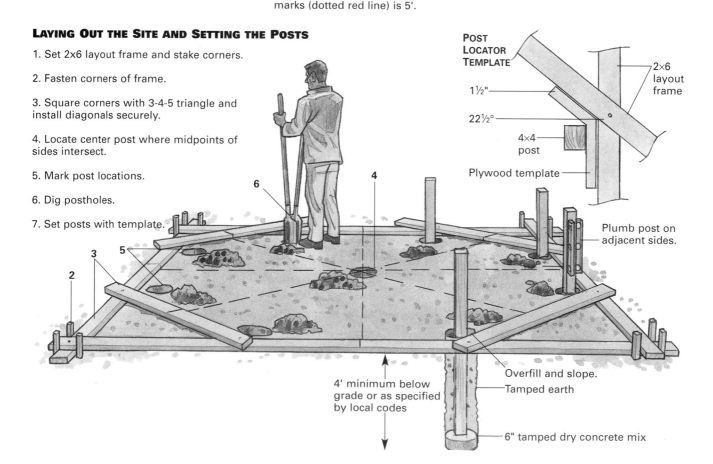

POST LOCATOR TEMPLATE

2×6 layout frame

1½"

22½°

4×4 post

Plywood template

Plumb post on adjacent sides.

4' minimum below grade or as specified by local codes

Overfill and slope.

Tamped earth

6" tamped dry concrete mix

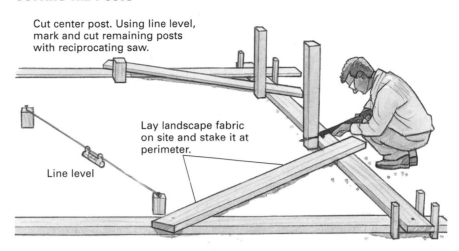

CUTTING THE POSTS

Cut center post. Using line level, mark and cut remaining posts with reciprocating saw.

Lay landscape fabric on site and stake it at perimeter.

Line level

DO YOU NEED A STEP?

A 2×6 floor structure at ground level with ¾-inch hardwood decking results in a finished floor height of about 7 inches. Most codes do not require a step or entry landing for this height. If you want to add a step for easier entry or for appearance, see pages 124–129.

If you install thicker decking or modify the design so the floor is more than 7½ inches off the ground, you may not have a choice—local codes may require that a step be built.

Mark each frame member 42 inches from the corner. Lay the diagonal on the frame and align the 5-foot marks on the diagonal with the marks on the frame sides. Fasten the diagonal to the frame with two 3-inch decking screws at each overlap.

MATERIALS LIST

FOUNDATION, FLOOR, AND WALLS
■ Posts	4×4×10', 5
■ Joists	2×6×12', 5
	2×6×10', 2
■ Subskirt	2×6×12', 4
■ Skirt	2×8×12', 4
■ Deck	2×6×12', 18
	2×6×10', 20
■ Studs, plates	2×4×8', 4
	2×4×10', 20
■ Header trim	1×12×12', 8
■ Sill	2×6×12', 4
■ Rail support	2×4×10', 4
■ Balusters	2×2, 75

ROOF
■ Area	220 sq. ft.
■ Shingles	2½ squares
■ Rafters	2×6×10', 8
■ Facing	1×12×12', 4
■ Roof boards	1×8×10', 35
or tongue-and-groove	2×6×10', 55
■ OSB or plywood	4×8, 8
■ Trim	1×6×12', 12

MARKING THE CENTER POST

The center post and beam keep the floor from flexing under a load. Locate the center post at the intersection of lines tied at the midpoints of the sides. Mark all post locations with spray marking paint.

SETTING THE POSTS

Set each post square to the frame and 1½ inches from it using the locator template shown on the opposite page. With the skirt in place, the floor will be 12 feet wide.

Set each post into about 2 inches of dry concrete mix at the bottom of the hole. The concrete will solidify with ground moisture. Hold the post against the template and tamp the soil around it with a 2×4. Plumb the post on adjacent sides as you go.

CUTTING THE POSTS

To cut the posts' ends to the same height, use a line level on a taut mason's line, as shown in the illustration above. Draw guidelines on the posts before cutting to ensure square cuts.

BUILDING A SLAB FLOOR

Although the gazebo illustrated in the plans on these pages employs a wood frame floor, you can use the same layout methods to install an octagonal concrete slab.

Lay out the site and mark the perimeter with spray marking paint. Remove the layout frame, excavate, build forms, and pour a concrete slab using the techniques shown on pages 120–123.

FRAMING THE FLOOR

The floor framing comprises a central beam and joists that are attached to 2×6 subskirt. The subskirt is then toenailed to the post tops. A 2×8 skirt covers the subskirt. The floor is covered with 1×6 or 2×6 hardwood decking.

INSTALLING THE SUBSKIRT

Boards for the subskirt are alternately cut at 45 degrees and 90 degrees, as shown in the illustration below. Measure between the corners of two posts for the first board A.

Install the subskirt one board at a time so you can fit each board to the actual post layout. Toenail the boards to the post tops with 10d spiral nails, and snug the miters together with 8d nails. After installing the first two boards, measure from the long corners of the subskirt.

CENTER BEAM AND JOISTS

The double 2×6 beam extends from the entry opening to the opposite facet, placing the decking perpendicular to the entry opening. If you want to install the decking with a different orientation, reposition the beam and joists. Draw the alterations on a scale drawing before beginning construction.

Install the beam with a double joist hanger. Mark the joist locations on the beam and subskirt (16 inches on center for 1× decking, 24 inches on center for 2× decking). Some joists are miter-cut at 45 degrees on one end to meet the angled subskirt.

SKIRTING AND FLOORING

Cut the skirt boards with 22½-degree miters and face-nail them to the subskirt with 10d rust-resistant finishing nails. Keep the top edge flush with the subskirt. Apply construction adhesive to the ends. Snug the miters with 8d nails.

SUBSKIRT AND SKIRT DIMENSIONS

58⅞"

2×8 skit

2×8 skirt
58⅞"

57⅜"
Board B
2×6 subskirt

45°   45°

57⅜"

Board A
2×6 subskirt

22½°

90°

Dimensions may vary according to post placement; measure before cutting boards. Alternate subskirt boards A and B around frame.

INSTALLING THE SUBSKIRT

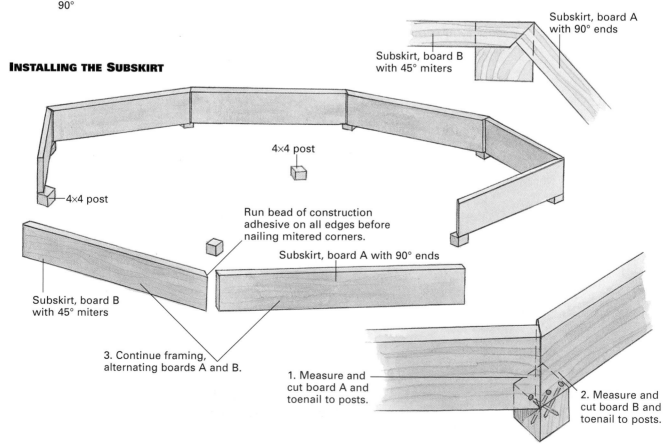

Subskirt, board A with 90° ends

Subskirt, board B with 45° miters

4×4 post

4×4 post

Run bead of construction adhesive on all edges before nailing mitered corners.

Subskirt, board A with 90° ends

Subskirt, board B with 45° miters

3. Continue framing, alternating boards A and B.

1. Measure and cut board A and toenail to posts.

2. Measure and cut board B and toenail to posts.

To keep insects out of a screened gazebo, staple fiberglass screening on top of the joists, overlapping the edges by 4 inches.

Start laying decking boards in the center of the doorway and work to the edges. Nail the flooring with 10d rust-resistant finishing nails. Let the ends run wild over the edge. Lay the boards for the last few courses in place but do not fasten them. To avoid narrow edge boards, rip the last boards to equal widths that fill the remaining space.

To cut the edges flush, measure under the decking to the skirt on each face. Mark the skirt position on the decking and snap a chalk line between the marks. Trim the decking along the lines with a circular saw, taking care not to cut into the skirt.

INSTALLING THE BEAM AND JOISTS

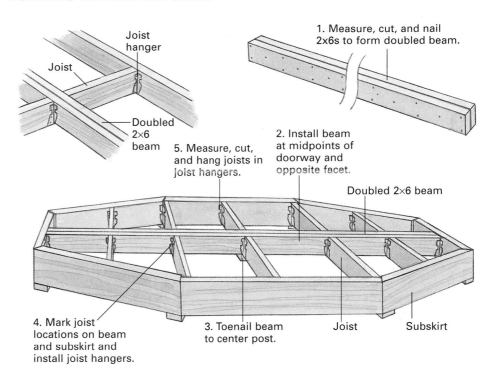

Joist hanger

Joist

Doubled 2×6 beam

1. Measure, cut, and nail 2x6s to form doubled beam.

2. Install beam at midpoints of doorway and opposite facet.

5. Measure, cut, and hang joists in joist hangers.

Doubled 2×6 beam

4. Mark joist locations on beam and subskirt and install joist hangers.

3. Toenail beam to center post.

Joist

Subskirt

INSTALLING THE SKIRT AND FLOORING

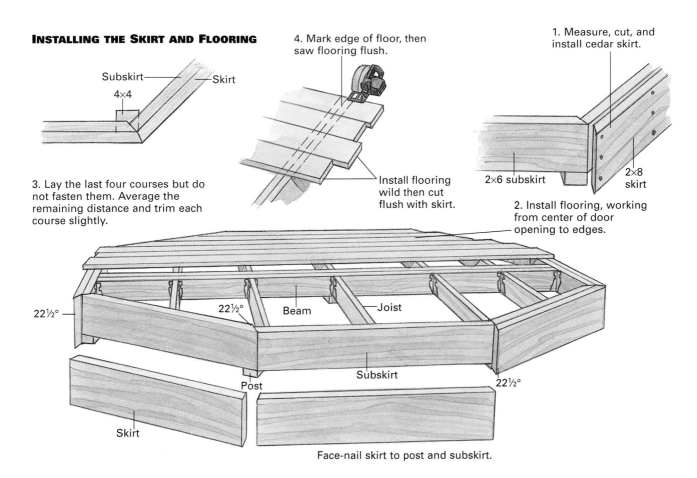

Subskirt — Skirt

4×4

3. Lay the last four courses but do not fasten them. Average the remaining distance and trim each course slightly.

4. Mark edge of floor, then saw flooring flush.

Install flooring wild then cut flush with skirt.

1. Measure, cut, and install cedar skirt.

2×6 subskirt

2×8 skirt

2. Install flooring, working from center of door opening to edges.

22½°

22½°   Beam

Joist

22½°

Post

Subskirt

Skirt

Face-nail skirt to post and subskirt.

TEST-FITTING THE RAFTERS

Because the floor and top-plate dimensions are the same, you can lay out, cut, and test-fit the rafters on the floor. This means you won't have to erect temporary rafter supports or climb up and down ladders to get the fit right.

The 2×6 rafters are strong enough to span the structures shown on these pages. If you plan to build a larger structure, consult a span table to see if you'll need larger rafters.

This method for test-fitting the rafters works for a closed roof, with or without a cupola. If you're building a gazebo with a cupola, refer to pages 194–196.

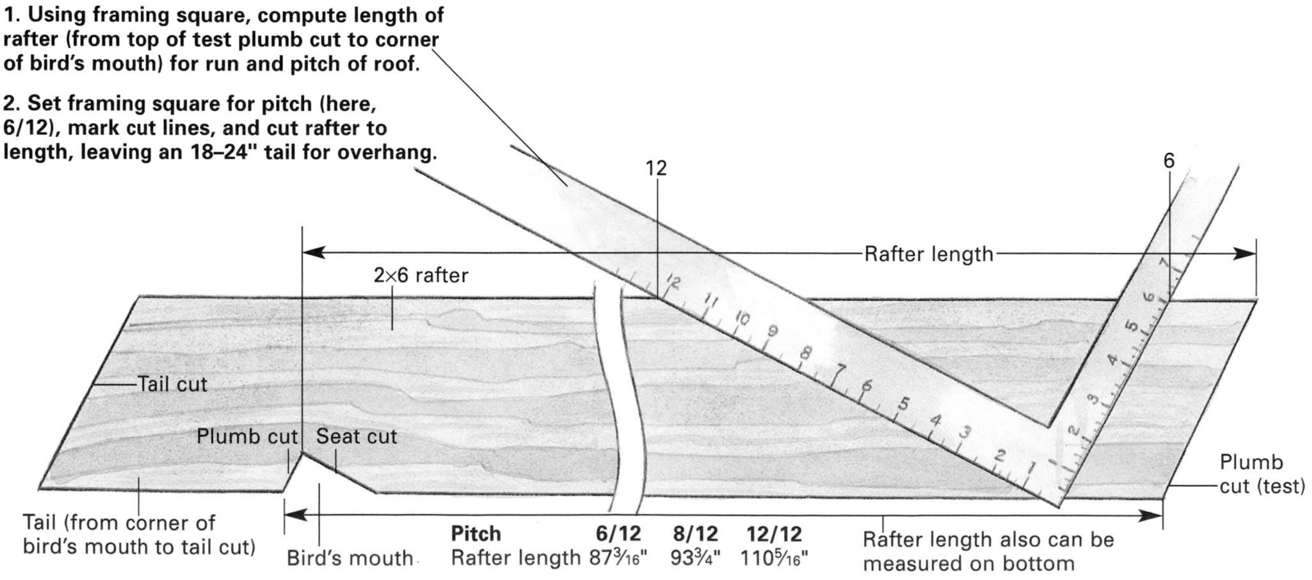

CUTTING THE ROOF CENTER POST

Cut the roof center post from a straight length of 4×4 stock of the same species as the other visible parts of the structure. The lengths shown accommodate any roof pitch and can be trimmed on the inside after you've tested the rafters.

Cutting the 4×4 as shown results in an octagon with 1½-inch faces—the thickness of the rafters. Mark the lines precisely with a sharp pencil and straightedge. Cut off the corners on a table saw.

Chamfer the post top to the angle of the pitch of the roof (see table, page 108). Mark the angle with a protractor—a plastic one works just fine.

TOP PLATE AND TEST RAFTERS

Measure the length of the top plates along the edges of the floor. Miter-cut the plate ends 22½ degrees. Cut a top plate for each side and mark the plates for position. Tack the plates along the floor edge, as shown on the opposite page.

Snap chalk lines between the midpoints of opposite faces. Mark the center of the floor (also the center of the roof peak) where the lines intersect. Then measure from an outside corner to the center to find the length of the rafter run.

Determine the rafter length for your roof pitch using the rafter scales on the framing square (see page 108). Rafter lengths for three roof pitches on a 12-foot gazebo are shown in the illustration below. Cut the rafters 18 to 24 inches longer than the calculated length to allow for the tails. Make the bird's-mouth

CENTER POST DIMENSIONS

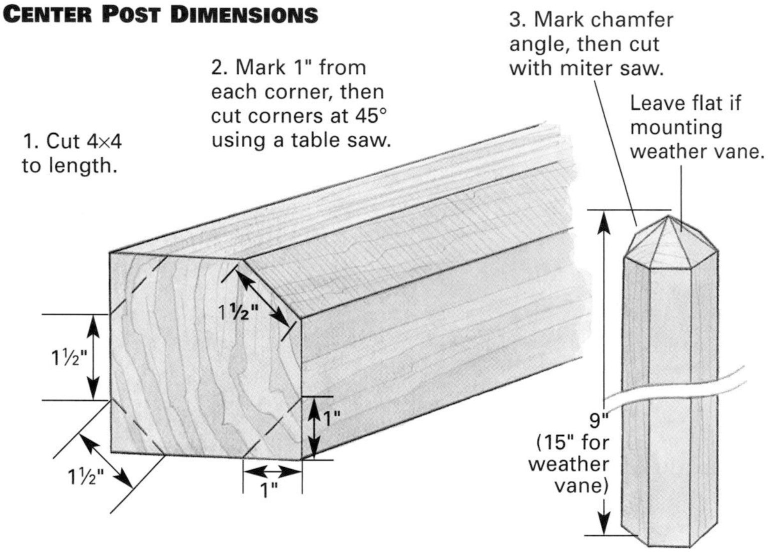

1. Cut 4×4 to length.

2. Mark 1" from each corner, then cut corners at 45° using a table saw.

3. Mark chamfer angle, then cut with miter saw.

Leave flat if mounting weather vane.

1½"

1½"

1½"

1"

1"

9" (15" for weather vane)

LAYING OUT A RAFTER

1. Using framing square, compute length of rafter (from top of test plumb cut to corner of bird's mouth) for run and pitch of roof.

2. Set framing square for pitch (here, 6/12), mark cut lines, and cut rafter to length, leaving an 18–24" tail for overhang.

12

6

Rafter length

2×6 rafter

Tail cut

Plumb cut | Seat cut

Plumb cut (test)

Tail (from corner of bird's mouth to tail cut)

Bird's mouth

Pitch	6/12	8/12	12/12
Rafter length	87³/₁₆"	93¾"	110⁵/₁₆"

Rafter length also can be measured on bottom

cut and test plumb cut on two rafters. Don't make the final plumb cut or tail cut or cut any more rafters until you have tested the rafters as described below.

TESTING THE FIRST RAFTERS

Make a temporary support from a 2×4 and two thicknesses of ¾-inch plywood to test the rafters. Doubling the plywood raises the 2×4 to the same height as the top plate. Cut the 2×4 to the height of the roof above the top plate, as shown at right. Screw two rafters to the support as illustrated.

Center the support on the decking, and place the rafters on opposite corners. If you don't like the way the pitch looks, or if the rafters don't fit, recut them. When the rafters fit properly, cut the final plumb cut 1¾ inches back from the first one to allow for the thickness of the center post. Trim the tail cut to the correct overhang. Lay out and cut the other rafters, using the test rafters as a pattern.

REMAINING RAFTERS AND ROOF

Shorten the 2×4 temporary support so you can tack the roof center post to it at the height of the roof. Then tack opposing pairs of rafters to the faces of the center post, keeping the post plumb.

Line up the rafters on the corners and recut any that need adjusting. Cut the roof sheathing pieces to fit, but don't fasten them.

Before you disassemble the rafters and center post, number the rafters and roofing sections so you can put them up in the same order. Mark the center post where it meets the bottoms of the rafters. Take apart the assembly and trim the post to the mark.

Then recut all the bird's-mouth plumb cuts ¾ inch deeper so the 1× facing can slide into place on the face of the wall later.

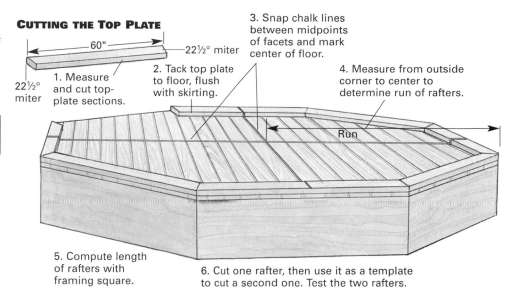

CUTTING THE TOP PLATE

60"

22½° miter

22½° miter

1. Measure and cut top-plate sections.

2. Tack top plate to floor, flush with skirting.

3. Snap chalk lines between midpoints of facets and mark center of floor.

4. Measure from outside corner to center to determine run of rafters.

Run

5. Compute length of rafters with framing square.

6. Cut one rafter, then use it as a template to cut a second one. Test the two rafters.

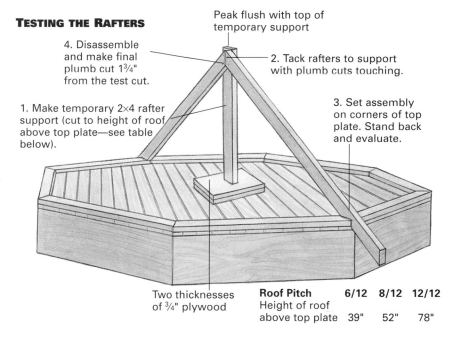

TESTING THE RAFTERS

Peak flush with top of temporary support

4. Disassemble and make final plumb cut 1¾" from the test cut.

2. Tack rafters to support with plumb cuts touching.

1. Make temporary 2×4 rafter support (cut to height of roof above top plate—see table below).

3. Set assembly on corners of top plate. Stand back and evaluate.

Two thicknesses of ¾" plywood

Roof Pitch	6/12	8/12	12/12
Height of roof above top plate	39"	52"	78"

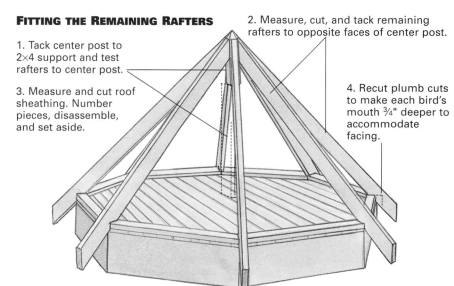

FITTING THE REMAINING RAFTERS

1. Tack center post to 2×4 support and test rafters to center post.

2. Measure, cut, and tack remaining rafters to opposite faces of center post.

3. Measure and cut roof sheathing. Number pieces, disassemble, and set aside.

4. Recut plumb cuts to make each bird's mouth ¾" deeper to accommodate facing.

BUILDING THE WALLS AND ROOF

The roof load rests on the studs, not the wall top plates, so walls are built with flat 2×4 headers above the openings instead of doubled 2× stock. This framing eliminates the extra expense of a doubled header and provides space to run wiring. The 1×12 facing provides lateral strength and keeps the header from sagging.

GAZEBO WALL FRAMING

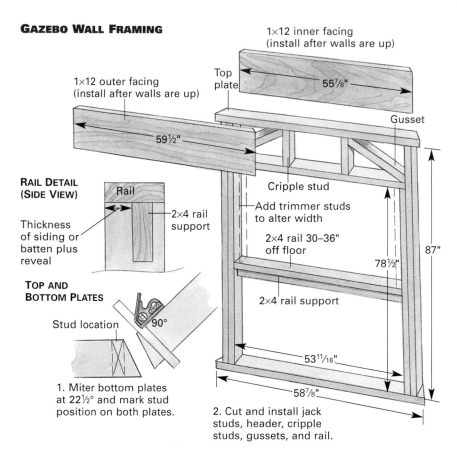

1×12 inner facing (install after walls are up)

Top plate

55⅞"

1×12 outer facing (install after walls are up)

59½"

Gusset

RAIL DETAIL (SIDE VIEW)

Rail

Thickness of siding or batten plus reveal

2×4 rail support

Cripple stud

Add trimmer studs to alter width

2×4 rail 30–36" off floor

2×4 rail support

78½"

87"

TOP AND BOTTOM PLATES

Stud location   90°

1. Miter bottom plates at 22½° and mark stud position on both plates.

53¹¹⁄₁₆"

58⅞"

2. Cut and install jack studs, header, cripple studs, gussets, and rail.

ERECTING THE WALLS

Preassemble and erect the walls one at a time. The dimensions shown place the bottom of the header 80 inches above the floor, the height of a standard door. This allows you to install a door later. The walls will accommodate any gusset design or decorative bracket and panels.

The rail height above the floor varies, depending on your preference. Stand the first wall up and experiment with the height of the rail. When you find the height that looks pleasing to you, mark it on the studs. Nail the rail support 1½ inches below the mark, set back from the front of the studs by the thickness of the balusters you will install plus a ¼-inch reveal. If the rail is a 2×4, assemble it as part of the wall frame. Rails 2×6 or wider are installed after the walls are up. Fasten the support and rail to the studs with 10d finishing nails.

When the basic framing is completed, cut and install jack studs or trimmers to reduce the opening sizes, if you prefer.

The 1×12 facing spans the studs, so wait until you have all the walls up before you nail it on. Determine the length of the facing boards by measuring the top plates from point to point on each facet. Cut the facing boards to that length with 22½-degree miter cuts at both ends. The interior and exterior boards are different lengths.

Install the facing boards to leave a ¼-inch reveal across the bottom of the header. If you want to build a shelf on the top plate, omit the

INSTALLING WALL SECTIONS

1. Install first wall section with temporary bracing. Leave bracing in place until roof is installed.

2. Assemble, erect, plumb, and brace remaining walls.

3. Measure, cut, and install 1×12 facing.

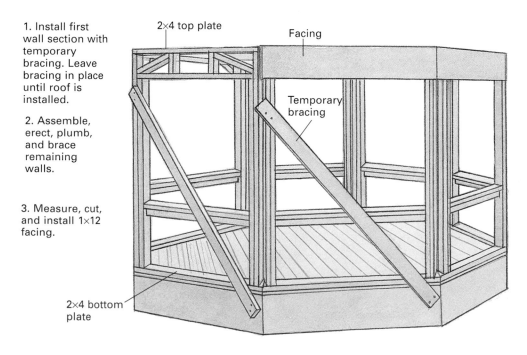

2×4 top plate

Facing

Temporary bracing

2×4 bottom plate

interior facing. Drill holes for electrical wiring before installing the interior facing or trimming the corner studs.

After you erect three walls, check their fit. If they don't meet satisfactorily, build the remaining walls in place, measuring them to fit. Tie the top plate joints with metal straps.

RAISING THE RAFTERS

To raise the roof, temporarily attach a long 2×4 to the bottom of the center post. Cut the top of the 2×4 square, and attach the center post with 2½-inch screws angled through opposite sides of the 2×4 into the bottom of the post. This way you can remove the 2×4 from below. Attach the first two rafters to opposite faces of the roof center post, and tilt the assembly through the opening to rest on top of the walls.

Attach the rafters to the center post with construction adhesive and framing screws driven with a drill/driver. Support the rafter tails as you raise the assembly to keep the rafters from pulling away from the center post. Set the rafters into the rafter ties and nail or screw them to the top plate. Fasten them into the rafter ties with framing-connector nails. Similarly attach the remaining rafters in opposing pairs. Remove the temporary 2×4.

ROOFING THE GAZEBO

You can install any type of roofing you prefer over the rafters. To install composition shingles over sheathing, bevel the bottom sheathing board or panel to the angle of the roof pitch, as shown in the illustration below. Use the table on page 108 to determine common pitch angles or use a bevel gauge to match the roof angle. (See pages 110–113 for information on shingles.)

RAISING THE RAFTERS

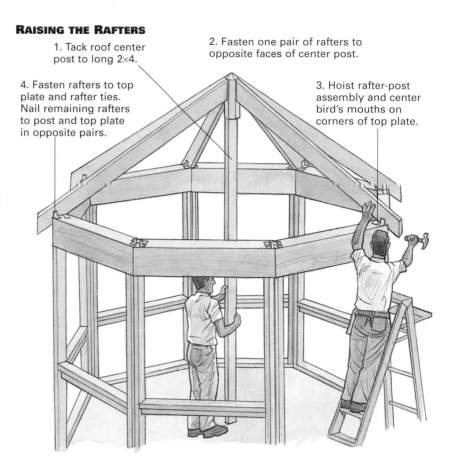

1. Tack roof center post to long 2×4.

2. Fasten one pair of rafters to opposite faces of center post.

4. Fasten rafters to top plate and rafter ties. Nail remaining rafters to post and top plate in opposite pairs.

3. Hoist rafter-post assembly and center bird's mouths on corners of top plate.

ROOFING THE GAZEBO

1. Bevel the bottom board to match rafter plumb cut.

2. Install roofing or sheathing from bottom to top.

2×6 rafter

Bird's mouth deepened to accept fascia

Fascia

Top plate

Stud

3. Install metal drip edge on eaves.

4. Staple felt paper and install shingles.

5. Seal gaps at center post with roofing cement.

Overlap felt paper.

BUILDING AND INSTALLING A CUPOLA

A cupola is built like a small roof, then installed on top of the main roof. Originally cupolas were built with open sides and served as a vent, allowing hot air to rise up and escape the building so cooler air could flow into the structure.

Although some cupolas are made for ventilation, most now are purely decorative.

This cupola can be added to any gazebo and modified to suit the style of the structure. The gazebo shown here is the open gazebo illustrated on the previous pages.

When constructing a gazebo with a cupola, build the main roof first and staple felt paper onto it. Next install the cupola and finally shingle both roofs at the same time.

DESIGN NOTES

The first question to ask when planning a cupola is: How high and wide should it be? The answer is a matter of style, so let your taste decide. Make side-view scale drawings of the gazebo, and sketch different-size cupolas on top to get an idea of how each would look. Rafter length can vary according to diameter and height, but a cupola roof looks best when its pitch is the same as that of the main roof.

The cupola base sections are cut from 2×12s, which are tall enough to accommodate the rafters on even a steep 12/12 roof pitch. The length shown produces a cupola that's about 30 inches in diameter. For a different size, multiply the desired cupola diameter times .416 to determine the length of the facets.

The proportions of a 2×12 base suit gazebos that are between 8 and 12 feet in diameter and roof pitches that are from 6/12 to 12/12. A 2×8 base made with 10-inch sections fits a smaller gazebo. On a larger gazebo make the cupola 3 to 4 feet in diameter with 2×6 cupola rafters.

To test your design, cut the pieces and assemble them with screws. Set the assembly on the main roof. If it looks too large or small, adjust the size of the base sections and recut the rafters. If the cupola looks too tall, for example, disassemble the base and rip the 2×12s to make them narrower.

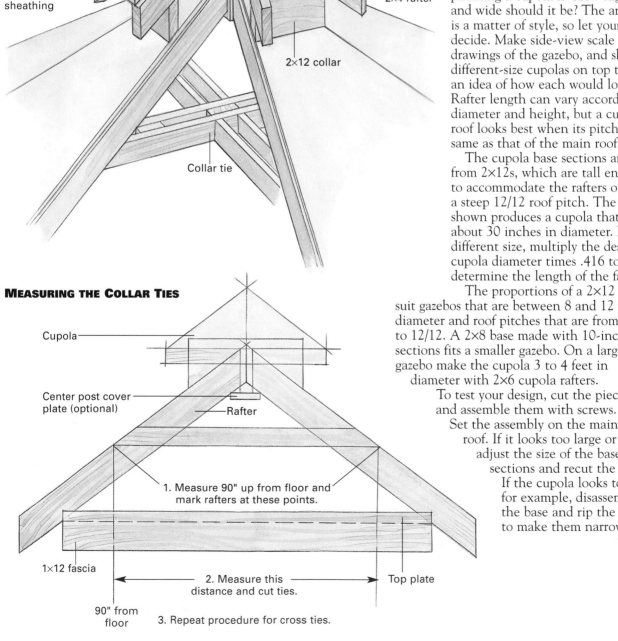

OPEN GAZEBO WITH CUPOLA (PERSPECTIVE VIEW)

Octagonal center post

Beveled 2×4

Composition or other shingles

Felt paper

1× or plywood sheathing

2×4 rafter

2×12 collar

Collar tie

MEASURING THE COLLAR TIES

Cupola

Center post cover plate (optional)

Rafter

1. Measure 90" up from floor and mark rafters at these points.

1×12 fascia

2. Measure this distance and cut ties.

Top plate

90" from floor

3. Repeat procedure for cross ties.

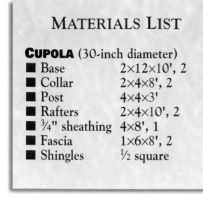

MATERIALS LIST

CUPOLA (30-inch diameter)
- Base   2×12×10', 2
- Collar   2×4×8', 2
- Post   4×4×3'
- Rafters   2×4×10', 2
- ¾" sheathing   4×8', 1
- Fascia   1×6×8', 2
- Shingles   ½ square

ASSEMBLING THE COLLAR TIES

1. Toenail collar tie A to rafters.

2. Toenail board B to rafter and face-nail to board A.

3. Attach board C.

4. Face-nail spacer D to A.

5. Attach board E to rafters and spacer.

6. Toenail board F to E and to rafter.

7. Toenail board G to E and to rafter.

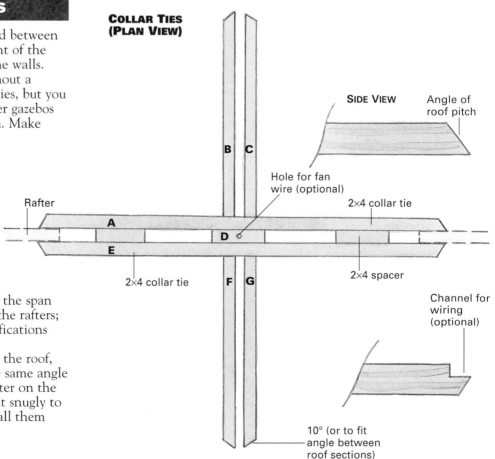

INSTALLING THE COLLAR TIES

Collar ties—boards attached between two rafters—keep the weight of the roof from pushing out on the walls. A 12-foot open gazebo without a cupola doesn't need collar ties, but you should install them on larger gazebos or any gazebo with a cupola. Make collar ties from 2×4 lumber for structures with 2×6 rafters; use 2×6s with 2×8 rafters. Install the collar ties before you put on the roofing or cupola.

Place collar ties 90 inches above the floor to accommodate the installation of a ceiling fan in an enclosed or screened gazebo. Make sure the span of the fan blades will clear the rafters; buy the fan or get the specifications before you install the ties.

The collar ties fit against the roof, so miter the top ends at the same angle as the roof. A 10-degree miter on the corners lets the collar ties fit snugly to the roof section. Don't install them square cut.

COLLAR TIES (PLAN VIEW)

SIDE VIEW   Angle of roof pitch

Hole for fan wire (optional)

Rafter

2×4 collar tie

2×4 collar tie

2×4 spacer

Channel for wiring (optional)

10° (or to fit angle between roof sections)

BUILDING AND INSTALLING A CUPOLA

continued

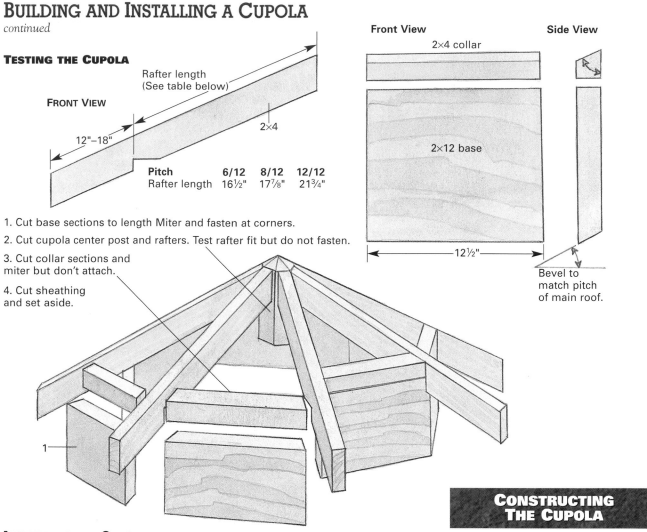

TESTING THE CUPOLA

FRONT VIEW

Rafter length
(See table below)

12"–18"

2×4

Pitch	6/12	8/12	12/12
Rafter length	16½"	17⅞"	21¾"

Front View

2×4 collar

2×12 base

12½"

Side View

Bevel to match pitch of main roof.

1. Cut base sections to length Miter and fasten at corners.

2. Cut cupola center post and rafters. Test rafter fit but do not fasten.

3. Cut collar sections and miter but don't attach.

4. Cut sheathing and set aside.

1

INSTALLING THE CUPOLA

1. Center base assembly on roof. Toenail to roof decking and install flashing.

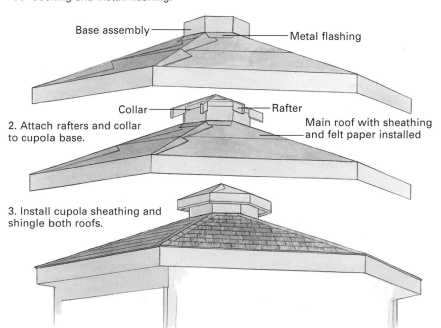

Base assembly

Metal flashing

Collar

Rafter

2. Attach rafters and collar to cupola base.

Main roof with sheathing and felt paper installed

3. Install cupola sheathing and shingle both roofs.

CONSTRUCTING THE CUPOLA

Cut the pieces in the order shown above. Cut the collar sections after you have fitted the rafters.

Assemble the base first. Miter the corners and bevel the bottom to match the pitch of the roof. Run a bead of construction adhesive on the mitered corners and assemble the base with 8d finish nails. Test the rafters following the same procedures you used with the main roof. Cut the cupola sheathing and number all the pieces. Then install the base assembly on the main roof.

Center the cupola base on the main roof and toenail it to the main roof rafters with 10d spiral nails. Install metal roof flashing around the bottom of the base, overlapping it at the corners.

Then toenail the rafters to the base, and the collar sections to both the rafters and the base. Nail the sheathing sections onto the cupola rafters and install the felt paper. Then shingle both roofs.

FINISHING AND TRIMMING

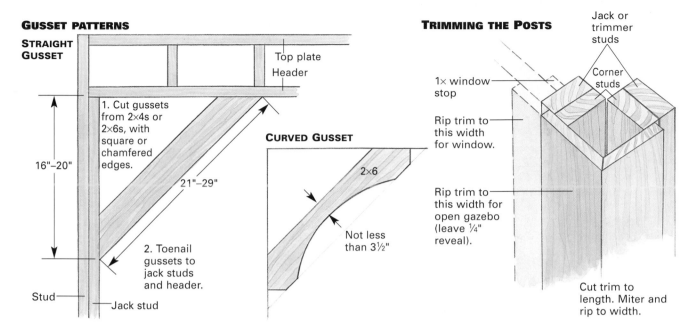

GUSSET PATTERNS

STRAIGHT GUSSET

Top plate
Header

16"–20"

1. Cut gussets from 2×4s or 2×6s, with square or chamfered edges.

21"–29"

2. Toenail gussets to jack studs and header.

Stud

Jack stud

CURVED GUSSET

2×6

Not less than 3½"

TRIMMING THE POSTS

Jack or trimmer studs

Corner studs

1× window stop

Rip trim to this width for window.

Rip trim to this width for open gazebo (leave ¼" reveal).

Cut trim to length. Miter and rip to width.

Finish the gazebo by installing gussets, post trim, and balusters. Page 235 shows decorative options.

and nail on the second piece. Snug the miters with 8d finish nails 6 inches apart from opposite sides.

INSTALLING THE GUSSETS

Gussets fit across the top corners of the openings. Their length and shape are matters of preference. To find the size you like best, start with a 2×4 that's 29 inches long, miter-cut at 45 degrees on both ends. Recut the miter at one end until you find a length you like. Then toenail the gusset to the studs with 10d nails. For curved gussets, make one overlength and test it by trimming from each end equally. Use the final one as a pattern.

INSTALLING BALUSTERS

Before you install the balusters, check local codes for spacing requirements. Cut the 2×2 balusters to fit between the rail and the bottom plate. Chamfer the ends. If you plan to inset them, fasten a 2×2 nailer across the bottom plate to provide a nailing surface. Experiment with three or four balusters to determine an interval that looks pleasing to you within the range required by code.

TRIMMING THE POSTS

Rip the trim for the corner posts from a 1×6. If you added jack studs to make narrower openings, you'll probably have to rip the trim from a wider board.

Measure the distance between the floor and the 1×12 facing (or from the bottom of the skirt if you want to carry the post line to the bottom) and cut the trim to length. Miter one edge at 22½ degrees and rip the other edge to the width needed. Install the trim with a ¼-inch reveal, as shown above. Fasten one piece of trim to the studs with 10d finish nails, apply construction adhesive along the mitered edge,

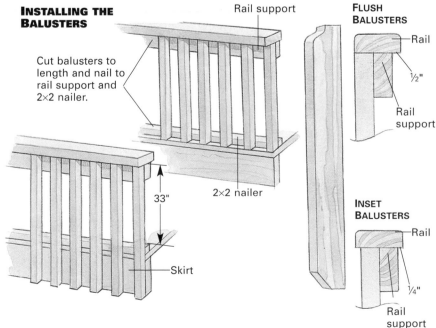

INSTALLING THE BALUSTERS

Cut balusters to length and nail to rail support and 2×2 nailer.

Rail support

2×2 nailer

33"

Skirt

FLUSH BALUSTERS

Rail

½"

Rail support

INSET BALUSTERS

Rail

¼"

Rail support

BUILDING A SCREENED GAZEBO

SCREENED GAZEBO

CUPOLA BASE

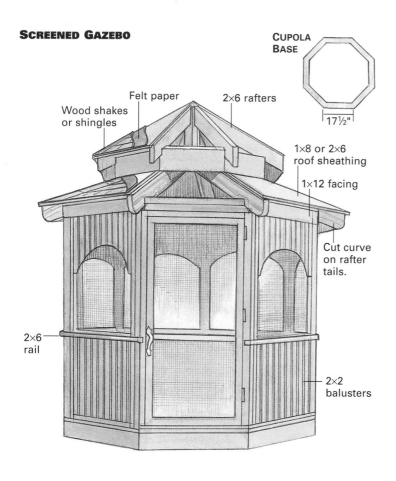

Felt paper

Wood shakes or shingles

2×6 rafters

1×8 or 2×6 roof sheathing

1×12 facing

Cut curve on rafter tails.

2×6 rail

2×2 balusters

17½"

Framing for the 9-foot-diameter screened gazebo is similar to the larger open gazebo described on the previous pages. Modifications include provisions for the screen panels and the door, shown in the illustrations on these pages. You can modify this design to build a larger gazebo, but screen panels for openings wider than about 48 inches require center supports.

FRAMING NOTES

Lay out the site with the frame shown on page 186, measuring 9 feet from side to side. Each facet will be about 43½ inches long; place the diagonals 32¼ inches from the corners. Build the floor, walls, and main roof following the procedures on pages 188–193. Construct the cupola as shown on pages 194–197. Build both roofs with an 8/12 pitch. The rafter length for the main roof (measured from peak to outer plate edge) is 70⅞ inches; for the cupola roof, 25¼ inches.

■ **INSTALLING THE DOOR:** To install a door, add jack studs to the entry opening to create a rough opening. Use either of the methods shown on the opposite page. For a door that is hinged to the framing, make a rough opening as wide as the door plus ¼ inch. To hang the door in a jamb, buy or build the jamb first, then make a rough opening to fit it. Position the jack studs to center the rough opening in the wall. The

INSTALLING SCREEN PANELS

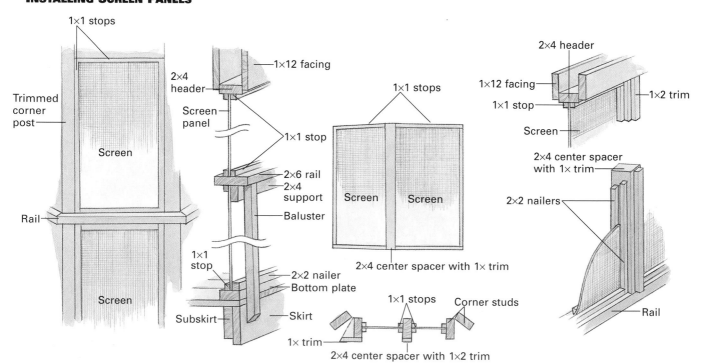

1×1 stops

Trimmed corner post

Screen

Rail

Screen

1×12 facing

2×4 header

Screen panel

1×1 stop

2×6 rail
2×4 support

Baluster

1×1 stop

2×2 nailer

Bottom plate

Skirt

Subskirt

1×1 stops

Screen   Screen

2×4 center spacer with 1× trim

1×1 stops   Corner studs

1× trim

2×4 center spacer with 1×2 trim

2×4 header

1×12 facing

1×1 stop

Screen

1×2 trim

2×4 center spacer with 1× trim

2×2 nailers

Rail

FRAMING THE DOOR

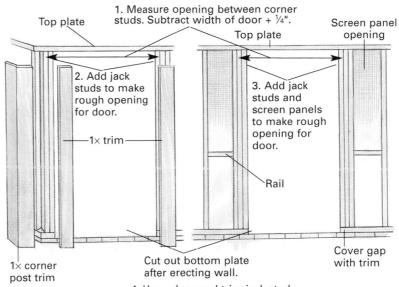

FRAMING A WIDE OPENING

Top plate

1. Measure opening between corner studs. Subtract width of door + ¼".

2. Add jack studs to make rough opening for door.

1× trim

1× corner post trim

Cut out bottom plate after erecting wall.

FRAMING A NARROW OPENING

Screen panel opening

Top plate

3. Add jack studs and screen panels to make rough opening for door.

Rail

Cover gap with trim

4. Hang door and trim jack studs. Install door batteries.

---

door shown is a commercial screen door with batteries added to match the design.

■ **INSTALLING THE RAILS:** Install notched 2×6 rails, as shown on page 192. Attach the rail support flush with the front edge of the studs so the balusters can extend down over the skirting.

■ **INSTALLING BATTENS AND BALUSTERS:** Cut the 2×2 balusters and window batteries. Chamfer the edges and nail the batteries 3 inches on center to the rail support and skirting. Tack the window batteries to the fascias above the openings. Make a cardboard template of the curve and trace the curve onto the batteries. Remove the batteries, cut them, and nail them on.

MATERIALS LIST

FOUNDATION, FLOOR, AND WALLS
■ Posts	4×4×10', 4
■ Joists	2×6×10', 8
■ Subskirt	2×6×10', 4
■ Skirt	2×8×10', 4
■ Deck	2×6×8', 6
	2×6×10', 13
■ Studs, plates	2×4×8', 48
■ Header trim	1×12×8', 8
■ Sill	2×6×10', 4
■ Rail support	2×4×10', 4
■ Balusters and batteries	2×2×8', 60

ROOF
■ Area	160 sq. ft.
■ Shingles	2 squares
■ Rafters	2×6×10', 8
■ Fascia	1×8×10', 4
■ Roof boards	1×8×10', 26
or tongue-and-groove	2×6×10', 40
■ OSB or plywood	4×8', 7
■ Trim	1×8×12', 12

CUPOLA (42-INCH DIAMETER)
■ Base	2×12×14', 2
■ Collar	2×4×12', 2
■ Rafters	2×4×12', 2
■ ¾" sheathing	4×8', 1
■ Fascia	1×6×10', 2
■ Shingles	½ square

■ **INSTALLING THE SCREENS:** Cut two sets of 1×1 stops to fit each opening. Nail in the outer stops. Measure each opening and make a screen panel for it with standard fiberglass screening and metal frame members available from home centers or lumberyards. Install the screens and nail in the inner stops to hold them.

CUTTING WINDOW BATTENS

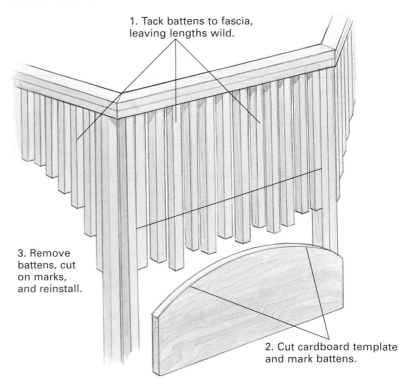

1. Tack batteries to fascia, leaving lengths wild.

3. Remove batteries, cut on marks, and reinstall.

2. Cut cardboard template and mark batteries.

BUILDING WALLS AND FENCES

Wonderfully versatile, fences and walls do far more for your landscape than mark property lines. They corral pets and keep out strays, frame things you want to showcase, and hide things you don't want to see. They can lift vines to new heights and knock down high winds. Fences define spaces, separating one from another. Walls impart a sense of permanence to the landscape, halting the erosion of the soil and standing firm against the vagaries of the weather. Time only enhances their beauty and your reputation for having the foresight to build them well.

Now that you've drawn your plans, had the materials delivered, and gathered your tools, it's time to turn your ideas into reality. Fences and walls start out with similar layout techniques. After that, construction can get a little more complicated. Most fences don't require much more than basic building skills. Wall building, however, can call for skills you've never used before and haven't had a chance to develop. Don't expect to start building large brick walls after only a day or two of practice. Start small and work slowly. You'll soon find your abilities growing right along with the size of your projects.

PROPERTY BOUNDARIES: WHERE TO DRAW THE LINE

Before you build a fence or wall on the edge of your property, know where the edge is. A plot map of your land (available at your local courthouse) will help, but you can be certain only with markers on the property itself. Use a metal detector to check for marker stakes. If they're not there get a survey to prevent boundary disputes and avoid questions that would arise when you sell your home.

At first you may not notice that this fence section is really a gate. By repeating elements of the fence bays in the gate and its frame, the homeowners have created an understated entrance to this garden.

Using spacers—one above the rail and one below—will keep board infill members parallel and evenly spaced.

Plumbing posts can be a chore if you're working alone. To make things easier hold the bracing as shown and when the post is level, grasp the brace and post firmly and mark the post where the brace intersects. Fasten the brace on the line you marked.

Rental yards carry engine-powered concrete saws that make short work of cutting masonry blocks. Be sure to wear protective clothing, goggles, and a dust mask when sawing concrete.

BUILDING TIPS
(SO YOUR WALL WON'T)

When building a *timber retaining wall*, use only timbers that are treated for ground contact. They are slightly more expensive than lightly treated timbers, but the less expensive timbers will rot and the wall will fail sooner.

For *dry-laid rock walls*, use flat sedimentary stones such as ashlar and flagstone. Lay the thickest and largest stones for the first course. Set the longest stones perpendicular to the wall as bond stones to tie the wall together.

When using *fieldstone*, sort by size. Use the largest stones for the first course, and use the small stones as fillers spaced uniformly throughout the wall.

WALL-BUILDING TECHNIQUES

Good walls, well made, add style to a landscape. Before you begin check local building codes for limits on wall height and setback, and plan your design so it harmonizes with the rest of your landscape.

Consider the materials already present in your landscape and the impact your new wall will have on its overall design. Choose materials that reflect the natural look of your region and the architectural style of your neighborhood, your house, and other landscape structures near it.

If the choices get to be overwhelming, take pictures of your site to a gardening center or a professional landscaper. They can help you narrow the alternatives.

As you consider the design features of materials, evaluate the amount of work each requires and strike a balance between design, budget, and your skills. Stacked landscaping timbers make wall building easy. So do dry-stacked walls—easy, but heavy. Mortaring brick and stone requires some special skills, so you may not want to tackle it yourself or without experienced help.

MATERIALS

CONCRETE BLOCK has strength and economy in its favor. Its functional appearance may limit where you use it.

BRICK has great versatility in its many surface finishes and patterns.

TIMBER is affordable and rustic, a quality that complements many landscapes.

STONE can bring with it high transportation costs, but nothing else might do in a woodland setting.

PRECAST DECORATIVE STONES, either pinned (with holes for inserting rebar) or interlocking, are self-aligning and take the guesswork out of positioning. They are especially useful if you need to build a retaining wall.

LAYING OUT A WALL

The technique for laying out a wall is much the same as laying out a fence (see "Laying Out a Fence Line" on page 214). First make batter boards from 2×4s and drive them into the ground 2 to 4 feet beyond the wall corners. Stretch mason's lines between the crosspieces of the batter boards. The lines should outline your wall, intersecting over the corners.

SQUARE? Corners must be precise. Use a 3-4-5 triangle to square the corners. Measure along two lines from the corner where they intersect—mark a point 4 feet from the corner along one line and a point 3 feet from the corner along the other line. Adjust the

DRAINING A RETAINING WALL

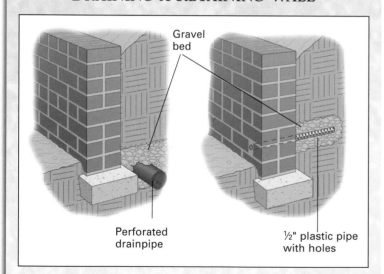

Gravel bed

Perforated drainpipe

½" plastic pipe with holes

Without adequate drainage water pressure can build up behind a retaining wall and crack it. To prevent water pressure from ruining all your hard work, dig a trench at least 8 inches deep and wide behind the foundation. Shovel gravel into it, making one end higher than the other. Lay perforated drainpipe, holes facing down, on the gravel. The slope of the gravel directs water away from the wall.

Another solution is to place ½-inch perforated plastic pipe every 4 feet along the wall in the first above-grade course. Cut an inch off adjacent bricks to fit the pipe. Build up mortar under the pipe at the back of the wall so the pipe tilts up into the backfill. Surround the pipe with a few inches of gravel as you backfill.

WORK CREW

Building a wall requires lots of lugging and lifting, so it's wise—and more fun—to have some volunteer help, at least two strong workers (more, if possible). If your friends have some experience and construction skills, so much the better. You'll discover that friends with the most building savvy will have fewer prior commitments if you mention the "builder's buffet" you'll be serving on the work site. (A pizza fulfills your obligation.)

lines until the marks are 5 feet apart. Tweak your mason's lines until all corners pass this test.

With the corners squared, drop a plumb line at each intersection and when the plumb bob comes to rest, mark the ground with a stake. Then stretch a line at the base of the stakes and use chalk or spray paint to mark the course of the wall.

FIRM FOOTING

Walls need better support than they can get from bare ground. Your choice of a gravel bed or concrete footings depends on the type of wall you build.

MORTARED WALLS: Mortared walls require footings twice as wide as the wall and deep enough to extend below the frost line.

Frost depth varies by region and soil type. In one area, for example, well-drained sandy soil may freeze to a depth of perhaps a foot, while just miles away clay soil may be frozen to a depth of 4 feet. Check with your local building department to find the frost depth for your area.

Build forms for the footings with 2×8s and tie them together with 1× scrap across the top to keep the weight of the concrete from bowing them. Make sure the inside dimensions—not the outside—conform to the footing width required. Once your forms are set and leveled, lay in rebar to provide reinforcement—two horizontal lengths (parallel to the edges) and vertical lengths at intervals appropriate for your materials.

DRY-STACKED WALLS: You won't need footings for a wall that is set without mortar, or "dry-stacked." Footings keep walls from cracking with frost heave, and because there is no mortar in a dry-stacked wall, there's nothing to crack. The pieces shift and settle with the frost. Dry-stacked walls do need a bed, however—a trench about 8 inches deep, as wide as the wall, with 6 inches of tamped gravel for drainage. And all stone retaining walls require a drainage trench to keep water from backing up behind them (see "Water Disposal," below).

RETAINING WALLS

Retaining walls must hold back the pressure of the earth behind them, so they must be designed with special considerations.

WATER DISPOSAL: If you are building a solid retaining wall on a sloped site, water running down the slope and the back side of the wall surface must not be permitted to build up behind it. When you excavate for a retaining wall, dig the trench wide enough for the first course plus an extra foot into the slope. Lay one or two courses. Then pour a 4-inch gravel drainage bed, sloping it 1 inch for every 4 feet. Lay 4-inch perforated drainpipe and 4 more inches of gravel. Cover it with landscape fabric and then with soil and sod. The drainpipe must end at a storm drain or a catch basin.

If your wall is dry-stacked stone or timber, the spaces between the materials will act as "weep holes" and let the water pass through. You can also drill 1-inch holes every 2 feet in the second course of a timber wall to improve drainage. Landscape fabric behind the wall will keep soil from washing through.

STAGGERED COURSES: When laying timber or stone retaining walls, each succeeding course must be staggered backward into the slope. Staggering adds strength and will keep the wall from bowing over time. To stagger the face set the front edge of each succeeding course about an inch back from the preceding one, using a batter guide as illustrated on page 206.

GREAT WALL OPTIONS

Don't build a plain old wall if you want something more attractive. Enhance your wall with special features. For example, incorporate a planter in a brick wall or enclose a waterfall that spills into a pool. Spice up your design with unique brick patterns.

For flowers or ground covers, interrupt dry stone or timber walls at random with exposed soil.

ESTIMATING MORTAR MATERIALS

Dealers can help you estimate your needs if you provide measurements and material preferences. They can also calculate the amount and cost of cement, mortar, and landscape fabric.

■ **AREA:** You can get a rough idea of some materials yourself, using a tape measure and pencil. Concrete block, brick, and landscape timbers have uniform dimensions, so it's simple to estimate how much of these materials you'll need. Here's how: Multiply the length and height of your wall to get its area in square feet. Then divide that total area by the dimensions of one piece of the material—one block, for instance—for a rough estimate of the number of pieces in the face of the wall. Remember to double that number if your wall is double the width of a single block or brick wall.

■ **WEIGHT:** Estimating stone is more difficult. Round stone is sold by weight: Eighty 25-pound stones make a ton. Your dealer can estimate the amount needed from the dimensions of your project.

These materials are too heavy to haul in a pickup. Have them delivered to your job site. Stone and brick are shipped on pallets and lifted with a hydraulic arm.

MORTARED STONE WALLS

LAYING MORTARED STONE

Laying stones of irregular size will result in mortar joints that are not uniform or straight. Use mason's line as a guide to keep the wall plumb. At its base the mortar bed atop the footings must be thick enough to fill the joints between stones. Use small stones to fill gaps and reduce the size of the mortar joints.

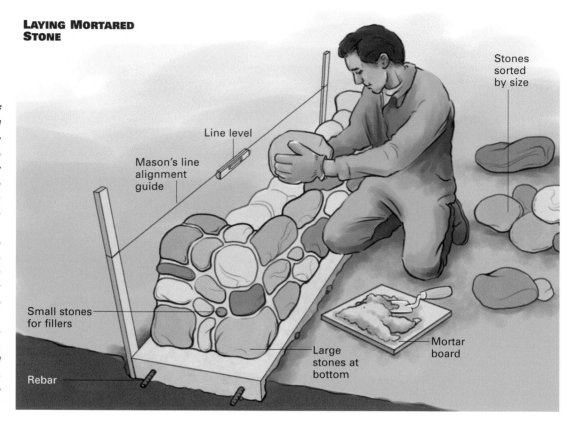

Line level

Mason's line alignment guide

Stones sorted by size

Small stones for fillers

Large stones at bottom

Mortar board

Rebar

"Like a rock." From poets to truck makers, people have turned to stone as the standard—the symbol of durability. Styles come and go, but stone stays. And with mortar, it also stays put. If that's what you want in a landscape wall, here's how to get it.

LAYOUT

Review "Laying Out a Wall" on page 202. Make batter boards from 2×4s and drive them into the ground 2 to 4 feet beyond the ends of your wall. Run mason's line between the batter boards to define the wall's edge.

TEST SQUARE: Be sure the corners are square— use a 3-4-5 triangle. From an intersection of your mason's lines, measure 3 feet along one line and mark it. From the same intersection, measure 4 feet along the other line. Adjust the lines on the batter boards until the diagonal measurement between your marks is exactly 5 feet.

Drop a plumb line at each precise corner point and mark each of the spots with a stake. Then stretch a line at the base of the stakes and use chalk or spray paint to mark the course of your wall.

Excavate for footings, retaining walls, and the drainage area (review "Water Disposal," page 203).

FOUNDATION

As you move your materials, you'll see why building mortared stone walls is heavy work. You'll also understand why the foundation has to be strong.

FOOTINGS should be as thick as the wall, twice as wide, and as deep as local codes specify. Lay in a 4-inch gravel base; level and tamp it.

REINFORCEMENT: In areas subject to frost heave, strong winds, or earthquakes, use rebar to strengthen any wall more than 3 feet high. Lay rebar along its length on each side and drive vertical lengths into the ground, leaving at least 2 feet exposed.

Pour the concrete and allow it to cure for a week. While it cures, you can prepare the rest of your materials.

COST CONTROL

You can cut your costs by filling the core of the wall with stones less attractive than those used on the wall's face.

To avoid wasted mortar, adjust batch sizes to the amount you can use in two hours. When laying a stone wall, the consistency of the mortar must be thick enough to support the weight of the stones without displacing the mortar.

SORT THE STONE

While the footings cure, sort the stones by size and appearance.

■ The largest will form the first course; use smaller stones as the wall rises.

■ The most attractive will be face stone, prominent on the wall's most visible surface.

■ Ugly stones have a place, but it's on the less visible side of the finished wall.

■ Long, flat pieces make bond stones, to be set perpendicular to the face of the wall. They tie it together from front to back.

■ Rubble, little stones, will function as filler.

CLEANER IS STRONGER: Now that everything is sorted, lay the first course next to the footing. Wash the stones with a pressure sprayer. They must be free of soil and clay or the mortar won't stick to them.

Keep the hose handy. You'll need it for mixing mortar and to wet the stone if you're laying sandstone or absorbent fieldstone. These stones absorb moisture rapidly, and wetting them will keep your mortar from drying prematurely. Nonabsorbent fieldstone and river rock don't need wetting.

MORTAR

Mortar comes in pre-mixed bags—or make your own from masonry cement, adding sand and water in quantities specified on the bag.

MIXING: For a job as big as a wall, rent a power mixer (or try to convince your kids this is an opportunity to spend some quality time together). Even with a mixer, you'll need one helper just to mix and move the mortar.

BEDTIME: Use a mason's trowel to spread a bed of mortar on the footing. The bed must be thick enough (at least an inch) to fill the cracks between stones in the first course. Start the ends of your first course with bond stones.

MOVING UP: Once a course is laid, wait until the mortar sets slightly (to keep from dislodging it), then lay mortar and stone for the next course. Fit stones as snugly as possible. Fill gaps with small stones and lay a bond stone every 6 to 10 square feet.

STRIKING: Use a ½-inch dowel to smooth the joints between the stones. Then remove any residual mortar with a stiff brush. To avoid mortar stains on the stones, do not wash the wall until the mortar is completely set.

CURING: It takes between 3 and 7 days for a mortared wall to cure.

MORTARED STONE

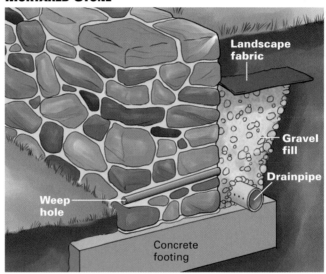

Mortared stone is the most permanent material. Pour a concrete footing as the base. A large drainpipe carries away most rainwater, and small drainpipe weep holes let excess water pass through from the other side.

POURED-CONCRETE WALLS

A poured-concrete retaining wall requires forming and placing a large amount of concrete, so consider hiring a contractor to build it.

The process involves wiring horizontal, vertical and 90-degree angle rebar in place before the footing is poured. Then vertical rebar is wired to horizontal rebar every 12 inches from the footing to the top of the wall. The rebar helps support the heavy wall. Forms are assembled at the front and back sides of the wall, and concrete is poured into the forms. When the concrete wall has cured, the forms are removed and gravel is filled into the space between the wall and the earth slope. A perforated drainpipe laid near the footing provides drainage behind the wall. The top foot of the wall is backfilled with soil.

Note that the footing is stabilized by earth fill on the front face and by the weight of gravel and earth on the back side of the wall.

If the wall is more than 3 feet high, the concrete forms need to be set so the base of the wall is thicker than the top and the face of the wall slants back toward the sloped soil.

DRY-STACKED STONE WALLS

To keep the weight of water runoff from destroying your retaining wall, install a drainage system. Lay perforated drainpipe in gravel so it can carry water away to a dry well or another area that will soak up the runoff. Add more gravel, then landscaping fabric. As you build upward, fill the area behind the wall with gravel, and finish off the top with soil and sod or plantings.

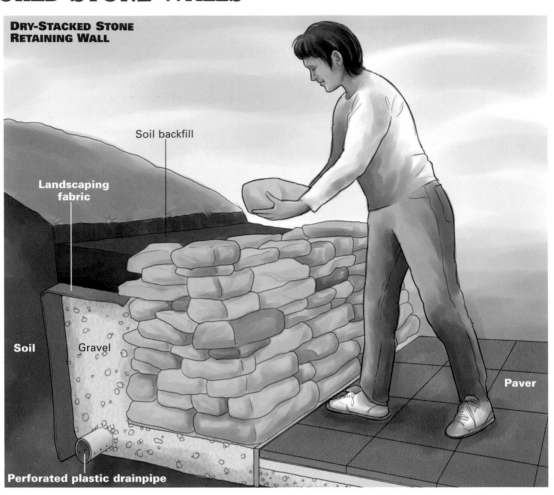

DRY-STACKED STONE RETAINING WALL

Soil backfill

Landscaping fabric

Soil

Gravel

Paver

Perforated plastic drainpipe

Building a dry-stacked stone wall requires patience and care. To make your work easier, have a crew on hand to help with the work.

SHOPPING FOR STONE

Make a batter guide from a board cut to the height of the wall, then cut at an angle along its length. Taper the guide 1 inch for every 2 feet of wall height. Tape a level to its straight side and use it to check the wall as you build it. When the bubble is centered, the angle is correct.

Take the measurements of your wall to your garden center or outdoor landscaping specialist. The dealer can help estimate the amount of stone you will need. When you

USING A BATTER GUIDE

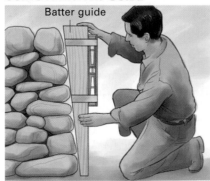

Batter guide

shop for stone, remember that round boulders are the most difficult to lay because they do not align well to the course below. Flat stones are much easier to stack and fit.

NO FOOTING REQUIRED

A dry-laid stone wall does not require a footing but does require drainage. Dig a trench at least 1 foot deep—check with your building department for soil conditions and excavation requirements in your area—and pour and tamp a 6-inch gravel or crushed-stone base.

If you're building a retaining wall, you will also have to cut into the slope—either straight or at the same angle as the finished face (see "Angling the Face," page 207).

Lay out the footing excavation with batter boards and mason's line, squaring the corners by measuring off a 3-4-5 triangle (see "Laying Out a Wall," page 202).

Excavate the footing trench to the depth required by local codes and lay the gravel bed. Level the bed and tamp it firmly.

PREPARATION

After you have dug and laid the bed with gravel, sort the stones by size and shape. Use a wheelbarrow to move the sorted piles along the length of the wall. You will use the largest stones for the bottom courses and smaller stones for filler.

As you're sorting set aside the longest stones for bonding (they will tie the wall together perpendicularly) and make a pile of the broadest ones for cap stones.

ANGLING THE FACE

Because only gravity and friction hold the stones in place, the face of a free-standing wall must be sloped (or battered) to carry the weight. Each succeeding course must be set back about 1 inch for every vertical foot. The face of each course must slant toward the center (or the slope on a retaining wall). Use 1×4 lumber to build a batter guide (*opposite, lower left*) to check the wall as you lay the stones.

MAKING THE WALL

Start with bonding stones at the ends of the wall, then fill in toward the center, keeping the front edges of the stones at a slight slant toward the center. Use the slope gauge you've

built—it will help you keep the angle consistent. Select stones that fit together as tightly as possible. Because gravity and friction hold the wall together, each stone should have maximum contact and surface bearing on the one below. Use small stones to fill any gaps and to stabilize the large stones. Lay another bonding stone perpendicular to the face of the wall at least every 6 to 10 square feet. Bonding stones lock the wall together front to back.

RETAINING WALLS

If you're building a retaining wall, you can excavate the side of the slope to the desired angle. Also excavate the drainage trench for gravel and perforated drainpipe.

After you lay the first course of stone, put landscape fabric behind it and fill the space between the wall and the slope with gravel. If the fabric is as long as the height of the wall, you can pull it up with each succeeding course, backfilling with gravel as you go. Landscape fabric will keep grass and weeds from growing between the stones, and it will let water drain out and keep the soil from washing through it.

DRY-STACKED DECORATIVE WALL

For stability in a dry stone wall, keep the batter sharp and lay bond stones every three or four courses.

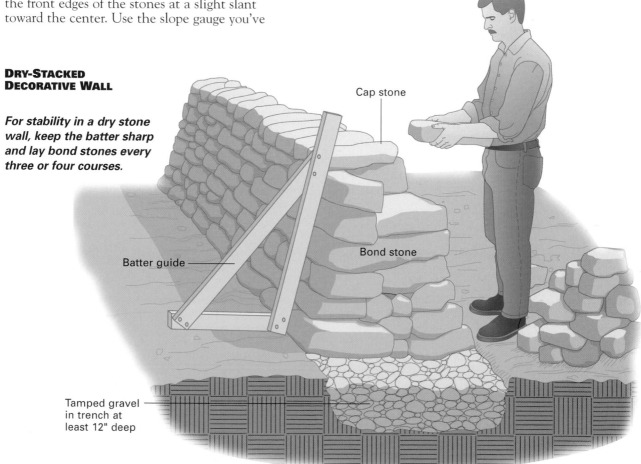

Cap stone

Bond stone

Batter guide

Tamped gravel in trench at least 12" deep

CONCRETE BLOCK WALLS

LAYING CONCRETE BLOCK

Mortar buttered on block ends

Concrete footing

Strike joints with steel tool

Use stiff brush to clean struck joints

Lay out the concrete blocks so the joints are staggered, as shown. For greater strength on high walls, use reinforcing wire in mortar between joints and fill the blocks with mortar.

Concrete block is inexpensive, durable, and relatively easy to install. And you can build in stages, working as your time permits.

FOOTINGS FIRST

Lay out and excavate for footings as described on page 204. Use batter boards and mason's lines and square the corners. Footing standards are the same as for other walls—twice the width of the wall and deeper than the frost line (at least as deep as the width of the wall).

REINFORCEMENT: Set rebar perpendicular to the footings to reinforce the wall against lateral or side pressure. About 8 inches from the bottom ends, bend the rebar to form a 90-degree angle and set the bent ends into the wet concrete. Place the rebar on 32-inch centers so they will extend up through the cores of the blocks.

To avoid injury while the footings are curing, tie red flags to the rebar tops.

ON THE LEVEL

Retaining walls must be level and plumb. Lay a uniform mortar bed so all joints will be ⅜-inch wide. Test each block for level and plumb. As needed tap the blocks with the trowel handle to level the blocks.

BLOCK LAYOUT

Let the footings cure for at least three days, then lay out your first course without mortar. String the blocks along the footings, leaving ⅜-inch gaps (the width of the mortar joints). Limit the amount of cutting by using only full or half-blocks.

CUTTING BLOCKS: Mark a line on both faces of the block. Strike a mason's chisel lightly alone the line, working around both sides until the block splits.

MORTARING

A simple mortar formula for laying blocks is one part masonry cement and 2½ parts mason's sand, plus enough water to make a workable consistency. Test the mortar with a mason's trowel: Scoop up some mortar, shake off the excess, then turn the trowel over. If the mortar is right, it will stick to the trowel.

Using a mason's trowel, spread a full bed of mortar on the footings, about 1-inch thick and completely covering the course. Push the end blocks down until there is about ⅜ inch of mortar between the footing and the blocks.

BUILDING LEADS

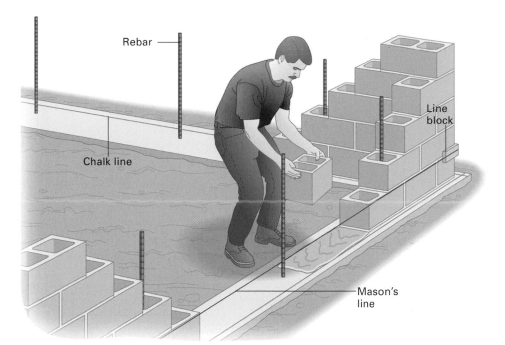

Rebar

Chalk line

Line block

Mason's line

A block wall calls for many of the techniques that apply to a brick wall. Chalk a layout line, then lay the first course in a 1-inch mortar bed. Build leads and string mason's line to maintain even courses.

After setting the end blocks, fasten a mason's line to align the intermediate blocks. Use a carpenter's level to make sure each block is level and plumb.

When you have completed the first course of blocks, lay reinforcing wire in the mortar to strengthen the joints.

Start succeeding courses at the corners so you have something to tie the mason's line onto. Constantly check for level and plumb as you proceed up the wall.

STRIKING: Press your thumb against the mortar joints; when the mortar is firm, use a jointing tool to strike the joints.

FILLING: After the blocks are laid, fill the cores that enclose the rebars with a pourable concrete mix.

CAPPING

Cap the wall with concrete or brick to keep water from entering the blocks. For a concrete cap, stuff fiberglass insulation into the cores of the top blocks to keep the concrete from falling in. Then trowel the cap onto the top of the wall.

STUCCOING A BLOCK WALL

Concrete block has an industrial appearance, but that can be remedied by stuccoing over it. First coat the blocks with a latex bonding agent. Then apply the stucco coats of the desired color.

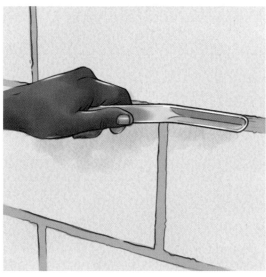

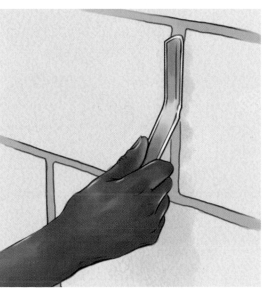

Finish the joints with a striking tool. Start with the horizontal joints and then strike the vertical joints. Jointing removes small mortar lodges that can trap and hold water, which could freeze and crack the mortar.

BRICK WALLS

LAYING A BRICK WALL

Lay a brick wall on a concrete footing. Note the line stretched between wood corner blocks as a guide to keep the courses straight. Walls more than a foot high require a double thickness of bricks.

The staggered pattern known as running bond is the most popular method of laying courses of brick. Use a carpenter's level to check brick alignment.

Line blocks and mason's line

Concrete footing

Check brick alignment with level

Brick can be laid in many decorative patterns: from flowing lines that fit informal landscapes to rectangular forms that accent formal styles.

FOOTINGS

If your wall is going to be no more than a foot high, such as a flower-bed border, you can lay it in a single row (one brick wide). Any wall higher than a foot should be laid in two rows (called wythes) with ⅜-inch spacing (the thickness of a mortar joint) between. Laid with these dimensions a wall can be spanned with a one-brick header.

Set the wall on concrete footings that are twice as wide as the wall and at least as deep as the wall's width (always deeper than the local frost line). Because soil varies check with your local building department to be sure your footing construction conforms to local requirements.

Lay out, excavate, and pour footings as described on page 204. Include the drainage area for retaining walls (see "Water Disposal," page 203). Drive batter boards and square the corners with mason's lines. Excavate the soil to the depth of the footing plus a 4-inch gravel base. Make forms if necessary and install rebar along the length on both sides and vertically at 2-foot intervals if your wall will be more than 3 feet high. Pour the footings and let them cure three to seven days.

MORTAR

Mix mortar for brickwork with 1 part portland cement, ¼ part hydrated lime, and 3 parts sand (or 1 part portland cement, 1 part masonry cement and 6 parts sand). Add water gradually as you mix. It should be plastic but not runny.

TEST MIX: Load up a mason's trowel; shake off the excess, then turn the trowel over. The mortar should cling to the trowel.

FIRST COURSE: Chalk a line for the front edge of the first course. String the first course along the center of the footings so only full or half-bricks are used to eliminate unnecessary cutting. Leave a ⅜-inch gap between bricks for the mortar joint. Mark the footings at the end of each brick to serve as a guide.

Trowel mortar on the footings about ¾-inch deep and make a furrow down the center of the bed to spread it. Lay the first course in parallel bricks, starting with the corners and working to the center.

SUCCEEDING COURSES: The arrangement of succeeding courses will depend on your choice of pattern (or bond). For a running bond start the second and alternate courses with a half-brick. Lay the corners five courses high so you have something to hold the line that will help you keep the courses straight.

Continue laying the bricks from both ends toward the middle, buttering the end of each brick before putting it in place. Then set the brick in the mortar and press it in position.

Be careful to maintain both the vertical and horizontal mortar joints at a ⅜-inch thickness. Use a level to check the bricks for level and plumb, and remove excess mortar with the edge of the trowel.

CLOSURE: Install the closure or last brick in the course at the middle of the wall. Butter both ends of the closure brick with mortar and set it straight down in the gap. When you finish the wall, cap it with a course of bricks laid on edge so no holes are showing.

BRICKLAYING TECHNIQUE

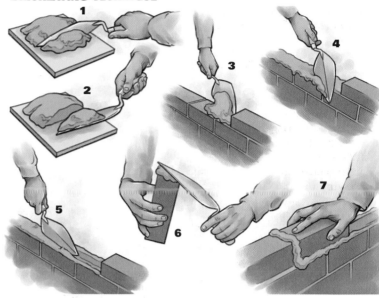

Follow these steps when laying brick: 1) Cut mortar from mortarboard. 2) Pick up mortar with a snapping motion. 3) Throw mortar with a sweeping motion and spread it evenly. 4) Cut off excess. 5) Lightly furrow the center of the bed. 6) Butter the ends of the brick with mortar using a sharp downward motion. 7) Shove the brick in place to force the mortar out of the joint.

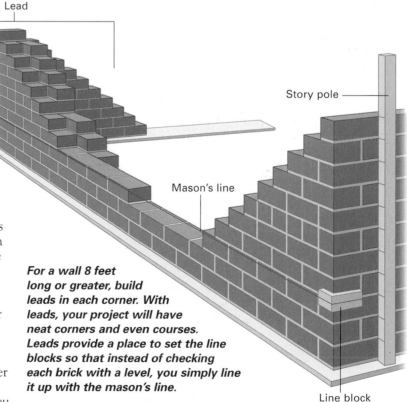

For a wall 8 feet long or greater, build leads in each corner. With leads, your project will have neat corners and even courses. Leads provide a place to set the line blocks so that instead of checking each brick with a level, you simply line it up with the mason's line.

PRECAST BLOCK WALLS

Precast block expands the capabilities of landscape designers and puts wall building within the reach of the homeowner. Attractive and effective, it's especially useful for retaining walls.

BEAUTY AND BRAWN

Decorative block has the color, texture, and shape to simulate natural stone. Some are cast in shapes that add expression to the face of the wall.

One type of precast block has alignment holes positioned to take the guesswork out of assembly. Others have interlocking lips that align the blocks and secure them in place.

EASY ASSEMBLY

No footings are required for precast block installation. Simply dig a trench and pour, level, and tamp a 4- to 6-inch gravel bed. To assemble, stack the blocks in tiers, interlocking their joints—or drive rebar through the alignment holes into the soil at the base of the wall. Some models require fiberglass pins to lock the stones together.

GREEN WALLS

Blocks cast in the shape of oversize flowerpots can be used to construct planted or "green" walls. Remove soil to position. Level the blocks and fill the planting area with the soil. Stairstep your design up the slope face and plant flowers or groundcover. Look under "Concrete Products" in the yellow pages of your phone book to find a manufacturer in your area.

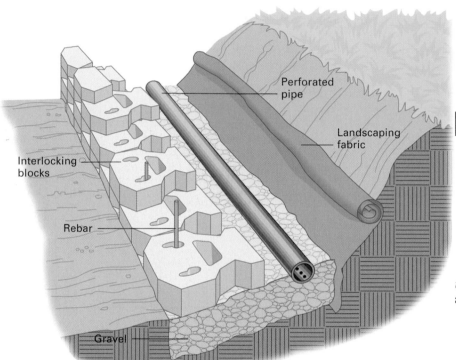

Perforated pipe

Landscaping fabric

Interlocking blocks

Rebar

Gravel

Sections of rebar or fiberglass anchoring pins help hold the blocks in place. Gravel and perforated pipe prevent damage from water pressure.

Some concrete blocks are self battering—made with a ridge along the lower back edge that hooks against the block below it.

These ridges also set each succeeding course back from the one below it. Interlocking blocks work best for walls that are no more than a few feet tall.

INTERLOCKING BLOCK

Landscape fabric

Interlocking blocks

Gravel fill

TIMBER WALLS

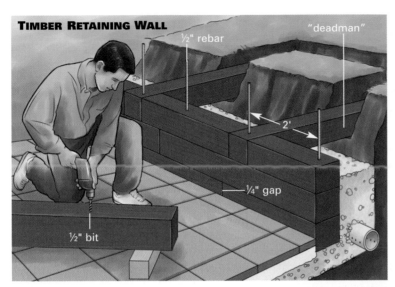

TIMBER RETAINING WALL

½" rebar

"deadman"

2'

¼" gap

½" bit

The first course of timbers is installed below grade. Use a chain saw to cut timbers as needed. The timbers rest upon a level bed of gravel. Position a perforated drainpipe at footing level, sloped ¼ inch per foot toward a storm drain or dry well (a hole filled with crushed rock). Lay landscape fabric over the drainpipe to prevent silt from plugging the drain holes. When the deadmen (see below) are in place, fill the area behind the timber wall with gravel.

Timber retaining walls, once built of railroad ties, now are most often made with commercial landscape timbers treated to resist moisture and insects.

ASSEMBLY

No footings are needed. Dig a trench about a foot deep and shovel in 6 inches of gravel for drainage. Wet, tamp, and level the gravel before laying the first course of timbers.

■ Drill ½-inch holes down through the base timbers and drive 18-inch-long rebar into the soil. Be sure the timbers are level along their length and across their width.

■ Position the second course of timbers so its front edge is ½ inch behind the front face of the first course. Stagger the joints.

■ Drill 1-inch weep holes every 2 feet in the second course—or leave slight gaps at each joint—to provide drainage through the wall.

■ Drill ¼-inch holes at each end and at 2-foot intervals along the timber length. Drive 10-inch barn spikes into the holes.

■ Continue laying up courses, each set back ½ inch from the one below it. Check often to be sure timbers are plumb and level.

For stability cut 4-foot timbers as deadmen (timbers set into the slope perpendicular to the wall). Dig trenches in the soil behind the wall and install the deadmen (above and right). Install deadmen at 4-foot intervals, at depths of 6 to 12 inches below the grade.

SAFETY PRECAUTIONS: Wear heavy boots, leather-faced gloves, and protective eyeglasses. Cut timbers with a sharp chain saw. Use a 2-pound sledge or mash hammer to drive the spikes holding timbers together.

DEADMEN (OVERHEAD VIEW)

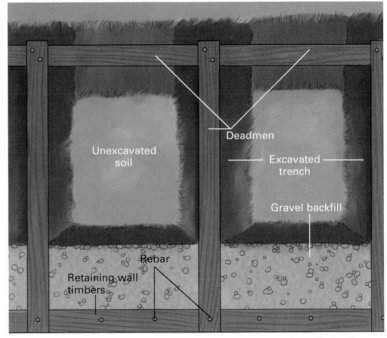

Deadmen

Unexcavated soil

Excavated trench

Gravel backfill

Rebar

Retaining wall timbers

Install deadmen every 4 feet, at depths one or two timbers (6 to 12 inches) below grade or below the top of the wall. Deadmen anchor the top of the wall to resist pressure from water or frost heave.

MAINTAINING TIMBERS

Termites and carpenter ants will consume a lightly treated timber wall. Buy .40-grade treated timbers for protection against them. Check the wall periodically for signs of insect infestation and use an aerosol insecticide to keep insects away. When the wall darkens with mildew and dirt, use a deck cleaner to clean it. Once a year use a sprayer to apply a clear wood sealer to exposed wood.

LAYING OUT A FENCE LINE

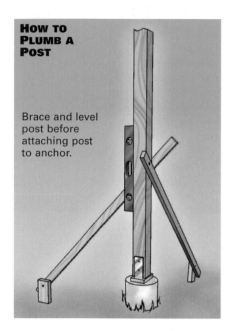

HOW TO PLUMB A POST

Brace and level post before attaching post to anchor.

Much of the privacy, shade, and ambience of a landscape comes from arbors, fences, gazebos, and other structures that use vertical posts. If the structure is to last, the posts need to be firmly anchored in the ground.

You have two techniques at your disposal—either bury part of the post in the ground or fasten it above ground to a concrete pier and footing. In packed soil that is not sandy or moist, set the post in an earth and gravel base. In sandy, loose, or moist soil, set the post in concrete.

Using batter boards and mason's line, lay out the perimeter of your fence or other structure and square the corners with a 3-4-5 triangle. (See page 97 for more information.)

Many fences and overhead structures have posts spaced 8 feet apart; your site and design may require different spacing. Lumber is sold in even-numbered increments, so space the posts in even multiples of feet to avoid wasting material.

If you use factory-made panels, place the posts precisely. Measure carefully or lay the panels on the ground to determine post locations. (If you're using prefabricated panels, you can mark and dig postholes as you go. This method involves setting a post, holding a panel in place, marking the next hole and digging it.)

DEPTH AND DIAMETERS

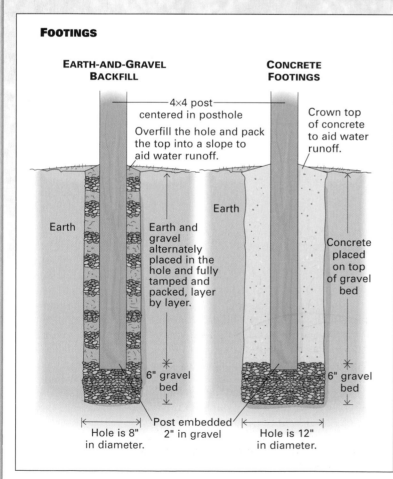

FOOTINGS

EARTH-AND-GRAVEL BACKFILL

CONCRETE FOOTINGS

4×4 post centered in posthole

Overfill the hole and pack the top into a slope to aid water runoff.

Crown top of concrete to aid water runoff.

Earth

Earth

Earth and gravel alternately placed in the hole and fully tamped and packed, layer by layer.

Concrete placed on top of gravel bed

6" gravel bed

6" gravel bed

Hole is 8" in diameter.

Post embedded 2" in gravel

Hole is 12" in diameter.

Here are some guidelines for posthole dimensions. Consult your local building department for information specific to your area.

Posthole diameter: The minimum diameter of the posthole depends on the footing:

■ Earth-and-gravel. Make your posthole diameter at least twice the width of the post. A 4×4 requires an 8-inch diameter, a 6×6 needs a 12-inch diameter.

■ Concrete footings. Make the posthole diameter at least three times the width of the post. A 4×4 post requires a hole 12 inches in diameter; a 6×6 requires one 18 inches in diameter.

Posthole depth: Terminal posts, as a general rule, have ⅓ of the total post length below ground (at a minimum depth of 24 inches) and ⅔ above ground. Thus a 6-foot terminal post should be 9 feet long, set in a 3-foot posthole. Line posts can be set slightly shallower. Line posts for a 6-foot fence can be 8 feet long set in 2-foot holes. Local codes may require depths below the frost line.

SINKING A POST

■ Using a posthole digger, dig a hole that is three times as wide as the post and ½ of its exposed length.
■ Shovel in 4 inches of gravel and set the post in the hole.
■ Plumb the post and brace it.
■ Then shovel in 2 more inches of gravel.
■ Complete the earth and gravel installation or fill the hole with concrete.

SETTING POSTS

Dadoed or mortised joints require posts cut to a precise height. With other styles let the height run wild and cut the entire line later. Here's what to do:

■ Divide the actual size of your posts by 2 (a 6×6, for example, measures 5½ inches thick) and move your mason's lines this distance away from their original position. This new position will place the line in the plane of the outside post faces, as shown.
■ Stand an end post in its hole and twist its base into the gravel bed about 2 inches. On two adjacent sides and about two-thirds up the post, pivot 1×4 braces on a single duplex nail (its two heads make removal easy). Then plumb the post on two adjacent faces with a 4-foot carpenter's level or post level, keeping the post face just touching the mason's line. Stake the braces securely, attaching them to the post with a couple of box nails or screws. Repeat the process for the other end post.
■ To help keep the intermediate posts straight, stretch another line between the end posts about 18 inches below their tops. Then set, align, and brace each successive intermediate post.
■ When all the posts are braced, shovel in the footing filler, either earth-and-gravel or concrete. Double-check each post for alignment and plumb. If you've installed concrete footings and you plan to fasten the rails and infill with screws, you can cut the posts and build the rest of your fence or overhead after the concrete sets. If you're going to nail your fence frame, wait until the concrete cures—three to seven days. In either case leave the braces in place.

CUTTING POSTS

If you've set the posts with their heights wild, now's the time to cut them to length.
■ Measure one end post from the ground to the post height and mark it. If the grade is level, snap a level chalk line from that point to the other end post. That will mark all posts

ALIGNING AND BRACING POSTS

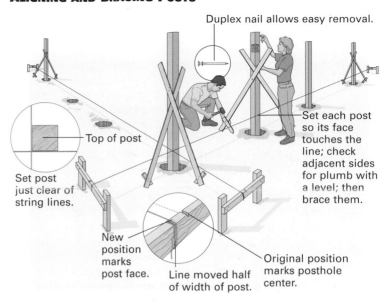

Duplex nail allows easy removal.

Set each post so its face touches the line; check adjacent sides for plumb with a level; then brace them.

Top of post

Set post just clear of string lines.

New position marks post face.

Line moved half of width of post.

Original position marks posthole center.

MARKING POSTS FOR CUTTING

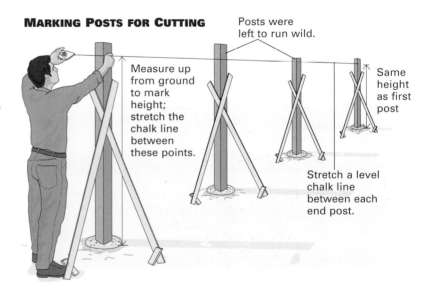

Posts were left to run wild.

Measure up from ground to mark height; stretch the chalk line between these points.

Same height as first post

Stretch a level chalk line between each end post.

at the same height. If you're building a contoured fence, measure the same distance up the other end post and snap the chalk line between them. Make sure all posts are marked and resnap the line if necessary.
■ Carry the marks around each post with a try square. If you're building a contoured fence, you will cut at an angle—carry the marks across the downslope and upslope faces first, then connect these lines on the fourth side.
■ Cut each post to height with a handsaw or a reciprocating saw. You'll be on a ladder, so be careful and, above all, patient. If you use a circular saw, start with it and finish the cut with a hand saw. Sharp blades make the job faster and safer.

Basic Fence Building

Most fences are made with 4×4 posts sunk into the ground, with two or three horizontal 2×4 rails that support vertical or horizontal boards or panels (often called the infill). Use materials that will resist rotting: pressure-treated lumber or naturally resistant species such as redwood, cedar, or cypress. Even if painted, untreated pine and fir won't last.

Laying Out and Setting Posts

Using the procedures discussed on page 202, lay out the site. If your fence runs downhill, refer to the illustrations (*right*) and cut the posts for a stepped or a sloped fence.

Start by stretching a taut line from one end or corner post to the other. If the ground is fairly level, or if you want the fence to follow the slope, attach the line at both ends the same height from the ground (you can use a water level to make sure the height is the same). Mark all the posts at the line and cut them with a circular saw.

If you want a fence that steps down (*right*), use the same method to establish heights but install fence sections that are plumb, then cut the posts.

Framing the Infill

Install rails: Cut 2×4 rails to span the outside faces of the posts or to fit snugly between them. For inside rails hold the rail in place and mark it. Attach the rails with rail hangers or predrill pilot holes for galvanized nails or screws.

Cut and attach infill: Cut all the infill at the same time, and make a spacing jig to speed installation. If the infill stock is wider than 2 inches, attach it with two nails or screws at each joint.

Stepped Fence

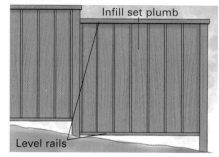

Install plumb posts on a sloped site as you would on a level site. For a stepped fence (above) attach level rails and then cut the posts. For a sloped fence (below) cut the posts and install the rails so they follow the slope of the ground. Install the infill plumb in both cases.

Sloped Fence

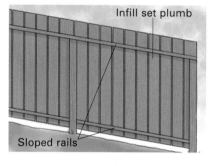

When the posts are set and cut, measure for inside rails. Use scrap wood to keep the bottom rail about 6 inches above the ground until you toenail it with 8d galvanized nails or use 2½-inch deck screws.

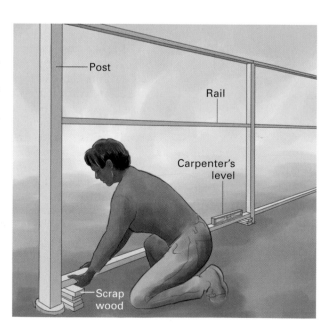

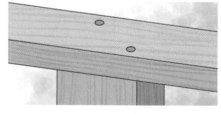

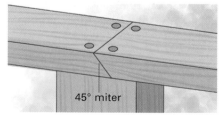

Fasten the top rail to the post in a diagonal pattern to avoid splitting the post. Miter adjoining pieces.

INFILL INSTALLATION TIPS

SPACING THE INFILL

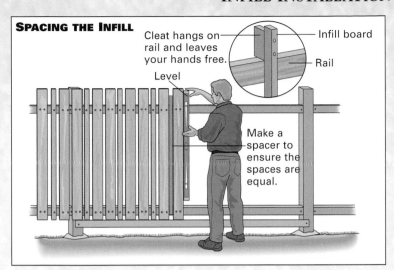

Cleat hangs on rail and leaves your hands free.

Infill board

Rail

Level

Make a spacer to ensure the spaces are equal.

CUTTING ANGLED INFILL

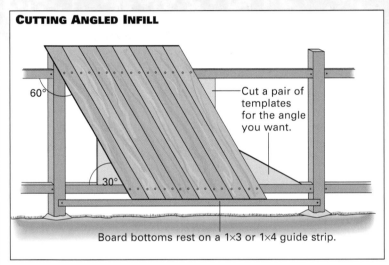

60°

30°

Cut a pair of templates for the angle you want.

Board bottoms rest on a 1×3 or 1×4 guide strip.

INSTALLING A KICKBOARD

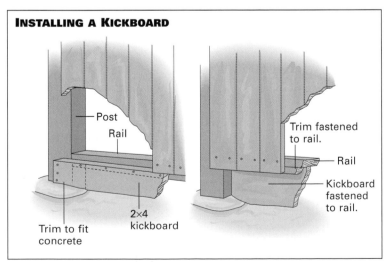

Post

Rail

Trim fastened to rail.

Rail

Kickboard fastened to rail.

2×4 kickboard

Trim to fit concrete

Whether your fence incorporates surface-mounted or inset infill, these tips will make fence building easier and result in a sturdier, better-looking job.

■ Don't scrimp on fasteners—either in quality or quantity. Galvanized or treated nails or screws cost slightly more but will last longer and stain the fence less than plain steel. Stainless-steel fasteners are the best choice. In addition to their own weight, fences have to carry extra loads imposed by rain, snow, wind, and climbing kids. Much of this stress falls on the fasteners—use plenty of them.

■ Hang boards plumb. Check the infill as you go—every few feet at least—with a 4-foot level (smaller levels may not be as accurate). If the infill has gotten out of plumb, take your work apart and correct it.

■ Equalize the spaces between pieces of infill. Make them regular with a cleated spacer; it will save you from measuring for each piece. Hang the cleat on the top rail so you can free both hands to hold the infill as you fasten it.

■ Keep angled infill even. Use a bevel square or make templates to properly position angled infill onto the frame.

■ Make bottom edges flush and smooth. Use guide boards to help place the infill (tack a 1×3 or 1×4 to the surface of the posts) unless your design intentionally calls for random lengths. Reposition the guide every few boards as you work your way down the line.

■ To finish a wild-top edge, chalk a line at the cutting height. Then tack a 1×3 or 1×4 guide so a circular saw's soleplate can ride on it. Set the blade deep enough to cut through the infill, but no deeper. Rest the saw on the cutting guide and cut the entire top of the fence in one pass.

■ Install kickboards. Kickboards will close the gap under the bottom rail, providing a more finished look and preventing animals from crawling under the fence. They also keep flat rails from sagging. Overlay them on the posts or inset them under the bottom rail; trim with a 1×2 if you want. Make the kickboard of pressure-treated lumber, heartwood, or a decay-resistant species like cedar or cypress because the board touches the earth and is subject to rot.

OVERHEADS AND AMENITIES

Even the most stunning deck or patio design feels incomplete without amenities—not only furnishings, but overhead structures that add both shade and delightful architectural accents and other elements that bring the comforts of home out into natural surroundings.

Like all aspects of good design, these amenities should not look like additions to your landscape. They should appear as integral elements of the landscape theme, reflecting both your sense of aesthetics and your lifestyle.

Including amenities is not tricky but does require careful planning. Consider your lifestyle first—how you want to use your outdoor structure. Dining and food preparation areas are a must for frequent entertaining. Outdoor lighting will extend the use of your space into the evening hours. An overhead structure or arbor will increase your enjoyment on sunny afternoons and it will also add a stunning design element to the entire space. Planters help separate one area of use from another.

Latticework is inexpensive and practical—it provides shade and lets in gentle breezes. Here it also tones down the massive character of this canopy. A canopy makes a great addition to a deck, providing privacy and partial shade.

Set just outside the kitchen door, this raised miniplatform deck provides an elevated view of the yard and adds an unusual architectural touch to the wider deck. The horseshoe-shape railing helps set off the deck even more dramatically. A clear sealer preserves the natural wood tone of the deck and railing.

PRETTY ARBOR

Frame a private dining nook with this elegant arbor. The materials are inexpensive and construction requires only basic do-it-yourself skills.

Build this neatly trimmed arbor on your deck and enhance its attractiveness by allowing vines to climb up and over it.

The lower rafters should span no more than 80 inches from beam to beam. For increased shade, top the arbor with lattice or 1×2s spaced 1½ inches apart. For less shade, space the rafters farther apart.

MATERIALS

- Wood: 6×6 posts, 2×10s, 2×2s
- Concrete mix
- Deck screws
- Tape measure
- Posthole digger
- Carpenter's level
- Shovel
- Backsaw
- Miter saw
- Circular saw
- Clamps
- Drill
- Saber saw
- Chisel
- Hammer

PLANNING YOUR ARBOR

For a freestanding arbor, sink posts at least 3 feet into the ground. For example, an 8-foot-tall arbor needs posts at least 11 feet long, so buy 12-footers. If possible, bolt some of the posts to existing deck posts or similar strong structural members.

LAYING OUT THE SITE

Lay out the arbor location using the techniques shown on pages 96–97 and square it with a 3-4-5 triangle.

PREPARE POSTHOLES
- Using a clamshell digger or auger, dig the postholes at least 30 inches deep or to the depth required by local codes.

SET THE POSTS
- Shovel several inches of gravel into the bottom of each hole and insert the posts. (You will cut them to height later.)
- Brace the posts temporarily so they are plumb (perfectly vertical). Use 3- to 4-foot 2×4s or 2×6s at the bottom and 1×4 or 2×4 angle braces anchored to stakes (*opposite, lower right*). Getting the posts both plumb and placed the correct distance apart may require shifting, but if you are off an inch or so, it won't be readily visible.
- Combine water and bagged concrete mix and fill the postholes. Work the mix up and down with a stout stick to remove all air pockets. Overfill each hole so that rainwater will run away from the post.

INSTALLING THE ROOF BEAMS

The frame supporting the arbor roof consists of doubled 2×10 beams. Collar pieces add a decorative touch and help mark the position of the beams.

INSTALL THE COLLARS
- Measure and mark the arbor height on one of the posts, then measure down 9½ inches.
- At this point, draw a line around the post using a small square.
- Miter the 2×2 collar pieces and attach them to the post, their top edges aligned with the lines you drew. Drill pilot holes and attach each collar piece with two 1⅝-inch deck screws.
- Working with a helper place a level on top of a long, straight board (as long as the arbor), then place one end of the board on top of the 2×2 collar. Mark for the collar heights on the other posts. Install the other collars in the same way.

CUT THE POSTS
- Set a short scrap piece of 2×10 on top of each collar piece; mark cutoff lines on post.
- Cut the posts with a reciprocating saw.

INSTALL THE BEAMS
- Measure the distances between the posts at the top and miter-cut 2×10s for the outer beam pieces. (It's OK to bend the posts an inch or two if they are not equidistant.)
- Working with a helper, place each beam piece on top of the collar pieces at either end and attach them by driving three 3-inch deck screws into each joint.
- Measure and cut the inside beam pieces. Laminate them to the outside beams using polyurethane glue and 1¼-inch deck screws driven every foot.

BUILDING THE ROOF

The arbor roof consists of notched 2×10 lower rafters set perpendicular to the upper rafters.

CUT THE RAFTERS
- Cut all the 2×10 rafters to length. The lower rafters are 2 to 3 feet longer than the

arbor width, and the uppers are 2 to 3 feet longer than its length.

■ On a photocopier, enlarge the pattern illustration below until it measures 9½ inches tall. Use it as a pattern for the rafter ends. Cut one rafter end with a saber saw and use it as a template to mark all the other rafter ends.

■ Also at this time cut the decorative ends, which slip over the arbor frame.

NOTCH THE RAFTERS

■ Cut the notches as shown. For the lower rafters and decorative ends, notch the bottom of each end so the rafters will fit over the beams. On top, cut a notch for the upper rafters to fit into. Cut notches on the bottom of the upper rafters for every lower rafter. Place all rafter notches an equal distance apart.

To mark the notches, clamp the upper rafters and all the lower rafters together. Mark their top or bottom edges all at once.

■ Cut the notches first with a circular saw, then a saber saw. Clean out the corners with a hand saw and chisel. As you work check to see that the notched rafters will fit tightly together.

SET THE LOWER RAFTERS

■ With a helper, set the lower rafters on top of the beams, spacing them evenly.

SET THE UPPER RAFTERS

■ Slip the upper rafters onto the lowers, fitting the pieces together. This requires

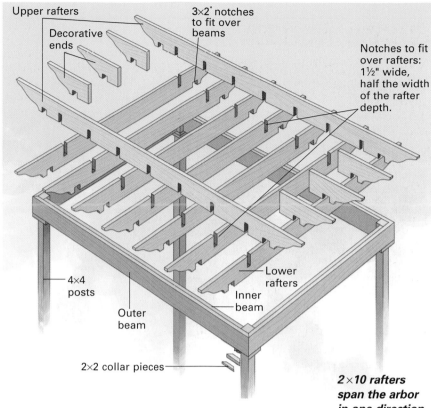

Upper rafters

Decorative ends

3×2" notches to fit over beams

Notches to fit over rafters: 1½" wide, half the width of the rafter depth.

4×4 posts

Outer beam

2×2 collar pieces

Lower rafters

Inner beam

2×10 rafters span the arbor in one direction, tied together by 2 perpendicular rafters that slip into notches near the scallop. Short, notched, decorative sections balance the design.

jiggling and tapping with a hammer.

■ Once all the pieces are put together, drill angled pilot holes and drive 3-inch deck screws everywhere a rafter rests on a beam.

■ If the structure wobbles stabilize it with angle braces.

APPLY THE FINISH

■ Apply two or more coats of stain, finish, or paint to the arbor.

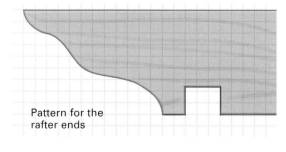

Pattern for the rafter ends

If the arbor seems wobbly, install a brace between the upper frame and the post.

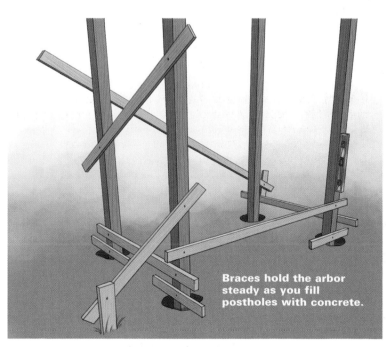

Braces hold the arbor steady as you fill postholes with concrete.

GEOMETRIC OVERHEAD

With squared ends and a strictly rectangular shape, this overhead is simple to build. Traditional homes call for a pressure-treated wood structure that is painted. For contemporary homes, use unfinished or stained redwood or cedar.

The rectangular grid of this overhead structure will cast a slatted pattern on the deck below. If you want nearly square shadows, space the 2×6 rafters and the 1×3 top pieces 12 inches on center. For less shade and a lower material cost, space them at 16 or 24 inches on center.

START WITH THE LEDGER

■ Cut a 2×8 ledger and a 2×2 nailer to length (as shown here, 10 feet long). The nailer helps support the 2×6 rafters so you don't have to use unattractive joist hangers.
■ Attach the nailer flush with the bottom edge of the ledger with glue and 6d galvanized box nails or 2-inch deck screws.
■ Cut the two 2×10 beams to the same length as the ledger.
■ On both the ledger and the top of one of the beams, draw layout lines for rafters at 12, 16, or 24 inches on center, depending on the amount of shade you want. Be sure the beam is crown-side up.
■ Mark a level line on the house, at least 7 feet above the patio or deck (here, 8 feet).
■ With helpers and steady ladders, lift the ledger and attach it to the house. (See instructions for installing the ledger to different surfaces on page 158.) This ledger does not need to be as strong as a deck ledger, but you'll need at least two fasteners every 16 inches to keep it from warping.

CLAD AND INSTALL THE POSTS

The 4×4 posts get their decorative interest from simple 1×4 and 1×8 cladding attached to opposite faces.
ON A DECK: At the rear of the deck, measure from the decking to the top of the 2×2 nailer and cut the 4×4 posts to that length.
■ Cut the 1×4 and 1×8 trim to the same length and nail trim to the posts with 6d galvanized casing nails, overlapping the 1×8s.
■ On the front of the deck, mark the post locations. (Use the methods described on page 166 for squaring the locations of posts.)
■ With a helper, raise each post, plumb it on two adjacent sides, and brace it temporarily with staked 1×4s.
■ Anchor the posts to the decking with predrilled 3-inch deck screws.
IN THE GROUND: Lay out the locations of the postholes as described above for on-deck post locations.

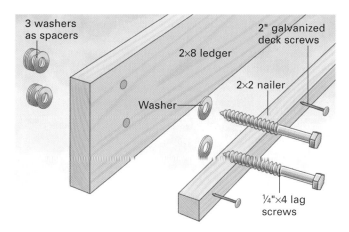

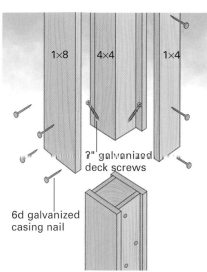

Adding 1× to a post bulks it up and covers knots and cracks. This treatment adds a crisp, professional-looking touch to the project

Attach a 2×2 to the bottom edge of the ledger, then attach the ledger using this or any of the other methods shown on page 158.

■ Dig holes and fill with 4 inches of gravel.

■ Set the posts straight in the holes, leaving them uncut for now—you'll cut them to height later.

■ Mark the posts about 1 inch above grade for positioning the bottom edge of the cladding.

■ Remove each post, install the cladding, reposition the posts, and brace them securely and plumb on adjacent sides.

■ Fill each hole with concrete, sloping the surface so water drains from it. Let the concrete cure for three days to a week.

■ With a helper, use a water level to mark the posts at the same height as the top of the 2×2 nailer. Transfer the cut line to all four faces of the post and cut the cladding and post with a circular saw and a handsaw.

INSTALL THE "CEILING"

Three components—double beam, rafters, and top pieces—complete the project and provide its distinctive character.

BEAMS: Determine how far you want the beams to extend beyond the posts, and mark and cut them to that size.

■ With a helper on a ladder at one post and you at the other, set the first beam flush with the top of the post, centered on the structure.

■ Tack the beam in place with duplex nails, then raise the second beam and tack it also.

■ Drill two holes centered on the posts and evenly spaced on beams, then fasten the beams with 5/16×8-inch carriage bolts. Remove the duplex nails.

RAFTERS: Cut the rafters so they will overhang the front beam by 2 or 3 inches.

■ Set the rafters on the 2×2 nailer and attach

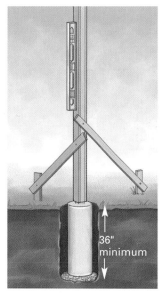

Set posts equidistant from the house (see page 159 for squaring corners). Brace and plumb posts.

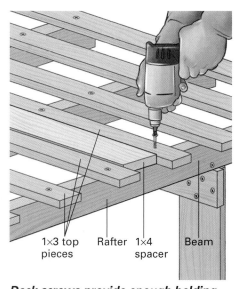

Deck screws provide enough holding power to attach beams to posts. Drive angled screws to hold rafters; one screw is enough for top pieces.

them to the ledger and beams at the marks you made earlier.

■ Use 2-inch decking screws driven at an angle into predrilled pilot holes. Then snap a chalk line at evenly spaced intervals across the tops of the rafters.

TOP PIECES: Cut the 1×3 top pieces to the same length as the beams.

■ Using the chalk lines on the top of the rafters, position the top slats and attach them with a single 2½-inch galvanized or coated decking screw at each point the pieces intersect a rafter. Predrill the holes to avoid splitting the wood—especially at the ends.

ATTACHED BENCHES

Versatility is the key to these bench designs—even though they're permanent. You can adapt the backless bench, *below*, to a patio by anchoring it to 4×4 posts sunk in the ground. The backed-bench design, *opposite*, uses existing deck posts for support and provides a useful substitute for a railing section.

There are some general rules for benches.
■ The seat height should be comfortable—15 to 18 inches from the surface.
■ The bench should look out on pleasant views.

■ Its location should encourage conversation.
■ Make the benches safe. The back of an attached bench—used instead of a railing—usually needs to be at least 42 inches high and cannot have open spaces wider than 4 inches (check with your local building department for bench-design requirements).

A BACKLESS BENCH

Use a backless bench on a low-lying platform deck or as a transition on a multilevel deck. The bench, *left*, with its support partially hidden, appears to float above the surface. Its 24-inch depth offers plenty of space for sitting and for resting food and drinks.

We've mounted it to the edge of a deck. You can bolt the posts to interior joists after removing the decking, notching it, and replacing it. This design uses decking screws as fasteners; carriage bolts and lag screws will provide stronger joints. They require additional drilling, however, and may not work if your deck construction won't allow you to get a wrench on them.

CUT POSTS AND FRAMING PIECES: Construct enough supports to install one every 4 to 5 feet.
■ For each bench, cut a 4×6 post, 2×6 front support, and seat cleats. Make sure the front support is long enough to reach from the bottom of the deck joist to a height of 15 to 18 inches.
■ Miter the ends of the seat cleats at 22½ degrees. (For a freestanding modification, cut the posts at 15 to 18 inches and bolt 2×6 feet to both sides.)

ASSEMBLE THE SUPPORTS: Fasten the two post sections—flush at the tops—with six or seven 3-inch deck screws driven into predrilled pilot holes.

Because its supports are partly hidden by the overhanging slats, this backless bench appears to float above the deck.

2×6 cleat   4×6 post   2×6 cleat

15"–17"

22½° cut

2×6 front support

Assemble each support from a 4×6 post and three 2×6s. Notch the decking so the front support can be attached to the deck joist or fascia.

Clamp 2×2s as an overhang guide; use ½-inch plywood for spacers. Adjust the spacing before attaching the last slats.

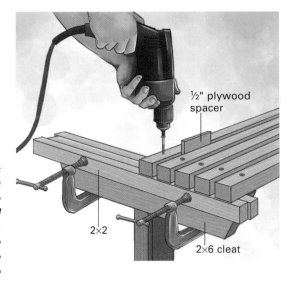

½" plywood spacer

2×2

2×6 cleat

■ Then center one cleat on the laminated post, hold it flush at the top, and fasten it with four or five 3-inch deck screws through predrilled pilot holes.

■ Attach the other 2×6 cleat in the same way.

FASTEN THE SUPPORTS: The front support needs to be snug against the deck joist, so notch the decking if necessary.

■ Use a post level to plumb the post in both directions (see page 160).

■ Predrill pilot holes at an angle through the 4×6 and through the face of the 2×6 beam, then drive 3-inch decking screws through the post and front support.

INSTALL THE SEAT SLATS: Cut twelve 2×2s to a length that will overhang each cleat by 3 inches. In order to keep the overhang consistent, clamp two 2×2s to the side of the cleat.

■ Lay the slats on a flat surface and mark pilot holes so they will be centered on the cleats.

■ Start the first slat with a ¼-inch overhang on the front of the cleats and fasten it with 3-inch deck screws at each support.

■ Fasten the remaining seat slats, using scraps of ½-inch plywood as spacers.

SEAT WITH BACK

This design uses existing rail posts for part of the framing. You can attach the bench without altering balusters or rails with most rail designs. However, the seat may look better if you remove all the balusters (building codes permitting, of course). If the rail posts are spaced more than 6 feet apart, install additional posts.

INSTALL THE SEAT SUPPORTS:
Each support requires two 25-inch 2×4 cleats—mitered on one end at 22½ degrees—and one 15-inch 4×4 seat post.

■ Cut the pieces and mark both sides of the rail post 15 inches above the decking.

■ Have a helper hold a 2×4 level at the mark while you drill pilot holes and drive three 3-inch deck screws.

■ Attach the other 2×4 to the other side of the post.

■ Then fasten the 4×4 post with two screws on each side and with angled screws to the deck.

CUT AND INSTALL THE BACK BRACE:
Use a circular saw to cut a 4×4 to the dimensions shown.

■ Attach the back support to the rail post with several screws.

INSTALL THE SEAT AND BACK SLATS:
Cut three 2×4s for the back and three 2×6s for the seat to the length of the bench (overhanging them 3 inches, if possible). Space them evenly and attach them to the 2×4s with two 3-inch screws driven into each joint.

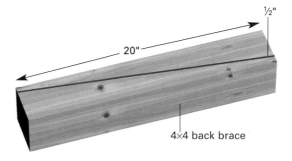

Anchor this seat to the rail posts for support. Use 2×4s for the back and 2×6s for seat slats. Place the bench where it can be part of a conversation area or where it faces a pleasant view.

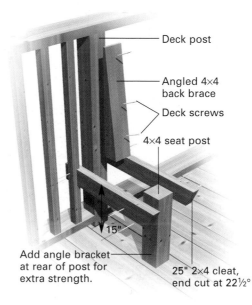

½"
20"
4×4 back brace

Use a chalk line or straightedge to mark the angled rip cut for the back brace. Mark both sides and make the cut with a circular saw. This cut is difficult; practice on a scrap first.

Deck post

Angled 4×4 back brace

Deck screws

4×4 seat post

15"

Add angle bracket at rear of post for extra strength.

25" 2×4 cleat, end cut at 22½°

Mark the deck post 15 inches from the decking and attach the cleats at the mark. Level and attach the seat post between the 2×4s and to the decking. Install the back brace with its bottom edge flush with the top of the cleats. Then fasten the back and seat slats.

FREESTANDING BENCHES

This bench, with its wide slats, will provide plenty of sturdy comfort and can easily be moved around the deck.

Benches made of dimensional lumber will not be lightweight, but they will be stable. And you'll be surprised how easily you can move them about your deck or patio to respond to changing shade patterns or entertainment needs.

"PICNIC-STYLE" BENCH

With its wide slats and shaped legs, this bench is reminiscent of a picnic table. Make the bench permanent by attaching it to joists below the decking or by setting posts in footings next to a platform deck or patio.

In a permanent installation, you can dispense with the bottom rails and braces, unless you want to keep the braces for a decorative touch. Choose any length and install a support every 4 feet.

CUT THE SCALLOPED RAILS: Each support requires a 22-inch 2×8 top rail and a 20-inch 2×6 bottom rail. (For more strength, install two rails on each side of the posts.)
- Cut the pieces to the proper length.
- Mark and cut each end of one top and one bottom rail. For the top rail, set a compass at 6½ inches and—with the compass point just at the corner of the board—mark the scallop outline on both ends as shown.
- Use the same technique to mark the bottom rail, setting the compass at 4 inches.
- Make all the cuts with a saber saw, then sand the curved cuts smooth.
- Use the first pieces as templates for marking the others.

Cut the 4×4 post and the top and bottom rails and attach them with deck screws. Fasten the brace after you attach the seat slats.

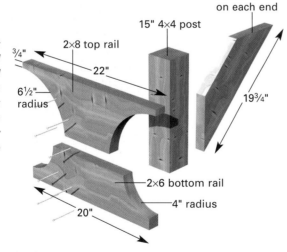

2×8 top rail · ¾" · 22" · 6½" radius · 15" 4×4 post · 2×6 brace, cut at 45° on each end · 19¾" · 2×6 bottom rail · 4" radius · 20"

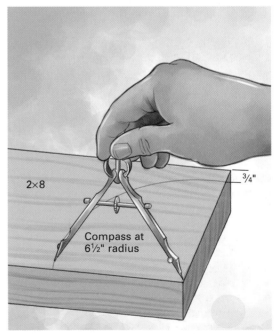

To scallop the top and bottom rails, set a compass just at the corner of the board and draw the arc.

2×8 · ¾" · Compass at 6½" radius

BUYING FACTORY-MADE WOODEN OUTDOOR FURNITURE

You may find wooden benches and picnic tables at a local deck yard priced only slightly higher than the cost of materials to build your own. Carefully check out the quality of the lumber and the fasteners; they may be wanting. You may be able to make a flimsy piece solid by strategically drilling pilot holes and driving a few screws. Don't buy pieces that have warped or cracked wood. You may be able to beautify and make untreated lumber rot-resistant by applying a stain or sealer (see pages 78–79).

CUT THE POSTS AND BRACES:
For each support, cut a 15-inch 4×4 post and a 19¾-inch 2×6 brace. Miter each end of the brace at 45 degrees.

ASSEMBLE THE SUPPORTS: Assemble the 2×8 top rails so they form a **T** flush with the top of the post and overhang by 9¼ inches on each side.

■ Drill pilot holes and drive four 3-inch deck screws.

■ Attach the bottom rail in the same fashion, flush with the bottom edge of the post and overhanging it by 8¼ inches.

CUT AND ATTACH THE SEAT SLATS:
Cut the three 2×8 slats to length. Then set your compass at 7¼ inches.

■ Center the point of the compass on the width of one slat with the pencil just touching the end of the slat.

■ Mark the curve on the corners, cut the curves with a saber saw, and sand smooth.

■ Lay the seat slats on the support assemblies. (Have a helper keep things from toppling over.)

■ Attach them at ¼-inch intervals with three 3-inch deck screws.

ATTACH THE BRACES: Turn the bench upside down and have a helper check each support for square as you position the angle-cut braces.

■ Drill pilot holes and drive deck screws through the braces into the posts.

■ Make sure each brace is centered on the middle seat slat, then fasten the braces with screws driven through the slat.

zigzag pattern so the screws won't split the wood along a grain line.

■ Spread a thin layer of glue and drive the screws.

■ Then laminate two legs, notch side down, to a 48-inch slat with a 41-inch slat between the legs.

■ Laminate the rest of the 48-inch slats until you have only one left.

■ Then fasten the remaining pair of legs, notch up, with a 41-inch slat between them.

■ Finish the bench with the final 48-inch slat. When the glue has dried completely, sand the surfaces smooth.

■ Use a belt sander to get the surface smooth and level. (Be careful—a belt sander can remove a lot of wood quickly.)

Take the time to sand the top of the bench smooth. Apply several coats of sealer, with no spaces between the slats—water may puddle.

BUTCHER-BLOCK BENCH

This design adapts butcher-block-table construction to create a multipurpose addition to your deck or patio. Increase the impact by building a companion coffee table using the same design and shortening the legs.

CHOOSE A LAMINATING METHOD: The seat slats and the legs are made by laminating 2×4s side by side with glue and predrilled 2¾-inch screws. Before you start, stack the slats in position and mark the sides of each pair for the screws. Stagger the marks so you won't drive screws on top of each other.

■ Cut the legs (one 15-inch and one 11½-inch 2×4 for each leg) and predrill them every 6 inches in a

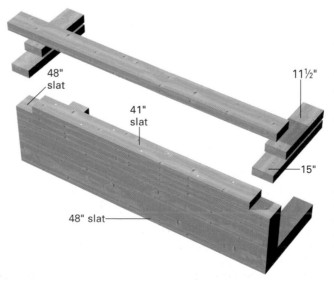

48"
slat

41"
slat

48" slat

11½"

15"

Start with a 48-inch slat, leg pieces, and a 41-inch slat. Align each slat carefully— flush at the top—and mark the positions; then laminate them with glue and screws. Stagger the screws to avoid splitting the wood.

PLANTERS

This bench and planter combination is large enough to hold small trees as well as flowers. The gaps between the bench slats permit water to run through, reducing the possibility of rot.

Planters put gardening within easy reach and help separate one section of your deck from another. Make them small enough so you can easily reach all of the soil and high enough so you don't strain your knees and back.

These planters are designed to hold soil, but you can use them for flowerpots as well—shuffle the foliage around and put your showiest flowers in prominent places. Size the planters so your pots can fit snugly inside.

You can build several planters in a day with a circular saw, drill, and basic carpentry skills. Just make sure that you start with all the materials on hand.

PLANTER-BENCH

A combination planter and bench lets you tend your plants while comfortably seated or is simply a pleasant spot to enjoy the foliage.

If you want a longer unit, build three or more boxes of the same size and either position them in a row or form a right-angle corner. Install seat slats between them.

START THE BOXES: For each box, cut nineteen 2×4s to the same length—24 inches is recommended. Working on a flat surface,

make square frames with lapped ends, *opposite.* Fasten the lapped ends with two 3-inch deck screws at each joint.

Next make a bottom with 1×4s. Cut the pieces to fit and fasten them to one of the 2×4 frames with ⅛-inch gaps for drainage.

Stack two courses of 2×4 frames on the one to which the bottom is attached, and fasten a 16-inch length of 2×2 to all the frame corners by driving 2½-inch screws into predrilled holes. Build the other box(es) to the third course using the same techniques.

BUILD THE BENCH: This design requires spacers to separate the bench slats. Using exterior plywood, cut 18 spacers ¼- to ½-inch by 3½-inches square Then cut seven 2×4 bench slats to the length you want the bench. Set the first slat on the third course of each box and attach it to the 2×2 corner brace. Fasten the remaining slats to each other by driving 3-inch screws through the spacers inserted between the slats.

FINISH THE PLANTERS: When the bench is completed, cut 2×4 fillers to fit between the last bench slat and the box corner. Screw them to the corner brace and to the bench slat. Then complete each box by attaching the last 2×4 frames to the corner braces.

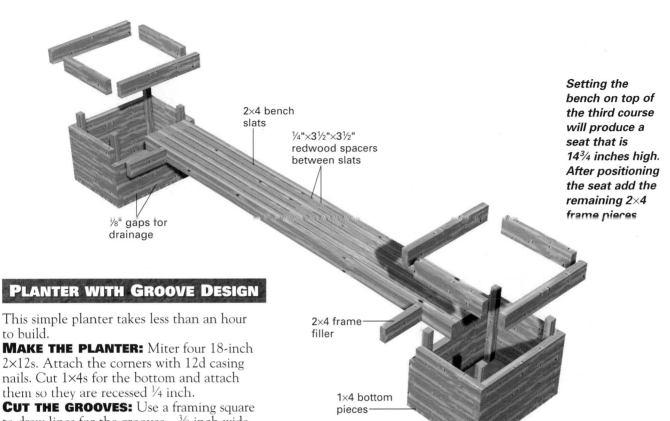

2×4 bench slats

¼"×3½"×3½" redwood spacers between slats

⅛" gaps for drainage

Setting the bench on top of the third course will produce a seat that is 14¾ inches high. After positioning the seat add the remaining 2×4 frame pieces

2×4 frame filler

1×4 bottom pieces

PLANTER WITH GROOVE DESIGN

This simple planter takes less than an hour to build.

MAKE THE PLANTER: Miter four 18-inch 2×12s. Attach the corners with 12d casing nails. Cut 1×4s for the bottom and attach them so they are recessed ¼ inch.

CUT THE GROOVES: Use a framing square to draw lines for the grooves—⅜ inch wide and 3 inches from the edges.

Set your circular saw to the desired depth (in this case, ⅜ inch), and use a speed square as a guide to make straight cuts along the lines. It will take three or more passes with the saw blade to produce a groove that is ⅜ inch wide.

Although it may appear complicated, this planter can be quickly built with common carpentry tools. If you are unsure of your ability to make precise 45-degree corner miters, practice on scrap.

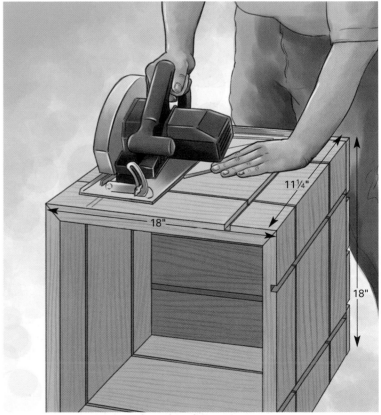

11¼"

18"

18"

Draw lines to mark the sides of each groove. Carefully set the blade of a circular saw to the correct depth. Cut the grooves. Each groove requires several passes.

LIGHTING

With a low-voltage lighting system, you can match the deck lamps with others along walkways or in the landscaping, creating a unified look all the way from the house to the gate.

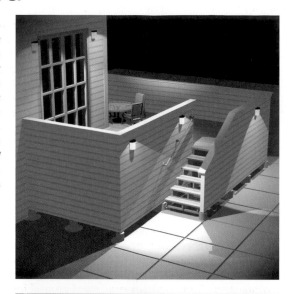

The small accent lights mounted under the steps and along the skirt of this deck show off its redwood tones and make the stairs easier and safer to use at night. The lamps are mounted directly to the surface, with only a small hole drilled for wiring.

If you need to run wire through areas that receive heavy foot traffic, bury the wiring in conduit for safety and convenience. Dig a trench to the depth specified by local codes. Join runs of conduit only with connectors designed for underground use.

Adding lights to an outdoor structure takes planning and care, but it's not difficult. Choose the system you prefer—either line voltage or low voltage.

WIRING A LINE-VOLTAGE SYSTEM

Line-voltage systems use the same AC power as in your house. Working with line voltage is easy enough for homeowners with experience doing their own electrical work.

LAYOUT: Using wooden stakes, mark where you plan to have lights, switches, junction boxes, and receptacles.

■ Tie colored lines between the stakes to show where to dig trenches for wiring.

■ Run the line to the power source.

CONDUIT: Cut away the sod where the wiring trenches will go.

■ Cut conduit to length and lay sections

in place. Attach fittings as you work. Avoid making sharp bends in the conduit. The wire should be able to slide through it smoothly.

■ Wherever the conduit will attach to a junction box or fixture, mount the junction box securely—to the side of the house, for example. Attach fittings to the conduit.

■ To run conduit under a walkway, dig on both sides of the path and drive an iron pipe through the ground with a sledge hammer. Push conduit through the hole as you pull the pipe out from the other side.

WIRING: Using a fish tape, pull wire through the conduit to each junction box and receptacle. Pull out several inches of wire at each location for making the connections.

■ Run wire from the beginning of the circuit to the house wiring, but don't connect it.

■ If you're uncomfortable finishing the wiring yourself, have a professional electrician complete the job. Otherwise wire the switches first followed by the junction boxes, receptacles, and fixtures.

■ Make sure all outdoor circuits have ground fault circuit interrupt (GFCI) protection and use waterproof gaskets on all exposed components. Point the open ends of all wire nuts downward so they don't collect water.

FINAL CONNECTIONS: Turn off the power at the main service panel. With all other parts of the system wired, connect it to the circuit you have chosen. Turn the power on.

■ Turn on each fixture to test the bulbs and replace the ones that don't work. If any fixtures are not getting power, turn off the electricity at the main service panel and

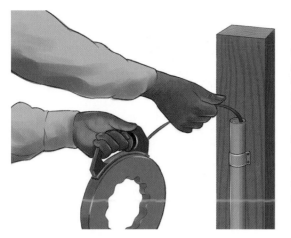

When the conduit is in place, you may have trouble pushing wire through it. To work around bends and over long distances, use a fish tape and pulling lubricant.

Tie the fixtures to the electrical supply lines with approved wire connectors. Turn on the power at the source to test the bulbs.

check the fixtures with a multitester. When all the fixtures work, adjust the lights at night to create the look you want.

CLEANING UP: When you are satisfied with the placement of your outdoor lighting, fill in the trenches and cover them with sod. Secure conduit and wires that extend above the ground. Now you're ready to enjoy an evening on your newly lighted patio.

WIRING A LOW-VOLTAGE SYSTEM

Low voltage is safe and easy to install. Buy a kit, which includes cable, lights, and a transformer that steps line voltage down so it is safe to touch. Some kits are designed to light surfaces, walkways, and stairways. Others show off plantings, walls, or fountains. Get a kit with a timer or a photovoltaic switch to turn the lights on automatically at dark.

■ Mount the transformer near an outdoor receptacle on the wall or on the same post as the receptacle, if possible.

■ Lay out the light fixtures and poke the mounting stakes into the ground. Dig a shallow trench for the cable, lay it in, and cover it. Plug in the transformer.

■ If you want to place lights on a railing or a fence, run the cable where it is out of the way, and fasten it with cable staples about every foot so it won't dangle. Use mounting plates that are designed for installing light fixtures on a horizontal surface.

■ Connect the parts of the low-voltage system to the transformer and then plug it in. Check each connection to be sure everything is finished.

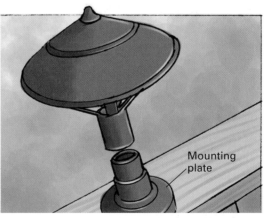

To install low-voltage lights on a railing, purchase a kit with mounting plates. Drill the hole then install the plate with the screws provided.

Mounting plate

Low-voltage system transformer

GFCI outdoor receptacle

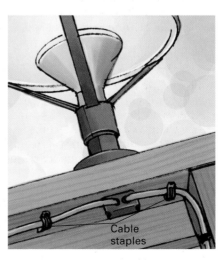

Run low-voltage cable alongside posts and under rails or wherever it will be least visible. Fasten it with round-topped cable staples; standard square-topped staples may cut the cable.

Cable staples

BUILD A FOUNTAIN

Build this quick fountain project in an afternoon. Inexpensive and easy to assemble, it brings the relaxing sound of water to your outdoor room. Because evaporation reduces the amount of water in the fountain, especially during hot or windy weather, fill it regularly to keep the water level high.

■ Choose a fountain location. Your fountain should be within reach of a garden hose and an outdoor electrical outlet. The location should show it to its best advantage—it will be the focal point of your patio. If the outlet isn't protected, have a ground fault circuit interrupter installed. For safety's sake also install metal conduit or PVC pipe between the outlet and the fountain to run the electrical cord through.

■ Dig a hole for the bucket. The bucket should fit snugly with its lip rising just above the surface of the soil. Cut a ½-inch-wide slit in the lip of the bucket with a handsaw for the pump's cord to pass through. Wipe the bucket clean.

■ Mark the center of the saucer on its back by measuring across the saucer horizontally and vertically, drawing a light line along the ruler. The center of the saucer is located where the lines cross. Drill a hole for the tubing to go through at this point using a ¾-inch masonry bit. Next drill several holes, any size, around the saucer for drainage. If drainage holes in the pots are too small for the tubing to pass through, enlarge them with the drill and masonry bit. Also drill additional drainage holes in the pots.

■ Rinse pots, saucer, and rock to remove dust that might clog the pump. Set the pump on a brick in the bucket, threading its electrical cord through the slit.

■ Thread the flexible tubing through the saucer, leaving just enough tubing underneath to reach the pump. Attach the tubing to the pump. Fill the bucket with water and place the inverted saucer on top of it.

■ Thread tubing through the center hole of the largest pot and the inverted. Set the pot on the saucer and fill it with river rock. The rock holds the tube upright. Thread the remaining tubing through the drainage hole of the top pot, then set it on the river rock.

■ Pull the remaining tubing up (don't stretch it) and fill around it with river rock. Cut the tubing so that the fountain spout is even with the rim of the pot. Attach the fountain nozzle to the end of the tubing.

■ Wipe dust from the fountain, then turn on the pump. Because soil around the fountain may become damp, plant this area with water-loving plants such as cardinal flower. Keep dirt out of the fountain as you plant.

MATERIALS

- ■ 5-gallon bucket
- ■ Submersible pump
- ■ Flexible water garden tubing long enough to run from the pump to the fountain
- ■ Fountain nozzle
- ■ River rocks
- ■ 14" saucer
- ■ 12" to 14" pot
- ■ 10" to 12" pot
- ■ 6" pot
- ■ Metal conduit wide enough to admit pump plug
- ■ Drill with ¾-inch masonry bit
- ■ Shovel
- ■ Knife or saw

This do-it-yourself fountain can add a splash to any outdoor room.

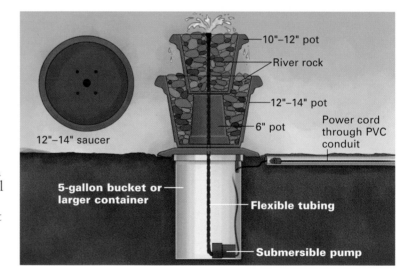

10"–12" pot
River rock
12"–14" pot
6" pot
Power cord through PVC conduit
12"–14" saucer
5-gallon bucket or larger container
Flexible tubing
Submersible pump

NOTES:

■ All pot dimensions refer to diameter.

■ Always wear eye protection when drilling.

■ If there is a chance of a small child pulling the fountain over, use PVC pipe instead of flexible tubing. Anchor the fountain with bricks in the bucket. Always supervise children near water features of any kind.

■ In cold climates store your fountain indoors to prevent the pots from cracking. Store the pump underwater so its seals won't dry out and shrink.

SELECTING A PUMP

Submersible pumps come in various sizes for pumping different amounts of water. The size of the pump you choose depends on the capacity of your water feature. Most small fountains and ponds require the simplest submersible pump, designed to recirculate 50 gallons or less. Larger ponds with waterfalls necessitate heftier pumps. Most pumps run economically, costing pennies per day. They require little maintenance.

PONDS

Ponds can make a big splash in any dry old patch of landscape. A garden pond adds sparkle to your yard, showcases goldfish and aquatic plants, and lures birds and other wildlife.

MATERIALS

Flexible pond liners have revolutionized the use of water in home landscaping. The liner is a low-cost, easy-to-install, custom-fit alternative to concrete or molded forms. Molded fiberglass ponds come in many sizes and shapes, but you should expect to pay extra for fanciful custom designs.

LAYOUT AND EXCAVATION

■ Outline the pond with a garden hose.
■ Remove the sod and excavate to a depth of 9 inches, sloping the sides at about a 20-degree angle. Leave a ledge—a shelf for aquatic plants—then dig again to a total pond depth of 18 inches. Slope this final excavation also. Your garden supply center can help you select attractive plants to place around the ledge.

LEVELING THE EDGE

■ Level the entire edge of the pond.
■ Center a post in the excavation area and extend a leveled 1×4 from the post to the edge. Mark a horizontal line where the 1×4 intersects the grade.
■ Dig to this depth around the perimeter of the pond, repositioning the board as you go. Your edging should be at least 2 inches above the lawn grade to prevent lawn runoff from contaminating pond water.

LINING THE POND

■ Line the pool bottom with damp sand and spread the liner over the excavation. Press the liner down and add 4 to 6 inches of water. The weight of the water will form the liner to the pool.
■ Adjust the liner to prevent wrinkles and fill in increments, adjusting as you go.
■ Fill the pond, lay flagstone or pavers on the pond edge, and cut away the excess liner.
■ Install a GFCI outlet to power a submersible pump so you can circulate and aerate the water.

A vinyl liner keeps this pond full and clear; use rocks or patio blocks to conceal the edges. Garden centers also offer rigid plastic pools in various sizes and shapes.

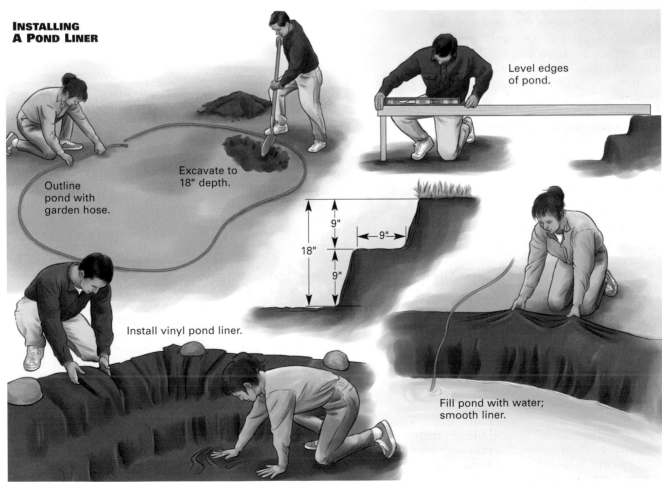

INSTALLING A POND LINER

Outline pond with garden hose.

Excavate to 18" depth.

Level edges of pond.

9"

9"

18"

9"

Install vinyl pond liner.

Fill pond with water; smooth liner.

ADDING STORAGE AND WORK SPACE

Adequate storage and work space make gardening and yard work more enjoyable. Build a shed that has the type of storage and work space you'll need.

Start by considering the garden tools you have, both hand and power. Organize your racks and shelves according to how frequently you'll use the tools to be stored on them. Find locations that allow easy access. Plan a place that keeps garden chemicals out of children's reach—perhaps on a high shelf supported from the rafters.

Hang long-handled tools on 12d nails driven into 1×4s nailed across the studs. Or for a more elegant rack, cut ¾-inch dowel rod into 6- to 8-inch lengths and insert them into holes drilled at an angle into 2×4s. To keep the angles consistent, make a jig with a predrilled hole.

Install adjustable shelf tracks to support 1× shelves. Screw and glue a lip along the front edge of each shelf for rigidity and to keep items from slipping off.

Suspended platform shelves transform overhead space into storage areas for light loads, and you can lay light but cumbersome items, from storm windows to long beanpoles, across the collar ties.

BUILDING A WORKBENCH

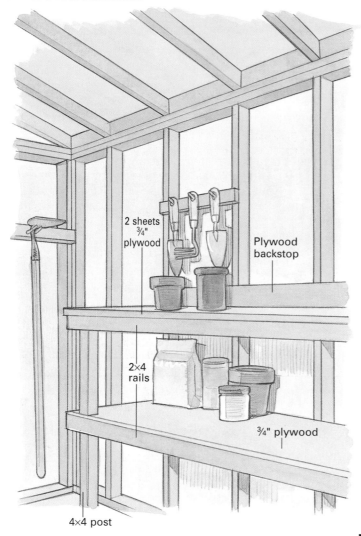

2 sheets ¾" plywood

Plywood backstop

2×4 rails

¾" plywood

4×4 post

INSTALLING HANGING SHELVES

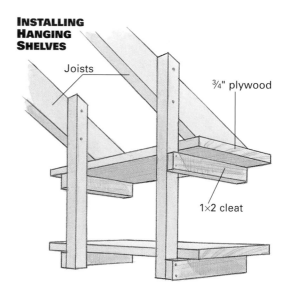

Joists

¾" plywood

1×2 cleat

HANGING TOOL RACKS

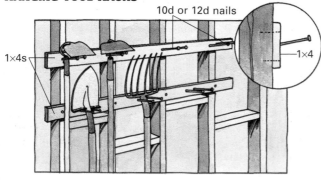

10d or 12d nails

1×4s

1×4

MAKING LIPPED SHELVES

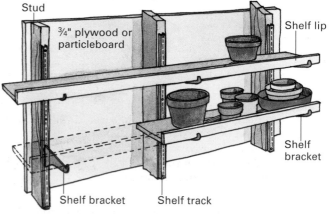

Stud

¾" plywood or particleboard

Shelf lip

Shelf bracket

Shelf bracket

Shelf track

DECORATIVE DETAILS

Customize your overhead structure or gazebo to match your landscape style by adorning it with spindle railings, slat railings, corner brackets, or friezes.

READY-MADE OR DIY?

You can purchase many designs from lumberyards or home centers, or you can make your own if you have a moderately well-equipped workshop. A local millwork usually offers custom parts and may have some stock items too, but expect to pay a substantially higher price there than at a home center.

Use the illustrations as a guide to make the pattern of your choice.

CUTTING DECORATIVE SLATS

1. Clamp three or four pieces of 1× stock to a miter-saw table and cut to length.

Miter saw

2. Trace the template onto one slat. Attach patterned slat to two more slats with brads or tape.

3. Cut template with jigsaw or band saw.

4. Make inside cuts with jigsaw.

Pattern drawn on top slat

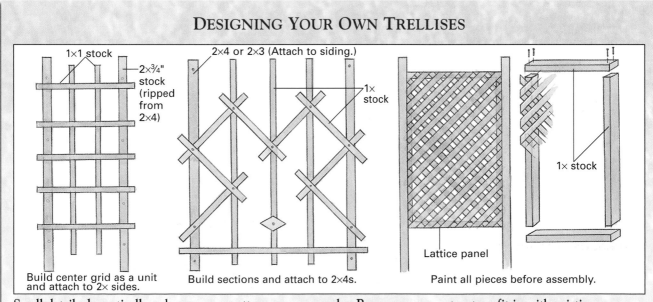

DESIGNING YOUR OWN TRELLISES

1×1 stock

2×¾" stock (ripped from 2×4)

2×4 or 2×3 (Attach to siding.)

1× stock

1× stock

Lattice panel

Build center grid as a unit and attach to 2× sides.

Build sections and attach to 2×4s.

Paint all pieces before assembly.

Small details dramatically enhance the appearance of even a small structure, such as the lean-to shed described in this section. Lattice panels are easy-to-construct accents that don't overwhelm the structure. The designs shown above are examples of the kind of lattice patterns you can make. By combining the strips at different angles, building panels of different widths, and installing similar panels on other structures, it's easy to create a design rhythm and a unity within your landscape plan. This is especially useful for making a new structure fit in with existing structures. Lattice comes in different widths. For most applications ⅜-inch strips hold up and resist warping better than narrower stock. For ease of installation buy premade lattice panels that attach to a frame.

GLOSSARY OF UNUSUAL TERMS

3-4-5 METHOD: A technique for checking whether a corner is square. Determined by marking a point 3 feet from the corner on one side and 4 feet from the corner along the other side. When the diagonal distance between the marks is 5 feet, the corner is square.

AIR-ENTRAINED: Term used to describe concrete suffused with tiny air bubbles, making it more workable and better able to withstand frost. Air entrainment requires the addition of a special mixture during the mixing stage.

BABY SLEDGE: A small sledge hammer, usually 2½ pounds, used for a variety of construction tasks and repairs where more weight is needed than can be supplied by a carpenter's hammer.

BATTER BOARD: A homemade tool constructed of 2x4s, used to set up layout lines.

BRICKSET: A wide-bladed chisel used for cutting bricks and concrete blocks.

BUTTER: To apply mortar on bricks or blocks with a trowel before laying them.

CANTILEVER: The portion of a joist, or of an entire deck, that extends beyond the beam

CRAZING: A pattern of hairline cracks about ¼ inch deep in the surface of a concrete slab. Caused by improper troweling.

CUBES OR BANDS: Pregrouped and bound quantities of pavers that will cover 16 lineal feet.

DARBY: A hand tool with a long sole made of smooth wood or metal, used for smoothing the surface of a concrete slab after initial leveling.

DOBIE: A small cement block manufactured specifically to keep reinforcing wire centered in a concrete slab.

DRY-STACKED WALL: A wall of masonry units (stones) laid without mortar.

EARTH-WOOD CLEARANCE: Minimum distance required between any wood and the ground; exceptions are made for pressure-treated or durable species lumber specified for ground contact.

EFFLORESCENCE: A white powdery substance that appears on masonry surfaces, caused by the leeching of chemical in the material.

HARD SCAPE: Those elements in a landscape that are made of wood, stone, or other hard, permanent materials.

ISOLATION JOINT: Strips of material installed in formwork to completely separate new concrete from existing construction or from other new construction. Allows sections to move independently of one another if the ground shifts because of influences like frost heave. Sometimes called expansion joints.

KDAT (KILN DRIED AFTER TREATMENT): Pressure-treated lumber that has been dried after being treated with preservative; more expensive than undried pressure-treated lumber but less likely to warp

MODULAR: A term describing a unit of material whose dimensions are proportional to one another.

MUD-JACKING: The process by which fallen sections of a concrete slab can be raised to level by injecting a mixture of mud and concrete under them.

PLASTIC CONCRETE: Concrete that has not hardened.

POP-OUTS: Small holes in a concrete surface. Caused by improper floating.

RUBBLE: Uncut stone, often used for dry-stacked walls.

SCRATCH COAT: The first coat of mortar or plaster, roughened (scratched) so the next coat will stick to it.

SCREED: A straight edge used to level concrete as it is poured into a form or to level the sand base in a form.

SEGREGATION: Separation of the elements of concrete, such as water rising to the top or aggregate sinking to the bottom because of overworking or bouncing (as in the motion of a wheelbarrow).

SETBACK: The minimum distance between a property line and any structure, as defined by local building codes.

SLEEPER: Horizontal wood member laid directly on ground, patio, or roof for supporting a deck.

SPALLING: Areas of pitting in the surface of a concrete slab. Caused by improper troweling.

STRIKING: The process of finishing a mortar joint.

STRINGERS: Heavy, inclined members that support stair treads; can be solid, with treads attached between the stringers, or cut out, with treads resting on top of the sawtooth sections.

SWALE: A shallow depression made in a landscape used to collect runoff.

WEEP HOLE: An opening made in a mortar joint to allow water to drain through.

USDA PLANT HARDINESS ZONE MAP

This map of climate zones helps you select plants for your garden that will survive a typical winter in your region. The United States Department of Agriculture (USDA) developed the map, basing the zones on the lowest recorded temperatures across North America. Zone 1 is the coldest area and Zone 11 is the warmest.

Plants are classified by the coldest temperature and zone they can endure. For example, plants hardy to Zone 6 survive where winter temperatures drop to –10° F. Those hardy to Zone 8 die long before it's that cold. These plants may grow in colder regions but must be replaced each year. Plants rated for a range of hardiness zones can usually survive winter in the coldest region as well as tolerate the summer heat of the warmest one.

To find your hardiness zone, note the approximate location of your community on the map, then match the color band marking that area to the key.

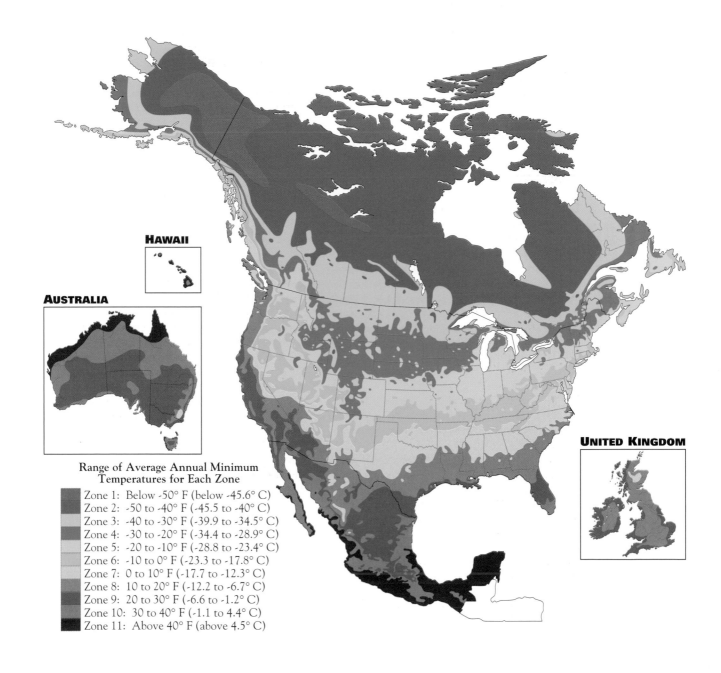

HAWAII

AUSTRALIA

UNITED KINGDOM

Range of Average Annual Minimum Temperatures for Each Zone

Zone 1: Below -50° F (below -45.6° C)
Zone 2: -50 to -40° F (-45.5 to -40° C)
Zone 3: -40 to -30° F (-39.9 to -34.5° C)
Zone 4: -30 to -20° F (-34.4 to -28.9° C)
Zone 5: -20 to -10° F (-28.8 to -23.4° C)
Zone 6: -10 to 0° F (-23.3 to -17.8° C)
Zone 7: 0 to 10° F (-17.7 to -12.3° C)
Zone 8: 10 to 20° F (-12.2 to -6.7° C)
Zone 9: 20 to 30° F (-6.6 to -1.2° C)
Zone 10: 30 to 40° F (-1.1 to 4.4° C)
Zone 11: Above 40° F (above 4.5° C)

INDEX

METRIC CONVERSIONS

U.S. Units to Metric Equivalents			Metric Units to U.S. Equivalents		
To Convert From	Multiply By	To Get	To Convert From	Multiply By	To Get
Inches	25.4	Millimeters	Millimeters	0.0394	Inches
Inches	2.54	Centimeters	Centimeters	0.3937	Inches
Feet	30.48	Centimeters	Centimeters	0.0328	Feet
Feet	0.3048	Meters	Meters	3.2808	Feet
Yards	0.9144	Meters	Meters	1.0936	Yards
Square inches	6.4516	Square centimeters	Square centimeters	0.1550	Square inches
Square feet	0.0929	Square meters	Square meters	10.764	Square feet
Square yards	0.8361	Square meters	Square meters	1.1960	Square yards
Acres	0.4047	Hectares	Hectares	2.4711	Acres
Cubic inches	16.387	Cubic centimeters	Cubic centimeters	0.0610	Cubic inches
Cubic feet	0.0283	Cubic meters	Cubic meters	35.315	Cubic feet
Cubic feet	28.316	Liters	Liters	0.0353	Cubic feet
Cubic yards	0.7646	Cubic meters	Cubic meters	1.308	Cubic yards
Cubic yards	764.55	Liters	Liters	0.0013	Cubic yards

To convert from degrees Fahrenheit (F) to degrees Celsius (C), first subtract 32, then multiply by $\frac{5}{9}$.

To convert from degrees Celsius to degrees Fahrenheit, multiply by $\frac{9}{5}$, then add 32.